College Sports Inc.

College Sports Inc.

The Athletic Department
VS
The University

Murray Sperber

Henry Holt and Company
NEW YORK

Published by Henry Holt and Company, Inc.,
115 West 18th Street, New York, New York 10011.
Published in Canada by Fitzhenry & Whiteside Limited,
195 Allstate Parkway, Markham, Ontario L3R 4T8.

Library of Congress Cataloging-in-Publication Data
Sperber, Murray.
College sports inc. : the athletic department vs the university /
Murray Sperber. — 1st ed.
    p.   cm.
ISBN 0-8050-1445-4
1. College sports—Economic aspects—United States.   2. College
sports—United States—Moral and ethical aspects.   3. College
sports—United States—Organization and administration.   4. National
Collegiate Athletic Association.   I. Title.
GV351.S64 · 1990
338.4'3796'071173—dc20   90-31838
                                                                  CIP

Henry Holt books are available at special discounts
for bulk purchases for sales promotions, premiums,
fund-raising, or educational use. Special editions
or book excerpts can also be created to specification.
For details contact: Special Sales Director,
Henry Holt and Company, Inc., 115 West 18th Street,
New York, New York 10011.

First Edition

Printed in the United States of America
Recognizing the importance of preserving
the written word, Henry Holt and Company, Inc.,
by policy, prints all of its first editions
on acid-free paper. ∞

10   9   8   7   6   5   4   3   2   1

For My Son
Oliver J. Sperber
(1982–1989)

"So cheerful, plucky, and good-tempered."

—Anna Sewell,
Black Beauty

Contents

PART TWO
Greed City: College Coaches' Salaries, Perks, Deals, & Scams

PART THREE
Toxic Waste: Recruiting Wars & Athletic Scholarships

Preface

*"What was allowed to become a circus—college sports—
threatens to become the means by which the public
believes the entire enterprise [higher education] is a
sideshow."*

> —A. Bartlett Giamatti, former president of
> Yale University and former commissioner
> of major league baseball

THE SHARPEST MEMORY of my first week in college is of walking toward
the Purdue football stadium on a sunny, cool September afternoon, the
noise of the marching band and the huge crowd in the distance, the
anticipation of seeing the Boilermakers play Notre Dame. That event,
over a generation ago, began a personal love affair with college sports.

During my years at Purdue, intercollegiate athletics was on the
margin of university life, but today, at Purdue and many other schools,
athletic programs are much larger than ever before. About a decade ago,
I began wondering whether and to what extent their increasing importance complements or corrupts the academic missions of their host
universities.

After studying these questions intensively for a number of years, I
came to one absolute conclusion: intercollegiate athletics has become
College Sports Inc., a huge commercial entertainment conglomerate,
with operating methods and objectives totally separate from, and
mainly opposed to, the educational aims of the schools that house its
franchises. Moreover, because of its massive hypocrisy and fiscal irre-
sponsibility, College Sports Inc. places many colleges and universities
under the constant threat of scandal and other sports-induced maladies.
This situation is intolerable for American higher education; a basic

redefinition of the role of college sports within the university is necessary.

I do not want to abolish college sports—I enjoy them and want them to survive. However, because the seriousness of the problems in college sports indicates systemic failure, I believe that only major surgery can save the patient. Therefore, throughout this book and particularly in the conclusion, I suggest a number of radical ways to restructure intercollegiate athletics.

Whether readers agree with my solutions or not, the research and arguments behind them will provide detailed and often surprising information about the nature of College Sports Inc., and will better prepare everyone connected to and/or concerned about higher education for an important and heated public debate in the 1990s: how to cure the corruption in American college sports.

Bloomington, Indiana
January 1990

Acknowledgments

MANY PEOPLE helped me with this book. Foremost were my friend and agent John Wright, and my sympathetic editor Bill Strachan: their constant support and savvy comments shaped the entire project and helped bring it to fruition. Special thanks also to Paul Strohm for saving me from making many large and small errors; and to Judd Kahn and Anne Rogin for their hospitality in Manhattan and excellent criticisms of the manuscript.

Friends and colleagues throughout the country aided me in many different ways. Among them were Bill and JoAn Chace, Tom and Jean Flanagan, Mark and Ann Shechner, Bill and Susan Fischer, Chris and Joanne Eustis, Howard and Shirley Maccabee, Michael Weiskopf, Frank Cioffi, Joe Ricapito, Fred Crews, Ralph Rader, Lynette Carpenter, Alison Juram, Ed Sedarbaum, and James Frey.

I am also very grateful to the persons whom I interviewed for this book. Whether they spoke on or off the record, they were invariably generous with their time and comments. Although I was able to fit only a small fraction of their words and names into the final text, they all greatly contributed to my knowledge of college sports and I thank them.

At my own school—Indiana University, Bloomington—many people encouraged and helped me. Among them were Vice President Ken

Gros Louis and his wife, Dee; Dean Albert Wertheim and former Dean Lew Miller; in the English Department, Mary Burgan, Don Gray, Chris Lohman, David Nordloh, Susan Gubar, Ken Johnston, Sheila Lindenbaum, Lee Sterrenburg, Scott Sanders, Paul Miller, Reba Amerson, Pat Risler, Stephanie Dobler, Elizabeth Rosdeitcher, Rebecca Rupert, and K. C. Smith; and in other parts of the university, Tim Long, Oscar Kenchur, Ed Gubar, Joan Sterrenburg, Tony Shipps, Dave Gallahue, George Walker, Sandi Lehrman, and Wayne Achterberg.

Finally, I am forever indebted to my father, Lawrence, my wife, Aneta, and my daughter, Giselle, for their constant patience and support, and to my son, Ollie, who was so inspiring in life and whose memory kept me company during the long hours in the library and in front of the computer.

College Sports Inc.

Introduction

"In interviews with UK [University of Kentucky] students, faculty members and administrators, a picture of two UKs emerges. One is a top-of-the-line $14-million-a-year athletic program, run largely by and for off-campus supporters; the other is a chronically underfinanced, 'fair-to-middlin' academic institution that seems to languish in the shadow of the 'Big Blue' [athletic] monolith."

—Item in the *Louisville Courier-Journal*

A GREAT NUMBER of myths shield college sports from casual scrutiny and burden any discussion of the subject. The following refutations of the most common myths should introduce the reader to the reality of contemporary college sports. Debunkings of other myths about the subject are in the main sections of the book.

Myth: College sports are part of the educational mission of American colleges and universities.

Reality: The main purpose of college sports is commercial entertainment. Within most universities with big-time intercollegiate programs, the athletic department operates as a separate business and has almost no connection to the educational departments and functions of the school—even the research into and teaching of sports is done by the physical education department.

The reason elite athletes are in universities has nothing to do with the educational missions of their schools. Athletes are the only group of students recruited for entertainment—not academic—purposes, and they are the only students who go through school on grants based not on educational aptitude, but on their talent and potential as commercial entertainers.

1

If colleges searched for and gave scholarships to up-and-coming rock stars so that they could entertain the university community and earn money for their schools through concerts and tours, educational authorities and the public would call this "a perversion of academic values." Yet every year, American institutions of higher education hand out over a hundred thousand full or partial athletic scholarships, worth at least $500 million, for reasons similar to the hypothetical grants to rock performers.

Myth: The alumni support—in fact, demand—that their alma maters have large and successful college sports programs.

Reality: Studies indicate that most alumni—people who were students at a particular school—contribute to the academic units of their colleges and universities and that only 1 to 2 percent of them donate to athletic programs. In fact, alumni often withhold contributions from their alma maters when the athletic teams are too successful or are involved in sports scandals: they are embarrassed by their schools' becoming "jock factories" and/or are angered by the bad publicity from scandals, and they believe that their college degrees are being devalued.

Other research indicates that the major donors to athletic programs actually are boosters—people who never attended the school, who give money only to the athletic department and in proportion to its teams' success on the field or court, and who refuse to contribute to the institution's academic programs.

Myth: College sports is incredibly profitable, earning huge sums of money for American colleges and universities.

Reality: One of the best-kept secrets about intercollegiate athletics—well guarded because athletic departments are extremely reluctant to open their financial books—is that most college sports programs lose money. If profit and loss is defined according to ordinary business practices, of the 802 members of the NCAA (National Collegiate Athletic Association), the 493 of the NAIA (National Association of Intercollegiate Athletes), and the 1,050 nonaffiliated junior colleges, only 10 to 20 athletic programs make a consistent albeit small profit, and in any given year another 20 to 30 break even or do better. The rest—over 2,300 institutions—lose anywhere from a few dollars to millions annually.

Because athletic departments are allowed to engage in "creative accounting," covering many of their expenses with money from their schools' general operating funds and other university sources, it is difficult to ascertain the full extent of their losses. One expert, Don Canham, longtime athletic director at the University of Michigan, estimated that "about 99 percent of the schools in this country don't balance their budgets in athletics." Canham balanced his, but the year after he retired (1988–89), Michigan's athletic program was, according to an NCAA official, "$2.5 million in the red."

Myth: The NCAA Division I men's basketball tournament makes millions of dollars for American colleges and universities.

Reality: Of the total revenue from the tournament, the NCAA keeps at least half or more for itself; for example, of the millions received from the 1987 tourney, the association distributed only 44 percent directly to the schools involved.

The new NCAA contract with CBS Sports will increase tournament revenue but, rather than share the pot o' gold, the NCAA plans to exclude a large number of schools from reaching into it. According to Tom Hansen, commissioner of the Pac-10, the NCAA may soon drop as many as 50 schools from Division I basketball, including four or five conferences. In addition, if past performance is any indication, the richer pot will increase lottery fever among the remaining 240 Division I basketball programs, with coaches engaging in "checkbook recruiting" and sparing no cost to build winning teams.

In the 1990s, Final Four squads will win the lottery (probably the perennial powers will triumph most often), the 60 other teams invited to the tournament will break even on their basketball program expenses, and the hundreds of also-rans will either pay large sums of money to purchase losing lottery tickets or be shut out entirely.

Myth: Schools receive millions of dollars when their teams play in football bowl games.

Reality: Often the numbers given in newspaper articles are for the "projected payout," whereas the actual payout can be much lower. Moreover, most participating schools must split their bowl revenue with other members of their conferences. As a result, when the headline announces that a Pac-10 team received $1 million for a bowl appearance, that school kept only $100,000 because of the conference's ten-way split.

In addition, athletic departments like to turn bowl and tournament trips into all-expenses-paid junkets for hundreds of people, including their employees and friends. Their travel, hotel, and entertainment costs often eat up the actual bowl or tourney payouts and transform post-season play into a deficit item!

Myth: The money earned from college sports helps other parts of the university.

Reality: Because athletic department expenses usually exceed revenues, any money earned by college sports teams stays in the athletic department. Moreover, athletic departments admit that they have no intention of sharing their revenue; an NCAA survey reported that fewer than 1 percent of all athletic programs defined their "fiscal objective" as earning money "to support nonathletics activities of the institution."

Rather than financially help the university, most athletic programs siphon money from it: for example, the enormous maintenance costs of stadiums and other facilities—used exclusively for athletic program events and by their elite athletes—are often placed in the "Buildings-and-Grounds" line in the university-wide budget, and the multimillion-dollar debt servicing on these facilities is frequently paid by regular students in the form of mandatory "Fees."

To cover athletic program losses, schools must divert money from their budgets and other financial resources. Thus funds that could go to academic programs, student scholarships, faculty and staff salaries disappear into the athletic department deficit.

Myth: College coaches deserve their high annual incomes because they generate huge profits for their athletic programs.

Reality: A few years ago, the athletic director at the University of South Carolina commented: "For someone to make $250,000 in the business world, he'd have to generate $60 million to $70 million in sales. When coaches say they're worth it, they don't know what's going on out there."

John Wooden, the most successful men's basketball coach in NCAA history, was never paid more than $25,000 a year by UCLA. Today, only a few coaches generate as much revenue for their schools as Wooden did for his, and the vast majority direct programs that lose money for their institutions. Nevertheless, the annual incomes of at least one hundred NCAA Division I men's basketball coaches, and seventy-five Division I-A football coaches, approach or top $100,000, and many program heads in the "nonrevenue sports" (so termed because they always lose money) like soccer, baseball, track, and swimming earn over $75,000 a year.

Myth: College coaches deserve their high annual incomes because they are the key to producing winning teams and are irreplaceable.

Reality: Sonny Smith, a longtime Division I men's basketball coach, commented, "It's a make-it-while-you-can thing. . . . If I quit tomorrow, there'd be three hundred names in the ring." Except for a handful of truly outstanding and innovative coaches, most of the others are interchangeable and can be replaced by any number of the "three hundred names in the ring." When Bill Frieder, making over $400,000 a year, quit the University of Michigan on the eve of the 1989 NCAA men's basketball tournament, an unheralded assistant, earning a fraction of Frieder's income, was given the top job. Under Steve Fisher, Michigan swept through the tourney and won the national championship.

Myth: Hired to be fired—that's the fate of most college coaches.

Reality: Firings are not the reason most college coaches change jobs. Coaches leave schools for a variety of reasons, most often to take better-paying positions, to quit jobs that are not working out, or to keep one step ahead of the NCAA sheriff. Only in a minority of cases are they asked to leave.

An analysis of the major coaching appointments listed weekly in the *Chronicle of Higher Education* over the last decade reveals the following typical sequence: the head man at Bigtime Sports U. quits in midcontract to go to the pros or to become an AD; the coach at Southern Jock State leaves his school to take the more lucrative package at Bigtime U.; the coach at Western Boondock sees a chance to move up and grabs the job at Southern; finally, if Western cannot hire another head coach, it offers its smaller package to an assistant at a major program or, in desperation, promotes one of its own assistants. When this Coach in Motion Play ends, at least three head coaches, as well as innumerable assistants, have changed jobs—not one of them fired by a college or university.

Myth: College athletic programs provide a wonderful opportunity for black coaches.

Reality: White athletic directors and program heads keep college coaching lily white by hiring their duplicates. In a 1987 study of the racial backgrounds of head coaches in football, basketball, baseball, and men's track at 278 Division I schools, only 4.2 percent were black. However, the real surprise was the percentage of black assistant coaches—3.1, lower than the percentage of black head coaches. On the other hand, another study of big-time programs found that over 50 percent of the football players and 70 percent of the men's basketball players, as well as a high percentage of baseball and track athletes, were black. Since 1987, the percentage of black head and assistant coaches in college sports has not changed significantly.

Myth: College athletic programs provide a wonderful opportunity for women coaches.

Reality: Women coaches, unlike blacks, once had a strong position in college sports. However, in the 1970s and early 1980s, male athletic directors and program heads took over women's college sports as well as the jobs of female ADs and many coaches. The most comprehensive study of this phenomenon shows that in the early 1970s, 90 percent of the athletic directors of women's college sports programs were female, whereas by 1988, the percentage had dropped to 16. In the same time span, the percentage of female coaches of women's sports teams went from the mid-90s to 48.

Paralleling the male takeover of individual jobs was the NCAA's cynical demolition of the main women's college sports group, the AIAW (Association of Intercollegiate Athletics for Women), and the NCAA's subsequent control of women's athletic programs.

Myth: Talented athletes, like other high school graduates, should enroll in higher education.

Reality: Only about 30 percent of American high school students go on to four-year colleges and universities; one subsection of these students, with little interest in and preparation for higher education, is nevertheless required to attend university—aspiring professional athletes in football and men's basketball.

An anomaly of American history—that intercollegiate football and basketball began before the professional versions of those games and excluded viable minor leagues in those sports—has created a situation that is unknown and unthinkable in other countries: *To become a major-league player in a number of sports, an athlete must pass through an institution of higher learning.* And to compound the problem, American schools now take on the training of young athletes in sports, particularly baseball and hockey, for which there *are* excellent minor professional leagues, as well as Olympic sport athletes for which there is a strong club system.

Myth: College athletes are amateurs and their athletic scholarships do not constitute professional payment for playing sports.

Reality: A school gives an athlete a "full ride" grant worth $5,000 to $20,000 a year in exchange for the athlete's services in a commercial entertainment venture, namely, playing on one of the school's sports teams. If the athlete fails to keep his or her part of the agreement and quits the team, the institution withdraws the financial package—even if the athlete continues in school as a regular student. Moreover, once the athlete's playing eligibility ends, the grant is usually terminated.

At one time in NCAA history, athletic scholarships were for four years and, once awarded, could not be revoked. In 1973, under pressure from coaches who wanted greater control over their players and the ability to "fire" them for poor athletic performances, the NCAA instituted one-year scholarships, renewed annually at the athletic department's discretion.

Under their current terms, athletic scholarships appear indistinguishable from what the IRS calls "barter payment for services rendered," thus making college athletes professional wage earners. In addition, a number of courts have found that the one-year grants constitute an employer-employee relationship between a school and an athlete.

Myth: College sports provides an excellent opportunity for black youngsters to get out of the ghetto and to contribute to American society.

Reality: Research by Harry Edwards, professor of sociology at the University of California, Berkeley, indicates that many athletic programs treat black athletes as "gladiators," bringing them to campus only to play sports, not for an education. The low graduation rates of black college athletes supports Edwards's thesis.

Most schools with major athletic programs, as well as many with smaller ones, recruit black athletes much more intensively and system-atically than they do regular black students. Moreover, some schools fund their "black gladiators" by diverting money from scholarship sources, such as opportunity grants, earmarked for academically moti-vated minority students. Thus, not only do the "black gladiators" fail to receive college educations, but many black high school graduates—whose academic potential is far greater than the athletes'—are deprived of the chance of entering university.

Myth: For college athletes, the opportunity for a university education is as important as playing intercollegiate sports.

Reality: Formal and informal studies indicate that most college athletes in big-time programs hope to play their sport at the professional or Olympic level, and they regard college as their path to the pros or the national team. That very few of these athletes ever achieve their dream is irrelevant to its power over them and its role in shaping their college careers, especially their willingness to devote as many as sixty hours a week to their sports and their inability to sustain a serious course of studies. Jim Walden, head football coach at Iowa State University, says that in his sport, "Not more than 20 percent of the football players go to college for an education. And that may be a high figure."

Myth: Athletes, like Bill Bradley and Tom McMillen, who were out-standing in sports and in the classroom prove that college sports works.

Reality: In any large sample of people in any endeavor, there are always a few at the end of the bell curve. In fact, the widespread notice taken of Bradley's and McMillen's success in both sports and academics suggests that intercollegiate athletics is a system that works for only a few. No one bothers to name all of the outstanding Americans who were once top college students but not athletes, because they are not unusual; higher education is supposed to produce them.

From their first day of college, however, athletes face a conundrum—how to be a "student-athlete"—that few can solve. Their only response is to erase one of the terms and to highlight the other: neglect a meaningful education and pursue sports fulltime, or, in a few cases, drop out of intercollegiate athletics and seriously go to school.

Most big-time athletic programs try to finesse this problem by shel-tering their athletes in special "hideaway curricula" and having them major in eligibility (the NCAA has minimal rules for "good academic standing" and playing eligibility). But time spent in a school's Division of Ridiculous Studies does not constitute a real college education. For the vast majority of athletic scholarship holders, the current system does not work; it also corrupts the host institutions and makes faculty, regular students, and the public cynical about the entire academic enterprise.

Myth: The high graduation rates of athletes announced each year by the NCAA and the College Football Association are accurate.

Reality: These rates are manipulated by the NCAA and CFA to produce the appearance of athletes doing well academically. Instead of basing the percentage of athlete-graduates at a school on the total number who began in an athletic program as freshmen, the NCAA and CFA do not count all those who transferred or who dropped out of school in "good academic standing." Because leaving in "bad academic standing"— i.e., flunking out—usually takes a grade point average *below D,* the NCAA and CFA exclude large numbers of academically marginal athletes from their pools, among them those who drop out after using up their college eligibility but have a D or better average. Not counting transfers has a similar statistical effect: many transfers do not graduate from their next institution, but their absence from the original pools raises the graduation rates.

Some schools even base their rates on only their senior class of athletes: such common pronouncements as "Of our senior student-athletes in football, 90 percent graduated this June" can mean "We based our rates on those ten football players who made it to the senior class—out of the thirty who started in our program as freshmen." Not surprisingly, after this numerical sleight of hand, the NCAA and CFA graduation rates reflect their propaganda, not reality.

Myth: The NCAA represents the will of its member colleges and universities and it tries to keep intercollegiate athletics in line with their educational objectives.

Reality: The NCAA functions mainly as a trade association for college coaches and athletic directors, implementing their wishes regardless of whether these are in the best interests of the member schools. Real power in the association resides in the forty-four-person Executive

Council and the twelve-member Executive Committee; for many years, a large majority of Executive Council and Executive Committee members have been athletic directors. These two groups control NCAA legislation, choose future council and committee members, and supervise the executive director of the association, currently Dick Schultz, a former coach and AD.

Myth: NCAA athletic programs sponsor teams in many sports, including Olympic events, because they want to give those sports a chance to grow.

Reality: Most athletic directors and program heads are empire builders. Through their control of the NCAA, they have instituted key legislation that ensures expansion—even though costly athletic department growth is not in the financial or academic interest of most of their schools.

The NCAA requires a minimum number of teams for participation in its various divisions, for example, for Division I-A, thirteen teams (men's and women's) in seven sports. If an institution fails to meet the requirement, the NCAA drops it to "unclassified membership," bars all of its teams from NCAA play, and penalizes it in various other ways.

The NCAA's rationale for the sports and team minimums is that schools should have "well-balanced athletic programs." In practice, these regulations serve the college sports establishment's self-interest: ADs and coaches want their programs to be as large as possible, and to employ as many administrators, assistant coaches, and athletes as possible. The NCAA, by locking athletic departments into a high number of sports and teams, deprives member institutions of a large degree of autonomy over their athletic budgets.

Myth: The NCAA can correct the problems in college sports.

Reality: The athletic directors and coaches who control the NCAA deny the existence of any significant problems in college sports. For them, the present system works well—after all, it provides them with extremely comfortable livings—and they see no need to repair it, except for some minor tinkerings.

Bo Schembechler, when head football coach at the University of Michigan, speaking for his fellow coaches and most ADs, once shouted at an audience of reform-minded college presidents, *"We are not the enemy."* Bo was wrong. But he was true to the NCAA's self-serving denials of any responsibility for the current problems.

The bottom line on meaningful NCAA reform is clear: the NCAA cannot solve the systemic problems in college sports because the coaches and ADs who control it are a central source of those problems. Moreover, the association will fight any attempts at real reform, even if—as is probable in the 1990s—College Sports Inc. begins to destroy the academic and fiscal integrity of some member institutions.

PART I

Old Siwash in Red Ink

THE FINANCES OF COLLEGE SPORTS

"We've got the deal spotted. If they [athletic programs] don't get enough money, they steal it out of the education budget."

> —Don Tyson, chairman of Tyson Foods
> and a member of the State of Arkansas
> Higher Education Committee

OVERVIEW: REVENUE

"N.D. WILL NOT MAKE MONEY ON ATHLETICS THIS YEAR
[1987–88]."

—Headline in the *South Bend Tribune*

WHEN NOTRE DAME loses money on college sports, what school's
athletic program is immune from red ink? Even the NCAA acknowledges the poor financial health of college sports. Its most recent study
on this topic, *The Revenues and Expenses of Intercollegiate Athletics
Programs,* polled 795 athletic programs and reported that the vast
majority lost money. Moreover, because only the big-time programs
have a chance at college sports' "pot o' gold"—lucrative bowl games
and the NCAA men's basketball tournament—most NCAA members
will continue to lose money indefinitely. In addition, the almost five
hundred NAIA (small-college athletic association) schools and the over
one thousand junior colleges cannot even buy a lottery ticket.

Like addicted gamblers, athletic directors often justify their annual
deficits by saying, "You have to spend money to make money." But the
odds of even a big-time athletic program capturing the pot o' gold are
long, and the risks—the multimillion-dollar outlay to build and maintain teams, coaching staffs, and facilities—are enormous.

There is an Italian expression that "A lottery is a tax on imbeciles."
The finances of most American college sports programs place their host
schools in the idiot's role.

*"Intercollegiate athletics is an area of university operations
that tends to be shrouded in secrecy."*

—*The Money Game: Financing Collegiate
Athletics,* an American Council on
Education report

Ascertaining the exact amount of red ink in college sports is difficult.
Because athletic departments are often autonomous units, not directly
supervised by a dean or other university official, they like to erect "Iron
Curtains" around their operations, particularly their finances. Even at
public universities they are unwilling to open their books. In addition,
because they frequently use "creative accounting" and try to remove as

15

many expenses as possible from their financial statements, they are adept at concealing their real losses.

In February 1988, the *Arkansas Gazette* headlined, SPORTS PUT [ARKANSAS PUBLIC] COLLEGES $6 MILLION IN RED, but later in the year, the paper discovered that because of various athletic department accounting practices, the $6 million figure was too low. In a typical maneuver, one Arkansas program had moved its athletic scholarship expenses—always a six- or seven-figure item—to another part of the university budget and had not listed them on its financial statement.

A few years ago in Florida, the regents of the state universities investigated the self-serving accounting methods of their state's athletic departments. They discovered a number of large annual deficits at the University of Central Florida in Orlando ($1.1 million), Florida A. & M. ($700,000), and the University of South Florida in Tampa ($655,000).

The chair of the Florida Board of Regents explained the core of the problem as "the general tendency of athletics administrators to overestimate the money that programs will bring in, then spend accordingly in advance. When faced with a shortfall, they have only two choices . . . ignore the bills or 'pay with someone else's money.' "

"Someone else" is usually the university, with money from specific budget lines or out of general funds; the students in the form of added, often mandatory fees; and, if a public institution, the taxpayers by the diversion of state subsidies.

> *"Athletic administrators have one of the sweetest deals*
> *going. They have lots of the goodies of corporate America*
> *and few of the financial headaches. They can spend*
> *whatever they want and every year Uncle University bails*
> *out the red ink. And the world hasn't caught on to their*
> *scam."*
>
> —A former NCAA Division I soccer coach

College Sports Inc. is an amazing hybrid of corporate and public agency America. The men and women who run college sports consider themselves corporate officers managing large businesses, amassing and guarding all revenue. They also reward themselves with the high salaries and perks of the corporate world. On the other hand, the executives of College Sports Inc. do not want the financial responsibilities of every other businessperson in America—not even paying utility bills. Instead, they prefer the "no bottom line" mentality of some public agency bureaucrats and allow their expenses to exceed their revenues. Then, at the end of the fiscal year, they claim that their College Sports Inc. franchise is really an educational unit of their school, like the math department, and they appeal to the central administration for extra funds to balance their books.

University authorities, whether through collusion, fear of bad publicity, or confusion about the real issues, have long cooperated with athletic administrators and covered their losses. Rarely do school officials point out the fallacy in the appeal for supplementary funds: an athletic program is *not* an academic unit. If, one year, the math department has a budgetary shortfall due to underenrollment, the university absorbs the financial loss because the mission of an academic unit is education, not monetary profit, and the value of teaching and research cannot be calculated in dollars and cents. However, the purpose of an athletic program is commercial entertainment, and if its expenses exceed its revenues, then, like every other business in America, it should be held accountable.

The present financial situation in college sports continues for two main reasons: athletic departments refuse to reveal their true financial situation, and the majority of Americans, including college graduates, current students, and even faculty, believe that College Sports Inc. is tremendously profitable and that the profits help higher education.

Athletic department secrecy, combined with the myth of great profitability, allows university and athletic program administrators to perpetrate and perpetuate this money "scam." If the public understood how these financial losses hurt the schools involved, especially their academic programs, major reforms might come to college sports.

CHAPTER 1

How to Become an AD & Confront, Ignore, or Personally Profit from the Red Ink

"We're not even really part of the school anymore, anyway. I work for the N.C. State Athletic Association. . . . You think the chancellor is going to tell me what to do? Who to take into school or not to take into school? I doubt it."

> —Jim Valvano, former men's basketball coach and athletic director at North Carolina State University

THE SITUATION that Jim Valvano described exists on many campuses. A more authoritative description was provided by a survey of sixty-five presidents of big-time college sports schools; a majority agreed that "the athletic director is the central and most powerful figure on campus in regard to all aspects of the program of student athletics. The president is clearly second in power."

The athletic departments of most schools with big-time programs are, according to the NCAA, "separate units entirely," with a greater degree of autonomy from their institutions than any academic department. At these universities, the athletic director's job is to operate the athletic program and to keep it in good standing with the NCAA. In effect, the athletic director runs the school's franchise—granted by the NCAA—in College Sports Inc., and he or she has control over all aspects of the franchise's operation, including its employees (staff, coaches, and student-athletes).

No other university official has a similar job. Deans and department heads spend their time and energies on academic matters; athletic directors focus on commercial entertainment. Even when deans and department heads consider budgetary questions, they base their decisions on educational concerns ("Is this research worth funding?" "Is this course, although cost-effective, a good way to teach this subject?"). Athletic directors, however, are in the entertainment business ("Should we schedule different opponents?" "Should we expand the marching band?"). Moreover, when athletic directors deal with student-athletes, it is usually in terms of NCAA regulations and penalties ("Is this quarterback eligible to play?") and the AD's concerns are analogous to a franchise holder having to please the company (the NCAA) that awarded and can suspend the franchise.

Athletic directors were not always executives with College Sports Inc. At one time, many held faculty appointments and they were involved with education and recreation (at schools with small athletic departments, this tradition continues). However, as intercollegiate athletics became a major entertainment business, ADs at the big-time schools evolved into self-proclaimed CEOs.

The career of Don Canham of the University of Michigan illustrates this transition. In 1968, Canham took over a department with a budget of, according to a sports business magazine, "around $3 million" and, in 1988, the budget "approach[ed] $20 million—the largest in the country—with an expected profit of a few hundred thousand." Canham is greatly respected by his fellow ADs because his program consistently made money (although in corporate America, a profit in the low six figures from a $20 million budget could quickly end a CEO's term in office).

Canham is important in the history of College Sports Inc. because he was one of the first athletic directors to use business techniques to promote his products. He recalls that at Michigan, in 1968, "we were projecting a deficit for the first time, and there were forty thousand empty seats in the stadium." So he began promoting the football team, taking "full-page ads in the Detroit newspapers, hawking season tickets. . . . It wasn't dignified to advertise," he admits, "I knew I was ruffling feathers, but I was positive that it was the wave of the future."

In later years, Canham also introduced mass-mailing techniques and a wide range of souvenir items to boost athletic department revenue. In the 1980s, he brought in computers to rationalize his department's business. Through it all, his Wolverine teams kept winning and filling the huge football stadium and basketball arena.

Canham's management style was "top-down," and as independent as possible from his university. Although Michigan, like all NCAA schools, is supposed to have administrative or faculty control of its athletic program, under Canham's directorship, according to the *Ann Arbor News,* the school's Board in Control of Intercollegiate Athletics was kept far from the decision-making process: Canham rejected "attempts by aggressive board members to delve too deeply into [athletic] department affairs or actually assert some control over the department's operation—although that's what the board is formally charged with doing."

During his long reign at Michigan, Canham was also criticized by faculty members for slighting his athletes' educational needs. An English professor in charge of the university's Composition Board said, "A great many of our athletes simply cannot read and write well enough to do normal college work at Michigan," and he accused the university of allowing athletes to earn "tainted degrees."

Canham shrugged off criticism and pointed to his teams' winning records and his department's financial health. At no point during his twenty-year career was he criticized—much less reprimanded—by the Michigan president or administration.

Canham is modest about his achievement: "I took over in an era when they needed a businessman, they needed a marketeer. The fact that we started it was incidental."

Don Canham, however, was the exception among athletic directors because his program consistently earned a profit. That he inherited one of the oldest and best athletic departments in the country, and had the good judgment to hire coaches like Bo Schembechler, were key components in his success. Putting the Michigan program on a solid business basis was the other part of the Canham formula—one rarely imitated by his colleagues or by his successor at Michigan.

> *"With its plush rugs, expensive paintings, big desk and striking view, [the Alabama AD's office] could be the office of a Fortune 500 company executive. And in many ways, there's no reason why it shouldn't be. After all, the man who occupies it, Ray Perkins, is every bit the businessman you'd find on Wall Street."*
>
> —Item in *USA Today*

Do athletic directors resemble real businessmen on Wall Street, or do their high annual incomes and opulent offices mask their limitations as business executives? When *USA Today* wrote about Ray Perkins in 1986, he was athletic director and head football coach at the University of Alabama, Tuscaloosa, receiving a base salary of $120,000 and perks totaling another $100,000 a year. His main qualification for the AD position was his record as an outstanding player at Alabama and in the NFL, followed by his success in various assistant and head coaching jobs. Under Perkins, one of the most famous franchises in College Sports Inc. languished, and, according to a sports business magazine, "By its own accounting, the Alabama athletic department lost more than $2 million in fiscal 1988, its third straight year in or near the red." Perkins subsequently left Alabama for the NFL Tampa Bay Buccaneers.

Perkins's successor, Steve Sloan, also a former football player and coach, inherited the fancy office and one of the more massive financial problems in college sports. In mid-1988, a headline in the *Birmingham Post-Herald* explained, IN DEBT $39 MILLION, TIDE [ATHLETIC PROGRAM] SWALLOWING ITS PRIDE.

Athletic directors have the salaries and perks of CEOs in corporate America, but very few of them have the training to deal with business problems. Perkins's and Sloan's route to the AD's office is still the most common one in college sports. When Mary Alice Hill applied for the athletic director's job at San Diego State, she was asked, "How can you be an athletic director when you've never played football?" (Ms. Hill got the job and soon lost it, blaming, in part, male locker-room politics for her demise.) More recently, the longtime assistant athletic director at Southern Illinois University, Charlotte West, well qualified for the top job because of her business and administrative training, lost out to Jim Hart, whose main credential was his experience as quarterback for SIU and the NFL St. Louis Cardinals.

Sports fans have long known that success as a player does not guarantee—in fact, often hinders—triumph as a coach. Unfortunately, when ex-players or coaches apply to become athletic directors, their sports records, not their business skills, are usually considered their main qualifications. This hiring practice helps insure that athletic departments will lose money and that ADs will be important enough public figures to have the clout to make schools swallow lots of red ink.

In the trappings of their office, athletic directors resemble CEOs but, in actual practice, they conduct themselves very differently. CEOs, no matter how large their corporations, always have an eye on the bottom line, the profit-or-loss number at the end of the financial statement. ADs tend not to worry about the bottom line because athletic departments have a Good Fairy to wipe away the red ink—the university.

The result is a tradition that allows ADs to operate free from the usual business constraints. Don Canham was an exception. In 1988, he wrote an article entitled "Paper Trail to Responsibility," in which he explained how some ADs fail to grasp even basic business practices: at Michigan, "only the business manager can authorize payment" on a bill, but in some other athletic programs, many people can issue purchase orders and pay bills with department money.

Canham also stated that, "Regardless of the size of an athletic department, the fiscal responsibility must start and end with budgeting. That may seem obvious but it is amazing how few institutions really understand it."

> "The [University of New Mexico] Lobo athletic program exceeded expected expenditures by $542,658.95 last year. At the same time, it came up $260,197.83 short on expected revenues . . . [for a budget deficit of] $802,856.78."
>
> —Item in the *Albuquerque Journal*

What occurred at the University of New Mexico in 1984–85 was a typical instance of an athletic director failing to understand Canham's dictum about fiscal responsibility and budgeting. John Bridgers, the AD, tried to explain away the red ink by attributing "much of the deficit to unexpectedly poor attendance at football games last season and to relatively low revenue generated by the Lobo Club, UNM's booster organization." The athletic director's excuse points to a key problem in many athletic department budgets: estimates are based on the expectation of a record year in football and/or men's basketball and maximum revenue from these sports and their boosters. However, for every championship team in the Western Athletic Conference, where New Mexico plays, there are eight also-rans. And in 1984–85, the Lobos finished 4–8 in football and 18–12 in basketball. Nevertheless, every year in every conference, many athletic programs budget and spend as if each of them will win the championship.

An examination of the New Mexico $802,856 deficit also reveals that most of the thirteen men's sports teams and administrative units were way over budget (football by almost $140,000), whereas, of the ten women's sports teams and administrative units, four stayed within budget and the other six were much closer to original budget projections than were their male counterparts. (This situation occurs at other schools and, in part, contradicts the widely held belief that women's sports are the main economic drain on athletic programs.)

The New Mexico athletic director survived this budget crisis and, in 1986, continued to draw his $64,903 salary and use his $95,000 expense account—reduced by 5 percent after the budget debacle. But in 1987, Bridgers retired and was replaced by John Koenig, former assistant athletic director at the University of Illinois, Champaign-Urbana.

Koenig's time at New Mexico was brief, and notable mainly for his attempt to hire Bobby Knight away from Indiana and for his alleged financial chicanery. While at Illinois, Koenig had overcharged his travel and expense vouchers from 1983 to 1987, receiving, according to newspaper reports, "about $11,000 in unauthorized reimbursements." An Illinois audit had turned up the double-dipping, and Koenig repaid the money to Illinois during the summer of 1987—four months *after* being named New Mexico AD.

In the summer of 1988, prompted by public disclosure of the Illinois discoveries, officials at New Mexico began examining their new AD's books and found "at least eight instances of double reimbursements for costs incurred on trips Koenig took in April and May," as well as the fact that their AD had spent $30,000 from an athletic department discretionary account "for such questionable expenses as symphony tickets, theatre tickets, tuxedo rentals, and ski lift tickets." Koenig blamed the double reimbursements on clerical errors by his staff, and he explained the $30,000 spending as "part of the job": "I've talked to a lot of athletic directors about these discretionary accounts, and these things aren't even questioned. This is the way they're used."

Nevertheless the president of the school pressured the athletic director to resign. Meanwhile, the local district attorney began an investigation of Koenig for "embezzlement, conspiracy, receiving kickbacks, and receiving a bribe from a public official." In March 1989, a grand jury brought a forty-seven-count indictment against the former AD, as well as eleven counts against his two top assistants, on these and other charges.

The indictments suggest that while New Mexico changed athletic directors, apparently it did not alter the financial climate in which its

AD operated. Unfortunately, what happened in New Mexico was not a Lobo aberration but typical of many athletic programs. With little supervision of expenditures, and infrequent outside auditing of accounts, money in athletic departments has a tendency to disappear, sometimes into the athletic director's pocket.

John Koenig would probably still be AD at New Mexico if his former boss, Neale Stoner, at Illinois had not gotten into trouble, forcing the audit of the Illini athletic department that turned up, among other things, Koenig's misappropriated $11,000. Like a chain reaction, the Stoner case led to Koenig and then back to the Illinois AD and his top assistants.

> *"He [the athletic director] may feel entitled to perks and live like a maharajah. He collects millions from men whose country club memberships and yachts are paid for by their companies. He may see nothing wrong with writing off hefty entertainment expenses to his company [the university] and having his yard and swimming pool fixed up at company expense."*
>
> —Item in the *Chicago Sun-Times*

When columnist Ray Sons wrote this description, he had Neale Stoner, former University of Illinois athletic director, partly in mind. Stoner's conduct at Illinois and his disregard of the differences between corporate and public life is typical of many ADs, especially in their desire for the lifestyle of corporate executives without the bottom-line responsibilities.

By College Sports Inc. standards, Neale Stoner's ten years as athletic director at Illinois were successful. He revived the Illini football program and sent it to three bowl games—although, during his directorship, that program was placed on NCAA probation three separate times. He increased athletic department revenue by filling the huge football stadium and by raising large sums of money from boosters—although his final budget had a $1.45 million shortfall. He was praised for his managerial skills but surrounded himself with old friends and cronies, including a college baseball coach whom he hired at $100,000 a year plus perks (the previous baseball coach, with a winning record, was paid $37,225).

Neale Stoner and the University of Illinois parted company in July

1988 after an audit of the athletic department discovered massive misuse of funds. Even though he agreed to resign, Stoner refused to apologize for—or even acknowledge—any misconduct on his part. He defended himself by explaining that what he had done was a "long-standing practice" at Illinois and at many other schools.

An internal University of Illinois investigation outlined the main complaints against Stoner: "unsupportable and unauthorized credit card charges" (he liked to treat his friends to expensive lunches and dinners—paid for with his athletic department credit card); "the use of maintenance personnel and . . . equipment for personal reasons" (he had university workers make thousands of dollars' worth of repairs on his house and cars as well as on those of two of his assistants); "the use of gifts-in-kind for personal benefit" (he and an assistant "solicited and received $10,752 worth of dry-cleaning services [for themselves and their families] in exchange for game tickets"); and "the use of [athletic program] funds for non-business travel" (he liked to travel in style, often with a large entourage, and pick up the bill—with athletic department funds).

One of Stoner's trips was to the 1987 Maui (Hawaii) Classic in which the Illinois basketball team played. The athletic program paid $12,000 for Stoner and a party of nine to go to Hawaii, ostensibly to see Illinois play—except Stoner and his party went to the Islands five days before the first Illinois tip-off. The Hawaii expenses included $5,000 in airfare for seven of the nine people, $6,000 for the rental of a condo for all nine, and $653 for one dinner for eleven people.

Discovering all the details in cases of athletic department financial abuse is always difficult. "There's a great deal of pick-and-shovel work here," an Illinois vice president/comptroller explained. "You have to track the rabbit all the way through before you know exactly what happened." This comment, and the amount of labor and money necessary for such audits, makes one wonder how many less sensational cases than the Illinois one go undetected.

This AD's money abuses also seem somewhat petty considering that his official salary (in 1986) was $86,000 and that he received perks worth over $25,000 a year. In addition, if the Illinois football or basketball team made it to a postseason bowl or tournament, he received a "bonus equal to [the] coaches' " bonuses and the "larger of two if both coaches get bonuses." (Such bonuses can be worth as much as $100,000.) Stoner also had an excellent retirement clause in his contract: "up to $500,000 guaranteed or $4,167 monthly for up to 120 months if [he] retires at age 65."

Throughout the Stoner case, the Illinois chancellor, Morton Weir, seemed perplexed by the college sports system and unable to find his moral bearings. At one point, Weir explained, "Some of the abuses have been standard procedure for more than twenty years and are clearly detailed in [our athletic] association records," and, the chancellor added, "Stoner has told me he didn't invent the system, that the records were there to see or be audited, and nobody did. That's regrettable, but true."

Stoner's defense—that it's okay to use funds in this way as long as you leave a record—wins an award for moral obtuseness. But not hypocrisy. This AD obviously believed that because his predecessors had done such things, it was correct for him to do so.

When the Illinois chancellor finally asked the athletic director to resign, Weir said: "I believe these [financial dealings] are improper. Neale strongly disagrees that [his] conduct was improper and points out that activities such as these predate his administration. I am also told that similar practices may be found within the athletic programs of many colleges and universities.

"To my mind," Weir continued, "that does not make these practices right, but it does provide a context and an extenuating circumstance which make them easier to understand. Whether this conduct in and of itself would have warranted [Stoner's] discharge will remain an open question."

The athletic director's refusal to apologize, or even to concede the least bit of wrongdoing, appears to the outsider as moral blindness, but within the context of College Sports Inc. it is almost predictable behavior. The chancellor's reluctance to state directly that the actions of the athletic director were grounds for dismissal is less understandable, especially considering that he is the head of one of the most important state universities in the country. Not surprisingly, Illinois later rewarded its former AD with a $300,000 settlement to his contract.

After he announced Stoner's resignation, Weir wondered out loud why all this had happened at his school and said, "I wish I knew the answer, and I hope to God it will stop."

A better question for Chancellor Weir and all heads of colleges and universities with major athletic programs is the old conundrum: How do you dismount from a tiger?

*"The payment of bonuses to athletic [department] personnel
who work in organizing a tournament is a common practice."*

—Item in the *Louisville Courier-Journal*

Neale Stoner was not lying when he told Chancellor Weir that all kinds of financial irregularities occur in the athletic departments of NCAA schools. Stoner could have pointed southeast about 255 miles to Louisville, Kentucky, and outlined how the AD at the University of Louisville disposed of $62,000 left over from a basketball tournament. Even more clearly than the Illinois case, the Louisville incident illustrates the inherent conflict between the business mores of an athletic department and the public service values of an educational institution.

In 1985, the University of Louisville hosted the Metro Conference postseason basketball tournament. The Louisville athletic director, Bill Olsen, and his staff worked hard and put on an excellent tournament, so successful that the final receipts showed a gross of $462,000. Olsen was obligated to give $400,000 of this to the conference in payment for assigning the tourney to Louisville, but $62,000 remained that no one had expected.

Olsen's solution was to send a check for $462,000 to conference officials and ask them, according to the *Louisville Courier-Journal,* to take the extra $62,000 and "write checks to 21 athletic department employees and four [Louisville] merchants." Metro Conference personnel cooperated with Olsen's scheme; the twenty-one athletic department employees received their cash bonuses, "which ranged from $300 to $5,000," and other employees could go to the merchants involved and pick up their gifts. Olsen also included something for himself; court testimony later revealed that "about $4,000 of the $7,500 sent to Jim Cooke [Buick Dealership, one of the merchants] was to go to offset the price of a car [Olsen] was going to purchase for his wife."

A few months later, however, the Louisville president learned of the bonus payments and reprimanded the athletic director. The president said that the AD should have cleared his bonus plan with the school's administration; the athletic director answered that there was no one in the administration supervising athletics at the time and that, as AD, he was in charge of such matters as the $62,000 tourney surplus.

After the facts of the case became public, the *Courier-Journal*'s excellent sports columnist at the time, Billy Reed, wrote a strong defense of the athletic director's conduct:

> The problem [Reed argued] goes back to March when Olsen and his
> staff put in 70-hour weeks, without overtime pay, to help U. of L. put
> on the best Metro Conference tournament in the league's history. . . .
> The large majority of these people earn less than $40,000 a year,
> many less than $30,000, some not even $20,000. Olsen himself
> makes less than $70,000. These are mere peanuts in an athletic
> department budget that, under Olsen, has grown to $8 million. . . .
> And with the $62,000 or so that he still had to show for his efforts,
> Olsen distributed bonuses among the little people who worked so
> hard for such little reward—assistants, sports information folks,
> secretaries and ticket personnel.

Reed then added the argument that is a never-ending mantra in all
discussion of athletic department financial maneuvers: "U. of L. had
engaged in a similar bonus program after the '83 Metro Tournament—
and . . . apparently it's fairly commonplace among universities that hold
such events."

Reed's defense of Olsen is totally tenable if one agrees with his
premise: an athletic department is a business and should be run like one;
thus, if the employees work particularly hard on a project and the
project generates a healthy surplus, the employees should be given
bonuses out of that surplus. This makes perfect sense and is the rule in
business America.

Only one problem exists with Reed's premise. According to the
NCAA Constitution as well as the charters of its member schools,
athletic departments are not set up officially as separate private businesses, and athletic directors are not autonomous CEOs. Most athletic
directors, however, want it all ways: when they have excess revenue and
wish to reward themselves and their employees, they become part of
corporate America and act accordingly; but when they overspend and
lose money, they become an integral part of higher education, embracing the NCAA Constitution and their host schools.

The Louisville case underlines this fatal contradiction between the
corporate and public aspects of College Sports Inc. Consider, in contrast, what happens in a purely academic unit of the same institution.

Since 1973, the language departments of the University of Louisville
have hosted a large Twentieth-Century Literature Conference. Every
year academic department secretaries and staff as well as the faculty
involved work extra hard, often long overtime hours, to insure the
conference's success. The pay scale for these employees of the University of Louisville is far lower than that for athletic department person-

nel, often half the pay of "the little people" that Reed sniffled over.

On a number of occasions, the Twentieth-Century Literature Conference has been more successful than anticipated, hosting more visitors and participants than planned, thus generating a surplus. Did any of this money go directly into the pockets of the staff and faculty who worked so hard? Could any of them go to local merchants for free gifts funded by the conference surplus? The answer, of course, is no, and most academics would find such an arrangement upsetting—not because faculty and staff are against money and gifts when appropriate, but because they believe that hosting an educational conference on a profit-and-loss basis opposes the basic premise of academic meetings, i.e., scholars and students gathering to share their latest research and ideas.

No doubt the president of Louisville, or someone in his administration, watches the profit-and-loss figures on the annual Twentieth-Century Literature Conference and, if there is too much red ink one year, inquires about its management efficiency, and if the losses grow, questions the feasibility of its continuing for too many more years. But simple profit or loss never impels a school to begin an annual conference or to end one. Wider educational concerns and issues are at stake: "How does this meeting benefit our faculty, other scholars in the field, our students, our academic reputation, etc.?"

No one ever asked such questions about hosting the Metro Conference basketball tournament. When putting on a tourney, the Louisville athletic department thinks in terms of profit and, like every professional sports club in America, asks: How will we make a buck out of this event? How much can we charge for tickets?" Unlike pro teams, however, College Sports Inc. franchises tend not to ask the follow-up questions: "If we don't make money out of this event, how will we cover our losses?"

Athletic directors like to say that they live in "the real world," and they accuse university presidents and faculty of existing in "ivory towers" where the inhabitants do not have to deal with business matters, particularly profit-and-loss statements.

In fact, the "unreal world" appears to be College Sports Inc., where athletic directors can play with their programs' revenues and not worry too much about the red ink on the floor.

To understand how athletic departments deal with—or, most often, fail to handle—profit and loss, a detailed examination of the revenues and expenses of athletic departments is necessary. This examination also provides an in-depth guide to the "unreal world" of College Sports Inc.

CHAPTER 2

Earned Revenue: Ticket Sales

*"ESPN's Beano Cook, about the possibility of adding a
12th game to the [college football] season: 'It's absolutely
insane. No matter how much money they [athletic
programs] have, it's never enough.' "*

—Item in *USA Today*

FILLING FOOTBALL STADIUMS with ticket-buying customers is College
Sports Inc.'s traditional method of generating revenue. However, attendance for college football games is down—last season a decrease of
close to 900,000 from the previous year for the lowest total in almost
a decade. And the NCAA, in its most recent *Revenues and Expenses
of Intercollegiate Athletics Programs* study, reveals that although
ticket sales are still the main source of revenue for big-time athletic programs, they are a decreasing percentage of the entire revenue picture,
and, in the smaller programs, they are not a dominant source of income.

The decline in football attendance is probably due to the proliferation
of college games on television. Not only does wall-to-wall telecasting
overexpose the big-time Division I-A teams, it also undercuts the
hundreds of schools in the lower divisions and outside the NCAA. In
comparison to the product on TV, all other versions of college football
appear "small-time," and potential spectators for those games are less
interested in attending these games.

Some of the athletic directors who run College Sports Inc. have predictable solutions to the ticket sales problem: add a twelfth regular season game and build bigger stadiums. When told of his school's negotiations for an extra game, the football coach at Arkansas said, "Like anything else, it's an athletic director's decision, and it's based on money. . . . They would schedule seventeen games if they could." And during the 1989 season some schools played twelve regular season games and ADs began to lobby the NCAA for a thirteenth.

The other solution is to add more seats to already mammoth stadiums in the hopes of assembling football teams that can win the college sports lottery. Athletic directors like to point to Michigan with its consistently sold-out 101,701-seat stadium as justification for plant expansion. And so the University of Kentucky, in a region without a natural recruiting area and thus a team usually in the bottom half of its conference standings, and in a relatively small college town with no nearby population centers, plans to expand its 57,000-seat stadium, adding 13,000 seats at a cost of $12 million. The hometown newspaper in Lexington commented, "Questions have been raised as to why UK, which seldom draws capacity crowds, would want a larger stadium." The Kentucky athletic director who began the project replied, "We feel there's sufficient interest to warrant expansion. And if we have winning teams, I think we'd pack the place."

But what happens if the football team loses, or just muddles along as the Wildcats usually do? Will all those fans come disguised, as the joke goes, as empty seats? In 1985, the San Jose University Spartans had a terrible season, and the following spring, the *San Jose Mercury News* reported that the football team's "2–8–1 record sank attendance and created a $250,000 [athletic department] deficit and a full-blown financial crisis" for the school. The 1985–86 San Jose athletics budget had been based on a "projected 20,000 average attendance and $315,306 in revenue for four home games . . . [but] the reality was average paid attendance of 8,800 and $105,477 in revenue." The newspaper pointed out that previous to this budget projection, the school's "best paid [average] attendance was 11,190 in 1983. In 1981, when the football team finished 9–2 and was nationally ranked, average attendance was 10,148." Again, an athletic department based its budget on projections for a year better than it had ever known.

*"They are called 'donations,' but there is little
philanthropy involved. Nearly every major college
institution now requires a donation to give a person the
right to buy the school's best season tickets. . . . The more
you fork over, the better the seats."*

—Item in the *Louisville Courier-Journal*

When Mary Alice Hill was athletic director at San Diego State in 1983–84, she faced an even worse problem than the one at San Jose: her Aztecs, after great years under coach Don Coryell, had entered the 1980s in a trough and were plowing lower; her average attendance had dropped from 35,000 a game to 20,000; and her department, which depended upon football ticket sales to carry its other sports, was running a deficit of $750,000.

Ms. Hill's solution—one that has become the norm with athletic departments—was to introduce "priority seating": fans who want season tickets in the best spots in the stadium have to make an extra contribution to the athletic department for the "right" to buy those seats. Even though the "donation" is tax-deductible, Mary Alice Hill, like all ADs who initiate this form of raising money, incurred the anger of many Aztec fans, especially longtime supporters who held good seats for no additional cost. Eventually the San Diego priority-seating plan was accepted but its implementation contributed to Ms. Hill's unpopularity and the eventual loss of her job as AD.

When the athletic director at Boise State University, in Idaho, tried to start a priority-seating plan at his school in 1982, the fan uproar was so great that it immediately cost him his job. In firing his AD, the Boise State president said, "I am concerned with collegiality and university-community relations, . . . I could tell this [priority-seating plan] was an affront to both of those things."

By 1990, however, because of the need to generate more revenue, athletic directors had introduced priority seating at about 90 percent of the big-time athletic schools and 75 percent of the smaller ones. The scheme has a number of drawbacks: most significantly, it binds ticket sales to the necessity of winning, thus increasing the pressure on coaches to get maximum production out of their student-athletes. Fans who are forced to pay top dollar are less likely to tolerate losing teams, and are less loyal than longtime supporters who pay only face value for their tickets. Priority seating, although a logical business innovation for

College Sports Inc., further removes intercollegiate athletics from its recreational and community origins.

Athletic directors, while increasing ticket sale revenue with priority seating, have also tolerated a major loss of this revenue through "leakage"—those spectators who gain free admission and whose dollars never enter the till. A state audit of the University of Missouri's athletic department books once turned up $125,000 in complimentary tickets; a report on leakage at Louisiana State University led the school's president to conclude that "eliminating LSU's complimentary ticket policy will generate about $450,000 if persons now receiving free tickets choose to purchase them." The LSU president also wanted to increase ticket sale revenue by ending the 50 percent discount that students and faculty received. However, discontinuing discounts to students and faculty—many schools have done this—does not address the main cause of ticket sale leakage—slack athletic department management.

> "Basketball is a budgetary winner for some institutions but net income from basketball is rarely sufficiently large to carry a significant portion of the costs of nonrevenue-producing sports."
>
> —The Money Game: Financing Collegiate Athletics, an American Council on Education report

One of the money winners in college basketball is the University of Louisville, located in a basketball-loving region and without competition from a major professional team. In the mid-1980s, Louisville decided to extract more money from its successful basketball program to help pay for its losses in other sports. From 1983, when a season ticket required a $200 donation, the price went, in 1985, to $500 plus face value of the tickets for ordinary seats in Freedom Hall. Fans who wanted a package of twelve choice season tickets for basketball and twenty-four for football had to pay $12,500 in 1984 and $25,000 in 1985.

When the price increases were announced, the Louisville Courier-Journal asked the school's basketball coach, Denny Crum, if he was "concerned about long-time season-ticket holders who can't afford the new donor rates." Crum replied, "There are different circumstances now for the university. . . . Those people have got their money's worth."

The *Courier-Journal* also printed a chart of the new seating arrangement in 19,000-seat Freedom Hall for the basketball season. Priority season tickets and public sale seats occupied all parts of the arena except for a student section behind one basket and a faculty and staff section in the second tier slightly behind and parallel to a basket. Of the seats in Freedom Hall, about 10 percent were allocated to the university community. (A chart of Louisville's football seating revealed a similar percentage for students, faculty, and staff.) In 1989, when the school increased prices again, it added more seats to the "priority" categories—some of the worst seats in Freedom Hall now require a "donation" to the athletic program.

Thus the University of Louisville sells almost all of its basketball and football tickets the same way any professional team does: as many season tickets as possible at the highest possible market price and the rest in individual game sales. In Louisville, the only difference between buyers of season tickets to the U. of L. teams and, say, purchasers of season passes for the Louisville Cardinal AAA baseball team, which shares its stadium with the U. of L. football squad, is that the college fans can write off a major portion of their season tickets as a tax-deductible donation to an educational institution.

One of the drawbacks to priority-seating plans like Louisville's is that they price students out of all but the worst football seats, and for basketball, almost out of the arena (at some schools, students are only allowed to buy tickets for a few games, often the least attractive contests on the schedule). This situation is particularly reprehensible at institutions where mandatory student fees go to the athletic department to help balance its budget and to pay the debt servicing on the stadiums and arenas. Yet, because of College Sports Inc.'s hunger for revenue, the day might come when big-time programs will admit only a small number of students to sports events, and those mainly as college atmosphere props for the TV cameras.

Basketball is not a certain source of revenue for athletic departments, especially beyond the charmed circle of the successful programs like Louisville's. Even though basketball is a low-capital-expense sport (fifteen scholarships and minor equipment costs), the NCAA's most recent edition of *Revenues and Expenses* reported that only 49 percent of the big-time basketball programs made a profit from the sport (based on ticket sales, media money, and other revenue), and merely 15 percent of the schools in all of the other divisions made money from it. Thus, at most institutions, basketball not only fails to carry the rest of the athletic department budget, often it cannot cover its own costs.

For College Sports Inc., football and men's basketball are the revenue-generating sports. Of the over ten thousand teams in other college sports, only a few baseball and hockey programs consistently make money, and occasionally a soccer or a wrestling team pays its own way. No school covers expenses in sports like swimming, track-and-field, gymnastics, volleyball, tennis, or golf.

The NCAA's most recent survey of *Revenues and Expenses* confirms the deficits for these "minor" college sports. Ticket sales are usually their only source of earned revenue, and in big-time athletic programs, these averaged $164,000, or 3 percent of total program revenues. Because the expenses for these sports—coaches' salaries, athletic scholarships, travel, equipment, facilities, etc.—are enormously high, usually $2 million-plus at a big-time school, the NCAA's term for them, "nonrevenue sports," is particularly apt.

> *"The football season can last from August 15 to January 1, and the basketball season from mid-October to the end of March. Some college baseball teams play almost one hundred games a season, with two-week road trips not uncommon."*
>
>   —D. Stanley Eitzen, professor of the
>   sociology of sport at Colorado
>   State University

Ticket sale revenue is obviously tied to the number of games played. For over a decade, some presidents of NCAA schools have argued that the length of college sports' seasons and the high number of NCAA-permitted games force student-athletes to neglect their studies. The former head of Georgetown University, the Reverend Timothy J. Healy, complained, "The length and intensity of seasons are positively ridiculous," and he called for specific cuts in the numbers of games played.

Educators like Father Healy are correct, but the NCAA, controlled by athletic directors, has usually rejected their arguments and proposals. Proponents of the status quo, as well as those ADs who want longer seasons, use a simple rebuttal: The more games, the more ticket sales and revenue, and the less money we'll lose.

In 1984–85, on the wave of the presidents' reform movement within the association, the NCAA Executive Council proposed a modest decrease in the number of contests in various sports—for example, a reduction of ten regular season baseball games. The membership refused to pass even these minor cuts. The president of the American [College] Baseball Coaches Association stated the majority position clearly: "With some institutions relying on ticket sales to help support the [baseball] team . . . a reduction in games would be devastating."

The proposals to cut the number of basketball games were particularly controversial and adamantly opposed. The attitude of Syracuse University, with one of the most prosperous basketball programs in the NCAA thanks to its huge Carrier Dome and an average of 20,000 spectators per home game, was typical of the big-time schools. When the Syracuse associate athletic director was asked how dropping a single home game would hurt his department's revenue, he replied, "Well, take twenty thousand fans, multiply that by eight dollars a ticket, add parking fees, concession sales, and any television revenue . . ."

More recently, at the 1990 NCAA convention, the presidents managed to pass a proposal to cut three games from the official basketball season. Again the athletic directors and coaches opposed it on economic grounds. Syracuse AD Jake Crouthamel argued that since his home attendance now averaged 29,000, his athletic program would lose "significant dollars" if any games were cut. However, the Presidents' Commission proposal does not go into effect until August 1992, and the ADs and program heads have vowed to overturn it before then.

Reducing the number of contests will affect revenue in two areas of college sports. At schools with prosperous basketball programs, cutting games, according to Louisville coach Denny Crum, "will hurt all the minor, non-income-producing sports. . . . If there is a shortage of income, it will be reflected in the budget of other sports, not in [men's] basketball and football." In addition, a reduction in games will slam the finances of the multitude of have-not athletic programs that rely on a few contests every year against Division I powers for their best paydays (these games are the most logical drops from the majors' schedules). Thus, reducing the official basketball season by even three games could severely weaken the precarious economic state of intercollegiate athletics.

———

Some critics of College Sports Inc. see its never-ending scramble for dollars as simple greed; however, a careful examination of the financial ledger, especially of such items as ticket sales, reveals necessity as well. And the main cause of this constant need for more revenue is mismanagement.

Attendance is on a gradual downward slope in football and a small upward incline in basketball because of the decision to overexpose these products. Attendance in other college sports is at the bottom of the mountain and shows no significant signs of movement; these bloated "nonrevenue" programs lose millions of dollars annually.

The bottom line on ticket sales, the traditional means of generating revenue in all college sports, is clear: they are flat and give no promise of improvement. However, unlike other American corporations in similar financial situations, College Sports Inc. cannot blame foreign competition. The athletic directors of America created their own problems.

CHAPTER 3

Earned Revenue: Guarantees

*"The [Georgetown] Hoyas hammered Shenandoah
114–40. . . . Shenandoah is a Division III cupcake from
Winchester, Va., that has produced two winning seasons
in the last 17 years. Its gymnasium seats 680.*
*"Why would a man volunteer his kids for 40 minutes
of impersonating a heavy [punching] bag?*
*" 'We got a real good guarantee,' said Dave Dutton,
Shenandoah's coach and athletic director."*

—Rick Bozich, *Louisville Courier-Journal*

ONE OF the most important but little-known duties of an athletic director
is to negotiate guarantees—the payments to visiting teams of fees and/
or percentages of the gate. Often large sums of money are at stake and
negotiations between ADs are more like poker table dealings than
academic discussions.

The Georgetown-Shenandoah game occurred because athletic directors of powerhouse programs like to schedule some home games against
weak opponents from obscure conferences, both to improve won-lost
records and to slip some mediocre contests into season-ticket packages.
The slang phrase that ADs use to describe the practice is "to buy" an
opponent. The ADs of the weak teams agree to send their players to
certain defeat and humiliation because the guarantees for these games
are often a major source of revenue for their programs.

In College Sports Inc., as in any branch of the entertainment business, the amount of the guarantee varies according to the gate potential
of the visitor. Weak opponents like Shenandoah receive a five-figure
sum that looks huge to them but is peanuts to the big-time programs.
The most attractive performers in college sports, the winningest teams,
demand hefty fees to visit. The athletic director at the University of

Miami explained last year that "the lesser [football] programs go for $80,000 to $125,000"—Cincinnati, Virginia Tech, and Toledo were among Miami's "lesser" visitors in recent years—"while the bigger schools are asking $175,000 to $250,000." Notre Dame and Florida qualified for these higher guarantees from Miami.

And when the Miami Hurricanes, who won a number of national championships in the 1980s, go on the road, they receive top guarantee payments. In 1984, the *Miami Herald* reported that "nearly $1 million [of Miami's athletic department revenue] will come from guarantees for showing up at away [football] games." As the Hurricanes continued to win later in the decade, the team's guarantee revenue increased and now approaches the $1.5 million mark, a profit of at least $500,000 (Miami pays out less than a million to teams that visit the Orange Bowl).

Yet, in 1984 the *Miami Herald* also reported, "In the past six years, the UM athletic department hasn't supported itself. It lost more than $1 million a year." And in 1988 the athletic director who presided over the football success, Sam Jankovich, admitted, "Still, we're not *making* money. Our institution costs are so much greater [than our revenue]" (his emphasis). The main reason that expenses outpaced revenues is that the Miami AD increased his athletic department spending from $5.8 million to $12.9 million in just four years.

As Miami proves, even millions of dollars from guarantees do not insure black ink. When the Reverend Edward "Monk" Malloy, the Notre Dame president, announced in August 1987 that his athletic program would lose money in the coming year, the reason he listed first was guarantees: of five home games in 1987, two were against Navy and the University of Southern California, and for those games "profits are to be split 50–50 instead of the usual 80–20." Someone should have told the good father that Navy did not deserve a 50–50 split, or even an 80–20 one, and that he should order his AD back to the poker table to work a better deal.

In the world of college sports, after all, an agreed-upon guarantee is not necessarily a done deal. Guarantees frequently come unstuck, as they did at the University of Akron, in 1985, after that school hired ex–Notre Dame coach Gerry Faust and decided to move to the top division (I-A) in football.

The first team on the home schedule for Faust's inaugural season was Salem College of West Virginia. Salem had previously agreed to a guarantee of $10,000, but when the visitors realized how badly the recently hired Faust and his upgraded program needed an opening win, they refused to come to Akron for less than a $20,000 guarantee. The Akron athletic director at the time, Dave Adams, explained Salem's jacked-up price and his acquiescing to it by stating, "I guess they decided that if they were going to come up here and take a beating, they were going to get paid for it."

Another Akron opponent that year, the University of Central Florida in Orlando, also didn't like its agreed-upon guarantee. Akron had an away-and-home contract with Central Florida and had already played there for a $25,000 fee; however, the summer before Faust's debut, the Floridians demanded more visiting-team money and said that they would pay the contract's $10,000 no-show forfeit rather than come for only the agreed-upon $25,000.

Dave Adams never called his opponent's bluff; instead, he paid Central Florida an additional $10,000 for honoring their original contract by showing up, making the new total guarantee $35,000. The Akron AD commented, "We got held up [by Central Florida] at the last minute."

Sometimes athletic departments also manipulate guarantee revenue in creative ways. In 1984, at the University of Nevada at Las Vegas, the Regents discovered that the athletic department was using "football game guarantee funds for recruiting players and other uses," i.e., they were taking the money set aside for guarantee expenses and spending it on other things in the hope that they could come up with the guarantee money when the payments were due. The UNLV athletic director defended this practice by pointing out that for fifteen of the previous sixteen years, the athletic department had operated by "advanced borrowing"—balancing this year's budget by adding revenue *expected* in the following year. When the Regents were told of the 1984 shortfall, they had to loan the university $400,000 to help cover the deficit.

> *"Money: The [Big West] Conference needs it badly. . . . For this reason Big West schools trap themselves into big-payday, no-win situations by playing road games against powerful Division I-A teams in [the Big West's] search of guaranteed paydays."*
>
> —Item in *Don Heinrich's College Football*

Guarantees show that for College Sports Inc. unethical conduct is often part of regular business procedures. Not only are signed contracts broken but, more significantly, when athletic directors schedule power-house teams against weak opponents, essentially they are selling their student-athletes for commercial gain. What other explanation is there for Georgetown's 114–40 mugging of the innocents from Shenandoah; Michigan's 104–66 battering of South Dakota State; and, in football, Florida's 58–0 smashing of the Indiana State Sycamores, and the humiliations that Big West teams endure when they visit the strongest football schools in the country—USC 66–10 over Utah State, Auburn 55–0 over Pacific, Oklahoma 73–3 over New Mexico State.

CHAPTER 4

Earned Revenue: Payouts from Bowl Games & Tournaments

"The NCAA doled out over $28.6 million to the 64 teams that participated in its Division I [1988 men's basketball] tournament including $1,153,000 to the Final Four teams."

—Item in the *Chronicle of Higher Education*

HEADLINES AND lead paragraphs such as the above imply that Kansas, Oklahoma, Duke, and Arizona all hit the $1 million-plus jackpot at the NCAA tourney. Further down in the story, if the journal is like the *Chronicle of Higher Education* and given to accuracy, the real numbers emerge: Arizona took home $138,000; the two Big Eight schools, $450,000 each; and Duke did best with $840,000. The reason, in the accounting term used by the NCAA, was "distributions."

Big-time athletic programs hope that the payouts from bowl games and tournaments will be a major source of revenue. However, unless they do not belong to a conference, they have to share their payouts with fellow conference members. Arizona's take from the 1988 NCAA tourney was so low because it participates in an equal-split payout plan with the nine other schools of the Pac-10. In this case, two Pac-10 teams earned money from the 1988 tournament: Oregon State gained $230,700 for its first-round appearance, and Arizona, $1,153,000; that total, split ten ways, equals $138,000 and change for each Pac-10 school. The Big Eight schools did better because five of their members participated and divided $3,691,000 eight ways. Duke did best of all because its conference, the Atlantic Coast, allows its members to keep first-round winnings as well as 70 percent of all other round earnings.

Most athletic programs work so hard for the pot o' gold and then keep only a percentage, often a small one, of it. In addition, for the NCAA basketball tournament, the pot o' gold is 50 to 60 percent of the total net receipts—the NCAA retains the rest to pay tournament expenses and to balance its own books.

Athletic directors must sometimes feel that the pot o' gold is as elusive as its location at the end of the rainbow. This is particularly true of football bowl payouts. Every year, newspapers print charts of the bowl games and their payouts to participating schools; rarely do they note whether the million-dollar figures are for "guaranteed" or "estimated" payouts and, if the latter and based partly on attendance, that the "actual" payouts can be much lower. In addition, some schools even move money to the bowl sponsors by agreeing to take huge allotments of tickets: although the University of Mississippi was ranked fifty-second nationally, the Liberty Bowl invited it to the 1989 game in part because Ole Miss guaranteed the sale of 20,000 seats.

In 1987, Indiana University's football team played in the All-American Bowl and, in 1988, the Peach Bowl. For each of these events, the reported payouts were $800,000, but the Indiana AD later admitted that these "appearances . . . brought the university about $250,000 each year." The distribution plan of Indiana's conference, the Big Ten, gives half of a payout to the participating school and splits the other half nine ways. Indiana's half of the All-American and Peach Bowl payouts was reportedly $800,000, but the school received only $500,000. The vanished $300,000 is typical of the appearance-versus-reality of bowl game payouts.

But even $250,000 a year is a substantial sum; what happens to the check from the bowl committee when the money arrives on campus? It stays in the athletic department. The average student or faculty member almost never benefits from a bowl or tournament payout. The exception that proves this rule occurred in the payouts from the 1987 All-American Bowl. The bowl sponsors announced that they were giving $100,000 to the general scholarship funds of the participating schools and they trumpeted the fact that this was "the first time in history that a bowl sponsor designated [payout] money for nonathletic purposes." Considering that by 1987, in the eighty-five years of postseason games, the bowls had paid out more than $400 million, the All-American Bowl's contributions to the academic scholarship funds of Indiana University and Florida State University came to one two-thousandth, or

.0005 percent, of all the money that bowls had sent to American colleges and universities.

> *"I have one question to ask regarding revenue sharing. Am I the only capitalist in this room? . . . All the games that Georgetown plays in and all the money that Georgetown wins, I'm going on record as saying that I think [the money] should go to Georgetown. I'm going to tell you the pity of it all. I don't think that I'm the only one that feels that way."*
>
> —John Thompson, head basketball coach at Georgetown University

Thompson was replying, at the 1988 NCAA convention, to the suggestion by a Division III college president that the association, and especially the major programs, be more generous in distributing payout money in order to help all the college sports programs in financial difficulty. Thompson's sentiments prevailed and, at present, a small number of big-time programs keep an increasing percentage of payout revenue for themselves. In fact, some ADs with perennially winning teams would like to change their conference splits and retain even more of the payout pie.

The argument for less equitable distribution is based on the appeal to capitalism that John Thompson articulated; its effect would be triage— throw overboard the huge number of athletic programs losing money and keep the few fat cats in the lifeboat. More payout money for the few would help them stay at the top of their conferences and more easily gain berths in postseason events; it would also insure that the large number of also-rans would trail behind at a greater distance each year. In the end, not only would the small-time programs sink but so would most of the Division I also-rans. At that point, those big-time programs left in the college sports lifeboat would play each other and have the "Super Conference" that many of their ADs have long dreamed about.

Most big-time athletic directors and coaches do approve of sharing some payout money with one group—themselves. Every year, the college football season begins with the Collegiate Kickoff Classic, held in late August—before classes at most schools start—at Giants Stadium in New Jersey. The payout from the 1988 Classic included $1.2

million to the National Association of Collegiate Directors of Athletics and $500,000 to the American [College] Football Coaches Association. The two schools, Texas A. & M. and Nebraska, received $690,000 each but had to split this money with their conferences. The largest payout, $2.5 million, went to the College Hall of Fame, a pet project of the NCAA and of most athletic directors and coaches.

When, in 1983, the plan for the Kickoff Classic was first announced, Joe Paterno, head football coach at Penn State, said, "It's typical of this association [the NCAA]. Every time we need a little more money for something, we just make the kids work a little harder. This means they'll have to start practice in the middle of the summer."

> *"The best of the bowls came up short on New Year's Day [1988] as the Rose Bowl turned in its worst ratings performance ever. By Jan. 2, the TV networks knew who the biggest losers were: Themselves."*
>
> —Headline in *Sports Inc.: The Sports Business Weekly*

A year after the above headline, the Rose Bowl was in even worse shape—its ratings had dropped from 16.5 in 1988 to 10.8 for its 1989 game (a rating point indicates approximately 900,000 homes tuned to a program). In addition, the seven New Year's bowls on TV in 1989, including the attractive "national championship game" between Notre Dame and West Virginia, had fewer total viewers than the six on TV the previous January 1. Because a huge proportion of the payouts from bowls are based on the TV revenue from the games, statistics such as these and the facts behind them must give the people in Pasadena and other bowl locations some anxious moments. Moreover, the 1989 figures did not begin a trend; from 1983 on, TV ratings for bowl games have declined—the Rose Bowl from 24.5 that year, and the Cotton Bowl and Sugar Bowl also by more than 50 percent.

New York advertising executives, in charge of buying commercial time on TV for their clients, believe that the "glut" of bowl games on television causes the lower ratings. As a result, they are paying less money for commercials. In 1986, NBC sold thirty-second spots during the Rose Bowl game for $222,000; a year later, for $205,000; and in 1988, for between $125,000 and $150,000. In 1989, NBC stopped broadcasting the Rose Bowl game.

In an article about NBC's dropping of the Rose Bowl, a sports business magazine wrote: "Declining Rose Bowl ratings, in part, led to the telecast's move to ABC. Plans are in the works to revive the game's popularity, but it won't be easy."

Nevertheless the proliferation, or "glut," of bowls continues, with new events beginning every year. The glamour of holding a bowl game attracts the new players, and each added bowl wants to move to New Year's Day as soon as possible.

For the 1989–90 season, the Cactus Bowl in Tucson, Arizona, and the Crab Bowl in Baltimore, Maryland, were to begin operations. In the NCAA's packet of instructions to the Baltimore people, the association probably did not include a list of failed bowls in northern cities: the Great Lakes Bowl in Cleveland, Ohio, one year of operation, 1947; the Aviation Bowl in Dayton, Ohio, one year, 1961; the Gotham Bowl, two years in the Big Apple, 1961–62; the Garden State Bowl, four years in the Meadowlands, 1978–81; and the Cherry Bowl in an all-weather indoor stadium in Pontiac, Michigan, two years, 1985–86.

The list of failed bowls nationally is much longer and, even during the late 1980s bowl boom period, such venerable events as the Bluebonnet Bowl suspended operations. The Houston, Texas, event owed over $400,000, and could not put on its 1989 game. That the bowl had continued for twenty-eight consecutive years carried little weight with the NCAA: Pay out or close up was its dictum.

> *"I recognize the tremendous financial crunch [in college sports]. But this [College Super Bowl] looks to me like somebody's just trying to make money. Football always seems to be the most convenient vehicle. It's just another greedy thing to do."*
>
> —Don James, head football coach at the University of Washington

In only one sport and one division does the NCAA not have a playoff and final championship game—Division I-A big-time football. Before the 1980s, some members of the association suggested a playoff and championship game but complications, especially over the format for arriving at the final two teams, always short-circuited the discussion.

Then the NFL Super Bowl came to be the single most important American sporting event, and college athletic directors noticed that there was an empty weekend in January between the completion of the AFC and NFC playoffs and the Super Bowl. What better way to fill it than with a College Super Bowl?

In January 1984, the NCAA appointed a committee to study the feasibility of the game and the playoffs leading to it. Some educators opposed the entire idea on the grounds that a championship tournament would keep football players from their studies for too long. In subsequent discussion, this argument disappeared under the weight of the real opposition: the various bowl committees, who feared that a College Super Bowl would relegate their events—which, at best, would be used as quarterfinal and semifinal games leading to the championship—to second- and third-rate status and a subsequent loss of prestige and revenue.

At the next NCAA convention, the members rejected the College Super Bowl proposal, mainly because they did not want to disrupt the bowl game system. However, the big-time football programs refused to let the idea of a playoff and championship game die. The College Football Association, representing sixty-six of the heavyweights, worked quietly on the concept and, in 1989, went public with a specific proposal for a sixteen-team playoff to begin in early December and to culminate in a championship game on the weekend before the Super Bowl. The educational arguments against this plan, particularly the lengthier season for football players, were again brushed aside. The AD of the Air Force Academy pointed out that "there are four or five sports at most schools that lose more academic days than football. Nobody says anything when Seton Hall's basketball team comes out west and stays three weeks during the tournament. . . . The academic argument is just not a factor."

And it isn't. The main opposition to the playoff and championship game proposal is economic, and it still comes from the bowl committees as well as from the two major conferences that do not belong to the CFA, the Big Ten and the Pacific Ten. (These conferences also have a long-term agreement with the Rose Bowl for their champions to appear in that game.) Because teams like Michigan, USC, and UCLA could contend for a national title, the CFA cannot unilaterally set up a championship system. However, considering the potential payout involved, it is an idea whose time has almost come, and if the money is right, the Big Ten and Pacific Ten might be willing to renegotiate their Rose Bowl contracts. If the College Super Bowl occurs, each bowl committee will have to accept whatever quarterfinal or semifinal game is handed to it, and because only six can be involved in the New Year's and early January rounds of the playoffs, the majority of bowls will die.

The argument over the football championship game suggests that College Sports Inc., in an apparently late stage of its economic development, has begun to devour its own—not only the student-athletes and the bowl games that have provided it with payouts for so long, but also the majority of its schools. Wayne Duke, longtime commissioner of the Big Ten, predicts, "A national football playoff would draw a further line of demarcation between the haves and the have-nots, and just the elites would be playing for the national football championship."

The dream of a College Super Bowl, a huge pot of money for the top college football teams, has begun to obsess some athletic directors. That a College Super Bowl, by forever excluding the also-rans, could become a nightmare for the majority of ADs is equally possible.

Before radically altering the present system, athletic directors should study NCAA history, especially the events of the early 1980s and what happened to all the money from TV that was supposed to cascade into athletic departments after two CFA schools, with the CFA's support, forever changed the rules on televising college sports.

CHAPTER 5

Earned Revenue: TV

*"There are three definitions as to why they did it [the CFA
schools' legal challenge of the NCAA's TV monopoly].
Greed, greed, and greed."*

—Gene Slaughter, athletic director at Capital
University, Columbus, Ohio

IN THE BEGINNING, there was Penn. During the 1940s, the University of
Pennsylvania, with some outstanding football teams, televised all of its
home games. When other schools started doing the same, some college
sports officials worried about the effect of TV on game attendance. In
1951, a majority of the NCAA membership, convinced that televising
college football had to be limited, passed the NCAA's first TV rule: one
national game a week on television and for only seven Saturdays in any
one region.

Penn challenged the new ruling; the NCAA declared the school a
member in "bad standing," and Penn's four visiting opponents for 1951
refused to come. Penn capitulated and the NCAA monopoly on televising intercollegiate football began.

For the next three decades, as both television and college football
increased in popularity, the NCAA refined its monopoly, eventually
enforcing a "limited appearance" set of rules: a school could appear on
TV only three times during a two-season period; also, games from each
of the twelve football conferences had to be telecast a minimum number
of times during the two-year period.

A myth has grown up about the days of the NCAA's TV monopoly of
college football: that all members of the association, including those in

Divisions II and III, received an equitable share of the wealth. In fact, as the *Chronicle of Higher Education* pointed out in 1975, "television money is heavily concentrated in a fraction of the NCAA's 700 member institutions," with the major football powers appearing the maximum allowed, and the minor ones the minimum. But appearance money was excellent: at the peak of the NCAA's monopoly, a school received $600,000 for a nationally telecast game.

Not everyone, however, was happy with the NCAA's control: the powerhouse football programs believed that they could earn even more money by being on TV as often as their winning teams merited; the networks complained that frequently they could not telecast the best games because the big-time schools had exhausted their allotment of appearances; and the fans wanted to see their favorite teams more often.

In 1976, sixty-one of the major football powers formed the College Football Association and immediately started lobbying within the NCAA for a TV contract that favored them, as well as for greater control over player eligibility and the terms of athletic scholarships. In 1981, the CFA began negotiating a separate TV deal with NBC-TV—a direct challenge to the NCAA's monopoly. Some educators saw the CFA's moves as part of a wider plan to expand big-time college sports, and they warned that "the prospect of huge television revenues . . . puts too much pressure on the institutions and the coaches to win at all costs, even if it means paying athletes, doctoring their academic transcripts, or violating rules in other ways."

The CFA backed away from its NBC contract and, in return, the NCAA agreed to restructure its major football division, removing over forty institutions, including all but one Ivy League school and the black colleges, from Division I-A status. This gave CFA members greater control over big-time football—except for the TV contracts. The CFA continued to press its TV demands and the NCAA refused to give in. In early 1982, the universities of Georgia and Oklahoma, with the CFA's backing as well as its help with legal fees, took the NCAA to court.

The case was heard in federal district court in New Mexico, and in his opinion in favor of Georgia and Oklahoma, Judge Juan Burciaga blistered the NCAA: "The court concludes that the NCAA controls over [televising] college football make the NCAA a classic cartel," and that the NCAA particularly discriminated against "the prominent pro- ducers, such as Georgia and Oklahoma . . . whose superior competitive practices have earned them prominence in the sport of college football [and they] wish to no longer suffer the economic injury visited upon them by the less prominent members of the cartel."

Judge Burciaga also ruled that one of "the most pernicious aspects" of the NCAA's TV monopoly was that "the viewers of college football receive absolutely no benefit from the [NCAA's] controls. . . . Consumer demand and the free market are sacrificed to the interests of the NCAA administration and its allies among the membership. . . . It is clear that [the] NCAA is in violation of Section 1 of the Sherman [Antitrust] Act." The judge concluded by ordering the NCAA to cease its monopoly over the televising of college football.

The parties to the case were not prepared for such a clear, unequivocal ruling. The NCAA had expected a version of the status quo and the CFA schools had hoped for a ruling partially in their favor, one that would provide leverage in future negotiations with the NCAA. Instead, as one of the lawyers for Oklahoma exulted, "It's a total blowout. It goes down the line with everything we contended."

Other commentators were less ecstatic. The athletic director at Eastern Kentucky University said, "The decision means the rich get richer and the poor can go to hell." The AD and football coach at Capital University in Columbus, Ohio, worried that his team "might be forced to compete on Saturdays directly with an OSU [Ohio State University] television network," and he wondered whether "it's going to put the small universities out of the football business."

Even some CFA people were less than overjoyed. Joe Paterno, the Penn State football coach, had been active in the CFA's opposition to the NCAA's TV monopoly, but he wanted a restructured system, not the total free market that Judge Burciaga ordered. "The idea," Paterno explained, "is to let the rich get a little richer while not letting them be hogs."

> *"There can be no doubt that the challenged practices of the NCAA constitute a 'restraint of trade' in the sense that they limit members' freedom to negotiate and enter into their own television contracts."*
>
> —Justice John Paul Stevens for the majority of
> the Supreme Court

The NCAA, with its teams of lawyers, fought Judge Burciaga's decision through the courts, and with the government joining the plaintiffs' side, the parties arrived before the Supreme Court in March 1984. In a truly sophistic argument, the NCAA's lawyers told the justices that "its tight control over football broadcasts had actually enhanced competition in the television marketplace, not illegally inhibited it."

In July 1984, the Supreme Court gave its verdict, voting 7–2 to uphold Judge Burciaga's decision. The majority opinion, written by Justice John Paul Stevens, reaffirmed that the college athletic programs of America were free to negotiate their own TV contracts. The dissenting opinion, by Justice Byron "Whizzer" White, an all-American at the University of Colorado in the 1930s, invoked a college sports world that had long since vanished, if it ever existed. White argued that the NCAA's former "television plan reflects the NCAA's fundamental policy of preserving amateurism and integrating athletics and education," and that his fellow justices err "in treating intercollegiate athletics under the NCAA's control as a purely commercial venture in which colleges and universities participate solely, or even primarily, in the pursuit of profits."

As with the Burciaga decision, the college sports community reacted immediately. Oklahoma City's *Daily Oklahoman* summed up the comments with, "Some said they won freedom, some said they won money, and some said they won chaos." Events proved the third group to be correct.

> *"In 1983, under the NCAA's non-competing agreements with ABC, CBS, and TBS, there were 24 games on television. . . . Rights fees for a national game amounted to $600,000 per team. In 1986, there were 66 games on television, with ABC, CBS, ESPN, TBS, and a myriad of syndicators [telecasting them]. . . . Rights fees for a national game amounted to $350,000."*
>
> —Keith Dunnavant, sports business writer

After breaking the NCAA's monopoly, the rich football programs did not get richer—in fact, everyone got poorer. Even Oklahoma, one of the plaintiffs, went from a per-game average of $425,528 for its regional and national TV appearances in the year before the Supreme Court ruling, to $188,302 the season after. The NCAA itself not only lost an immediate $5 million—its share of the old monopoly package—but by November 1984 had paid out almost $1.3 million in legal costs and was still in various courts attempting to work its way around the original decision.

The NCAA also tried to alter the decision by changing the laws that the courts had sustained. In 1984, the association got its friends in Congress to hold subcommittee hearings on its TV plight and to push for an exemption of NCAA football from the antitrust laws. Walter Byers, longtime executive director of the association, argued that "college football is [now] in a buyer's market, it is not a seller's market," and he predicted that TV revenue would find a new and lower level, causing athletic programs to lose millions of dollars. However, the television networks prodded Congress to stand by the Sherman Antitrust Act, and it did.

Byers was right: when the final contracts were signed for the 1984 football season, the new total was $30.8 million, startlingly below the $74 million that the colleges and universities had been scheduled to receive for 1984 under the old monopoly deal. Helping the TV networks and cable companies drive such hard bargains were the TV ratings for college football for 1983: 9.8, a record low to that point. In 1984, the ratings dropped further, into the 4.0 range.

The sugarplums that the CFA schools had envisioned when they embarked upon the legal challenge to the NCAA soon turned to sour grapes as many athletic directors questioned the wisdom of the original move. But there was no putting the monopoly back into the bottle; each school and/or conference had to scramble for itself and deal with the TV powers as best it could. In 1984, Notre Dame managed to equal the $1.4 million it had received in 1983 under the monopoly, but to do so, the Fighting Irish had to appear on television eight times instead of three as in the previous year, and to please the networks, the school had to set five different starting times for six of its home games, inconveniencing and upsetting its fans.

Few schools, however, were able to equal their previous TV revenue. Some, like the members of the Southern Conference, were excluded from TV entirely and, instead of dividing up an expected $1 million to $1.5 million, received nothing. The AD at Appalachian State, a member of the Southern Conference, admitted, "I've been out rattling the tin cup. If you can find anybody who says they're making as much or doing as well, I'd like to know who they are."

Athletic directors soon realized that the drop in football TV revenue was not a temporary phenomenon, but most were unprepared for the new, deregulated climate, which included such dangers as dealing with cable syndicators. As a result, some schools suffered additional financial blows. In 1985, when Metrosports of Pittsburgh went bankrupt, various Big Ten and Pacific Ten universities lost between $400,000 and $500,000 each on this syndicator's default.

The *Chronicle of Higher Education,* reporting Metrosports' bankruptcy, noted, "The financial difficulties of Metrosports and other syndicators are not surprising, industry representatives say. Syndication is a volatile business in which takeovers, mergers, and reorganization of financially strapped companies are common." In their campus offices, did school officials ever wonder about their swim in the shark-infested waters of TV syndicators, and whether all the red ink splashing about had anything to do with the academic missions of their universities? Apparently not—no school is on record as having tried to bring its athletic department under control even at this most favorable moment for such a move.

If, in the mid-1980s, school officials had forced athletic directors to adjust their budgets to the huge loss of TV revenue, they might have brought some fiscal sanity to athletic departments. Instead, they allowed ADs to pursue a mainly futile scramble to make up the lost revenue and—the worst error—to maintain spending at pre-1984 levels. The result was greater deficits for a larger number of programs and an accelerating loss spiral that continues to this day.

> "After five years [1984–89] in which revenues from television have declined as much as 60 percent, representatives of college football's heavyweight organizations have joined forces to seek federal approval of a proposed unified television package."
>
> —Item in *Sports inc.: The Sports Business Weekly*

Instead of facing the new financial reality, many of the big-time athletic directors continue to flail against it, and in the least imaginative ways. In 1988, under the auspices of the NCAA and the CFA, they held a series of meetings and hired lawyers to plan a resurrection of the old monopoly. John Weistart, a Duke University Law School professor and an expert on sports law, commented: "I hear much from athletic directors saying that they want to reduce the supply and raise the price. That is exactly what was wrong before."

Weistart also pointed out that the proliferation of football games on TV "is precisely what the Supreme Court ordered. Most importantly, it is a state of affairs that the antitrust law will continue to require." The Federal Trade Commission enforces this law, and in April 1989 it put the big-time athletic directors on the defensive by beginning an investigation of the current football TV packages, especially the CFA's, and the Big Ten–Pacific Ten deal. Thus, no matter how much the ADs want to return to the past, they will have to live with the consequences of their original actions.

In the history of college football, the Georgia-Oklahoma legal play will go down as one of the all-time blunders, easily surpassing Roy Riegels's wrong-way run in the 1929 Rose Bowl. No amount of effort will change the score of that game or the result of the CFA schools' lawsuit.

> *"Rights fees [for basketball] are flat. Ratings have tended to be flat because they've been splintered. . . . There are a lot of games on TV now [1988–89 season] for which people [athletic programs] are getting no money, zero."*

> —Dave Gavitt, commissioner of the Big East Conference

Before the 1980s, no national TV network took regular season college basketball very seriously—the main reason the NCAA never attempted to monopolize its telecasting. The major networks had their games-of-the-week sandwiched into Saturday and Sunday slots between bowling and *Trash Sports from Hawaii*. The ratings depended mainly on the matchups but were sometimes respectable.

Then ESPN appeared. In its early period, the first sports cable network needed to fill twenty-four hours a day and it would televise almost anything. Polo from Palm Beach, however, did not build audiences, whereas college basketball had fans whom ESPN hoped to attract. "We were in a weak bargaining position then," an ESPN executive explained. "The conferences were able to say, 'Look, you take thirty or forty of our games, or you'll have none of them.' "

In the early 1980s, college basketball ratings showed real strength, especially on the major networks for their games-of-the-week: NBC had a season-long average of 6.5 in 1981, and CBS a 5.5 in 1982. These ratings not only convinced ESPN to televise more basketball but they also attracted independent syndicators, who threw increasing numbers of games onto the tube.

By 1984, oversaturation was a problem. Ratings began to sag and NBC offered conferences and schools less money for the 1985 season. Then ESPN, whose college basketball ratings had dropped 21 percent from '83 to '84, cut back on its number of telecasts.

As ratings continued to decline—both NBC and CBS slipped to 4.6 in 1986—and payouts decreased, many of the syndicators remained in the game, ever hopeful of a jackpot, ever willing to telecast more contests, and if they failed, ready to skip out on their payments to colleges by declaring bankruptcy. Surveying the situation in 1986, Peter Lund, then president of CBS Sports, saw "no end to the proliferation of televised college basketball in the near future."

Athletic directors cooperated in the oversaturation. For an ESPN contract, the Ohio Valley Conference agreed *to start games at midnight*; and the more sedate Big Ten consented to tip off at 9:38 P.M. on Monday nights for the same network. One major syndicator related how, "At times in negotiations [with networks] we've had to get a conference commissioner out of the room because he's willing to give his product away just to get on. People say, 'We'll *buy* the time, just get us on' " (speaker's emphasis). (Almost every conference commissioner is an ex-AD or athletic department administrator.)

For the 1989–90 season, an all-time record number of games are on television. Meanwhile, lost in the mindless scramble of college basketball programs trying to appear on TV are the student-athletes who have to play in the games. Big Ten teams frequently return home from Monday night away contests at 4:00 and 5:00 A.M., but the next morning, the players are supposed to go to class (athletes have morning classes because of afternoon practices). An Indianapolis sportswriter commented that although the players are "exhausted . . . [no one] cares. They are merely pawns in a money-making game that extends far beyond the basketball floor." The irony is that, in this situation, the franchises in College Sports Inc. not only abuse their employees but do not gain that much money from their efforts. Bob Knight says, "This is for the damned dollar—and it isn't even a big dollar."

Because of oversaturation in the 1980s, TV revenue from basketball never increased significantly enough to help the majority of athletic programs end their annual deficits. The hope for the 1990s is that the millions received from CBS for the NCAA men's basketball tournament will solve the financial problems in college sports. However, the unwillingness of the powerhouse schools and conferences to share their winnings makes an equitable distribution of the tournament money unlikely. If the past indicates the future, the rich athletic departments will build stronger basketball teams and will win a larger share of the pot o' gold; the hundreds of also-rans will spend increasing amounts of money trying to break into the golden circle.

> *"Please note that this revenue generated from television*
> *has no strings attached and may be used for any purpose.*
> *We do not tell college athletics how to spend their money,*
> *we do not tell the NFL, we do not tell the NBA, golf,*
> *tennis—they are free to spend that money as they choose."*
>
> —Neal Pilson, president of CBS Sports, in an
> address to the 1988 NCAA convention

Pilson, a frequent spokesman for the television industry, then added a comment that he probably thought put him on the side of academic seriousness: "It is money the schools can use for libraries, for scholarships, professors' salaries, research and new classrooms, or for new football stadiums, recruiting athletes or raising coaches' salaries. The choice is yours to make."

Is it really? As a TV executive with extensive experience in college sports, Pilson should know that athletic programs, because of the nature of their finances as well as their frequently incompetent management, need every penny of TV revenue they can generate. More important, his analogy with pro sports underlines the schools' true lack of choice: *if universities spend their TV sports revenue on academic items, their athletic product will deteriorate*—not having state-of-the-art facilities, not recruiting the most talented athletes, and not paying coaches the market price will definitely dilute the product—and then *CBS and the other telecasters will pay less money to televise college sports events.*

Beneath this TV executive's high-minded rhetoric there appears to be an attempt to distance the television industry from the very problems in college sports that it helped create: the professional demands upon the student-athletes and the totally commercial atmosphere in which big-time athletic programs must exist in order to produce the highest-quality athletic product for TV.

On the weekend after Pilson spoke, both the Harvard at Cornell and the Memphis State at Tulsa basketball games took place. The former game was between two schools that fulfill the criteria for much greater emphasis on academics than on athletic programs; the latter featured two "jock factories" with the best facilities, players, and coaches that money can buy. CBS telecast Memphis State at Tulsa as well as a game featuring the University of Nevada at Las Vegas.

CHAPTER 6

Earned Revenue: Miscellaneous, Including Corporate Sponsorships

"Those of my colleagues who have protested the appearance [of the Dallas Cowboys' cheerleaders at halftime] apparently have misconstrued the function of institutions of higher learning in our society. Everyone knows that it is the unique mission of the university to provide great spectacles of sex and violence."

—Paul D. Bush, economics professor at
California State University at Fresno

IN COLLEGE SPORTS, with budgets tight and deficits omnipresent, athletic directors frequently turn to nontraditional ways of generating revenue. One sports business magazine described the situation with the headline CRISIS: THE MOTHER OF INVENTION and the subhead "Innovators at a few schools have taken action to forestall bankruptcy and scandal."

Russ Sloan, AD at Fresno in the early 1980s, was a pioneer. In 1982, he discovered a way to turn a scheduled football road game with Utah and a $25,000 loss (because of road expenses) into a nice profit. First, he canceled the Utah trip and invited Weber State, for a moderate guarantee, to Fresno; then he made a deal with the Dallas Cowboy cheerleaders to provide halftime entertainment and he convinced boosters to put up the $20,000 needed to bring the act to Fresno. Sloan was proud of the result. "We made about $70,000 instead of losing $25,000," he said. "That's a $95,000 decision on my part."

This AD's only problem was that many members of the Fresno faculty interpreted his move as sexist and undignified. A hundred faculty members signed a petition that, in part, read, "We believe this [appearance by the cheerleaders] is demeaning for women and a counterproductive use of university resources." However, the head of the boosters' Bulldog Foundation defended athletic department operations with the argument, "College sports is a business now, it's a business." In subsequent years, Fresno has steadily enlarged its athletic program and has become an even bigger business than in Sloan's day.

Another athletic director who believed in college sports as a business was Bob Brodhead, nicknamed "Bottomline Bob" for his imaginative ways of handling and raising money at Louisiana State University. Before taking the top job at LSU, Brodhead had been a coach and financial officer with a number of professional teams, including Portland of the now-defunct World Football League and the Miami Dolphins. About the WFL job, he said, "I was a master at deficit financing," and he claimed that this experience helped him in college sports.

One of Brodhead's first financial innovations at LSU was to sell the back of the football tickets to McDonald's. In exchange for putting their ads on the tickets, the AD explained, "they completely pay for the cost and printing of tickets. They pay the actual invoice costs, but it amounts to about $16,000 we don't have to pay." In recent years, many other athletic departments have started selling the backs—and sometimes even the fronts—of their tickets.

Brodhead was also more aggressive about placing and selling the LSU logo on a variety of items as well as about collecting a royalty when others used it. In addition, as he and other ADs discovered, the logo business can work both ways in college sports: athletic departments can earn money when their athletes wear commercial insignias on their uniforms. By the mid-1980s, this practice became so widespread that the NCAA stepped in because, according to its spokesman, "Athletes were beginning to look like walking billboards. Uniforms were beginning to have sponsors' names on them that were bigger than the name of the university."

Another Brodhead innovation at LSU was to build two huge computer-controlled message boards near the campus sports center. Some faculty and staff objected but the athletic director replied, "Critics will say the pylons are trashing up the campus and overcommercializing Tiger sports, but that's just part of 'doing business' for any university that wants to make it big in intercollegiate athletics. I've said since I got here that intercollegiate sports is one of the biggest businesses in the world. It's entertainment and nobody is entertained by watching someone lose all the time. We have to be competitive at the national level and that takes money."

For Brodhead, part of doing business and winning apparently included bugging his own office in order to overhear comments by subordinates as well as by visiting investigators from the NCAA. In 1985, LSU won the bidding war for seven-foot-one-inch Tito Horford of the Dominican Republic, and when he enrolled at LSU, the NCAA came to Baton Rouge to interview him. Brodhead offered them the use of his bugged office for the interview. The athletic director claimed he had installed "the electronic listening devices . . . to uncover an information leak in the athletic department."

Brodhead was convicted of violating the federal law on electronic eavesdropping and was sentenced to two hundred hours of community service. LSU fired him, in part for the office-bugging incident and also for accepting, according to newspaper accounts, "a free trip to a Mexican resort from a Baton Rouge businessman" as well as receiving "improper payments for a radio appearance from a broadcasting company owned by the same businessman." For all of Brodhead's transgressions, his talent as "Bottomline Bob" kept him in the athletic directors' profession: after LSU, he became AD at Southeastern Louisiana University.

By the late 1980s, no deal seemed off-the-plate to revenue-hungry athletic directors. In 1988 the Temple University AD arranged to play the home half of a series against the defending NCAA champion, the University of Kansas, in Atlantic City, New Jersey, under the sponsorship of the Showboat Hotel and Casino. The casino agreed to pay the rental fee on Convention Hall in Atlantic City and to give Temple a $100,000 guarantee in return for having its name and logo plastered onto the event. (According to press reports, Temple planned to give Kansas "the same $15,000 guarantee it paid Temple when the Owls played in Lawrence, Kansas, two years ago.")

Even after being criticized for this tie-in to professional gambling, the Temple University president approved the Atlantic City date, and his AD said that he saw "nothing wrong with the deal." But before Kansas could comment, the deal was called off and the game moved to Temple's home arena in Philadelphia: according to the *Philadelphia Daily News*, NBC Sports, which had television rights to the game, was unhappy with the Atlantic City location and the casino connection.

"Our surveys tell us that most athletic directors have their backs to the wall financially. Anything that can help college athletics survive, we're all for, and corporate sponsorship can do just that."

—John R. Davis, president of the NCAA at the time of the comment

Corporate sponsorship, with all its gleaming manufactured images and big bucks, is what contemporary athletic directors seek most. It started in the mid-1980s when a number of companies began sponsoring bowl games and such hybrids as the John Hancock Sun Bowl and the Sea World Holiday Bowl appeared on TV to perplex New Year's viewers. Then the venerable Sugar Bowl became the USF&G Sugar Bowl. The bowl committees—and the corporations—at first worried that the public would not like the new situation; the public relations director of the Sea World Holiday Bowl commented, "People are slow to accept some kinds of change, and I think tradition gets in the way," but, he predicted, corporate sponsorship of college sports was here to stay.

To soften up the public, some corporations used ingenious P.R. campaigns. For the 1989 Rose Bowl, Burger King, one of the bowl sponsors, sent educational packets to thousands of primary schools west of the Mississippi. Burger King hoped to reach between five million and seven million kids with an "in-school educational program" that focused on the history of the bowl game's Tournament of Roses, and that connected its name to the Rose Bowl and the universities of the Pacific Ten and Big Ten.

Corporate tie-ins to College Sports Inc. seem inevitable, not only to bowls but also to the athletic programs of individual schools. San Diego State University has been a leader in the scramble for this new form of revenue. The school sells each home football game to a different business, including, in 1988, Texaco, Sea World, El Cajon Ford, and Smith Barney, and it also has three full-season sponsors, one of which, Agua Caliente Race Track, has a very problematic ownership history. The athletic director at San Diego State had no trouble convincing the school's administrators of the wisdom of corporate sponsorship because he had a very powerful argument on his side—his athletic department was running $1 million in deficit and needed every cent it could raise.

At the University of Denver, the athletic department enlisted fifteen corporate sponsors last year and, in return for their money, put their names, logos, and ads on everything from arena signs to parking lot receipts. The sponsors included Coors beer and Anheuser-Busch; that alcohol consumption, especially of beer, has reached epidemic proportion on campuses across America did not bother the University of Denver. An associate athletic director explained, "What we try to do is provide a vehicle for corporations to associate with higher education while complementing our own programs."

In 1989, a group of almost sixty NCAA athletic programs met to discuss the formation of a consortium to sell themselves, as a bloc, to major corporate advertisers. The AD at San Diego State, pushing the consortium idea, explained: "It's time to drag college sports, kicking and screaming, into the marketplace of national sponsorship."

For the fall 1989 football season, some universities in the conservative Big Ten allowed, for the first time, corporate billboards and logos in their stadiums. A midwestern sports columnist, writing about the traditional football game between Purdue and Indiana University, asked, "So, how far away is [it from being] the Farm Bureau Old Oaken Bucket Game, permanently assigned to the Hoosier Dome [home of the NFL Colts]? Probably only as far away as the first sufficiently large check."

Not all athletic directors, however, embrace corporate sponsorship. Tom Shupe at Wichita State, an AD who has worked hard to erase his university's image as the most penalized NCAA school, says of the hustle for corporate sponsors, "Prostitution is probably too harsh a word—but selling out may not be in the best interest of an institution image-wise."

Robert E. Lehr, associate AD at Yale, wonders what will happen when corporate sponsors, upon whom athletic departments could increasingly depend, "begin to demand input in the decision making of the department." Lehr asks, "Are we foolish enough to think that six- and seven-figure patrons are going to be satisfied with signage, mentions, and preferred seating?"

Ironically, some corporations are also questioning their sponsorship of college sports—not for ethical but for practical reasons. To use the advertising jargon, companies are encountering four main problems: Clutter, Ambushes, Jinxed Jocks, and Measuring Impact.

USA Today explains Clutter: "It's getting tough to tell the Miller Lite Lineman of the Year from the Old Spice Rookie of the Year, the John Hancock Sun Bowl from USF&G Sugar Bowl." Clutter produces less bang per advertising dollar. Similar duds occur with Ambushes, when, at the same sporting event, the ad or logo of one corporate sponsor crowds out an ad of another company in the same business.

Jinxed Jocks are the other edge of the athletic publicity sword. Corporations are happy to have their names associated with a winning college football team until the day the school's star halfback is charged with a criminal offense or the program is investigated by the NCAA. SMU is reported to have lost "$250,000 in major corporate sponsorships" after being put on NCAA probation, and the new SMU athletic director admits, "We are [now] starting over. We have to re-establish a certain amount of credibility and work twice as hard to get half as much revenue."

In addition, for corporations, measuring the effectiveness of their sponsorship of college sports is almost impossible. One sports business magazine asked, "Do people really go out and buy more life insurance if they enjoy the John Hancock Sun Bowl?" And a marketing executive explained, "There's no way, really, to set the criteria. It's not like an in-store promotion you can measure by units sold."

Thus, as with so many aspects of advertising, there may be less to corporate sponsorship than meets the eye. Advertisers are notoriously fickle and trend-driven; if they decide next year that sponsorship of college sports is "out," then all of those athletic directors who put this form of revenue into their budgets as a permanent item will discover the same kind of hole that the loss of the TV monopoly caused.

But with the optimism of true lottery players, many ADs do not consider the financial risks inherent in corporate sponsorship and are chasing it as their last and best hope for a massive infusion of new revenue. That a few will succeed is as inevitable as the few winners of this weekend's lottery; that the majority will raise a lot less than they hoped for, as well as much less than they need to balance their books, is also certain.

> *"I don't want to see us prostitute sport and the educational process just to take that dollar in [through corporate sponsorship]."*
>
> —Robert E. Lehr, associate athletic director at Yale University

Beyond the financial and practical concerns, College Sports Inc.'s pursuit of corporate sponsorship raises serious ethical questions for higher education. Since their inception, colleges and universities have tried to protect the integrity of the academy from outside encroachments and blandishments. Schools have never sold their names and, by implication, their integrity to business interests. However, athletic departments, as commercial entertainment ventures, see nothing wrong in peddling themselves, wrapped in their host universities' names, to corporate or any other kind of sponsors.

This practice undermines one of the fundamental tenets of American colleges and universities—their independence. To the public, schools stand apart from corporate America. To allow athletic programs to acquire sponsors will inevitably change the way the public perceives higher education. It could also change the public's willingness to fund colleges and universities. That school presidents and other administrators are willing to allow this to happen, and for a paltry amount of money, is not simply shortsighted but shameful.

CHAPTER 7

College Sports Revenue & the IRS

*"The tax-exempt status that the IRS accords universities
depends on their serving educational purposes. The
interest of the IRS in athletics programs is likely to be
aroused sooner or later."*

—John Timothy Young, tax attorney

BY THE LATE 1980s, Congress and the IRS showed increasing interest in
the "unrelated businesses" of institutions like universities. Many tax
experts charged that tax-exempt "businesses on the side" such as huge
gift shops and big-time athletic programs are abuses of the law and
deprive the Treasury of millions of legitimate tax dollars. Congressman
J. J. Pickle, chairman of the subcommittee looking into this question,
pointed out that when Congress wrote the law, it clearly "did not want
charitable organizations . . . running unrelated commercial ventures,"
and that the time had come "to insure that the original intent of
Congress is preserved."

Universities have always argued that athletic programs are educational endeavors, not "unrelated businesses," and that the money they
earn should be as tax-exempt as the tuition dollars generated by English
departments. Today, however, when ADs proclaim that they run huge
businesses, the equation of big-time athletic programs to academic
departments is not remotely valid.

The legal turning point in this question came with the 1983 and 1984
judicial decisions concerning the NCAA's TV monopoly. Because Judge
Burciaga and seven Supreme Court justices based their rulings, in part,
on the premise that intercollegiate athletics was a business and its TV
monopoly violated antitrust laws, the traditional defensive line of college sports as an educational activity was broken.

Since then, the IRS has become more aggressive. A few years ago, it sent the Michigan athletic department a tax bill on the money earned from the sale of advertising space in football game programs, and it also fought a tax court case with the NCAA over the same source of revenue from the association's basketball championship programs. Michigan and the NCAA argued that their sale of advertising was part of their tax-exempt educational function, but the IRS was able to collect both bills. Possibly these cases will set a precedent for other IRS attempts to collect taxes on the "unrelated business" activities of college sports.

The profits of America's athletic departments, however, will not prove an abundant source of tax dollars. If the IRS audits these programs, it will find mainly red ink and mismanagement. (Of course, it could file "unreported personal income" claims against the employees who siphon off money and also against the athletes who accept under-the-table payments.)

But if the IRS and the legislators who write the tax laws look closely at athletic department financial statements, they will find millions of untaxed dollars in booster donations and sales of priority seats. This money, so crucial to the existence of nearly every athletic program, is the single greatest tax abuse perpetrated by College Sports Inc.

Every year, supporters of athletic programs give an estimated $400 million—$150 million in priority-seating "donations" and the rest in other kinds of gifts—to help their favorite college sports franchises stay afloat. Every year, most of this money—targeted for an "unrelated business" of the university—is entered on the donors' income tax forms as "contributions to education" and excluded from tax payments. Congress and all ordinary taxpayers should be outraged by this massive tax loophole.

> *"What you're talking about here is taxpayers subsidizing someone buying tickets to a football game."*
>
> —Dom LaPonzima, public affairs officer for
> the Baltimore, Maryland, IRS office

When increasing numbers of athletic programs established priority-seating plans in the early 1980s, the IRS began to question whether these were legitimate donations to education—as the "donors" and recipients claimed—or whether these gifts were merely part of the ticket price. In 1984, the IRS ruled that because a priority-seating "donation results in a special benefit for the contributor, the donation cannot be considered charitable and is therefore not deductible."

The NCAA and its Washington allies caught the IRS's kickoff on priority seating and roared back up the field. Within a month, the IRS announced that it would delay implementation of the ruling while it studied the issue further. In January 1985, the IRS held public hearings on the ruling and the NCAA rounded up all the usual suspect arguments about amateurism and education.

If common sense as well as a straight interpretation of the tax law had been the deciding factors, the IRS would have won. Richard L. Kaplan, professor of law at the University of Illinois, presented one of the most cogent arguments: "A 'gift' of, say, $500 made to obtain the seats is no gift. It's just the price of the goods offered for sale. . . . Let's call a spade a spade; the people subscribing to these athletic programs have no intention of benefiting the university generally. They want good tickets." He concluded that, "the IRS should reissue and enforce its ruling vigorously."

But the IRS exists within the political climate of Washington, and the NCAA, like the NRA, has lobbying power out of proportion to its national popularity. The IRS subsequently issued a compromise ruling on priority seating: through a complicated formula, athletic departments could decide how much of the donation was "a prerequisite to the purchase of tickets" and how much was not, with the latter part being tax-deductible. Not surprisingly, many athletic departments reported low "prerequisites" on their priority seats, allowing purchasers to write off the rest as donations.

The NCAA, however, was not satisfied with this procedure and, in 1988, asked its friends in Congress to introduce legislation to change priority-seating payments to a 100 percent tax deduction. With no sense of irony, the NCAA wanted the proviso placed in the addendum package to the Tax Reform Act.

Some opposition to this tax giveaway surfaced, and so, on the last day of the One Hundredth Congress, the NCAA agreed to a compromise bill: 80 percent of priority-seating payments as tax-deductible. In addition, any boosters "who were previously denied the deductions can file for tax refunds."

Entering the 1990s, massive illogic envelops the tax situation of big-time athletic programs. Clearly they are "unrelated businesses" attached to their host universities, but money that goes to purchase tickets to their sports events is considered a legitimate donation to education. In addition, all other donations to help keep these businesses afloat are also tax write-offs.

In an era when governments at all levels are starved for tax dollars and, in turn, starve authentic educational endeavors, a major entertainment industry and its supporters get a free ride. But someone has to pay for this—the ordinary citizens whose tax dollars are, in effect, subsidizing College Sports Inc.

CHAPTER 8

Unearned Revenue: Booster Club Donations

"Some [college] presidents look the other way when the booster clubs generate millions for athletics while the academic programs are starved for gift support. My own untested hypothesis is that athletics breeds gifts for athletics but not for much else."

—Robert Atwell, president of the American Council on Education

ONE OF the fastest-growing areas of athletic department revenue is supporters' donations. When the NCAA began its financial studies in 1965, this source accounted for 5 percent of total revenue at big-time football schools. By 1985, it had increased to 13 percent and a significant $712,000 annual average per program. Since the last survey, these contributions have grown every year, helped in large part by the fact that they are tax-deductible.

Texas A. & M. has experienced typical growth in this area. In 1965, its supporters' organization, the Aggie Club, raised only $60,000. Twenty years later, the club gave $2.5 million to the athletic department. With money comes power: in 1982, the Aggie Club was instrumental in hiring football coach Jackie Sherrill away from Pitt and signing him to a $1 million multiyear contract; a club official, H. R. "Bum" Bright, made the offer to Sherrill without the knowledge of the university president or the incumbent football coach. The *Dallas Morning News* commented that Bright, at the time also the owner of the Dallas Cowboys, and the boosters "delivered the message that [college] athletics are now big business—and should be treated as such."

"It has been our experience that athletic success does not correlate with alumni giving. . . . In fact, we have the opposite problem here. We are forever trying to convince people that we keep athletics in perspective, that this is first and foremost an academic institution."

—Richard Conklin, vice-president of the
University of Notre Dame

One of the central myths about college sports is that "the alumni demand it." In fact, the majority of people who support and donate money to athletic programs are not alumni, and to term them such both fuels the myth and obscures their real relationship to the university.

Alumni are the graduates or former students of a particular college or university: rarely do more than 1 to 2 percent of them contribute to their alma mater's sports teams. *Boosters, on the other hand, have no connection to a school other than their support of its teams.* For example, the I-Club, the main boosters' group for University of Iowa athletics, has over eight thousand members who were never students at the university.

A number of sociologists have studied the differences between alumni and boosters. Their work reveals that alumni are interested mainly in the academic programs of their schools and prefer to give money to those programs—in part, to insure that the value of their college degrees does not decline—and they are much less concerned about and sometimes even hostile to athletic programs. Boosters, however, focus almost exclusively on college sports teams and seldom give money to the educational units of the schools that house those teams.

The situation at Stanford University is typical of many institutions with big-time athletic programs. Bruce Hinchliffe, a Stanford administrator who has worked with alumni and boosters for almost twenty years, explained in an interview that "a very large percentage of our alumni are, basically, indifferent to sports." By way of illustration, Hinchliffe mentioned all of the former graduate and professional school students, as well as the female and even male undergraduates, who do not care for organized sports. At his school, there is a gulf between this large group of alumni who are extremely generous in their support of the university's educational units, and the boosters in the Buck/Cardinal Club who give money to the school's athletic program.

Even the Notre Dame alumni are less interested in sports than is generally believed. A major study of their attitudes concluded: "When asked about their motivation for contributing to the alumni fund . . .

[they] ranked the following as most important: alleviating the university's financial need, keeping private higher education viable, and recognizing Notre Dame's academic promise. At the bottom of the motivational scale . . . [was] endorsement of Notre Dame's athletic success."

Notre Dame, of course, is also famous for its boosters—the "subway alumni"—and their generosity toward its athletic teams. Richard Conklin, a high official at the university for many years, offered this comment about them: "We at Notre Dame have had extensive experience trying to turn athletic interests of 'subway alumni' to [academic] development purposes—and we have had no success. There is no evidence that the typical, nonalumnus fan of Notre Dame has much interest in its educational mission."

In fact, the nature of booster club appeals for money makes this situation inevitable. Club fund-raisers tell boosters how much the athletic program is hurting financially and urge them to dig as deeply as possible to support it. After Booster Ed pays for his priority seats and also contributes to the Save the Jocks Drive, he has little left over—and less inclination—to give to the physics department's scholarship fund.

Another tenacious myth about alumni and college sports is that they give or withhold donations according to the won-lost records of their schools' teams. In 1979, two University of Kentucky sociologists, Lee Sigelman and Robert Carter, examined 138 Division I schools and found "no relation between athletic success and giving. Some evidence that success depresses giving." A 1983 follow-up study confirmed the previous results and also found that "it was schools with poorer football records that received more generous gifts to their annual [educational] funds." (Observers explain the "negative reaction" as alumni being embarrassed by their schools' becoming "jock factories," and withholding contributions during times of great athletic success and/or scandal.)

Booster club support, however, was different: the Kentucky sociologists found a "strong relation between football success and donation to athletic programs," and they were even able to quantify that connection: "For every 10 percent improvement in football success, the unstandardized regression coefficient leads us to anticipate an increment of $125,160 in outside donations to the athletic program."

The researchers concluded that "when winning or losing a football game has such direct financial repercussions on the economic viability of the athletic program, college football ceases to be a sport in the classical sense and becomes a battle for financial survival instead."

In the 1980s, other studies recorded similar results, and even those that attempted to refute the Kentucky work sometimes offered evidence to support its conclusions. One such study discovered the astounding fact that *throughout UCLA's basketball championship years, that school had "a much lower than average rate of donations from alumni" than did the other schools in its conference* (emphasis added).

Concomitant with the other myths concerning alumni support is the belief that schools that dare to drop or de-emphasize a sports team will be hit with the wrath—emotional and financial—of their alums. Only anecdotal evidence exists to refute this assertion but it is important. According to the *Chronicle of Higher Education.* "Donations to Tulane University rose by $5 million in 1986, the year after the institution dropped basketball; annual giving at Wichita State University nearly doubled the year after officials suspended its debt-ridden football program."

Wichita State presents a particularly interesting case because, as one official said, "There were warnings that enrollment would drop dramatically and that fund-raising would fall off" if the school discontinued football. In fact, "Enrollment climbed . . . and giving jumped to more than $25.5 million from just under $13.5 million" in the last football year. The president of the school, Warren Armstrong, who had been severely criticized by the local press and boosters when he made the decision to drop football, commented, "If a person's support is solely based on the athletic program, I think it's probably misplaced in the first place." Other Wichita State officials made the point that "the lack of reaction to the university's decision indicates how soft the [booster] support was to begin with."

Thus the sociological and anecdotal evidence suggests a crucial distinction between boosters, on one side, and the vast majority of alumni on the other. When referring to boosters, many athletic department fund-raisers use the euphemism "Friends of the University"; in fact, boosters are usually fair-weather friends, given to extreme temperature changes, particularly if a university's athletic teams are not winning. (The head fund-raiser at USC said in 1988, "We're doing great now [in generating money], but we know we're always two football losses from a deficit.")

Regular alumni, however, once mobilized, are loyal to and have a deep affection for their alma maters; moreover, they see their connection to a school as a lifetime commitment, a tie that transcends this year's football and basketball won-lost records. Alumni are not oblivious of their schools' athletic teams, but they place them below the horizon as a criterion for giving or withholding money—except if athletic success or scandal becomes so visible that it jeopardizes the academic seriousness of a school and the value of its alumni's degrees. Then they give less.

> *"In fact, any effort to control these [booster] groups has been largely superficial since the need for the resources these groups provide is so great. . . . Athletic directors tend to hold ideological and behavioral similarities to boosters. . . . Therefore, athletic directors rarely provide a source of resistance to booster enthusiasm and involvement."*
>
> —James H. Frey, associate professor of
> sociology at the University of
> Nevada at Las Vegas

Booster clubs have an amazing degree of autonomy from the universities to which they are nominally affiliated. Many are set up and run as private foundations, and the athletic director is the only school official active on their boards. Other booster organizations reside within athletic departments, with their staff on department payrolls. Some athletic departments even utilize both types of booster clubs, inside and foundation, to allow maximum flexibility in moving money around, especially payments to coaches and athletes. (Because private foundations do not have to open their books, serious scrutiny of their finances is almost impossible.)

In a survey of booster clubs in North Carolina, the *Raleigh News and Observer* pointed out that they "are big business, headed by financially savvy executives employing computers and [large] staffs. . . . For example, [East Carolina University] Pirates Director, Richard B. Dupree, taught business at ECU for five years before taking over the club last year."

At North Carolina State University, according to the same newspaper, "the Wolfpack Club owns and maintains the College Inn, a converted motel . . . that houses 300 athletes." From 1981 on, the Wolfpack Club also was in charge of ticket sales, game programs, and some concession stands at the school's sports events. In 1987, an internal university audit "was critical of two areas of responsibility assigned to the Wolfpack Club. One involved the handling of souvenir and novelty sales at rock concerts staged at Reynolds [the school's arena]. The other involved catered meals to rock performers." The Wolfpack Club, like all booster foundations, is protected by the tax-exempt status of the school's educational mandate.

For all the gleaming sports complexes and shiny office furniture, the slipshod nature of intercollegiate athletics' business operations frequently emerges. Concerning the booster club at East Carolina University, less than two months after praising its professional setup, the Raleigh paper printed the headline FANS' FAILURE TO MEET PLEDGES PUTS ECU ATHLETICS IN THE RED. The article related that the ECU athletic department "owed $573,873 as of June 30," and "a major reason for the loss was the failure of the school's athletic booster club, the Pirates' Club, to meet its pledges to the athletic department budget."

Even with clubs that deliver their pledged money, such as at the University of North Carolina at Chapel Hill, a large percentage of a booster's contribution goes for overhead: at UNC ten years ago, "$400,000 went for club office expenses—paying the seven-member staff, keeping the club computer running, and paying for activities to promote contributions." In 1990, the overhead figure is much higher.

In addition, like their AD colleagues, many booster club directors are often overpaid and develop a taste for expensive perks. Under the guise of raising funds from rich donors, club executives travel extensively, usually staying in the best accommodations because, as they explain, "To talk to rich people, you have to look rich." And, like ADs, booster club directors often have trouble separating personal expenses from business costs. Last year, South Carolina newspapers revealed the travel and expense account of the former director of the University of South Carolina Gamecock Club. Apparently, he enjoyed going to such events as the Talladega 500 stock car race in Alabama, taking his wife with him on out-of-state excursions, and treating university employees to lunch in Columbia—all bills listed as business expenses and, according to his AD, "approved under the policies of the athletic department."

Bonus to Head Football Coach . . . $25,000.
Bonuses to Assistant Coaches . . . $15,000.
Renovation of Weight Room . . . $15,285.

—Sample booster contributions, from an
NCAA pamphlet

The NCAA not only sanctions booster clubs but in its *Public Relations and Promotion Manual* encourages schools to establish them. In the manual's article "Athletics Fund Raising: How to Get Started," John Novotny, former head of the main booster club at the University of Kansas, explains his premise: "Athletics fund-raising organizations are the most logical way to generate resources for financially starved athletics budgets." Novotny advises booster clubs to solicit "contributions, whether they are checks, cash, stocks, bonds, or deferred gifts through wills and bequests."

These are only the standard money-raising ploys, and many clubs have moved beyond them into very creative concepts: at the University of North Carolina at Chapel Hill, according to the *Raleigh News and Observer,* some "boosters take out a life insurance policy with the Educational Fund as the beneficiary. The club gets the insurance benefits and the donor, in addition to getting athletic tickets, gets the tax advantage of writing off his premiums." (Contrary to its name, the main instruction with which the UNC Educational Fund is concerned occurs in the football stadium and basketball arena.)

Another creative ploy is endowments: at various schools, including some Ivy League ones like Yale, the head coaching position in football and sometimes in basketball is endowed; i.e., a booster donates a very large amount of money and the interest on that money is given annually to the coach to supplement the latter's already large salary. The University of Southern California has raised an endowment of $1.5 million for the head football coach and $250,000 for each position on the football team. Although USC uses the player endowment money to offset football expenses, if endowing positions catches on with boosters, the day may come when this year's starting player at each position will, like the endowed coaches, personally receive the interest on the endowment.

Another popular target for booster club endowment is athletic scholarships. The Aggie Club at Texas A. & M. has endowed almost four hundred for its athletic department. In addition, the "donations" for priority seats are often applied to athletic scholarship costs—the rationale being that this truly makes them gifts to education and not money for fifty-yard-line seats.

Money to coaches is also a standard gift of booster clubs. At most big-time Division I schools, the football and basketball coaches have among the highest, if not *the* highest, annual incomes of any university employee, including the president. Often a portion of the coaches' money comes from booster payments—the Aggie Club's to Jackie Sherrill—or in performance bonuses. Because of NCAA rules, the booster payments are not allowed to be called "salary" or be on a regular basis, but money is channeled through such subterfuges as the boosters guaranteeing the coach a much higher income for his TV show than his ratings merit or than the TV station will pay.

In the early 1980s, when the regents of the University of Nevada at Las Vegas lost patience with the deficit spending of the school's athletic department, they forbade basketball coach Jerry Tarkanian from accepting an annual $24,000 booster supplement to his salary. One problem with the regents' order, however, was the actual amount "Tark the Shark" was receiving. According to a newspaper account, "One boosters' club member questioned the $24,000 figure. He said that Mr. Tarkanian had been receiving about $80,000 a year from organizations such as his." The regents, the boosters, and the coach eventually straightened the matter out, and as Tark the Shark's teams went on to NCAA Final Four rounds, he greatly increased his annual income.

The amount of money given by boosters can be substantial. Like all athletic department financial records, accurate and current figures are hard to come by, but, five years ago, the *Miami Herald* placed booster donations to Clemson University and the University of North Carolina at Chapel Hill at $5 million each, and the universities of Georgia and Florida at close to $4 million each. As long ago as 1983, the *Des Moines Register* reported that the University of Iowa collected a little over $3 million from its boosters, a sum that "accounts for more than half the school's athletic budget and exceeds the entire academic budgets of several U of I departments, such as pharmacy, nursing, and graduate colleges."

But like all of the large financial figures in college sports, booster donations are not always one hundred cents on the dollar. Novotny talks about "deferred gifts through wills and bequests," which means the athletic department does not see the money until the donor dies and the will is probated. The changing of a will or even the loss of the money that is supposed to be given is hardly an unknown phenomenon; considering the fickleness of boosters, the incidence of such occurrences is more common than athletic programs acknowledge. An official of the University of Florida's Gator Boosters warned the *Miami Herald* that when it printed revenues from booster clubs, to "Keep in mind that the booster figures are tricky. What do you count? Deferred giving? In-kind deposits?" The latter refers to gifts of goods and services that boosters donate to—or trade with—athletic departments for tickets and/or perks.

The softness and unreliability of booster club money has long worried athletic departments and the universities that house them. Every big-time program, as well as many smaller ones, count on this source of revenue but they have no way of predicting the amount that will come in each year. Boosters are capricious, and if a particular situation displeases them—an unpopular coach, a losing streak, a star player dropped for academic reasons—they are liable to cut back on or even withhold donations, but athletic directors budget booster contributions as if they were "hard" revenue. In fact, ADs should consider them "soft" money, similar to academic grants that depend on short-term results to insure renewal—in this case, winning teams.

Complicating the problems with booster donations is the fact that, according to an NCAA expert, "90 percent of money raised comes from 5 to 10 percent of the donors." At Purdue University, for example, the most generous donors belong to the "Directors" group of the John Purdue Club and give a minimum of $2,500 a year; last year, they numbered 192 of the 4,612 club members (as opposed to the over 260,000 living alumni of the school). Pleasing these heavy hitters can be difficult. Moreover, of all boosters, they are the quickest to anger when a sports situation upsets them; with anger comes the closing of checkbooks.

These statistics on the number of major donors deflate another myth about college sports: that great hordes of alumni and boosters surround most schools and will destroy all administrators, including presidents, who do not promote big-time athletic programs. The real numbers reduce the mythical tribe to a rather small band of deep-pocketed individuals, many of whom have no affiliation with—nor affection for—any part of the university other than its sports teams.

"The booster problem is worse than it's ever been. It's become especially acute because institutions must attempt to obtain financial support from booster organizations and then worry about not turning over control of their programs to these same people."

—Wayne Duke, longtime commissioner of the
Big Ten Conference

Boosters tend to become very proprietorial toward their favorite college sports teams—the Purdue "Directors" title suggests the role these people see themselves playing in Boilermaker athletics. The biggest contributors often regard their five- and sometimes six-figure donations as "investments" in their favorite programs. In their opinion, this money not only grants them certain perks—the best box seats, special parking spaces, the ear of the AD and of the coaches—but also entitles them to a say on how the college sports franchise should be run.

As happens in pro sports, where the wealthiest fans buy and operate teams, sometimes the most prominent boosters actually take over their favorite college athletic programs. The $1 million hiring of Jackie Sherrill as coach and athletic director by the Aggie Club, led by H. R. "Bum" Bright, illustrates how that group ran Texas A. & M.'s athletic program. Throughout the 1980s, similar incidents occurred; Don Canham, former Michigan athletic director, bluntly stated, "I'm fearful that more and more industrial types and other wealthy people are trying to use their money to control a college football team or a basketball team as if it were a professional franchise."

When boosters "operate" college sports programs, they create multiple problems for the universities involved. Boosters are usually can-do business types and the distinction between ethical conduct and succeeding by any means is often unclear to them. When this syndrome is combined with their sense of ownership of a college sports team and their desire to see that team win at any cost, they ignore NCAA and all other rules. The stories of boosters giving recruits and college athletes illegal gifts are legion. In the history of the NCAA's policing of intercollegiate athletics, almost half of the approximately two thousand penalties have involved boosters abetting coaches in various violations.

Thus the revenue from booster donations has as many minuses as pluses. Athletic departments desperately need this money but it is "soft" and unreliable. Moreover, these dollars come with strings that are not only attached but can strangle an athletic program. If boosters spark an investigation, the resulting NCAA penalties, financial and others, can easily outweigh whatever money the boosters have given, and so can the accompanying notoriety.

> *"Big-time athletic schools love to talk about the great publicity produced by their sports programs. I just don't buy that. Sure, they get their names in the daily sports pages and on TV for free but how does that help their academic missions or their fund-raising? More probably, they're only convincing the public of their lack of educational seriousness."*
>
> —A development officer at an East Coast university

One of the central myths about college sports concerns the great publicity that it supposedly generates. At best, publicity from intercollegiate athletics is a two-edged sword: successful sports programs receive lots of media coverage, but when negative incidents occur in an athletic program, media attention intensifies and the bad publicity tarnishes all parts of the institution. These days, universities like Oklahoma and Kentucky are mainly known to the public for their sordid sports scandals, whereas their serious educational endeavors are ignored. Not surprisingly, schools in this situation often have difficulty raising money—not only for their athletic programs but also for their educational units.

In the year after the boosters of Southern Methodist University earned their favorite football team the most severe NCAA penalties, alumni gifts declined by over $1 million. The university vice-president in charge of the alumni association described SMU alums as "in a holding pattern. They seem to be saying, 'We're going to wait and give when the university has rid itself of these [college sports] problems, and when it seems to be back on course.' "

When a major scandal occurred at Memphis State University in the mid-1980s, the *Memphis Commercial Appeal* headlined, SETBACK IN MSU FUND-RAISING FEARED FROM PROBE'S FALLOUT. A school official admitted, in mock understatement, "When there is this much adverse publicity, there are some people who are not thrilled with having their names associated with the university."

The negative-publicity blade also swings back at a university when the attention generated by successful athletic teams overshadows academic programs and the institution gains a reputation as a "jock factory."

Alumni give approximately $2 billion a year to their alma maters, but the largest donations to colleges and universities do *not* come from alumni and boosters but from private foundations and corporations (not for "advertising signage" but to underwrite research, chairs, academic scholarships, etc.). Last year, these sources gave an estimated $3.45 billion to American higher education. According to the *Chronicle of Higher Education,* university fund-raisers have long warned that a school with a big-time sports program risks being "known as a 'football factory' [rather] than as a first-rate university" and could have trouble obtaining grants, especially from the major foundations.

A fund-raiser for an East Coast research university put the problem in human terms: "The foundation people who control the big bucks are often graduates of Ivy League or small liberal arts schools like Amherst and, frankly, they're prejudiced against jock factories. Whether it's justified or not, they tend to believe that schools with highly successful sports teams are not really serious about having first-rate academic departments."

That private philanthropies take a dim view of jock factories and their attendant ills was underlined by an editorial in their newsletter, *Foundation News,* that "urged the foundations and corporations that give money to colleges and universities to make the integrity of a school's athletic program one of the conditions for providing grants."

Thus one of the most common myths about college sports—that they generate great publicity and raise lots of money for schools—is not substantiated. Publicity from intercollegiate athletics is a two-edged sword that can easily swing back and injure a university, costing it millions of dollars.

CHAPTER 9

Unearned Revenue: Student Fees & Assessments

*"Student fees pay most of the athletic department bills at
most state-supported Virginia schools playing major
college sports. . . . The high price of subsidizing sports
programs plays a pivotal role in making tuition and fees at
these schools among the highest in the nation."*

—Item in the *Richmond Times Dispatch*

THE NCAA's financial report on college sports places the mandatory
"fees" and/or "assessments" that students pay to athletic departments
under "Unearned Revenue." This designation is appropriate but, considering how schools often obtain this money, the term "Consumer
Fraud" might also apply.

At almost every college and university, when students register for
classes, there is an item on their bills listed as "Activity Fees." Students
assume that this is for their use of the recreational sports and other
activity facilities; rarely does the bill indicate that, at many schools, part
of their "Activity Fees" payment goes to the athletic department and is a
significant source of its revenue. At a decreasing number of universities,
the "fee" entitles students to some form of admission to sports events;
other schools treat this money as a straight "assessment" and give
nothing in return.

The bottom line on this revenue item is clear: whether an individual
student likes college sports or not, plans on attending events or not, he
or she must still pay these charges.

In the last NCAA financial survey for Division I football schools, the
money raised from student fees and assessments averaged $1,196,000
per athletic program, and was anywhere from a single-digit percentage

to 60 percent of total revenue. At institutions with smaller programs, and less access to outside money, students provided from 30 percent to 85 percent of athletic department funding; for example in the 1986–87 academic year at Virginia Commonwealth University, they contributed $1.9 million of the $2.2 million total revenue. In terms of an individual registration bill, according to the student newspaper at William and Mary, each student there paid "more than $500" a year (in 1987–88) to the school's intercollegiate athletics program.

Taxing the populace in hidden and unfair ways is a historic cause of political grievance. One athletic director warns that the collection of student fees could result in "the tea party on campus." Perhaps if American college students understood how College Sports Inc. extracts money from them, they would be less passive about it and, as a result, would consider throwing some athletic programs overboard.

> *"Students don't have a say as to where the student fees for athletics go and the athletic department expects us to vote on the fees without comment."*
>
> —David Baker, two-term student body
> president at Virginia Polytechnic
> Institute and State University

The NCAA requires that all member institutions have a committee or board "in control of intercollegiate athletics," and, at many schools, students sit on this board. The NCAA, college presidents, and athletic directors point to these committees as proof that students have control over their fee and assessment dollars. This assertion is not true.

Democracy is almost unknown in the country of Intercollegiate Athletic Committees and Boards. Elections rarely occur: usually the school president, with input from the athletic director, appoints the board, including the student and faculty members, and chooses well-known supporters of the athletic program. In addition, very few presidents and athletic directors grant the boards any real power: the official NCAA pamphlet *Athletic Committees* indicates that *at only 4.4 percent of member schools are the "Functions of the Athletic Committee . . . Largely Regulatory"* (emphasis added); all other boards are either completely or partly "Advisory." Most important, these boards almost never have control over athletic department finances—usually they are not even allowed to examine the books, never mind the booster foundation records. Yet these boards are supposed to be the instruments of student control over their fee and assessment dollars as well as faculty and institutional control over intercollegiate athletics.

The particular students on the boards, as the NCAA pamphlet indicates, are neither representative of the entire student body nor impartial concerning athletic department matters. The student official most often serving on athletic boards—on 45 percent of them—is the head cheerleader! The student body president sits on 21.9 percent of the boards; the editor of the student newspaper on 16.4 percent; and the student head of intramurals on 11.4 percent. The student manager of athletics and the head of the campus organization of athletes are also on some boards. Considering the impotence of most athletic boards, it is surprising that administrators and ADs even go to the trouble of stacking the student members in this way.

The experience of the student representatives on the athletic board at Virginia Tech is fairly typical. In 1987–88, with Virginia Tech trying to recover from a major sports scandal, the student body president, David Baker, wanted to inform himself about the athletic department's operations. He particularly wanted to study the budget because each of his constituents contributed a mandatory $108 a year to it—for a total of over a $1 million of the athletic department's revenue. Baker sat, with two other students, on his school's athletic board—its function is advisory, not regulatory—and, as he explained in an interview, "I tried to learn about the athletic department but there is so much to learn and they really don't help us learn."

One of the incidents that upset the student board members was that, during their term, the school administration raised the mandatory athletic fee by 40 percent without consulting them or the board. As for the budget, Baker commented that the athletic department "tries to run it through without a lot of consultation. They tell us that the Board of Visitors [the trustees] are coming and we need to vote on the budget right away. We don't get a serious chance to look at it. This spring [1988], they gave the whole athletics board forty-five minutes for a $5 million budget."

Baker was reelected student body president for 1988–89 and he asked the administration to reappoint him to the athletic board. "I even starred my name on the [committee assignment] form to show them how serious I was," he said in a subsequent interview. "But they appointed a freshman instead of me." Considering his experience on the board, Baker would seem to be a logical choice. But, in most cases, experience on an athletic board is exactly the qualification that school presidents and athletic directors value least.

> *"[At the University of Maryland] $2 million—or almost a third of the athletic [department] receipts—were forcibly extracted from the students as athletic fees. Many students, including graduate students and those on highly restricted budgets, have very little interest in sports, yet are forced to pay the fee."*
>
> —Barbara R. Bergmann, professor of economics at the University of Maryland

In an excellent analysis of athletic department finances at Maryland, Professor Bergmann pointed out the unfairness of the fee system and also questioned "whether student fees should fund intercollegiate competition for a small number of" elite athletes, especially in minor sports "out of which most students do not even get entertainment." She also mentioned that at her school, "Intramural sports . . . are funded as part of the regular academic program," and not helped in any way by the $2 million athletic department tax on the students.

Like other forms of taxation, athletic department fees and assessments often carry extra hidden costs. At many schools, like Maryland, intramural sports and other recreational activities are funded separately by the school and/or students. At other institutions, administrators help pay athletic department expenses out of "Auxiliary Services" funds, i.e., money for the bookstore, student housing, cafeterias, etc. If there are profits from "Auxiliary Services," they send them to the athletic department instead of putting them into student activities—their traditional target. If "Auxiliary Services" is just breaking even or losing money, some administrators still squeeze it for dollars for college sports. When money is diverted from, or not reinvested in, "Auxiliary Services," it lowers the quality of campus life and all students—sports fans and non fans alike—suffer.

On occasion, university administrators take money directly out of student academic funds to help balance the athletic department's books. At the University of Nevada at Reno in 1983, $175,000 was moved from the "student-union fund" to help cover the athletic department's deficit. In previous years, this fund had paid English composition teachers and also contributed to the library. The president of the university explained, "Some say the money was supposed to be used for academic purposes only. The problem is, we had difficulty keeping the athletic program on a break-even basis, so we had to find the money somewhere."

More efficient is the tried-and-true method of extracting money from students—raise the mandatory fees and assessments by fiat. Because of athletic department mismanagement, students at the University of Houston were forced to pay an increasing proportion of the bill through most of the 1980s.

When a 1982 university audit of the athletic department revealed a $3.4 million deficit, the school's main response was to order an increase in "the athletic department's share of student fees from $400,000 in 1985 to $900,000 in 1986 and $1.72 million" the following year. Moreover, the school president said that the subsidy would have to rise to about $2 million a year for the late 1980s.

The Houston students did not go gentle into that red-inked night. The students, almost 70 percent of whom were part-time and/or evening students and not interested in a high-powered college sports program, protested the unfairness of the raised fees. Their elected leaders complained that the school "has had to cut money from other fee-supported activities, such as handicapped-student services and the health center."

The president of the university replied, "Somebody always gives up something. We have to get it [the money] from somewhere."

Complicating the Houston controversy was a major scandal involving the football coach and a number of his players in a long-term illegal-payoff scheme. At one point, the student senate passed a resolution calling for "the abolition of the intercollegiate athletic department," and "an end to student and university financing of athletics by 1990."

Like all student resolutions on athletic programs, the Houston one was advisory and nonbinding. Only the student fees and assessments for athletics were enforceable and apparently irrevocable.

Throughout the 1980s, students at American colleges and universities paid constantly rising tuition, room and board, and incidental fees. On many campuses, student fees and assessments for intercollegiate athletics are close to their saturation point. When athletic directors consider these facts, along with the demographic certainty that fewer students, paying increased tuition bills, will attend university in the coming years, ADs encounter a source of revenue without real growth potential.

This situation, no doubt, particularly saddens ADs: in the last decade, of all sources of unearned revenue for College Sports Inc., students have proven the most dependable and the least demanding.

CHAPTER 10

Unearned Revenue: State or Other Government Support

*"There's a popular belief in North Carolina that the
taxpayers don't foot the bill for intercollegiate athletics.
"It isn't so."*

—Item in the *Raleigh News and Observer*

SOME CRITICS of college sports describe it as "the tail that wags the
university dog," i.e., that athletic department needs so dominate the
attention of school presidents and administrators that they neglect more
important concerns—the education of their students. Nowhere is this
situation more obvious than in the "State or Other Government"
funds—money that could go to education—that schools use to bolster
athletic programs. This diversion of taxpayers' dollars prompts questions about the very reasons for having intercollegiate athletics, especially in an era when the academic units of most colleges and
universities go begging for money.

The NCAA financial survey lists only *"Direct* State or other Government Support," but this total is probably less than 50 percent of the
public monies used for college sports. Even the listed amounts are
considerable: in the last reporting year, 1985, the athletic departments
of Division I football schools received an average of $736,000 of the
taxpayers' dollars. The survey also noted that for all public institutions
in the NCAA, well over two-thirds benefited from government support
of their athletic programs.

The athletic departments of state schools in Illinois provide a typical
example. In 1983–84, they received $7 million of their funding from

the public purse, and in subsequent years, the Illinois government has increased its support. In California, the amount of state funding per athletic program is often substantial: in 1988, Cal State at Fullerton received $2.5 million from the taxpayers. Even in smaller states, governments generously support college sports: in Alaska, in 1988, the athletic program at the University of Alaska at Anchorage received $1.2 million from the state; and in Montana, in 1983, the athletic departments of the University of Montana and Montana State were given $961,000 and $1.34 million, respectively.

One of the great public relations myths perpetrated by athletic directors is that their programs have to be self-supporting and do not interfere with the funding of academic units. Some ADs are fond of promoting this myth with the maxim "Every tub [must stand] on its own bottom." To bolster their assertion, these athletic directors cite state laws that prohibit taxpayers' money going to intercollegiate athletics. In fact, only sixteen states have any sort of law to this effect and, in most of them, athletic directors and college administrators have long ago figured out ways to circumvent the laws.

The most common ploy is to have an academic department, usually physical education, pay the salary of a coach. In North Carolina, as the *Raleigh News and Observer* revealed a few years ago, "More than 100 faculty members on 15 University of North Carolina System campuses are doing double duty as physical education instructors and coaches. The tab for these services . . . $2.3 million this year—is paid by taxpayers through funds appropriated to the UNC System by the Legislature." The problem is that many of these academic employees were not doing double duty; they functioned mainly as coaches, and only a small percentage of their time, if any, went into teaching phys ed.

In a number of states, including Kentucky, university administrators get around their state laws by placing intercollegiate athletics under "Student Services," and funding it with public money in the "Auxiliary Services" budget. In other states, sometimes to circumvent laws, other times to keep up the pretense that the taxpayers are not paying for college sports, schools waive tuition for athletes or pay it out of the academic scholarship fund. In these cases, the "Jock Subsidy" is not direct but the hole in the university's financial books is as real and must be made up by dollars from other, often academic, revenue sources.

Direct subsidies for athletics at public institutions are relatively easy to trace; indirect ones at those schools as well as at private colleges are more difficult to spot and can involve very large sums of money. One of the best explanations of how indirect subsidies work was given by the judges of both the district court and the U.S. court of appeals in their decision on Temple University's challenge to Title IX, the equality for women's sports provision of the 1972 Education Act. Temple claimed that, as a private school, it was exempt from this federal law. The courts replied: "Even though the athletic program does not receive federal dollars directly . . . the program benefits from governmental aid to other branches of the university. *Federal money to those other branches allows the university to divert other funds to the sports program*" (emphasis added).

One of the standard ways that schools do this is to put tax dollars into the General Operating Fund and then move money from the G.O.F. into the athletic department (some people call this "money laundering"). Understandably, most public as well as private institutions are reluctant to disclose how much money is involved. Neither does the NCAA offer any dollar-and-cents figures on this source of "Unearned Revenue," but it does provide some interesting percentages. In response to a questionnaire, over 50 percent of all athletic departments admitted that they received "financial assistance from the general operating funds of the institution in deficit years." To the question whether university funds regularly helped pay for nonrevenue sports, 42 percent responded "Yes." By all accounts, this percentage has increased in the years since the survey.

The judges in the Temple decision used the word "divert" to describe the movement of funds; this seems too mild a verb for what can occur. In a famous case at Washington State University, the school administration took $2.2 million of state funds to bolster the athletic program. In addition to the direct subsidies, a faculty senate report charged that "substantial but unknown amounts in indirect support from state funds" were also channeled into college sports. The faculty was particularly upset because, during this period, the school had cut funds to academic departments, and a number of them, because they were short of teachers, had to refuse qualified students admission to their programs.

Another egregious case of direct and indirect subsidies occurred at Utah State University in 1988, when the state's economy was in bad shape. The school administration slashed the academic budget, and the faculty and staff accepted a $500,000 reduction in their medical insurance benefits, but the athletic department was allowed to run up an $800,000 deficit. To cover this loss, which included a greatly increased football budget for a new coach, the university moved money from academic funding. The faculty was upset: "In this time of retrenchment," a professor of business administration asked, "the real question is, 'Where do our priorities lie?' "

For Utah State, apparently a main priority was chasing the college sports' pot o' gold. The athletic director justified his spending with Excuse No. 1 in the *AD's Handbook*: "With a winning season, we could . . . possibly start turning a profit. Sometimes you have to spend money to make money."

Professor Barbara Bergmann, an economist at the University of Maryland, explains the real reason direct and indirect subsidies are always demanded: "When the school wins, the sports budget has a tendency to expand to spend its 'profits.' When it loses, the losses are made up from within the university."

Throughout the 1980s, San Jose State experienced athletic department deficits—and employed similar solutions. In 1986, San Jose president Gail Fullerton commented, "The problem is that all departments are competing for scarce money. . . . The faculty sees money to athletics as money out of their programs. I think a lot of them would be more supportive if the [athletic] programs were self-supporting."

No doubt faculty would, but this promised land is never reached at most American colleges and universities. In fact, because of the way that athletic departments forecast revenue—as if every year will produce bowl and NCAA tournament bids and maximum booster donations—shortfalls are almost inevitable. An annually self-supporting athletic program is almost an oxymoron.

> "A five- to six-million-dollar program ought to be able to generate its own revenue without resorting to public funds. Taking state tax money places you in a position of people being able to say you're taking money that could be used for general education."
>
> —Dick Schultz, executive director of the NCAA

Schultz made this comment when he was athletic director at the University of Virginia, and he added, "I know public money is tempting but I like to be able to look professors in the eye." Now that he has become head of the NCAA, Schultz has shown no inclination to convince the membership, especially the athletic directors who occupy most of the key Executive Council posts, of his position on this issue.

A specific recommendation on this question was made in 1988 by the Carnegie Foundation to the state of Arkansas. In a special report on higher education in that state, commissioned by a council of state business leaders, the Carnegie investigators urged the legislature "to bar the transfer of huge sums of money from educational to athletic accounts, which has become a perennial practice at several state universities."

The Carnegie criticism was based, in part, on the $6.3 million deficit run up by Arkansas athletic departments in 1986–87, and covered by taxpayers' dollars. The Carnegie Foundation was not alone in its recommendation; a large statewide poll found that "almost 75 percent of Arkansans favor limiting state spending on college athletics . . . [and] 71 percent favor requiring college athletic programs to be self-supporting."

When the athletic department of the University of Wisconsin at Madison had an estimated $5.9 million deficit in 1988–89, and a $9.5 million one forecast for future years, the *Milwaukee Journal* also polled the taxpayers on who should mop up the red ink: 78 percent said they were against "the use of state tax money."

Nevertheless many school officials and athletic directors are hooked on this money, and if they cannot get it directly, they obtain it through subterfuge. That some university presidents are complicit in this use of tax dollars is a sad commentary on their priorities.

If the public believes—as opinion polls indicate—that the educational missions of American colleges and universities are more important than their franchises in College Sports Inc., it will put political pressure on elected officials to end this use of tax dollars.

OVERVIEW: EXPENSES

"If [athletic program] costs are going to go up on one side, and the revenues are going to stay the same, then there's got to be some containment in there to deal with these costs."

—Dick Schultz, executive director of the NCAA

THE AUTONOMY of athletic programs makes overspending almost inevitable. Of all parts of the university, only athletic departments are so self-contained that when asked to justify expenses, frequently they answer solely to their own employees—their business managers. All other units of the university have to explain their spending, usually item by item, to deans and to central administration comptrollers.

Academic departments, in addition to internal university scrutiny, are regularly evaluated by professionals from outside institutions—accreditation panels—and no academic department can deny them full access or is immune from their penalties for serious infractions, including the cancellation of degree-granting powers. Athletic programs, however, face no such regular auditing or penalties.

Thus the potential for financial mismanagement is built into the structure of College Sports Inc. Rather than use their independence to build strong, self-supporting enterprises, athletic programs too often indulge in financial chicanery.

The NCAA's *Revenues and Expenses of Intercollegiate Athletics Programs* is a useful guide to the sea of red ink in which most athletic departments swim. The section "Analysis of Expenses" focuses on the costs of salaries, athletic scholarships, travel, equipment, supplies, and other items. The NCAA's official numbers, however, are probably far below the actual expense totals in college sports: the figures were supplied by those athletic departments that voluntarily responded to the survey (in all likelihood, the more prosperous ones), and the numbers were uncertified, i.e., the NCAA accepted whatever figures were sent it.

In addition, the survey excludes the costs of women's sports. The NCAA does this "to maintain comparability with prior-year financial

92

trends," but, as a result, the frequent AD complaint that women's-sports-are-dragging-us-down-financially is invalid here. The survey also places "additions to property, plant and equipment, and certain types of debt-service payments for principal and interest payments" in a separate section, both for accounting reasons and because so few athletics programs acknowledge these costs. Yet even with these omissions, *the official NCAA expense figures for men's intercollegiate athletics are enormous and growing.*

For the last reporting year, 1985, Division I schools with football teams averaged $4.6 million in expenses, a 286 percent increase from 1973. Schools in other divisions had six-figure expenses, but with increases ranging from 212 percent to 374 percent during the twelve-year period. Expenses for some of these years were related to inflation but, as the survey points out, for the 1982–85 period "a 12% increase in average total expenses would be considered normal," whereas in college sports the increase exceeded 112 percent for each division in this period.

Expenses must also be seen in terms of revenues. The $719,000 average expense bill for Division II football schools would not be so significant if revenues met or exceeded that amount. However, with almost every cent of revenue accounted for and huge sums of expenses missing, these schools admitted average losses of $300,000. For Division III schools with football teams, the losses averaged $268,000, and, in all divisions, deficits for institutions without football teams were between $53,000 and $280,000.

In addition, in its "Forecasts of Average Total Expenses," the survey sees a deteriorating situation. It predicts that, in a period when revenue was expected to be flat, total expenses for Division I football schools will have increased from $4.6 million in 1985 to $6.75 million in 1989, that the expenses for Division II football schools will have gone over $1 million by that year, and that costs in all other athletic programs will have increased by comparable increments.

In the end, however, the NCAA provides only global and abstract statistics. To comprehend the meaning of these numbers—how athletic departments spend and waste enormous amounts of money—a detailed analysis of the main categories of expenses and, wherever possible, of expenditures is necessary. The NCAA survey provides a map but, for a full understanding, it is essential to travel up the rivers that feed the sea of red ink.

CHAPTER 11

Salaries

"The problem at [the University of] Maryland [athletic department] was one of organization. They were completely overstaffed. They had far more people than they needed."

> —Don Canham, former athletic director at the University of Michigan, after a consulting visit to Maryland

THE SINGLE greatest expense for most athletic departments is salary payments to personnel. The NCAA survey lists these as averaging $1.4 million annually for Division I football schools, or 30 percent of all acknowledged operating expenses. Payroll dollar figures for Divisions II and III averaged much lower but, as the survey pointed out, and it is particularly true of these smaller programs, "In some cases, salaries are paid from institutional funds . . . and may not be included in expenses of the athletics program."

Payroll costs at schools in the highest echelon of college sports far exceed the NCAA's average. In 1986, the University of Michigan listed its athletic department's "salaries, wages, fringes" at $4 million, and the year before, the University of Georgia placed its "personal services and staff benefits" at $2.73 million. Almost a decade ago, the American Council on Education reported, "In the semipro programs, coaching and other staff salaries may bear little relationship to other salaries within the institutions unless state laws or personnel regulations require comparability." When there are such regulations, athletic departments have various ways, usually with the help of booster organizations, of getting around them and paying their employees, especially the coaches, more.

Since the ACE report, athletic department salaries have remained significantly higher than the pay for comparable academic faculty and staff. A major reason for this pay discrepancy is that autonomous athletic directors establish their own and their employees' pay rates, whereas academic department heads, when setting pay for themselves, faculty, and staff, have to bargain every year with supervising deans. Athletic department personnel, however, do not like to compare their salaries to those of faculty members; they prefer to see themselves in the same league as corporate America and they reward themselves accordingly. Thus athletic department personnel are able to have it all ways—a corporate pay scale, and a public service institution absorbing the red ink.

> *"College football coaches [were] led by Texas A & M University's Jackie Sherrill, whose $110,865 a year base salary tops Gov. Mark White's $94,348 a year. . . . Four [Texas] university coaches and athletic directors earn more than $90,000, records show."*
>
> —Item in the *Dallas Morning News*

The most comprehensive study of the salaries of athletic directors and football and basketball coaches was done by *USA Today* a few years ago (made possible by Gannett's financial resources and willingness to employ Freedom of Information laws when confronted with athletic department intransigence). Beginning with the A's, the paper discovered that, in 1986, Alabama AD and football coach Ray Perkins received a base salary of $120,000 and perks worth another $100,000. Alabama has a big-time football program; the University of Alaska at Fairbanks does not play football, yet its AD had a base salary of over $61,000, plus benefits. The list continues, with most big-time athletic directors receiving over $75,000 a year, plus perks and benefits.

Even though athletic directors set their own salaries, they are rarely the highest-paid employee in their department. That honor usually goes to the football and/or men's basketball head coach.

The University of Iowa provides a good example of the regular pay scale in College Sports Inc. In 1987–88, Hayden Fry, the football coach, had the top salary in this athletic department—$103,400 (because of the various deals that he, like all big-time coaches, had on the side, his total annual income was close to $250,000). Men's basketball coach Tom

Davis was second to Fry in salary at $82,500, and he also had other sports income. Athletic director Bump Elliott received at least $70,000 annually and various perks.

The head football coach and men's basketball coach are sometimes called the "full professors" of the athletic department. At Iowa, in comparison to these coaches' salaries, the average pay for academic department full professors was much lower, $51,000 a year.

In 1987–88, the salary average for the nine assistant football coaches at Iowa was almost $50,000, and the two men's basketball assistants were at $47,200 and $45,200. These eleven coaches also had income supplements through money earned at camps and clinics.

Assistant professors at Iowa were on a much lower salary scale. Although a Ph.D. is required for this faculty rank, the average pay for assistant professors was $32,800 a year.

In the wake of the football and men's basketball coaches came the personnel in nonrevenue sports. At Iowa, these totaled thirty-two coaches and, in salary, they were led by the head man in wrestling at $54,100, and the head women's basketball coach at $53,800 annually. The other Iowa head coaches in nonrevenue sports were paid between $43,700 and $29,250 annually, but many of them had such built-in income supplements as profitable private summer camps on university property.

In most athletic departments, coaches' salaries eat up less than half of the personnel budget. The dispersal of the rest of the salary money provides an insight into the daily workings—and bloated payrolls—of contemporary athletic departments.

> *"The number of full-time personnel involved in the administration of intercollegiate athletics increased 35.9% between 1966 and 1972. The number of part-time personnel in the form of fund raisers, public relations directors, and information or media liaisons increased 53%."*
>
> —Professor James Frey, "The Organization of American Amateur Sport: Efficiency to Entropy," in the *American Behavioral Scientist*

Frey's statistics on the growth of athletic department personnel in the 1966–72 period must be complemented by the NCAA's figure that athletic department expenses—personnel being the largest—*increased 300 percent from 1973 to 1985.*

A detailed analysis of a typical big-time athletic program, Indiana University at Bloomington, provides some sense of the people on the payroll and how much they make.

At Indiana, in 1988–89, the top administrator in the athletic department was Ralph Floyd, the AD, with an annual income of $87,000 and perks. Beneath him were five associate directors and one assistant director, whose salaries averaged $42,524. The average annual salary for an associate professor in many departments at Indiana University the same year was much lower: in History, $36,841; in English, $33,489; and in Slavic Languages (including Russian), $31,676.

Many of the full-time employees of an athletic department provide direct support to the various teams. In 1988–89, the Indiana athletic department's doctor earned $71,550 a year, higher than his equivalent colleagues at Indiana University's School of Medicine, and much higher than the doctors working in Student Health Services. Under "Training Room" on the "Athletic Department Salaried Personnel" roster, nine full-time and part-time people were listed, a number of them paid in part by the school's HPER (Health, Physical Education, and Recreation) Department. The basketball trainer received $40,995, and the football trainer $36,860. In addition, the "Strength Director," in charge of the "Weight Room," earned $30,325 a year. (This state-of-the-art training room, like all athletic department facilities, is available only to athletes on intercollegiate teams.)

As part of an elite athlete's training, a great deal of equipment is necessary and, at Indiana, three full-time employees, as well as many part-time helpers, are in charge of everything from swimming goggles to tackling dummies. Beyond the physical necessities for athletes are the mental ones, particularly staying eligible for NCAA competition. The I.U. athletic department employs four full-time academic counselors—the head one earned $38,560 last year—and as many as 150 part-time tutors to help its athletes pass their courses.

But no college athlete runs onto a field without a large administrative staff setting everything up beforehand. On the I.U. athletic department roster, four employees were listed under "Business Office," the highest salaried one at $44,500 per annum, and assisting the AD in his office were four full-time employees. In the "Ticket Office," seven full-time, full-year employees toiled away, with salaries of $40,400 and $32,200 for the ticket director and his top assistant, respectively. Most of the tickets sold were for five home football games and fifteen home basketball games, and for these events many part-time ticket sellers were employed.

To put the best face on its business, the I.U. athletic department had four full-time P.R. people and a number of part-timers. The sports information director annually earned $35,625, significantly more than the assistant professors in I.U.'s School of Journalism. In addition to the word-flacks, the department had two full-time photographers as well as part-time assistants. Their main duties were to take team pictures and public relations shots (all major newspapers and magazines that cover college sports send their own photographers). The head photographer's salary was above that of some assistant professors of fine arts (the academic unit that teaches photography).

With this kind of annual payroll to cover, not surprisingly, the I.U. athletic department has its own fund-raising unit, called the Varsity Club. Last year it employed eight full-time people and many part-timers for a six-figure total payroll. This booster organization must raise an estimated $400,000 to cover its own salaries, office and other expenses, especially its large travel and entertainment bill, before it can contribute a single penny to athletic department revenue.

For 1988, there were 123 employees—including coaches, but excluding hundreds of part-timers—on the Indiana University "Athletic Department Salaried Personnel" list. Did these people deserve their various paychecks and perks (among other goodies, for many of them, free travel to away games as well as to a bowl and NCAA tournaments)? It is impossible for an outsider to say. None of them, however, taught over two hundred students a year as did the average faculty member in English and many other departments. Nevertheless, for 1989–90, the athletic department projects that "Salaries, Wages, and Fringe Benefits" will increase to a total of $4.66 million, almost 35 percent of its expenses.

Examining athletic department salaries not only prompts questions about program spending, but when comparing them to faculty salaries, the issue of university priorities arises. Administrators once defended high athletic department payrolls by arguing that "college sports makes lots of money for the university" and the people who generate these dollars should be rewarded accordingly. At very few schools is this argument still valid. Therefore, it is totally illogical for administrators to allow these high payrolls to continue and at the same time to subsidize the deficits created, in part, by these employees.

Most faculty members do not "make lots of money" for their schools—but that is not their job. They are supposed to teach, do research, and help their institutions carry out their educational missions. However, in American society, the standard measurement of the worth of an individual's work is the size of his or her paycheck. Faculty members make a distinction between the public service sector and corporate America and do not expect the latter's high pay scale. Nevertheless, when most assistant, associate, and full professors are paid significantly less than athletic program personnel, they have to interpret this as a comment by their schools on the value of their work.

CHAPTER 12

Athletic Scholarships

"The problem that I hear discussed at this [1988 NCAA] convention and other conventions is expenses. The rising costs are based on the fact that we have more athletes. At the University of Michigan, when I first became athletic director [twenty years ago] . . . we had 250 athletes, varsity athletes. Today we have 600 varsity athletes."

—Don Canham, former Athletic Director at
the University of Michigan

DON CANHAM is not being entirely accurate—his salary costs were not the same when he began at Michigan as when he retired ($4 million)—but, in 1986, his athletic scholarship bill was $2.4 million and rising. According to the NCAA financial survey, "Grant-in-Aid" expenses are growing exponentially: for Division I football schools, an average of $556,000 in 1981 to $860,000 in 1985, the last reporting year; schools in other divisions had 138 percent to 750 percent increases for this item in this period. Since the survey, according to a sports business magazine, "Financial aid to athletes is draining budgets, rising 10% to 15% a year, while revenues are largely flat." By the year 1995, the cost of this item to athletic departments may be 100 to 150 percent above the 1985 level.

The NCAA prefers the term "grant-in-aid" to "athletic scholarship": the new phrase is apparently more pleasing to them than the more accurate "athletic scholarship," with its clear indication of college athletes receiving money solely on the basis of their sports abilities.

Like football players, NCAA-approved athletic scholarships come in a variety of sizes and shapes. The most expensive are "full rides": the athletic program pays all tuition and fees, books required for courses, room and board, and miscellaneous expenses such as tutoring. The least expensive are "partial grants," where only a percentage—usually between 33 and 50 percent—of an athlete's costs is paid. Most big-time programs have at least two hundred athletes on full scholarship and an even higher number on partial grants. In addition, athletic departments sometimes give scholarships to student managers—formerly known as "water boys" (at Indiana, of the eleven student managers for football, most receive full or partial grants, as do the basketball managers). With a year in residence at a public institution now costing each student from $6,000 to $12,000, and at a private college as much as $20,000, paying for hundreds of grants is an enormous expense for all athletic programs.

According to the NCAA's financial survey, for Division I schools with football teams, athletic scholarships comprised 17 percent of their acknowledged total expenses; for institutions in other divisions, these costs were as high as 30 percent. One way to comprehend these percentages is to examine the athletic scholarship line for specific schools. In its 1985 budget, the University of Georgia listed this item at $2.04 million. In 1987, Big Eight Conference schools averaged $3.7 million in grants. Stanford University, in 1987–88, paid $4.73 million for athletic scholarships.

As at most private schools, Stanford's tuition costs are high, and once the other perks of an athletic scholarship are added in, the value of a single grant comes to about $18,000 a year. At that price, when Andy Geiger, the athletic director, starts with 95 freebies a year in football, adds 30 in men's and women's basketball and another 185 for the athletes on the school's seventeen other intercollegiate teams, he has spent close to $5 million. Geiger says, "Every time they raise tuition here I cringe, and they always raise tuition here, so I always cringe."

According to the NCAA survey, breaking down the percentage of athletic scholarships per sport reveals that 55 percent of the grant money at Division I schools with football teams went to players in that sport, 10 percent to basketball players, and 35 percent to athletes in other sports.

One of the unjustified excesses of big-time athletic programs is the number of football scholarships. In Division I-A, most football coaches give ninety-five full rides, and they insist that this number of scholarship players as well as a contingent of fifteen to thirty "walk-ons"— nonscholarship athletes—is necessary for a competitive team. NFL clubs, with much longer and tougher schedules, manage to get by with forty-five players. (All attempts within the NCAA to start to control expenses by reducing the number of football grants have failed because of the power of big-time football coaches.)

Schools like Stanford, however, with large nonrevenue sports programs, reverse the usual percentages on athletic scholarship expenses: in 1987–88, 40 percent of its grant money went to football and men's basketball, and 60 percent—$2.83 million—to nonrevenue sports. The Stanford situation illustrates the other major excess in athletic scholarship expenses: the support of elite athletes—at Stanford, over two hundred—in sports that will never pay their own way.

> *"A number of institutions that award grants-in-aid to participating athletes do not report these costs as operating expenses of the athletics program, because the amounts are paid by institutional funds outside the control of the athletics department."*
>
> —*Revenues and Expenses of Intercollegiate Athletics Programs*, published by the NCAA

The NCAA's caveat about the figures on grants-in-aid is rather understated: "outside the control" is a polite way of saying that many athletic departments have such direct access to university funds that they can tap into them regularly, usually annually, to lay off part or all of the cost of their athletic scholarships. No academic department, even one with the most intellectually gifted students, has this access to university scholarship money.

Athletic departments accomplish their financial sleight of hand in a number of ways: they convince the central administration to pay for athletic grants out of student scholarship funds, and/or they exert influence over financial-aid committees. This latter maneuver involves channeling money to athletes on a direct or a loan basis, and the effect is to give athletes money and *not call it an athletic scholarship.*

The intent behind the various maneuvers is to move this expense away from the athletic department's books and also, in many cases, to get around NCAA rules on the number of grants allowed in certain sports or for certain divisions. No matter what the intent, the result is that scholarship and financial-aid money that could go to regular students is siphoned off to the athletic department.

The financial-aid end run has become so blatant and abused that at a recent NCAA convention, Proposals 92 and 93 were introduced. The former "would prohibit athletic department officials at Division III institutions from serving on the college's financial-aid committees and from being involved in decisions about financial aid offered to athletes. No. 93 would preclude Division III institutions from considering athletic ability as a criterion in developing a financial-aid package." Division III was singled out because its schools are not supposed to give any athletic scholarships, but many of them cheat through financial-aid maneuvers. Proposal 93 was passed and immediately many Division III schools began to lobby against it, claiming that they could not enforce it.

The NCAA attempted to reform the financial-aid situation in Division III but apparently it does not want to confront this issue in higher divisions. If it did, it would have to deal with such financial-aid strategies as the University of Nebraska's "county scholarship" plan, a key component of the school's successful football program. Each year, the Nebraska athletic department harvests large numbers of unofficial grants funded by boosters and awarded to promising football players throughout the state. The county scholarship holders come to the university as walk-ons and, not surprisingly, many more make the team than in other big-time programs.

The university will not confirm that county scholarships exist but Dave Gillespie, the Nebraska assistant coach in charge of walk-ons, admitted that forty to fifty are on the varsity in any year and "that 90 percent of Nebraska's walk-ons are in-state students." At the beginning of the 1988 season, of the forty-four starters and backups at each offensive and defensive position, twenty-five had come to the school as walk-ons; on most other big-time college football teams, no more than a handful of walk-ons ever become starters or backups. Nebraska's county scholarship plan allows the football coaches to give their NCAA-authorized grants to only the most outstanding in-state players and to many out-of-state athletes.

The NCAA acknowledges the existence of such athletic scholarships in one of its most widely distributed pamphlets, the *NCAA Guide for the College-Bound Student-Athlete*. "If you receive a scholarship from your high school or local civic or booster club," the association advises potential college athletes, "tell your college recruiter so he or she can notify the school's financial-aid office." And—the NCAA doesn't add—so he or she can get the cost of your grant well away from the athletic department's books.

Another standard financial-aid ploy is the Pell grant end run. These federally funded grants for needy students have a ceiling of $2,100 per recipient, and many athletes, especially poor blacks, easily qualify for Pell grants on the basis of financial need. The NCAA rule is that an athletic scholarship holder can only take a maximum of $1,400 (for Division I athletes) and $900 (for other divisions) of Pell grant money. The rationale for these ceilings is that athletes are already receiving a large amount of remuneration from their regular grants-in-aid and the fiction of their amateur status must be maintained.

Some athletic departments, however, do not pass on the money from Pell grants to their athletes—instead they reduce an athlete's scholarship by the amount received from the government. In addition, a number of programs abuse both the Pell grant rules and the NCAA limits on this money. In the mid-1980s, in Tennessee, the *Memphis Commercial Appeal* discovered that at some state universities, "a larger percentage of athletes than of students in general received federal Pell grants." Memphis State had an amazing appetite for these grants: one year, sixty-three football players acquired them, and of this group, fifty-four "indicated [that] their home address was that of one of four football coaches," i.e., the coaches were filling out the forms for the players and dispersing the money. After the NCAA investigated Memphis State, it charged that the school had "exceeded the permissible limit for such aid under NCAA legislation" by $58,940.

Memphis State's NCAA sin was not in using Pell grants to help pay its athletic scholarship bill but in going over the NCAA's limits (which the association subsequently raised). Unfortunately, Pell grants, with their admirable aim of helping needy students go to college, have become, like tax-deductible booster donations, one more way of getting the taxpayers to subsidize College Sports Inc.

No matter how athletic departments fiddle their grant-in-aid bills—by using university scholarship and/or financial-aid funds and/or Pell grants—they cannot escape rising tuition and other college costs. The Department of Education estimates that "tuition at the average public university will rise 70% to 80% between 1988 and 2000," and other college expenses may increase even more. A sports business magazine predicts that "[athletic] scholarship costs at a school like Alabama . . .

will jump from its current [1989] level of $3 million to about $6 million annually" in the year 2000.

In trying to feed this growing grant-in-aid monster, athletic departments will appeal to their universities for even more money from regular scholarship and other funds, and many administrators will yield to these requests. This will occur at a time when increasing numbers of serious and talented students will urgently need help financing their college educations. Money that could go to them will be given instead to athletic programs.

CHAPTER 13

Travel & Recruiting

"The most significant hidden cost in intercollegiate athletics is recruiting."

> —*The Money Game,* published by the
> American Council on Education

WHERE TO FIND and put hidden costs? *The Money Game* gives one suggestion: in many athletic department budgets, "recruiting costs are not separated from travel as a general athletics budget line item." Travel costs also contain some of the worst abuses of athletic program spending; often a huge entourage of hangers-on (all expenses paid by the athletic department) goes along with the team, and, when recruiting, coaches spare no cost. The acknowledged travel bills of athletic departments reveal some impressively high numbers. The NCAA financial survey lists "Team and Other Travel" for Division I football schools at an average of $554,000 in 1985, or 12 percent of their total expenses. For most other kinds of athletic programs, travel averaged around 15 percent of total costs but in the $100,000 range.

As always, the big-time programs spent far above the average: the University of Georgia, in 1985, placed its "Squad Travel" expense at $835,860, and its "Travel—coaches, recruiting and scouting" at $591,522. From 1985 to 1990, however, with airline ticket prices increasing by as much as 100 percent, athletic program travel bills have lockstepped up.

> *"Travel is expensive in more ways than dollars and cents.*
> *At a small Division I school like ours, the travel money*
> *goes into flying the basketball team around. But,*
> *according to NCAA rules, we've got to have lots of teams*
> *in other sports in order to play big-time basketball. So we*

106

*end up with most of our athletes driving around in vans
during the middle of the night, eating fast food, and
missing class."*

—Professor James Vincent, Robert Morris
College, Pittsburgh, Pennsylvania

Most big-time athletic programs spend at least half of their team travel money on football; in Georgia's case, over $400,000 in 1985. Basketball teams play more games than football squads but travel lighter; a major Division I team, in 1990, puts about $100,000 into this item. For nonrevenue sports, travel costs vary: college baseball teams, especially at northern and midwestern schools, take long and expensive exhibition trips through the Sun Belt each spring; soccer teams, particularly in Division I, hopscotch around the country in pursuit of berths in the NCAA postseason tournament; and in other sports, like tennis, teams travel widely in order to play suitable opponents. (Team travel to NCAA tournaments is paid by the association.)

The structure of College Sports Inc. works against rational spending on travel. Not only does the NCAA require members to have large numbers of teams in various sports (thirteen squads in at least seven sports for Division I-A schools with football programs), it also demands that teams play at their divisional level—no matter what the geographic location of their opponents.

A few years ago, the University of Akron upgraded its football team to Division I-A, and to qualify for an NCAA-approved schedule in 1988, it had to play as far away as the University of New Mexico and Auburn University (Alabama), as well as entertain schools from equally distant places. Thus, the football teams of Long Beach State, Fullerton State, and New Mexico State took the long, expensive flight to Cleveland's Hopkins Airport, and their travel was paid, in part, by the host school's guarantees.

The NCAA's built-in travel costs, particularly for nonrevenue sports teams, burden the majority of members. Big-time athletic programs spend about $300,000 a year transporting their nonrevenue squads; many smaller Division I programs cannot afford this price tag and often try to cut corners, even at the expense of their athletes' health and educations. A faculty member at Robert Morris College in Pittsburgh explained: "This year [1989], I had some volleyball players in a class and these kids had to take van tours along the East Coast—and get hammered wherever they played—so that our basketball team could compete in Division I and go first-class. Not only did the volleyball players fall behind in my course but they also never seemed to get much sleep or enough to eat."

After a full season of divisional travel, a few teams go to postseason events, including NCAA tournaments. The travel bills for these also illustrate the association's attitude about this expense. In 1987, for example, the NCAA men's and women's skiing championship was held at the University of Alaska at Anchorage. Receipts were $4,826 but expenses were a whopping $161,000, almost $102,000 of that amount in transportation costs and $24,000-plus in per diems. Fifteen of the seventeen teams came from the "Lower 48," ten from as far away as New England.

When the NCAA schedules meetings, it also likes to gather at wonderful vacation spots, many of them far away from the campuses of the coaches and officials involved. In 1987, the NCAA lacrosse meeting took place in Monterey, California, even though every major lacrosse school is on the East Coast. The same year, the NCAA ice hockey meeting was in San Diego, far from the college hockey hotbeds of New England and the upper Midwest. The men's and women's skiing meeting—after the championship was held in Alaska—was on Amelia Island in Florida. And the list goes on, with each year bringing new all-expenses-paid travel opportunities to the athletic department personnel involved.

In corporate America, travel expenses are a flexible item and, in tight times, can be cut. In College Sports Inc., the only way to save on travel is to change the structure of the enterprise and the attitude of the people who run it.

> "It's somewhat of an irritant to many of our [NCAA]
> members when they read in the papers that they are
> getting x number of dollars for [bowl games or
> tournaments]. . . . They have to use that money to pay for
> all the additional people they take with them, from
> university presidents down. That eats up the money real
> fast."
>
> —Tom Jernstedt, NCAA official

Often the major expense in team travel is picking up the tab for all the hangers-on. The more important the sporting event, the more people who want to be aboard the gravy train. Athletic departments, never too cost conscious with losing teams and during economically difficult times, become Santa Claus when their teams are winning and compete in bowls or tournaments.

During the Patrick Ewing years, Georgetown's sports promotion director, Brian McGuire, was in charge of the athletic department's travel. Among his other duties were arranging charter flights—one time he had to rush "$87,000 to Chicago in two days to guarantee a 'Stretch 727' aircraft"—and moving a large entourage, including a fifty-piece band, to the team's various tournament sites. He explained that the spending of travel money accelerates "as you get further into the tournament, [because] you're getting more and more money, so it's easier to rationalize spending it." After the tournament is over, and all the bills are in, many participants are tapped out.

The Louisiana State Tigers played in the 1985 Sugar Bowl in New Orleans, only a short distance from LSU's campus in Baton Rouge. After the game, the *Baton Rouge Morning Advocate* reported that "the Sugar Bowl Commission withheld $65,823 from its settlement check with LSU to cover such LSU expenses as $21,275 worth of complimentary tickets, $3,504 for a staff party, $8,125 for a New Year's gala and other university expenses." Among the latter, even though their homes were up the road in Baton Rouge, athletic department personnel spent $13,625 on hotel accommodations, including babysitting for their children. In addition to billing the Sugar Bowl Committee for all of its New Year's fun, the LSU athletic department got its own university to pay "$9,539 for post-game meals for 525 people and bought $1,474 in beverages for about 400 people at a post-game celebration." What makes the LSU–Sugar Bowl adventure noteworthy is that thanks to Louisiana's Freedom of Information laws, the story emerged (many other athletic programs spend as much or more in similar circumstances but their lips and books are sealed), and though the LSU athletic department knew that their expenditures would become public because the local and state newspapers had been investigating their finances for a number of years, they went ahead and spent the money anyway.

Athletic department travel expenses even earned a Golden Fleece Award for government mismanagement from Senator William Proxmire. He discovered that the 1983 Army-Navy game, held in the Rose Bowl in Pasadena, had cost the taxpayers "at least $100,000 . . . and maybe considerably more" because large numbers of cadets and midshipmen had been flown from the East Coast to California. The athletic departments of the Army and Navy had originally promised, when they switched the game from its traditional site in Philadelphia, that the West Coast trip would not incur any extra costs. After the event, they had to swim through the red ink and call for a life preserver of extra money—instead of from Uncle University, from his richer relative, Uncle Sam.

Often the most profligate spenders of athletic department travel money are athletic directors themselves. Frank Broyles of Arkansas is a figure of probity among his peers, yet in 1988, Little Rock's *Arkansas Gazette* revealed that "the Razorback Scholarship Fund Inc. frequently pays [Broyles's] travel and entertainment expenses . . . but keeps few details about them." Among the facts that did emerge was that this AD liked to stay at the Waldorf-Astoria in New York and run up sizable hotel bills: $1,439 for one short visit, including $303 in room service charges. Broyles also traveled around the country and wrote off hundreds of dollars of entertainment expenses in such places as New Orleans and Rancho Mirage, California.

Nevertheless, by all accounts Broyles is an honest man and a good athletic director. In his case, as in many other instances of profligate athletic department spending, the system more than the individual is to blame. With a minimum of financial accountability, no one can be overly surprised at stories like LSU's Sugar Bowl trip or Frank Broyles's New York visit. The unindictable offense in this kind of spending is that it siphons off revenue from other parts of the athletic program and/or the university. And frequently, the resulting deficits are covered by funds that could go to academic units and students.

> *"I never had to justify making a [recruiting] trip to see a kid because of the money it would cost. What you have to worry about is losing a kid because you didn't make that one last trip. You spend a lot of money in this business just covering your ass."*
>
> —The football recruiting coordinator of a
> southern school

Recruiting is a key part of the lottery quest in college sports. Pepper Rodgers, former head football coach at UCLA and Georgia Tech, once wrote, "I can coach good players, but I can't do a damned thing with bad ones. *No* coach is that good at his job. . . . In coaching there are three important things: recruiting, recruiting, and recruiting" (his emphasis). With this rationale, coaches will go anywhere and pay almost anything to land the best players. As a result, recruiting costs are enormous.

In his thorough 1988 study of these expenses, Tony Barnhart of the *Atlanta Journal* estimated coaches' recruiting travel at $150,000 a year for the average Division I-A football team. The widely accepted gauge that football accounts for 50 percent of all recruiting costs moves this item to a total of about $300,000 a year for all sports. As always, the biggest athletic programs exceed the average: in 1985, the University of Georgia athletic program acknowledged $591,000 for this expense, and, no doubt, these costs have subsequently increased.

Georgia's high number resulted, in part, from its coaches' use of as many as six private planes for football recruiting. Other schools also borrow, lease, or own planes for this purpose; Bob Pittard, recruiting coordinator at Georgia, explained, "It's a lot more expensive than commercial travel but . . . I don't want to lose a player because somebody else had more contact than we did. It's an expense I feel is worthwhile."

For Georgia, these plane rides are not all short hops around the South. In college football, and even more so in basketball and in many nonrevenue sports, coaches recruit nationally as well as regionally. Not long after Louisiana Tech's women's basketball team joined the NCAA, its budget was set at $200,000, much of it for recruiting. Other women's basketball programs have done the same; they all hope they can sign the top women basketball players in the country. Recruiters for major football and basketball programs are on the road for as many as 250 days a year, and they travel the nation and, increasingly, overseas in the hunt for and wooing of the best high school athletic talent.

The second most costly item in recruiting travel is bringing prospects to campus; when they fly from distant locations, expenses go up accordingly. Barnhart estimates this expense at $45,000 per major football program. Many schools, however, are far above this average because of their hang-the-expenses attitude. A few years ago, an audit of Georgia's athletic department revealed that it had spent travel money for such frills as renting helicopters to ferry potential recruits from the airport in Atlanta to the athletic facility in Athens, seventy miles away.

The NCAA allows athletic programs to bring in eighty-five prospects in football, fifteen in men's basketball, fifteen in women's basketball, and varying numbers in other nonrevenue sports. In addition to their travel, the host department must pay to house and entertain potential recruits during their on-campus visits. Barnhart puts this expense at about $50,000 for football, but it is a budget item with great elasticity. At Georgia, in 1985, the athletic department paid $2,500 for five hundred bobwhite quail so that visiting high school athletes could have some fun shooting the birds. Probably it was touches such as this that raised the average cost of each football signee at Georgia that year to $16,500. (These are the estimates on legal on-campus recruiting; the costs of the many illegal benefits that prospects receive during recruiting are hidden in various athletic department slush funds and, therefore, impossible to quantify.)

> *"At one time, the president of Kansas State University advised me he thought they could get by with* half *the recruiting budget in football as Nebraska. And I had to inform him he had it the reverse. Kansas State needed* twice *the recruiting budget of Nebraska, because Nebraska had the tradition to attract the recruit"* *(speaker's emphasis).*
>
> —Chuck Neinas, executive director of the College Football Association

In addition to the coaches' and the prospects' travels, there are other substantial—almost bottomless—recruiting expenses, and always athletic departments willing to pay them.

Recruiters like to bury high school athletes in printed and visual material, including elaborate videotapes. Barnhart estimated that $65,000 was spent on these items in 1988 by the average big-time football program. On occasion, more than recruiting propaganda is used to convince an athlete to sign with a school. In 1988, a thousand dollars in fifty-dollar bills tumbled from a package of videotapes sent by University of Kentucky assistant basketball coach Dwane Casey to the father of Los Angeles recruit Chris Mills, and set off the most recent Kentucky basketball scandal.

College recruiters cannot live without their knowledge of and contacts in high school sports. An estimated $5,000 a year of athletic department money is spent on "Dues & Subscriptions" to maintain this lifeline. In addition, there are coaching clinics that the college staffs hold for high school coaches: these cost about $20,000 a year.

In staying in touch with high school coaches, their players, and the players' parents and friends, recruiters run up enormous telephone bills. Usually these are *not* listed as recruiting costs but are shifted over to athletic department office expenses, and, at some schools, put onto the university-wide telephone bill. Barnhart offers no estimate for this item but, in 1981, one authoritative study put "telephone recruiting costs . . . as being in excess of $50,000 annually." Almost a decade later, recruiters are reaching out to a lot more people and paying higher telephone bills.

Sending those special recruiting brochures and videotapes is also expensive, and athletic departments like to go first-class to demonstrate their seriousness and sincerity to prospects. The Kentucky package to Chris Mills's father was sent by Emery Worldwide Air Freight and, according to a newspaper account, was "one of at least 66 Emery Worldwide envelopes assistant coach Dwane Casey has sent during his two seasons as a UK recruiter." Like the phone bill for recruiting, postage and shipping costs are usually moved to the main athletic department office budget, and from there, if possible, to the university-wide postal service. An informed estimate places this recruiting expense at $25,000 a year.

Barnhart lists other items for football recruiting: "Equipment— $10,000"; "Professional Services—$8,000"; "Student Help— $7,000"; and the athletic department's old and true friend, "Miscellaneous—$17,000." Equipment can vary from the rental of VCRs and film projectors for a coach's show-and-tell performance while on the road, to water beds for visiting recruits. Professional services can entail medical examinations of prospects as well as legal advice when recruiting gets sticky. Students help recruiters in a number of ways, from licking envelopes to entertaining visiting prospects.

"Miscellaneous" can include any item that the fertile, free-spending minds of athletic department personnel can conceive. Bill Dooley, a football coach with a history of extravagant spending, justifies recruiting expenses with this anecdote: When he was at the University of North Carolina at Chapel Hill, a prospect who had rejected UNC for Clemson told him that the deciding factor was the soft-ice-cream machine in Clemson's student union and UNC's lack of one. Dooley promptly ordered a machine installed at North Carolina, a true "Miscellaneous" recruiting expense—if his athletic department actually paid for it.

Finally, there is the cost of recruiting personnel. Most assistant coaches, whose main if not sole duty is recruiting, are on the regular athletic department salary list, but some programs pay legal and illegal recruiters out of their recruiting budget. In 1988, Cleveland State admitted that it had an "assistant coach" on its basketball staff who lived in Boston, almost never made it to practices or games, but had landed four Boston-area players for the team. Cleveland State paid its Massachusetts recruiter $56,000 annually. The NCAA acknowledged that this arrangement in no way violated its rules.

A decade ago, the American Council on Education estimated that for big-time athletic programs, the total bill for recruiting, including personnel, was $400,000. Calculating this cost in 1990 adds $100,000 to the base number for inflation, and another $200,000 for athletic department expansion in recruiting personnel and procedures—a $700,000 total. Because many schools are above the average—Georgia admitted to almost $600,000 just in recruiting travel costs in 1985—some athletic programs now spend over $1 million annually on this expense. At that price, if in an average year a school signs twenty-five new football players, ten basketball players (five men and five women), and fifteen freshmen for its main nonrevenue sports, the cost is $20,000 each.

These figures raise serious questions for the universities involved. In economic terms, does it make sense to spend $20,000 to bring in a "full ride" athlete and only a fraction of that amount to recruit a regular student—even though the students will become the school's future alumni and important benefactors? More significantly, in social terms, should an institution of higher education pay huge sums to recruit potential pro athletes but relatively little to find and attract future scientists, doctors, teachers, and other citizens? When university presidents and administrators absorb their athletic programs' deficits—and thus underwrite the million-dollar recruiting expenses—they provide disturbing answers to these questions.

CHAPTER 14

Equipment, Supplies, & Medicine

[1989] Totals for Football Equipment Costs:

Team	=	*$150,340*
Coaches	=	*$10,660*
Practice	=	*$41,666*

Total Initial Investment = *$202,666*

—From a confidential study on
equipment costs for a new
Division I-A football team

ATHLETIC DEPARTMENTS like to go first-class, and because last year's equipment is often hard to recycle, their tendency is to buy new supplies rather than to maintain old. Division I-A football teams carry about 125 players a season, and their equipment expenses usually reach six figures annually.

Helmets with face masks or bars cost $125 each and come in a variety of models. Major college teams usually keep at least 250 helmets on hand because of player preference on type and fit. The price tag for 250 helmets is $31,250.

Shoulder pads are also expensive—$125 a pair—and 250 are usually stocked, as well as special kinds, such as Donzi orthopedic pads at $250 each. Game pants cost $45 apiece and teams use two sets (home and away); game jerseys also require two sets and cost $35 each. Most football teams need 600 pairs of shoes (three different types) for a season and, at an average of $50 a pair, the cost for this item is $30,000. Then there are knee pads, thigh pads, hip pads, socks, jocks, girdles, and miscellaneous equipment at varying prices. The total cost of equipping a Division I-A football team is about $150,000, or $1,200 a player.

Coaches also need equipment. With at least ten on each Division I-A staff, the cost of sweat pants and shirts, T-shirts, jocks, shorts, and shoes is high. Then for game days, two sets (home and away) of shirts, pants, jackets, rainwear, and other clothing are necessary. The "Equipment Costs" study puts the total for coaches' supplies at $10,660.

Football teams also require expensive practice equipment: large blocking sleds at $3,000 a pop; close to a hundred dummies ("stand up," "half moon," "full moon," etc.) at a minimum of $60 each; three pairs of goalposts at $3,700 a pair; and many miscellaneous items, such as running tires ($785 a set). When the bill for practice equipment is added up, $40,000-plus is a standard amount.

Thus, before a single ticket is sold, a new Division I-A football team has spent over $200,000 on equipment, and an established one almost half that amount.

Football is the most expensive sport to outfit, but athletic programs with ice hockey teams pay up to $1,000 to suit up each player, and even basketball and baseball squads provide uniforms that start at $100 apiece, and warm-up jackets that cost another $100 each.

Once the athletes take the field, they need footballs ($75 each) or basketballs ($60 each) or other equipment. Then there are hockey nets and wrestling mats and pole vault pits and, if an athletic program really wants some high equipment costs, it can sponsor a gymnastics team and outfit a gym with at least $50,000 worth of vaults, high beams, rings, etc.

While other units of the university recycle paper and use the backs of old tests for secretarial notepads, athletic departments insist upon first-class equipment and supplies. Even with established programs, the acknowledged bill for these items at the University of Kentucky in 1986 was $213,000 for football and $33,500 for basketball. In 1985, the University of Georgia grouped all its expenses for sports equipment and supplies in only two budget lines, for a total of almost $600,000.

The NCAA survey puts the average for equipment and supplies at $218,000 for Division I schools with football teams, and it shows all other kinds of athletic programs averaging around $40,000 on these costs. In percentage terms, equipment and supplies come to anywhere from 5 percent to 12 percent of an athletic department's total expenses.

*"It might be wise to stamp the football itself with the
Surgeon General's warning that playing intercollegiate
football may be hazardous to your health."*

—A comment in a study in the *Physician and
Sportsmedicine*

Keeping players in new uniforms and supplied with top-of-the-line
equipment is only a part the cost of preparing elite athletes for competition. Preventive, emergency, and rehabilitative medicine have become
an enormous expense for many athletic programs. Almost ten years
ago, a team physician for the Penn State football team estimated the
medical costs for football at his school as $326,000, or an average of
$1,437 per player. The doctor concluded, "Intercollegiate football is
big business, and, as in any business, success or failure ultimately rests
on the merits of the product produced."

In the 1980s, the only item that inflated as rapidly as college tuition
costs was medical expenses. A conservative estimate would add 50
percent to the Penn State figures and another $300,000 for the medical
expenses in the school's other sports, for a total of about $800,000. If
there are 400 elite athletes on some form of athletic scholarship, the
average medical bill per performer runs about $2,000 (this excludes
medical insurance).

As they do with most of their expenses, athletic programs try to
divert their medical costs to other university accounts. At some schools,
the athletic department has no doctors officially on its payroll but uses
the medical personnel of the student health center. Because the majority
of these professionals' time is taken up with the care of elite athletes,
they cannot see many student patients—even though the health facility
is funded out of mandatory student fees. At other schools, in addition to
student health center and/or its own medical personnel, the athletic
department uses private doctors and surgeons on an annual retainer or a
per-case basis. Sometimes these fees are paid by the department but
often they are assumed by the central administration.

Even when athletic departments pay medical costs, frequently they
treat game and practice injuries, and skimp on preventive procedures.
In an NCAA-sponsored survey done at the University of North Carolina
at Chapel Hill, the researchers concluded that the best way to prevent
football fatalities and major sports injuries was through "stringent
physical examinations" that could turn up "concealed disorders." The

researchers admitted, however, that "physicals sufficiently thorough to detect such disorders can cost upwards of $200 per player . . . and colleges [in various divisions] are unable to afford them" for their large number of athletes. Some of the Division I-A programs do include full physicals for their football players—often at the insistence of their insurers—but many schools, especially lower division ones, often have only cursory examinations for the majority of their intercollegiate athletes.

> *"The right of the people to be secure in their persons, houses, papers, and effects, against unreasonable searches and seizures, shall not be violated . . ."*
>
> —From the Fourth Amendment to the United States Constitution

A new and increasing medical expense for college sports programs is the purchase and use of drug-testing machines or the payments to outside laboratories to conduct drug tests. In 1986, the Ohio State athletic department paid $150,000 for these tests, up $100,000 in just two years. That same year, the University of Tennessee spent $100,000 for its drug tests. In 1986, the NCAA began testing athletes for eighty-one substances (many legal, including caffeine) at its championship events and acknowledged that "about 3,000 such tests will be performed this academic year at a cost of about $950,000," or over $300 a test. That same year, the president of the University of Wyoming estimated that, for his school, each "comprehensive [drug] test could cost as much as $800." However, with state-of-the-art technology needed to detect the latest drugs and to counteract test "masking" substances, a complete workup on a single athlete, such as was administered at the 1988 Olympics in Seoul, now costs at least $1,000. Moreover, many medical experts dispute the accuracy of even the state-of-the-art tests.

Athletic directors and coaches are very much in favor of testing, not simply for "vocational" drugs like steroids but also for "recreational" ones. Most ADs and coaches endorse drug testing because it gives them greater control over their athletes. Even when schools make the tests voluntary, coaches can coerce their athletes to comply. Vince Dooley, the longtime football coach at Georgia, explained, "One weapon a coach has is that he determines who plays." Dooley offered his players a simple choice: take the tests or forget about playing.

The NCAA is all for drug testing, not only for its good P.R. value, but because it helps to insure that college sports are honest and that TV sports viewers, including the millions who bet on college contests, will continue to tune in. (If the viewing-betting public came to believe, as happened at Tulane a few years ago, that college athletes were shaving points or dumping games because of drugs, the already fragile TV ratings and payouts could disintegrate.)

Testing, especially the full-spectrum variety, is increasingly expensive and many athletic directors, invoking the media attention on the issue, have been able to persuade administrators to assume this cost out of university funds.

When college officials receive the five- and six-figure bills from outside labs or even the discount ones from their own facilities, do they ever wonder what this new and growing athletic department expense has to do with higher education? Administrators can offer defensive reasons for drug testing: they have to prevent a steroid scandal; they have to avoid an athlete overdosing on cocaine or being arrested for selling it. But the simple facts of drug testing dramatize the difference between College Sports Inc. and university life. Athletic programs endorse drug testing because it helps protect their investment in their athletes: drug use can lead to uncontrollable behavior on and off the field and undercut the militaristic discipline that coaches try to impose on players. No administrator can truly justify this expense in terms of his or her school's academic mission.

The history and political science departments, however, can offer very good reasons why mandatory drug testing of college athletes may violate the U.S. Constitution, especially its provisions on unreasonable search and on freedom from self-incrimination. The law school can point to recent court decisions in favor of those athletes, such as Simone Levant, a diver at Stanford, who have challenged compulsory testing. Other educators can argue that unless one equates college athletes with airline pilots and believes that public safety is in danger if the jocks go untested, this infringement of basic liberties is not justified. However, very few schools bothered to consider these objections before accepting the NCAA's drug test demands.

For most institutions, protecting their athletic programs' investments in and control of athletes, as well as avoiding potential embarrassments, outweighs any concerns about abrogating constitutional liberties. The increasing expense of drug testing, in monetary and especially in ethical terms, is one more example of how College Sports Inc. corrodes the traditional values of the university.

CHAPTER 15

Insurance

"Behind every sportsman in America stands a lawyer."

—James K. Coyne, president of the American
Tort Reform Association

IN THIS litigious age, the Rock of Gibraltar or the Good Hands of Allstate should be painted onto football helmets instead of a school's logo. In 1988, the owner of Rawlings Sporting Goods, when his firm exited from the helmet business, declared that "the cost to insure our company against helmet-related lawsuits was more expensive than the cost of manufacturing the helmets themselves."

In the late 1960s, over twenty American companies made football helmets for secondary schools and colleges. Fifteen years later, and after $46 million had been paid in lawsuit settlements, three helmet manufacturers remained. Then Rawlings departed and Bike tried to sell out. Only Riddell, a division of MacGregor, stayed firmly in the market, along with a number of offshore companies.

The owner of Rawlings explained: "Most football-related neck and spinal cord injuries are not caused by defective helmets but poor coaching and improper playing tactics. . . . Coaches instill a win-at-all-costs aggressiveness in their players. The results—too frequently— may include the flagrant spearing and illegal tackling which can cause spinal injury" and monumental legal settlements.

In these lawsuits, the lawyer for the plaintiff—often a young athlete left paralyzed for life—goes after the helmet manufacturer and, in recent years, the coaches, medical personnel, and the college or university sponsoring his client's team. With more athletic programs buying helmets from offshore companies—which tend to disappear into the Taiwanese mist when the first pretrial hearing date is set—tort lawyers will increasingly sue the schools involved.

All universities carry liability insurance—someone might slip on the pavement outside of the student union—but no comparable unit of the university is required to pay such high premiums as the athletic department. The University of Oklahoma athletic program spent $107,000 on liability insurance in 1986; the University of Georgia's insurance bill for intercollegiate sports, in 1985, was $89,000. Other schools, depending upon the number and kinds of sports in their athletic programs, pay varying costs: in 1986, Kansas kept the cost at $35,000, but Colorado paid $60,000, in part because of that school's high-risk skiing program.

In addition, schools have begun to insure their star athletes. In 1989, Bobby Humphrey, a running back with the University of Alabama, skipped his senior year because of an insurance dispute. According to newspaper accounts, "Although he was insured for $1 million through Lloyd's of London, he wanted coverage of at least twice that amount" for his final college season, in case he was injured so severely that he could not play pro football. Humphrey, Alabama, and Lloyd's were unable to reach an agreement and he went into the NFL supplemental draft. In the 1990s, the cost of this item for athletic departments could rise exponentially as more athletes demand greater individual coverage.

Schools with small college sports programs do not escape the burden of carrying substantial insurance. Lower-division NCAA institutions as well as NAIA schools and junior colleges face the same risk of a sports injury as Alabama—in fact, often they assume a greater risk because their equipment and supervision are not as good. Concordia College in Nebraska saw the premiums on its liability insurance for intercollegiate athletics increase from $7,000 to $30,000 in four years in the 1980s and, rather than pay that high figure, insisted that its athletes insure themselves before participating.

Finally, there are major insurance problems in nonrevenue sports. A gymnast falls from the high rings and cracks his skull, a hockey player slips to the ice and an opponent's skate cuts a neck artery—any number of serious if not catastrophic injuries can occur in these sports. It makes no economic sense that, in addition to all the other costs in nonrevenue athletics, schools also pay high insurance premiums to subsidize elite athletes in dangerous sports.

> *"Look, there's only one reason why anyone goes to*
> *Bermuda to start an insurance company—and it isn't the*
> *weather."*
>
> —Tony Schrader, deputy commissioner for
> insurance for the state of Iowa

In one of its more enlightened moves, but only after its usual machinations, in 1983 the NCAA established a group catastrophic insurance plan. How that plan came about and what it reveals about the association's attitude toward college athletes is an important story.

In the early 1980s, after a number of major lawsuits by former college football players left paralyzed as the result of practice field injuries, the athletic directors and coaches who run the NCAA decided to protect themselves by instituting a group catastrophic insurance plan. The NCAA's agreement with its insurer, the Ruedlinger Company, contained such stipulations as, "To qualify for the benefits, an athlete must spend $10,000 on medical care as a result of the injury. The athlete must also waive his or her right to sue the institution or its personnel in connection with the injury." Personnel was defined as "coaches, trainers and other" athletic department employees. One journal reported that the athlete's waiving of the right to sue "is particularly attractive to schools and colleges." Just to make sure that the injured athlete understood how paralyzed he or she really was, the policy added another stipulation: if the athlete "decides to sue instead of taking the benefit package, the insurance company will pay the university's legal costs and any judgment against the institution or its personnel."

For the NCAA, the main problem with the Ruedlinger catastrophic insurance plan was not the antiathlete clauses but the fact that Mr. Ruedlinger's primary underwriter was a company that he partly owned and had chartered in Bermuda. The deputy insurance commissioner of Iowa explained that "insurance companies in Bermuda are not required to have as much money in reserve as are insurance companies operating in the U.S." Under pressure from various state agencies such as Iowa's, the NCAA had to back out of the Ruedlinger plan.

Eventually the association signed with State Mutual Life Assurance of Massachusetts. For many injuries in this package, however, catastrophic coverage does not kick in until $25,000 in medical costs have been paid. Some of the harsher aspects of the previous plan were eliminated but the new floor means that schools have to carry extra liability insurance to cover the costs up to $25,000, or that the injured athlete has to come up with that amount.

Only about half of all college athletic programs decided to carry the NCAA or any other catastrophic insurance. Unfortunately, The Citadel was in the absent half when a football player, Marc Buoniconti, the son of a former all-pro linebacker, broke his neck in a 1985 game. Left a paraplegic, Buoniconti sued the school for $22.5 million but, after a difficult trial and to avoid future ones, settled for $800,000. When Northeastern University was sued by a former swimmer, paralyzed in a training accident, it too lacked catastrophic insurance and paid out the major share of a $7.5 million settlement.

Future prospects for containing the liability insurance expenses for college sports are not good. In 1988, the *Chronicle of Higher Education* quoted a prediction by some insurance experts that liability premiums "could become so prohibitive that sports programs might cause colleges more trouble than they're worth."

That liability insurance costs will prove the straw that breaks the muscle-bound back of intercollegiate athletics seems unlikely; that they could cause a major reassessment of some college sports programs, especially the economic viability of many nonrevenue teams, is a possibility.

CHAPTER 16

Legal, Public Relations, & Office Costs

"A college's chances of winning a lawsuit are slim if injury or death occurs during practice drills that are dubbed 'suicide drill,' 'death run,' or the like."

—Herb Appenzeller, athletic director and
professor of sports management at
Guilford College, North Carolina

LEGAL EXPENSES are an unpredictable item for most athletic departments. There are good—i.e., quiet—years and then there are awful ones, such as 1988–89 at the University of Kentucky when the school spent at least $450,000 in lawyers' fees and other legal costs during the NCAA's investigation of its athletic program.

The University of Georgia athletic association had such a quiet legal year in 1984 that it listed under "Legal Services" expenses of only $276. In 1985, however, the Jan Kemp lawsuit began and the athletic association's legal bill was $97,668 (Kemp was fired from her job teaching jocks and sued). Much of the cost of that lawsuit was paid out of other university funds. For almost a decade, Temple University disputed the government's Title IX provision for equality for women's sports and paid hundreds of thousands of dollars in lawyers' bills. Stanford has supported diver Simone Levant's lawsuit against the NCAA's mandatory drug-testing rules but has incurred some hefty legal bills along the way and will pay even more as the NCAA takes the case to higher courts. (The NCAA budgeted $1.75 million in legal fees in 1988–89.)

When faced with a legal problem, many athletic departments turn to their university's in-house lawyers and have them carry the legal—and financial—ball. Even when outside lawyers are necessary, their fees are often paid by extra funds allocated to the university's legal office. This is especially true for costly liability suits. Ironically, often the more legal trouble an athletic department gets into, the less of its own money goes to paying the bill.

Guilford College's Herb Appenzeller, an expert on sports law, predicts that "the number of sports-related lawsuits is likely to rise . . . as will the amounts of money awarded successful plaintiffs." Professor Appenzeller and his associates suggest various defensive moves that athletic departments can make to short-circuit these lawsuits, one of the most important being, "Inform athletes of the inherent risks of activities, and have them sign a waiver form indicating that they understand the risks. Even if such waivers were not recognized by a court [because of their coercive nature], they would indicate to the court that the institution had actively sought to maximize safety." Similar waivers, usually called "Consent Forms," are used by the NCAA and many athletic departments to show that their athletes "voluntarily" submitted to drug tests.

As with so many aspects of College Sports Inc., legal considerations help turn the athletic program–athlete relationship into an adversarial one. What began long ago in a spontaneous and informal way, when a coach, usually a faculty member, gathered some students together for sports activity and fun, has become, in our era, a full-fledged employer-employee relationship. And like most businesses in America, the franchises in College Sports Inc. seek all possible legal protections to neutralize their employees'—athletes'—rights.

Universities, however, have not been as adept in negating the legal claims of former coaches. Last year, the University of North Carolina at Chapel Hill settled with former football coach Dick Crum for $800,000. In neighboring Georgia, in the early 1980s, the state court of appeals, in a landmark decision, agreed with Pepper Rodgers, fired football coach at Georgia Tech, that the school was not only liable for payments on his entire contract but also owed him money from media fees and other income that he would have earned if he had continued as coach. Rodgers's claim and large settlement began a series of lawsuits by ex-coaches that grows in number each year.

The legal costs of college sports, especially the huge bills caused by athletic department transgressions, are at odds with the academic purposes of the host schools. It makes sense for a university to go to court, as some have in recent years, to defend a professor's right to do research on a controversial subject, but what educational point is served when a

university fights a multimillion-dollar lawsuit brought on by a catastrophic injury in a "suicide drill" or some other sports activity?

> *"An atrocious amount of athletic funds are wasted*
> *basically to benefit one player [the Heisman Trophy*
> *candidate]."*
>
> —Gordon S. White, Jr., longtime *New York*
> *Times* college football writer

The above quote refers to the campaigns that college "sports information directors"—P.R. flacks—stage for their Heisman Trophy candidates. In June 1988, the athletic department at the University of Iowa
launched an $11,000 publicity campaign on behalf of the football
team's quarterback, Chuck Hartlieb, and two teammates, Marv Cook
and Dave Haight. The Iowa plan included mass mailings to all Division
I-A football coaches and members of the Football Writers Association
as well as advertisements in major sports publications like the *Sporting
News.* That none of these players received a single first-place vote—of
over nine hundred cast—in the final 1988 Heisman Trophy balloting
marks Iowa's publicity splurge as one of the least effective athletic
department investments in college sports history. It also suggests that
the multitude of glossy P.R. campaigns neutralize each other and, in the
end, most voters cast their ballots according to the on-field performances of the athletes.

The P.R. campaigns for Heisman Trophy candidates are the most
visible manifestations of sports information work. Less well known but
part of the regular routine of all athletic departments are the many
brochures, pamphlets, and stats sheets produced for the media. "Keeping the media happy" is every sports information director's goal, and he
or she goes to great lengths to accomplish it (all SIDs list their office *and*
home phone numbers at the top of all handouts). In addition to supply-
ing basic information to the media, SIDs and their assistants also
operate as "spin control doctors," trying to soften a coach's scatological
remarks about a certain player or explain away a halfback's recent
altercation with the police.

As with all aspects of athletic department finances, ascertaining how
much is spent on sports information is difficult. Some schools put their
recruiting brochure expenses into this budget line; others move costs
such as stats sheets to "Game Expenses." In 1985, Georgia listed under
"Sports Promotions" expenses of $70,413, but the year before, this

item was only $24,390. Why this expense increased almost threefold in a year is inexplicable, unless, in 1985, the Georgia athletic program conducted a massive P.R. campaign to counteract all the bad publicity it received from the Jan Kemp lawsuit. In addition, Georgia listed $31,911 in 1984 for "Awards"; some athletic departments lump this expense into "Sports Promotion" because that is the point of most of the awards.

This year, Indiana University's athletic department paid at least $150,000 in salaries to its sports information personnel. If this figure is added to Georgia's $70,000 for "Sports Promotion" (nonsalary) costs, and $32,000 for "Awards," a sum of around $252,000 is probably a fair estimate for a major athletic department's spending in this area.

That figure surpasses the costs for the main information office— sometimes called the "News Bureau"—of many colleges and universities, which serves the entire campus (no school allocates funds to academic departments for individual information units). Science departments would like to tell the world about their latest research and, in so doing, help raise money for future research; English departments would like to inform the public about growing illiteracy in America, new teaching methods to combat it, and the funds needed for these programs. To do so, these departments must go through their school's information office—an agency so traditionally underfunded and understaffed that few academics seriously consider using it. But if a football coach spits into the wind, a sports information person is there to gauge the velocity, wipe off the coach's face if necessary, and interpret the move for the media, as well as provide 8-by-10 glossies of the event and samples of the spit.

> "... program administration, office supplies, certain salaries and communication expenses are examples of expenses that usually cannot be identified with specific sports."
>
> —Revenues and Expenses of Intercollegiate Athletics Programs, published by the NCAA

The NCAA survey lists miscellaneous costs such as the above at a $1,571,000 average for Division I football schools in its last reporting year, 1985. This came to 33 percent of total acknowledged expenses for these programs; for all other classes of athletic departments, the percentages for this item ranged from 25 to 34. In other words, "The Team Behind the Team" eats up one-third of every athletic department dollar at the average Division I football school and as much or almost as much at other schools.

Of all parts of the athletic department budget, office expenses—which should be easy to track because they involve a steady flow of invoices and receipts—are often the most difficult for an outsider to document. Frequently, these expense lines are receptacles for items moved from other parts of the athletic budget and placed here for cover. The University of Alabama, for example, for its fiscal 1987 expenditures listed an "Operating Fund" line—defined as including "administrative costs, sports information, band, etc."—that totaled $2,440,693. The final figures are huge and seem exact, but neither Alabama nor any other athletic department is willing to break them down in detail for the public record. If some athletic departments revealed their actual "Other Expenses," they would publicly acknowledge their fiscal mismanagement; the rest of the university might not understand the intricacies of recruiting expenses, but the cost of paper and stamps and office personnel is well known.

When Don Canham, then AD at Michigan, visited the University of Maryland athletic department in 1986, he and three visiting colleagues "looked at everything—from computerization to scheduling to the management and organization of the department." He found Maryland "completely overstaffed. They had far more people than they needed." As a result of Canham's recommendation, Maryland laid off seventeen athletic department staffers.

Canham's story makes athletic departments sound as rational as many corporations or small businesses. His visit to Maryland, however, must be placed in context. The Maryland administration called him in because its athletic department was in chaos, reeling from the death of Len Bias, from the prolonged attempt to fire basketball coach Charles "Lefty" Driesell, and from various moves to force out AD Dick Dull. In addition, the school's president, John Slaughter, had become chair of the Presidents' Commission of the NCAA and needed a clean house at home. If this conjunction of events was necessary for this school to move, it is unlikely that many other institutions with bureaucratic overload will act at all.

Athletic programs, however, claim to be modernizing—at least, many have started to use computers in their daily affairs. Some departments employ the machines for event scheduling and budgeting, but for others, computers nicely fit one of the athletic staffs' traditional goals—control of athletes. According to a sports business magazine, many "coaches and academic counselors . . . link their microcomputers to data bases on the university mainframe, which store [class] schedules and academic records of student-athletes" and, in this way, more easily monitor their charges.

Contrary to the Buckley amendment to the General Education Provisions Act, which mandates the confidentiality of all student transcripts, some athletic departments gain access to the private records of their athletes and use the information for their own purposes. That university administrators cooperate with this illegal procedure is hardly a surprise. If, on the other hand, a faculty member wants to validate a student's claim that he received straight A's last semester, the registrar will—quite properly—not reveal the information.

Big Jock is watching. Last year, one athletic department in the Midwest wanted hard information on which instructors favored its athletes and which were indifferent or hostile to them. Using its university's mainframe and the previous ten years of transcripts for all athletic scholarship holders, it compiled a statistical profile of the grades each faculty member had given to the athletes in his or her courses. With this information, the athletic department's academic advisors were able to steer the athletes to certain professors and away from others.

"In the past," boasted the tutor who conceived of the computer survey, "we had to rely on rumor and hearsay and we were forever getting stung by some professor who turned out to be a hard-ass, even though so-and-so on the track team had said she was okay. Since we did the survey, we haven't been wrong once and our athletes' grades have gone up an average of 20 percent. My AD thinks I'm a genius and calls me the 'Tutor of the Century.' "

This AD's definition of the word *tutor* is as new as his employee's use of computers. That other athletic departments will follow this procedure is as certain as their constructing a new and better weight room because their rival, Northern Jock U., just installed a state-of-the-art facility. As in the Defense Department, computers are part of the new gadgetry that athletic departments demand for the "Athletics Arms Race." That the machines will enable athletic programs to cut their bureaucratic expenses is about as likely as computers accomplishing that for the Pentagon.

CHAPTER 17

Capital Expenditures, Debt Servicing, & Maintenance

"I'm not sure we should build places for gladiatorial display rather than build classrooms to benefit a wider variety of folk."

—Dan Blue, state legislator, North Carolina

IF IVY-COVERED HALLS represent an era when colleges were student-teacher centered, what statement do today's multimillion-dollar glass and steel "athletic complexes" make about the current preoccupations of American higher education? In the controversy over the 1980s construction of the $35 million Dean Smith Arena at the University of North Carolina, built during a faculty pay freeze, some members of the university community "feared that the modern state-of-the-art building . . . would come to symbolize an overemphasis on athletics and the increased influence" of the booster club. After the building was completed, "That symbolism has come to pass" for many UNC faculty and students. (Quotes from the *Chronicle of Higher Education.*)

For these groups at UNC, the school's basketball team seems disconnected from the university. It plays in an arena where the booster club controls seating and has relegated almost all the faculty, students, and staff to the upper deck. One professor explained, "A lot of the discontent concerns the fact that it's more like a professional arena, like we have a professional team here with corporate sponsors."

Gleaming new arenas, however, are integral to College Sports Inc. Instead of learning from Chapel Hill's symbolic overemphasis on college sports, North Carolina State University, in Raleigh, has begun

130

construction on a $40 million basketball palace next to its campus that, according to news accounts, will also "host everything from tractor pulls to pro wrestling, roller derby to circuses." In Winston-Salem, Wake Forest University recently opened a $20.2 million "coliseum," and the University of North Carolina at Greensboro inaugurated a $15.7 million "complex."

The state of North Carolina does not have a lock on new college sports facilities. Two years ago, the University of Tennessee in Knoxville completed an arena that was supposed to cost $30 million but ended up at $43 million-plus, and, according to one sports business magazine, "stands in the middle of Big Orange Country as a lesson in how *not* to build an arena" (original emphasis). Last year, Boston College built an athletic facility for $25 million; Kansas State, one at $17.5 million; the University of Alabama at Birmingham, $12 million; Illinois State University at Normal, $17.4 million; and, next year, Cleveland State will open one of the most expensive of all, at $47 million.

A questionable aspect of this construction mania is the number of traditional athletic have-nots involved: add to those on the above list the new athletic buildings at Saginaw Valley State College, $18.7 million; at Wright State University, $20 million; and at the University of Hartford, $9.8 million. These institutions argue that their new, expensive facilities will turn them into athletic haves, but this claim overlooks the nature of the Athletics Arms Race—the haves are not standing still. Michigan State has a $45 million center coming on line in early 1990; the University of Connecticut at Storrs has a $24.5 million one scheduled for completion this year; San Diego State, a $30 million one in 1991. Moreover, many of the above figures are provisional because, as the University of Tennessee arena proved, every uncompleted building can easily slip into the Cost Overrun Twilight Zone.

To pay for this construction, athletic programs use a variety of financial schemes, including tax-free bonds, but their main fallback strategy is the diversion of university funds or an increase in student "activity fees."

In 1988, Purdue University announced plans for "the construction of a $6 million, 110,000 sq. ft. indoor [football] practice field and weight training facility." Over $3 million came from "unrestricted gift funds" (those donations not clearly marked for a specific use, for example, checks with only the name of the university on the "Pay to the Order of" line). Thus, many contributors to this school, including well-meaning alumni who probably thought they were donating to academic programs, had $3 million of their money go toward the building of college sports facilities. In addition, the Purdue administration lent $1.5 million to this project; administrators could have as easily lent that money to any number of worthy academic units and/or students.

> *"They've got a $50-million to $60-million capital*
> *investment in their football plant at U.T. [University of*
> *Texas at Austin]. Try amortizing that at 5 or 6 percent,*
> *and you will see the program is actually losing money."*

—John Silber, president of Boston University

For many major athletic programs, Silber's comment, made over fifteen years ago, is even truer today (except for the low interest rates on construction loans). The most visible symbols of College Sports Inc. are its huge stadiums and arenas; ironically, the most overlooked cost in intercollegiate sports—one that the public as well as students and faculty rarely consider—is hidden in the financing of those athletic complexes. Very few schools build a stadium or an arena with cash up front; once the money is borrowed, someone has to pay the interest charges—service the debt—every year. (Purdue was unusual in financing its facility mainly with cash but could do so because of the relatively low price tag.)

The NCAA financial survey, for accounting reasons and also because only a minority of athletic departments are willing to assume their "Debt-Service Cost[s] and Capital Expenditures," places these items on a separate chart. The average for the responding Division I football schools (28 percent of the membership in this category) was $546,000 in 1985, the last reporting year. Two years earlier, however, they put these costs at $824,000 (probably because of the high interest rates of the early 1980s). For all other schools with athletic programs, only a small percentage acknowledged paying for these items.

The NCAA provides average figures; well above the average are those of the big-time programs. In 1985 the Georgia athletic association had a capital outlay of close to $230,000, a capital outlay transfer of over $1.5 million, and a debt-service bill of $1.4 million, for a total of $3.16 million on these costs.

In the 1980s, the Alabama athletic department went on a $24 million building and capital purchase spree—including $1.5 million for a private jet. When the interest payments are added in, the final bill is expected to be $39 million. For 1989, Alabama's debt-servicing cost was $3.1 million, more than the estimated expenses of the football team.

Athletic programs like Alabama's that service their own debts are in a minority. More typical are schools like Kent State University, where the students have been paying off the construction bonds on the football stadium since 1971 with millions of dollars of their "activity fees," and will continue to do so well into the twenty-first century. An even more egregious case of soak-the-students occurred when George Mason University in Virginia built its indoor Patriot Center in the mid-1980s. The school financed the construction by saddling present and future students with the repayment of $16.7 million in State of Virginia revenue bonds. The debt load averages out to a mandatory $100 a year per student—whether they ever attend an event in the arena or not—and repayment will also go on into the next century.

The 1980s was a boom period for construction of college sports facilities. Many schools, in their willingness to accept this increasing indebtedness, reflected the Reagan administration's cavalier attitude toward the mounting national deficit. In the 1990s, to continue this capital expenditure expansion, universities will have to assume an even larger debt-service burden and, as is being done with the national deficit, pass an enormous part of it on to future generations. If schools make this choice, it will indicate, in large part, the nature of their commitment to higher education.

> "At first, when the Dallas Cowboys did it [build skyboxes],
> it was thought to be an extravagance. But then they
> started popping up all over the place. . . . Now, it's like
> one guy [in college sports] does it and the next has to
> follow."
>
> —Bob Bockrath, assistant athletic director at
> the University of Arizona

One of the ways that many athletic departments hope to pay for their new stadiums and arenas is the renting of skyboxes. But before any income can come from the corporate and/or booster fat cats in their lofty perches, the skyboxes have to be built. More capital outlay, more debt servicing.

The University of Kentucky recently decided to construct twenty-six skyboxes for its football stadium at an estimated cost of $3 million. Whether Kentucky, with a team usually in the bottom half of its conference standings, can rent the boxes and pay back the $3 million is an open question. At Boston College in 1988, according to a sports business magazine, "a $7 million stadium renovation [was] being financed by leasing 28 skyboxes, which [were] expected to bring in $341,600 starting [that] year." At this rate, BC will never pay off the $7 million: even at 5 percent interest a year—$350,000—the skyboxes will never earn enough to retire the debt. Moreover, will the revenue from these skyboxes drop if Boston College's football team continues to lose? It was 5–17 during the last two seasons.

The amount of revenue derived from skyboxes is also dependent upon favorable IRS rulings. The Tax Reform Act of 1986 now prohibits skybox holders at professional sports events from claiming their rental cost as a tax write-off. Athletic departments, however, argue that skybox rentals in their stadiums are legitimate donations to higher education. Presently, under the priority-seat compromise, the IRS permits an 80 percent deduction on these rentals—thus the taxpayers help subsidize the wealthiest college sports fans—but this obvious tax abuse is vulnerable to reinterpretation by the IRS and the Congress.

Even more than priority seating, skyboxes symbolically exclude the university community. Although most ADs salivate over the supposed income that skyboxes will bring, an occasional school objects to them. An official at the University of Washington explained, "We decided that they don't fit in with the college atmosphere in the Pacific Northwest. The elitism and the college spirit don't go hand in hand."

In the early years of intercollegiate sports, faculty, students, alums, and townspeople stood together on the sidelines or sat in a rooting section in the stands. Eventually this evolved into some fans—those who could pay extra—obtaining seats on the 50-yard line or at midcourt, but in the present era even the pretense of big-time college games being held for the university community has vanished. Skyboxes are an ever-present and symbolic reminder of the distance between College Sports Inc. and the university.

> ". . . universities also pass on the actual costs of athletics
> by using various strategies to pay some overhead
> expenses—such as stadium utilities and upkeep—from

*the general budget. In effect, state money intended for the
general academic and administrative operation of the
university winds up subsidizing athletics, which isn't
supposed to happen."*

—Wayne Young, chief staff aide for the
regents of the State Universities of
Florida

So many schools absorb the maintenance costs for their athletic departments that this expense is usually excluded from any discussion on the
financing of college sports. Like debt servicing, maintenance is an item
that athletic programs want to keep far away from their books. If they
were responsible for these two expenses, the true extent of their financial losses would be better understood, and the people now paying the
bills—the taxpayers and/or students—might be less willing to do so.

Maintaining athletic program facilities is enormously expensive.
Football stadiums—used five or six times a year—need special year-
round care because of the stress on concrete during cold winters and hot
summers. A 1988 in-house memo at the University of Cincinnati admitted, "The University has been advised by T.H.P. Limited, an engineering consulting firm, that Nippert Stadium's concrete will last no more
than five (5) more years . . . [and] replacement will cost approximately
$15 million according to the latest estimates." Even the artificial turf
substances in football stadiums, especially the popular Astroturf, can
cost up to $3.2 million to install, and other turfs, like PAT, up to
$100,000 a year to maintain.

Those schools that require their athletic departments to pay for
maintenance and associated costs provide a yardstick for these expenses. In 1986–87, according to a newspaper report, the athletic
department of the University of Missouri at Columbia reimbursed the
school $671,000 "for rent at the Hearnes [Athletic] Center, mainte-
nance, and utilities." (Whether this bill also included maintenance on
the football stadium is not clear from the report or subsequent inquiry.)
At Alabama, in 1987, the athletic department paid $762,000 on "build-
ing maintenance" and $602,000 for "repairs/replacements."

Missouri and Alabama are in a small minority of athletic programs
held accountable for these items; among all Division I-A schools,
however, there are almost no exceptions to one rule—the stadiums,
arenas, weight rooms, etc., are for the exclusive use of the elite athletes.
Thus the cost per user is enormously greater than for any other facility

on campus, averaging thousands of dollars per athlete: the maintenance costs for the library and classroom buildings average a few dollars per student user, and many of these structures are badly maintained and need repair.

Even with a mundane item like maintenance costs, the contradictory relationship between an athletic department and its university is seen. Big-time athletic programs are supposed to be self-sufficient entertainment businesses, but they demand and usually receive free rent and maintenance. Academic departments also do not pay rent or maintenance fees but they are *not* profit-oriented businesses—their purpose is to educate students and conduct research. Athletic programs have no such educational rationale and, as ADs always proclaim, "Anybody who says this ain't a business doesn't know what's involved" (C. W. Ingram, a longtime AD). Unlike other businesses in America, however, most of the franchises in College Sports Inc. are unwilling to pay rent, repairs, cleaning, or even their utility bills.

> *"Colleges and universities need to spend at least $20 billion if they hope to save their crumbling and outdated buildings, a new survey has found.*
> *"Classroom buildings, laboratories, and offices need nearly $15 billion in work, while the cost of fixing auxiliary facilities . . . totals more than $5 billion."*
>
> —Item in the *Chronicle of Higher Education*

If American colleges and universities were wonderfully rich and could afford every expense proposed to them, the construction, debt servicing, and maintenance of athletic facilities would not be a serious issue. In fact, the opposite is true—most schools are rattling the tin cup for faculty pay and basic amenities, and not able to improve or even maintain their physical plants.

In 1988, an authoritative survey of university facilities estimated the total cost of needed repair at a minimum of $20 billion and possibly as high as $50 billion. The core problem is that most schools indulged in "deferred maintenance" throughout the 1980s—doing only essential repairs and no preventive measures or upgrading of plant—with the inevitable result that many buildings now require massive and costly repairs. According to the survey, "research institutions" (many Division I football schools) need "an average of $49.1 million each";

"doctorate-granting institutions" (large private and some public schools), $22.3 million each; and "liberal-arts institutions" (Division III schools), $7.5 million each. Thus some of the universities that have spent the most on their new athletic complexes now require the largest transfusions of cash to keep much of their physical plant from disintegrating.

How schools and their supporters, private and public, face this crisis will determine the future of many American colleges and universities. That so much money in the past decade has gone into athletic department facilities and so relatively little into academic ones is a terrible indictment of America's higher education system and the values upon which it is increasingly based.

SUMMARY: HOW THE POT O' GOLD BECOMES THE TIN CUP

"Most Division I schools don't show a profit with sports. The odds against that are only slightly less than the high school kid who dreams of playing in the pros [actually making it].

"But every [school] is chasing the dream of joining the elite, being one of the few who make money. To do so, the popular conception is, you have to spend more money to get there."

—Richard Lapchick, director of the Center for the Study of Sports at Northeastern University

THE DELUSIONS of many athletic directors and their supporters are only matched in American society by the faith of addicted lottery players. As the financial analysis of College Sports Inc. shows, only a small number of athletic programs consistently make money and even those few are extremely vulnerable to the mischances that cause losing—on the field and at the cash register—seasons. The University of South Carolina athletic department did so well in the 1980s that it built up a reserve fund but, as its business manager said, this fund is critical because "if your quarterback breaks his leg on the first play of the season, you've got [financial] problems." (Whether South Carolina had to go into its reserve fund in 1989 as a result of the Tommy Chaikin steroid scandal is a question that its athletic department refused to answer.)

Yet, like true lottery players, college sports believers possess a faith and hope that seem unshakable. A few years ago, the University of North Carolina at Asheville decided to move from an athletically successful NAIA program to NCAA Division I. The AD explained that his school was losing money in the NAIA, whereas in NCAA Division I, "the potential revenue is greater." The key word is "potential," but the present reality is a large increase in spending. UNC at Asheville had to augment its athletic budget by "some 40 percent, to around $600,000," to make the move, with the major added cost being the funding of twelve teams in at least six sports to meet the NCAA's minimum regulations for Division I participation for nonfootball schools.

138

At Asheville, increased student fees bankrolled the additional expense. But a $600,000 annual budget allows this school to buy only one small lottery ticket and, as any experienced Division I athletic director can attest, this amount of money will not go very far in big-time college sports. Even the UNC-Asheville AD admitted that "it will be a long time before we make any money in intercollegiate athletics," but he added the perennial cry, "But I think we have a chance."

University administrators at schools like UNC-Asheville, with Division I ambitions, usually argue that big-time college sports accomplishes a number of things for an institution: (1) it attracts attention to a school; (2) it increases academic prestige; (3) it boosts student enrollment; and (4) it builds school spirit. Administrators at all schools also use these arguments to justify paying the deficits of their athletic programs.

No factual data substantiate the positive-publicity argument; much evidence points to the opposite—the negative fallout from college sports scandals and a "jock factory" image.

The second assertion, that big-time college sports helps the academic prestige of a university, is clearly invalid. Academic prestige is tied to academic achievement: among other indicators, the average SAT or ACT scores of the freshman class, the GRE and other scores of the seniors, and, most significant of all, the teaching and research achievements of the faculty. Various educational groups try to quantify academic prestige in national polls that rank schools and their departments. Success in college sports only enters into the prestige equation in a negative way: the educational authorities who vote in these polls are often prejudiced against jock factories and tend to discount their educational and research achievements (Notre Dame and USC have long suffered in the prestige rankings because of this phenomenon).

Third, is there a correlation between big-time college sports and increased student enrollment? This phenomenon is totally unproven; more important, even if it were true, is it desirable? Those students who apply to a school primarily because of the fame of its sports teams give strong signals about their lack of academic seriousness. Every school has its beer-and-circus contingent, but if their number reaches a critical mass, then the learning environment of the entire institution changes. Teaching or attending class on a Friday when a large number of students are absent because of a football or basketball weekend becomes a negative experience. Being in class on a Monday when students have not returned or recovered from their sports weekend seems a waste of time. In this atmosphere, even the serious-minded quickly become cynical and demoralized about the educational process.

Fourth, do major intercollegiate athletic programs build school spirit? All of the evidence on this, pro and con, is anecdotal. When a school's team wins a championship, many members of the university community claim to feel good about it; however, for every champion there are many more losing teams and disappointed fans. A more important refutation of the school spirit assertion was discovered by this writer while doing interviews for this book: at institutions with big-time programs, most regular administrators, faculty, and students told private horror stories about coaches and athletes of their acquaintance who had received financial and/or academic privileges forbidden to all other members of the university community. ("Coach Kick-Ass is allowed to skim $X from his travel budget"; "Danny Dunk was in my Forensics 100 class but one of the basketball managers took the exams for him," etc.) These tales of corrupt practices emerged as regularly at institutions known for abiding by NCAA rules as at those with a history of NCAA probations, and the stories were usually narrated in a spirit of resigned inevitability ("This is the way that college sports works here, and because our athletic department is so powerful, there's nothing anyone can do about it"). The frequency of these negative anecdotes, as well as the scarcity of stories about the positive and unifying effect of college sports, suggests that big-time athletic programs create mainly distrust and opprobrium in their university communities. Thus College Sports Inc. does not seem to build school spirit; it breeds cynicism.

A final test of the assertions about the positive effects of big-time college sports is to examine the converse: after the NCAA banished seven of the eight Ivy League schools from its top rank in 1983, these institutions suffered "zero loss" of academic prestige and student enrollment. Other schools, such as the University of Chicago and New York University, that have downgraded or even dropped athletic programs experienced no decline in enrollments as a result. And those colleges that have never left Division III, such as Amherst, Kenyon, and the Claremont, California, group, are well-known, academically prestigious, and well-attended institutions, not noticeably lacking in school spirit.

Thus, the main reasons for embracing and sustaining a franchise in College Sports Inc. appear fallacious. Yet athletic department personnel and their supporters, including many university administrators, prefer the myths to the financial and educational realities.

*"[Division I is] like being in a poker game where you have
the second- or third-best hand, but they keep bumping up,
and bumping up, until you have trouble staying in."*

—Lansing G. Baker, president of Utica
College

Although the Wonderland of College Sports Inc. often resembles the
terrain that Alice journeyed through, the laws of financial and even
ethical gravity sometimes apply. The stories of how Utica College and
Seattle University moved from Division I to III are cases in point.

When Utica College, a small upstate New York school affiliated with
Syracuse University, decided to play big-time college basketball in
1980, it hired former NBA coach Larry Costello to bring it to the top
rung. Unfortunately, what began as $50,000 start-up costs grew over
the years, especially as the NCAA increased the number of sports and
teams required for membership in Division I (from eight in 1980 to a
high of sixteen in mid-decade).

As costs increased, Utica College did what many financially strapped
athletic programs do—accepted away games against powerhouse teams
so that the small school could have some big paydays. In this regard,
college sports resembles pro boxing, where journeymen fighters show
up in a popular contender's hometown and "go into the tank" for a good
purse. The Utica athletic director admitted, "The travel was crazy, and
it wasn't fair to the kids to play teams they didn't have a chance against.
It felt like we were selling our souls."

In 1988, Utica College made the decision to drop out of Division I,
end athletic scholarships, and massively cut its athletic department
deficit. The school also began to emphasize recreational and intramural
sports—an area impossible to promote during the years when all of its
sports money and energy went into its Division I programs.

*"Seattle University President William Sullivan still is being
asked, 'Why did Seattle U drop sports?'
" 'We didn't,' he says. 'We dropped the semipro
program. We decided not to pay people to play for us.' "*

—Item in the *Seattle Times*

Seattle University did not have an ordinary college basketball program.
Among its great players had been Elgin Baylor and the O'Brien twins,
and in one twelve-year period it had gone to the NCAA tournament nine
times, including to the final game in 1958. To cut a program with such

an illustrious history as well as strong booster support took courage but, in 1980, Father William Sullivan, the school's president, swung the ax. Ironically, the school had the money to continue in Division I, but Father Sullivan decided that the financial questions in big-time college sports were being asked incorrectly. He rephrased the query: "Should an institution like Seattle be placing such large amounts of money into subsidizing a program for a handful of students—one that in many ways contaminates the educational ideals of a university?"

Father Sullivan, like many educators, felt that "any school that runs a big-time athletic department—with special classes, tutors, the whole thing," was moving too far from its primary academic mission, the best education for all of its students. In 1980, the Seattle president, with backing from his faculty and board, but in the face of booster howls and threats of closed wallets, as well as dire predictions about enrollment declines, shut down his school's franchise in College Sports Inc.

Two years later, enrollment was up, moreover, without the financial burden of a big-time athletic program, the school was able to move an extra $135,000 into undergraduate academic scholarships. Four years later, enrollment had continued to increase and some of the money saved because of the decreased athletics budget now went to academic scholarships for minority students—ironically, many more black students were now in Seattle's classrooms than during the period when a small number of blacks played Division I basketball in its arena. In addition, the school began emphasizing intramural and club sports and, by the end of the decade, many more of its students were participating in these activities than ever before.

What about alumni contributions? In 1986, *Sports Illustrated* reported that "alumni have actually been donating more dollars to the school, in significant increments, every year since the decision was made." Father Sullivan said, "We were told there wouldn't be any more alumni support. But it's clear that with a few exceptions, alumni support their universities because of their education—and not because of the fact that for a few times during the course of their undergraduate years they sat in the bleachers and watched somebody else dribble up and down the court or run across a field."

> *"In the last two years, schools that are led by two good friends of mine have won the NCAA [men's basketball championship]. When that happens, you can't help but*

*say to yourself, 'Wouldn't that be nice?' Then, after you've
said that, you need to say, 'What about the hundreds of
schools across the country that are pursuing that great
mythical championship and spending millions and
millions of dollars doing it and endangering their own
educational ideals and integrity and never making it?' "*

—Father William Sullivan, president of
Seattle University

The University of Baltimore certainly qualified as one of Father Sullivan's "hundreds of schools" trying to reach into the NCAA Division I pot o' gold but never making it. On the basis of some success in Division II (it won the men's soccer championship in 1975), and a persuasive athletic director, it moved to Division I in 1979. But in the 1980s, as the NCAA raised the ante in the membership poker game, the University of Baltimore lost more money and became unhappy with life in Division I.

In the early 1980s, Baltimore did a cost analysis of its college sports program and concluded that the university was spending a large amount of money on 115 elite athletes—who would not have attended if they had not received athletic scholarships—and that an even greater sum of money was needed to make the school's teams competitive in Division I. In addition, according to a report on the situation, because most of the athletic department's revenue came from student fees, "it was obviously inequitable that 80% of student fees was supporting the activity of 115 student athletes and only 20% of that same revenue was available [for the health center and other services] to the remaining 5,185 students."

The facts from the cost analysis were so clear that they led the school's administration to the logical next step—drop intercollegiate athletics entirely and put the money into other activities, including recreational sports, for the benefit of all the school's students.

If cost analyses were done on all the athletic programs in the NCAA, NAIA, and the junior college associations, the conclusions for the vast majority of schools would be similar to the University of Baltimore's. That most schools will not undertake such examinations and that even fewer would implement their conclusions is the sad truth of American university administration.

*"Once an institution tastes the water in the [big-time
college sports] well, it's hard to give it up."*

—Lewis A. Cryer, commissioner of the
Pacific Coast Athletic Association

Many schools get to taste the water in the big-time college sports well, but only a very few are able to nourish themselves annually with long swallows from the font. That so many become bewitched after a brief taste and that the spell continues to grip athletic programs dying of financial thirst is a testament to the magical powers of sports and media in American society as well as to the myth-making abilities of College Sports Inc.

In the 1990s, however, the spell may be broken by the coming financial crunch that experts, some of them inside the NCAA, predict. If that time of reckoning occurs, many schools will face a hard decision: either stay in the increasingly expensive Athletics Arms Race and try to maximize their sports product by becoming more professional than at present, or drop out of Division I or II and cut their losses by spending much smaller and more easily raised amounts of money on a few intercollegiate teams. The Michigans and Georgias will stay in the race without undue financial strain (although continuing to risk scandals such as the Jan Kemp affair); many more schools will sweat, hem and haw, and eventually drop out. A few of this latter group—the Seattles and Baltimores of the future—will willingly go to Division III or beyond; many others will start to sink, flailing and screaming, in the sea of red ink, but will eventually swim for the Division III and NAIA lifeboats.

Whatever happens in college sports in the 1990s will not occur overnight or with calm deliberation. That change will come because of the monumental financial problems seems as inevitable as upheavals in the American economic scene because of the country's huge deficit. Colleges and universities can either prepare for the changes, placing their academic priorities foremost, and act wisely and in their self-interest, or they can behave foolishly, giving in to vocal ADs, coaches, boosters, and the NCAA, and throw more good money at their athletic program deficits. As many government programs have proven, throwing even enormous amounts of money—much larger sums than the NCAA will distribute from its 1990s TV deals—at systemic problems solves nothing. The finances of College Sports Inc. are a systemic problem.

From a rational point of view, the choice for American colleges and universities seems simple and the course of action clear. But in the Wonderland of college sports, to take the logical course will require courage from school administrators, the same kind of guts that Father William Sullivan showed at Seattle University.

A pessimist would predict that irrationality and the lobbying efforts of the college sports establishment will win, that schools will waste more and more money—funds increasingly needed by other parts of the university—on their franchises in College Sports Inc. An optimist would argue that the inexorable financial facts will bring schools to their senses, and presidents and boards of trustees will step in and straighten the situation out.

This section, "Old Siwash in Red Ink," has tried to present the financial reality of College Sports Inc. Readers have to decide whether they are pessimists, optimists, or in between. Some readers—concerned students, faculty, alumni, and taxpayers—could even help shape the decisions of individual schools and move from silent observers to participants in the coming Big Game.

PART II

Greed City

COLLEGE COACHES' SALARIES, PERKS, DEALS, & SCAMS

"People who say I'm greedy are either jealous or fragile."

> —Jackie Sherrill, replying to criticism of his $267,000 annual income package to coach and be athletic director of Texas A. & M.

OVERVIEW: HOW THE SUPPLY & DEMAND FOR COACHES DEFIES ECONOMIC GRAVITY

"For someone to make $250,000 in the business world, he'd have to generate $60 million to $70 million in sales. When coaches say they're worth it, they don't know what's going on out there."

—Bob Marcum, former athletic director at the University of South Carolina

THE NUMBERS are astounding. At least fifty college football and men's basketball coaches earn $250,000 or more in annual incomes and the ones close to the quarter-million mark are trailing far behind the leading money winners.

Rick Pitino makes between $800,000 and $900,000 a year from coaching men's basketball at the University of Kentucky. Jim Valvano, men's basketball coach and athletic director at North Carolina State University, acknowledges that he took in at least $750,000 a year. Around the $600,000 mark, especially if their teams do well in the NCAA tourney, are Denny Crum of Louisville, John Thompson of Georgetown, and Jerry "Tark the Shark" Tarkanian of the University of Nevada at Las Vegas. When, in 1989, Arizona's Lute Olson turned down the Kentucky job, he was able to renegotiate his annual package in Tucson to over $600,000, prompting the Arizona student newspaper to comment, "He doesn't deserve to receive any more, not while student services are at an all-time low at this financially burdened institution."

In college football, coaches' annual incomes are equally high. Lou Holtz of Notre Dame is reported to be making between $500,000 and $700,000 a year, depending upon the number of speaking engagements (at up to $20,000 each) that he is willing to hustle. Approaching or above the $400,000-a-year mark are Bobby Bowden at Florida State, Dennis Erickson of the University of Miami, Howard Schnellenberger of the University of Louisville, and Steve Spurrier at Florida.

These are the stars of the profession. More significant is the fact that the average annual income for at least 150 NCAA Division I men's basketball coaches and 100 Division I-A football coaches tops

149

$100,000. At most of these institutions, one or more coaches have a larger annual income than any faculty member, and often earn more than the president of the school. Moreover, in twenty-nine states, at least one college coach—usually at a public university—makes more than the governor.

Even in nonrevenue sports, many head coaches do surprisingly well. At least 25 women's basketball coaches and numerous head men and women in college baseball, hockey, soccer, swimming, and track-and-field earn between $50,000 and $75,000 a year.

> *"It's a make-it-while-you-can thing. You can be replaced at the drop of a hat. If I quit tomorrow, there'd be three hundred names in the ring."*
>
> —Sonny Smith, longtime Division I men's basketball coach

Most intercollegiate athletic programs lose money, and even those few that report a profit show small ones. Some coaches earn what CEOs of major corporations make, but no coach in any sport, no matter how big the school's stadium or TV contract, generates $10 million a year in profit for his franchise in College Sports Inc. Even the team of a very successful coach like Bob Knight at Indiana only brings in a fraction of that amount. Moreover, as Sonny Smith says, coaching exists in a buyer's market, where for every opening there are hundreds of applicants. Therefore, *why are coaches' annual earnings so out of whack with the supply-and-demand laws of their labor market?*

"There's only one Bob Knight and he's worth his weight in gold," the argument goes. Indeed, only one Bob Knight exists, and, as in every line of work, he is one of those individuals who introduce innovations and profit from them. But for every Bob Knight in college basketball, there are dozens of coaches with very average records to prove their ordinariness. Nevertheless, they too earn hundreds of thousands of dollars a year.

Bill Mallory, the other revenue-generating head man at Indiana University, is a typical journeyman coach. He got a leg up on his football coaching career with winning seasons at Miami of Ohio; then he had nine years of break-even, winning, and losing campaigns at Colorado and Northern Illinois (as good as 10–2, as bad as 3–8); and similar results in six years at Indiana (5–6 in his most recent season). Nevertheless, Mallory, who seems interchangeable with most of his Division I-A counterparts, earns over $150,000 a year—as do many of his colleagues, as will many of the assistant coaches who will one day be promoted to head jobs, as will the ex-pro coaches who will shuttle back to the college ranks. *Most college coaches can be replaced by any number of their peers—but their annual incomes only increase.*

Not only is this proposition proven by Steve Fisher taking over at Michigan and winning the 1989 NCAA men's basketball title but, as a recent article pointed out, he "was not the first coach ever to have been handed a Final Four team." The list includes Rick Pitino, who took a Providence College squad, with four of the five top scorers having been recruited by his predecessor, to the NCAA Final Four in 1987. Michigan rewarded Fisher with a $370,000-a-year package; Kentucky signed Pitino for at least twice that sum—although he has yet to top his 1987 triumph.

College coaching is supposed to connect to the university and be governed by some of the same supply-and-demand laws that apply to all university personnel. But it doesn't. The head football coach at Ohio State earns close to $400,000 a year, as does the men's basketball coach. These annual incomes dwarf the school's average pay of $57,900 a year for a full professor.

Historically, faculty salaries are low because of the supply-and-demand laws of the academic labor market. At Ohio State, as elsewhere, for faculty in the humanities and other areas where there is little or no outside demand for their services and a high number of applicants for their jobs, schools maintain a low pay scale (there are some Ohio State assistant professors who earn around $25,000, and the average is $35,300); for faculty in chemistry and business and other fields where the university competes with private industry for personnel, the school pays above its average.

Universities enforce labor market rules upon all of their faculty and staff—except for the athletic department, and particularly the football and men's basketball coaches. Schools compete with no outside business for the services of most "program heads"—relatively few coaches each year receive job offers from pro sports or allied fields—but university administrators allow coaches to have much higher incomes than their schools' most distinguished professors.

The same inflation that has driven the finances of College Sports Inc. has included coaches' incomes in its upward flight. At one time, administrators kept coaches' salaries in line with those of faculty; John Wooden reportedly received an annual salary of $25,000 from UCLA during most of his NCAA championship years. But in the current era, coaches' salaries, perks, and deals have increased many times since Wooden's not-so-distant day; yet only a minority of current coaches generate as much revenue for their schools as Wooden did for UCLA.

Thus, like the finances of College Sports Inc., coaches' salaries and compensation packages defy the laws of economic gravity. Only a combination of show business hype and lottery fever keeps these annual-income balloons in the air.

> "It's a disease. You think you can become the next [L.A.] Rams coach."
>
> —Rey Dempsey, longtime college and pro football coach

Not only do most coaches believe that they will hit the lottery jackpot but—and this is the worst effect of the disease of college coaching— the university administrators who approve their income packages share the coaches' dreams and delusions. When a school takes on a new coach, it is often willing to pay top dollar because it believes that this head man or woman might just turn around a losing program and get to the promised land of bowl games and the NCAA basketball tourneys. If the coach is young and moving up from the assistant ranks or a lower division, the university also indulges in the fantasy that this person might be the next Bob Knight or Lou Holtz. But even when the coach is a journeyman, administrators rationalize, "He didn't have a real chance at his last stop, Old Siwash. He didn't have full administrative support [i.e., enough money] for his program there. Look at his record: when he was with Northern Jock U., he once went to the Tequila Sunset/Obscure Bowl, and he promises he can do better with us. He has a reputation for running a clean program—the NCAA never put his current program on probation even though they investigated—and he'll bring his black assistant, who's a great recruiter, with him. So, give him the $180,000 package he's asking for—that's only $30,000 more than he's making now."

The key person in the hiring of any coach is the athletic director, and, not surprisingly, most ADs, usually ex-coaches, share the lottery fantasy. Moreover, an athletic director is not a disinterested party when it comes to establishing the salaries and compensation packages for coaches. As their boss, it is in the AD's self-interest to keep the coaches' incomes inflated so that, as the officer directly above the coaches, he or she can also receive a very substantial salary and perks.

If the same hiring rules applied to coaches as do to faculty, ADs would have to offer income packages in line with the university's usual budgetary constraints. But athletic departments do not operate under rational economic or university budget rules, thus ADs feel no need to enforce market discipline on coaches' income packages or their own.

CHAPTER 18

The Source of the Pressure on Coaches to Win

"There's just an insurmountable pressure on coaches today. I don't think coaches should develop loyalty to an institution. You should go in and get as much as you can, market yourself, win and stay ahead of your situation."

—Joe Gottfried, former head basketball coach
at Southern Illinois University, now athletic
director at the University of South Alabama

MANY COACHES argue that they deserve their high incomes as compensation for the win-or-else pressure placed upon them by their schools. They also claim that this pressure causes the transience and cheating in their profession. These arguments have become so accepted that they deserve inclusion in the pantheon of myths about intercollegiate athletics.

Charlie McClendon, longtime LSU football coach and now director of the American Football Coaches Association, offers a different point of view on coaches' pressure: "The greatest pressure is within yourself, not outside. Coaches put pressure on themselves. I didn't know that until my last four or five years."

Schools, especially those with big-time athletic programs, want their teams to win, but, considering the amount of deficit that they tolerate with losing squads, and their fear of bad publicity from messy coach firings, the win-or-else argument seems exaggerated. McClendon pinpoints the real source of pressure on coaches—themselves. Most coaches are extreme Type A personalities, perfectionists who want to excel at any cost. When Syracuse basketball coach Jim Boeheim, earning over $300,000 a year, won his three hundredth college game last year, he said, "I don't get much pleasure from winning, that's why winning three hundred doesn't mean that much to me. I do get a lot of displeasure out of losing, though."

Woody Hayes was the archetypal football coach. When, during the 1978 Gator Bowl game, Hayes punched a Clemson player who had intercepted an Ohio State pass, he was acting out his frustration at his team's failure to do what he had ordered, their lack of perfection. That Hayes, after years of coaching triumphs, including national championships and Rose Bowl victories, was still driven by an intense perfectionism indicates how the pressure on this coach came from within. If Hayes had rested on his successes, and lost lots of games, Ohio State would have been very slow to ease him out. Only a public act of extreme irrationality forced the school to retire—not fire—him. Appropriately, the best book on this coach is titled *Woody Hayes and the Hundred-Yard War.*

By all accounts, Bob Knight is driven by a similar perfectionism. Knight is also a coach who has tenure at his university and thus is economically and professionally secure for the rest of his working life. Moreover, even during his losing seasons, no Hoosier supporter ever whispered that he should be fired. Nevertheless, Knight drives himself and his players with the same intensity that he showed twenty-five years ago in his first head coaching job at West Point.

Hayes and Knight are models for their coaching peers. In addition, many of their assistants, including Bo Schembechler and Mike Krzyzewski, have gone on to head coaching jobs and have become the next generation's role models. Some of the followers are as secure in their jobs as Hayes was and Knight is, yet drive themselves with a hyperperfectionism worthy of their idols. This pressure is separate from any real or imagined win-or-else edicts that their schools issue or imply.

"Pressure to Win Tempts Basketball Coaches to Cheat."

—Headline in the *Dallas Morning News*

The argument that external pressure is the main reason coaches cheat is like the excuse "The devil made me do it"—it's the fault of outside forces and has little to do with the character of the criminal. Since in Division I, most schools put a relatively similar amount of pressure on their coaches to win, why doesn't every coach break the rules?

Coaches who cheat do so for the same reasons that some gamblers try for an illegal advantage. They are extremely competitive, obsessed with winning, and will bend or break the rules to obtain the winning edge.

They subscribe to the dictum that "Winning is the only thing," that losing is not merely defeat but also a loss of self-worth. When gamblers or coaches cheat and succeed, they consider themselves "smart" and they show no remorse or inclination to stop. Only when caught do recriminations and blame—"Pressure from the school made me do it"—appear.

Richard "Digger" Phelps, head of Notre Dame's men's basketball program, has long argued that external pressure is not the main source of coaches' cheating. He says of himself and his colleagues, "You choose the job you want to take. You decide who you want to recruit—the type of person. You also decide who you want to have surround that program as far as alumni, boosters, and friends. And you also decide what you want to do with the NCAA rules."

Probably the difference between coaches who cheat and those who play by the rules is less personality type than attitudes toward the game and toward authority. Cheating coaches believe that the end—winning—justifies any means. Honest coaches believe in "the level playing field" and want to win within the rules; they also understand that cheating undermines authority. But belief in rules and authority is an abstract and fragile concept; won-lost records and huge sums of dollars are physical and bankable items. That many coaches push aside the abstractions and charge for the tangibles is not surprising.

Coaches who cheat successfully do not talk about it. Only convicted coaches discuss the subject and, like many criminals, they blame "the system"—the supposed win-or-else pressure—for their personal troubles. The other pressures—the attraction of jackpot-size annual incomes and the competition with their peers—are not part of their tales. However, these forces connect directly to coaches' internal drives and are probably more powerful motivators than any real or imagined pressure from their schools.

> *"A coach simply must resign himself to the fact that he is no longer involved with the educational process, but with entertainment."*
>
> —Ralph "Shug" Jordan, Auburn football coach 1951–76

At one time, the majority of college coaches were mentors to their student-athletes and considered themselves teachers. In addition to their coaching duties, they taught regular courses (not always phys ed) and remained at their institutions for most if not all of their careers. From the beginning of college sports, however, some coaches proved adept at marketing their coaching skills and selling them to various schools. A number of the most famous figures in college sports history, men like Pop Warner and John Heisman, began the movement that split college coaching into two main categories—the full-time entrepreneurial coach versus the divided-time teacher-mentor.

In recent decades, schools have employed increasing numbers of full-time coaches and fewer teacher-mentors, especially in sports like football and basketball. Even where teacher-mentors are still hired and assigned regular classroom as well as coaching responsibilities—in Division III, the NAIA, junior colleges, and some NCAA nonrevenue sports—full-time coaches are encroaching fast.

The gulf between the full-time, especially the big-time, coaches—who "head programs"—and the teacher-mentors—who "teach and coach"—has never been greater. Program heads are in the entertainment business; teacher-mentors are involved with students and education. Few Division I "head men," especially in football and basketball, see the inside of a classroom on a regular basis; they devote their energies to administering their programs and promoting their careers. They also do not spend much time with their players; the pressures of recruiting and of speaking engagements put them on the road for many days of the year. Assistant coaches and athletic department personnel attend to the players. The "head honcho" may not even run most practices, and during games, especially in football, often the main assistants, the offensive and defensive coordinators, call the plays. But the program head does appear for press conferences, TV shows, and other personally profitable occasions. A big-time coach is many things but he or she is not, in any recognized sense of the term, a college teacher.

The evolution of intercollegiate athletics into College Sports Inc. could put teacher-mentors on the endangered-species list. As athletic departments increase in size and specialize their personnel, they replace teacher-mentors with program heads. There is an irreconcilable difference between program heads and teacher-mentors, the same split that exists between the entertainment business of College Sports Inc. and higher education.

CHAPTER 19

The Coach in Motion Play

*"Less than 11 months after he told the University of
Cincinnati and the city that he planned to make his home
here, UC football coach Watson Brown disclosed Tuesday
that he was leaving to take a similar position at Rice
University in Houston."*

—Item in the *Cincinnati Enquirer*

ACCORDING TO the American Football Coaches Association, head football coaches remain at an NCAA Division I-A football program for an
average of 2.8 years. Even when other divisions are factored in, the
average stay is only 6.8 years. Similar statistics used to prevail for men's
basketball coaches, but now in Division I, like molecules being heated
by NCAA tourney and TV fever, coaches are moving increasingly fast
and have surpassed the football rate. Almost 50 percent of all head
basketball coaches changed jobs between 1986 and 1989.

Coaches move for a variety of reasons: (1) to take a better-paying
position; (2) to leave a job that isn't working out; (3) to stay one step
ahead of the NCAA sheriff; and (4) because they've been asked to leave.

Watson Brown earned nearly $100,000 in his year at Cincinnati but
he departed to take the head job at Rice and an annual income package
of $240,000 for a minimum of six years. Brown only stayed at Rice for a
year and then moved on to Vanderbilt. Tom Penders, between 1986 and
1988, went from the head basketball job at Fordham to Rhode Island to
the University of Texas at Austin. Penders's move to Rhode Island was a
medium step up, where he increased his pay and perks, but the Texas
position put him into the bigger bucks with an annual income over
$125,000. Penders remarked that Texas has "given us everything we've

wanted," including a pair of ostrich boots. "They cost more than the car I was driving at Rhode Island."

Lou Holtz had a winning record at Arkansas and was earning close to $400,000 annually, but in 1984, because he made some TV commercials endorsing the reelection of Senator Jesse Helms of North Carolina, Holtz's working conditions became difficult at his school. Rather than hassle with Arkansas state and university officials opposed to his using his coaching position to endorse a political candidate, Holtz quit and four days later accepted the head job at Minnesota (from where he subsequently resigned and moved to Notre Dame).

Another reason for coaches to call a Motion Play is to avoid an NCAA investigation. A number of program heads routinely cheat on recruiting and athletic scholarships and then depart for a new job because, as one coach explained, "Some guys operate on the theory that it's harder to hit a moving target." Larry Brown typifies this kind of head man. He left UCLA ahead of an NCAA investigation and subsequent punishment, and then, weeks after his Kansas team won the 1988 NCAA championship, departed for the NBA. When, a few months later, the NCAA announced its investigation of Brown's Kansas program, the *New York Times* headlined, IN TROUBLED TIMES, LARRY BROWN SKIPS TOWN AGAIN.

Coaches' firings also get the headlines, and sometimes handwringings from editorial writers who point to them as the major source of evil in college sports. *Contrary to myth and coaches' self-serving propaganda, firings are not the reason behind most coaching changes. The Coach in Motion Play, with its Shuffle Effect, is the main cause.*

Follow these bounding coaches. When Joe B. Hall retired—he was not fired—from the head job at Kentucky, Eddie Sutton, at the time the head man at Arkansas, sought out Hall's old position. Sutton negotiated and accepted a nice pay package with Kentucky (an increase from an estimated $300,000 at Arkansas to at least a half million in Lexington).

With Sutton gone from Arkansas, that university needed to find a head basketball coach, and the winning applicant was Nolan Richardson, at the time the head man at the University of Tulsa. Richardson's move left the Tulsa spot open and along came J. D. Barnett, from Virginia Commonwealth University, to fill it. Into the Virginia job went Mike Pollio, head at Kentucky Wesleyan. Finally, this shuffle ended—into Pollio's slot moved Wayne Chapman, an assistant at Kentucky Wesleyan. Other assistants at the various schools involved also moved, some with the old head coach to his new school, some to other assistant jobs, at least one to a lower-division head position.

As a result of this particular Coach in Motion Play, these four coaches significantly increased their annual incomes. Not one of them had been fired by his old school and, presumably, each had departed with time remaining on his contract. Moreover, these coaches left their former programs, including all of the players whom they had recruited, in the lurch.

A few years later, the Kentucky head coaching job started another massive Coach in Motion Play. Because of an NCAA investigation, the Kentucky AD who had hired Sutton resigned and was replaced by the Vanderbilt head basketball coach, C. M. Newton. To Vandy jumped Eddie Folger from Wichita State, and his former assistant moved up. Then, with NCAA prodding, Sutton quit, and Rick Pitino of the New York Knicks took his job.

As for the rest of the original four, J. D. Barnett stayed at Tulsa and Nolan Richardson remained at Arkansas (though he interviewed for the Ohio State position). However, Virginia Commonwealth coach Mike Pollio quit and went back to his home state, this time with Eastern Kentucky. Into his VCU slot came Sonny Smith from Auburn; to that school flew Tommy Joe Eagles from Louisiana Tech, replaced by Jerry Loyd from South Plains J.C. in Texas. *In all of these shifts, not a single coach left his school as a result of being fired for a losing season.*

The Kentucky shuffles are typical of the majority of coaching changes in big-time college sports. On occasion a firing will begin the process but the movements along the line occur because other coaches choose to break their contracts and move to what they perceive as better jobs. Often, because a coach abruptly leaves a school, the athletic director will panic—the next season may be only a few months away—and rather than carefully hire a new coach, the AD will sign a journeyman candidate and pay too high a price. All of this occurs at colleges and universities where faculty members, especially in the present era of affirmative action, are hired through an open and deliberate process, usually taking many months, and for the labor market price.

Contrary to current myth, most schools are reluctant to fire a coach in midcontract. Rather than aid a college sports program in its lottery quest, a departing coach disrupts it. A new program head has to be hired, that person usually institutes different methods and brings in new assistant coaches and athletes. Rarely does a new head coach instantly turn around a losing team or keep a break-even one moving along as successfully. Yet, every year many colleges and universities engage new program heads and suffer the accompanying change and flux— not because they fired the old coach but because he or she left for another job.

One final and often overlooked point about coaches in motion is that few dismissed head coaches are required to leave their schools. Just as in the old bureaucracies of Eastern Europe where, even after a demotion, an official was guaranteed a job, most athletic departments offer some sort of administrative position to a discharged coach. The pay and perks are not as lucrative as when the coach headed a program, but the job puts food on the table. Universities, on the other hand, are rarely so generous when they ax staff or instructors or nontenured faculty.

In 1971, Bob Knight replaced Lou Watson as men's basketball coach at Indiana. Watson, until his retirement sixteen years later, passed his postcoaching career as a well-paid administrator in the I.U. athletic department, with such responsibilities as supervising various facilities.

Don Morton spent three years as head football coach at the University of Wisconsin at Madison compiling an awful 3–21 record in Big Ten play but the school did not fire him. In November 1989, the university announced that Morton would be "reassigned within the athletic department," and that his annual income would remain above $100,000. No faculty member who fails a three-year review is treated as kindly at Wisconsin or any other major school.

When, in 1989, Don Donoher was eased out of the head basketball job at the University of Dayton after twenty-five years—the last three with a 38–50 record—he admitted, "They've given me an awful lot of chances here. I wish I could have let us out of the hole we're in, but it didn't happen." Donoher was asked by Dayton to "assume other administrative duties with the university" and was assured of a position until retirement.

This coach, however, went off to become one of Bob Knight's assistants at Indiana. Like Donoher, many demoted program heads refuse the administrative sinecure and prefer to stay in the coaching hunt.

CHAPTER 20

Costs to Schools & Athletes from the Coach in Motion Play

"Notre Dame never would have fired me. I resigned because I felt I needed a fresh start and Notre Dame needed a fresh start."

—Gerry Faust, former Notre Dame
football coach, presently
University of Akron head coach

WHEN SCHOOLS pursue the college sports lottery, they tend to suspend normal economic and athletic common sense. On occasion, a powerful coach will not only extract a huge sum of money for his annual income package but will also insist that the school pump millions into his program and, to satisfy his ambitions, even move his team to a higher division or a more select grouping within a division. The signing of Gerry Faust by the University of Akron illustrates the illusions and wasted dollars that can accompany the Coach in Motion Play.

In 1985, when Faust was on the market after his mediocre years at Notre Dame, Akron decided to hire him at his six-figure asking price and to agree to his main program demand—that the school move its football team to big-time Division I-A. Akron had been successful with a modest Division I-AA program, but to bring in Faust it had to reassign its former football coach, Jim Dennison, to an athletic department administrative role (he eventually became AD and Faust's superior).

The ex–Notre Dame coach held out the promise of success in big-time college football and sold his new school the program head's standard line—"To win big, you've got to spend big." If Akron had hired this coach in the same thorough way in which schools normally engage faculty and other employees, it would have inquired into the reasons for his failure in his last job. It would have discovered that Faust's lack of college coaching experience—he had only coached high school football before coming to Notre Dame—had apparently limited his effectiveness as a program head. According to South Bend sportswriters, Faust was unable to work well with the assistant coaches whom he inherited or to attract first-class replacements when he made staff changes. Moreover, some of his Notre Dame players said that he treated them more as high school athletes than as college players and potential pros—their preferred self-image.

The one thing Faust did learn well from his first stop in big-time college football was how to spend money. After his initial six months at Akron, the school's athletic department had a $585,306 budget deficit, much of it from the new coach's overspending and the rest from a shortfall of projected revenue that his program failed to generate. (During the previous years, while in Division I-AA, Akron's athletic department had lost around $100,000 annually, and in 1982–83 had a surplus.)

In just half a year, Faust went over budget on such items as recruiting and employee travel expenses ($57,000 over); telephone bills, including the installation of a new $10,000 computer and wire system ($52,000 over); feeding the team during five road game trips (almost $59,000 over); and transporting the team to practice ($12,000 over). On the last item, rather than use an excellent practice field on campus, the new coach insisted on busing his players to the team's home stadium, the Rubber Bowl.

What did Akron receive from Faust's spending spree? In his opening season, the team he inherited from Dennison was 7–4, playing mainly a Division I-AA schedule against such opponents as Middle Tennessee, Murray State, and Morehead State. The previous year in Division I-AA, Akron had gone 8–3 and made the playoffs.

After Faust's debut season, the school decided to throw more money into his program and, for the following budget year, approved a 24 percent increase in athletic department expenditures. It also invited Frank Broyles, the AD at Arkansas, to advise it on athletic department finances. Broyles told Akron that "it would take a $3 million annual subsidy from the university to maintain a $4.5 to $5 million budget during the next five years," and this was the minimum necessary to play in Division I-A. The Akron administration accepted this proposal even though the school is in an area of high unemployment and faculty and community groups had criticized its spending priorities.

Akron officials justified their long-term commitment to huge athletic department deficits by arguing that a big-time coach like Faust would deliver winning teams, fill the Rubber Bowl, and generate sufficient revenue to wipe out the deficits.

Has Gerry Faust created those teams? In 1987, still with a basically Division I-AA schedule and including such new opponents from that tier as Delaware State and Nicholls State, Faust's team was 4–7. In 1988, Akron added some big-time opponents (it lost to Auburn, 42–0) but also Division I-AA Arkansas State (it lost to them too). The Zips ended with a 5–6 record and, more significantly, in the final "Jeff Sagarin College Football Computer Ratings," they ranked 105th, ten places *behind* Rice (0–11). Their home attendance averaged 8,841 per game. Not without reason did the *Sporting News* rate Akron in 1988 as the "worst program" among all Division I-A independent schools. In 1989, with an easy schedule, Akron managed a 6–4–1 record: they beat two lower-division teams and lost or tied three others for an 89 computer ranking (behind Vanderbilt, 1–9).

But Gerry Faust is a professional optimist and continues to expound his "We will win" line. Whether he is a competent big-time college coach remains unproven. The only certainty in the Akron situation is that the new regime has cost the school a huge amount of money and the institution has gained little in return other than negative publicity and bad feelings from many faculty, alumni, and community people.

If Gerry Faust had stayed at Notre Dame (he could have had a well-paying administrative post there), Akron probably would have remained in Division I-AA and continued with modest financial losses and on-field successes. Very possibly, all parties involved, including Gerry Faust, would have been better off if he had not spun in motion.

> *"Michigan State football coach George Perles will receive a $45,000 annuity [with payments for as long as Perles or his wife lives] that has been added to his contract."*
>
> —Item in *USA Today*

Hiring a program head under contract to another school usually does not involve any extra expenditure of money—except to the coach for the pay package—but when universities sign coaches from the pros, the big-leaguers tend to bring in their lawyers. When Michigan State hired George Perles from the Philadelphia Stars of the USFL, the pro team hit the university with a $1 million lawsuit but ended up settling for $175,000 of the university's money. When, a few years later, the Green Bay Packers tried to tempt Perles back to the pros, Michigan State paid out more money, adding a $45,000 lifetime annuity onto Perles's $200,000 annual income package. Perles is a successful coach and, like many in his category, he is able to convince his school to pay these hefty fringe benefits for his services.

But even mediocre coaches cost their schools extra money. Frequently, dismissed coaches sue their former bosses for breach of contract and the schools end up adding large amounts in legal fees and settlements to their already considerable college sports costs. Rarely, however, do universities sue coaches who jump contracts for the greener Astroturf and dollars of another institution. Colleges and universities do not hesitate to threaten or instigate legal action against regular employees, including faculty, who leave without fulfilling or satisfactorily settling their contracts, but generally they allow coaches to resign untouched. Possibly schools fear bad publicity if they sue a coach, but normal legal and business logic would dictate such action.

In the 1970s, Washington State University achieved an athletic program triumph—not on the field but in the law courts—by being the first institution of higher education to sue a departed coach and to win a settlement. With two years remaining on his Washington State contract, Warren Powers, the football coach, left for the head job at Missouri. His old bosses took him to court for breach of contract and obtained a $55,000 settlement. Unfortunately, this case did not begin a trend.

The most outrageous and unjustified payoffs, however, occur when coaches cause NCAA investigations and penalties and universities still prefer to "settle" rather than to fire them outright. Administrators do this even though a standard clause in most coaching contracts absolves the school from its obligations if the coach violates NCAA rules. When Mike White, after years of incurring NCAA sanctions and negative publicity for the University of Illinois, finally quit, the school rewarded him with a $300,000 settlement. Barry Switzer settled with the University of Oklahoma for $225,000 during its recent troubles. After the NCAA put Texas A. & M. on probation for over twenty-five violations during Jackie Sherrill's regime, the school waved goodbye to this football coach and AD with a $684,000 cash settlement and a house. And when Danny Ford resigned in 1990 at Clemson, with the NCAA cops at the gates, he was rewarded with a settlement that could top $1.1

million. In College Sports Inc. and the NCAA, apparently a coach's crime does pay.

> *"Dick Vitale [commenting] on high school players signing*
> *early for college and then seeing the coaches change*
> *schools—'I think the kids should be allowed to be re-*
> *recruited for two weeks in April.' "*
>
> —*USA Today,* quoting TV commentator and
> ex-coach Dick Vitale

When an athlete signs an NCAA Letter of Intent with a school, he or she acknowledges agreement with Item 4 of the letter: "I understand that I have signed this letter with the *institution* and not for a particular sport" (original emphasis). This item originates in the NCAA's fiction that college athletes are regular students.

In reality, as Dick Vitale and every other informed commentator make clear, outstanding athletes choose a particular school primarily because of the program head's ability to train them for professional sports, and their schooling is a distant consideration. (Vitale offers the statistic that "nine out of ten athletes pick a school because of the relationship with that coach.") Thus, why penalize the athletes if the coach suddenly leaves? Let them move with the coach, one argument goes, or at least be rerecruited by other coaches. At present, if a program head skips out of an obligation to one school, he or she can begin work at a new school immediately; however, according to NCAA rules, athletes who want out of a letter of intent can lose up to two years of college eligibility and have to sit out for those two years.

In 1989, when Miami football coach Jimmy Johnson recruited high school all-American Darren Krein, he assured the player that he was not leaving Miami for the Dallas Cowboys. On the basis of the coach's promise, Krein signed, and shortly after, so did Johnson—with the NFL team. The recruit then wanted to go to another school but Miami insisted that Krein fulfill his "commitment" to them or suffer the NCAA two-year penalty. Meanwhile, the Miami athletic program replaced Johnson with Dennis Erickson from Washington State—although this coach had three years left on his contractual "commitment" to that school!

On the face of it, Vitale's and similar arguments for giving athletes the same freedom as coaches make perfect sense—except their premise is that college sports are professional in nature and both coaches and players should enjoy a free labor market. The NCAA, controlled by coaches and as old-fashioned a cartel as exists in America, prefers a restricted labor market for the players as well as the legal fiction that athletes are students, not employees (an athlete is not even allowed to appeal an NCAA ruling—only a coach or a school has that right).

This controversy, however, points to the increasingly professional nature of College Sports Inc. An important part of this phenomenon is the movement of coaches, players, and personnel into pro sports and back.

> *"Jack Pardee, former coach of the Houston Gamblers of the U.S. Football League and other professional football teams, to football coach at U. of Houston."*
>
> —Item in the *Chronicle of Higher Education*

Each week, the "People in Athletics" column, where the above Pardee item appeared, and similar columns in daily newspapers track the coaching and personnel movements in college and professional sports. A fired pro coach will become a program head at a university or a successful college coach will move on to the pros. Assistant coaches also take part in the shuffle: a pro assistant will move to a head college job, a head man at a school will become an assistant in the pros, or an assistant at one level slides into a similar slot at the other. In addition, the assistant ranks at both levels are constantly replenished by recently retired pro athletes.

The interpenetration of professional and college coaching is so complete that most big-time coaches consider a position in the pros and one in College Sports Inc. as merely separate stops on the same career line. For them, there is much less difference between a pro job and a major college job than between the latter and a teacher-mentor appointment in Division III.

Jack Pardee's career is instructive. Pardee played college football at Texas A. & M. and had a successful pro career with the Los Angeles Rams and the Washington Redskins. His first coaching job was as an assistant with the Redskins; then he had stints as head coach of the Chicago Bears, the Redskins, and the Houston Gamblers of the USFL before becoming program head at the University of Houston. After a successful stay with the Cougars, he recently moved to the NFL Houston Oilers.

Unlike Pardee, however, most ex–pro football coaches do not receive a second shot at NFL head jobs and often come to permanent rest in College Sports Inc., mainly because many more university positions are available. This limited competition from the pros should deflate the college coach's labor value but, since the market is illogical, it has no effect. In the same way, deflation should have occurred when the United States Football League disbanded and a large number of qualified coaches needed work. Schools hired many ex-USFLers, including Pardee, but the annual income packages continued to inflate.

Professional basketball is also tied in to the college game. Elevation from the college ranks, as well as shuttling back and forth, is about as common as in football. Larry Brown went from the Denver Nuggets head job to UCLA to the New Jersey Nets to the University of Kansas to the San Antonio Spurs. (Brown was also head man at Davidson but never coached a game there before he moved on.) When Brown signed with San Antonio for a multimillion-dollar contract, Dick Versace, another coach who has moved between the colleges and pros, exclaimed, "He hit the lottery. Larry Brown hit the lottery." Although more nomadic than most, Brown's journey illustrates the interchangeability of head jobs in pro sports and College Sports Inc. as well as this coach's astounding devotion to self-interest.

One side effect of this basketball phenomenon is the intrusion of pros into the women's college game. When jobs are unavailable in the men's college or pro game, some male ex-pros use women's basketball as their entry point into coaching. Steve Mix, former NBA standout, was one of the first ex-pros to take a head women's basketball post when he accepted the job at his alma mater, the University of Toledo, and others have followed. Such moves not only shut out some female coaches from this sport but raise questions about the appropriateness of imposing male and pro sports values upon women players.

College Sports Inc.'s assimilation of the pro game and its coaches has occurred with as much velocity in many of the non-revenue-generating sports as in football and basketball. College hockey coaching, once the preserve of prep school types, is increasingly open to ex–National Hockey League players, often with pro hockey ideas about playing the sport. Gordon "Red" Berenson, one of the first American college graduates to play regularly in the NHL, has moved back and forth between NHL coaching jobs and university ones, including stops with the St. Louis Blues and the University of Michigan (his present post). Often, as in Berenson's case, the coach learned the college scene before spending time in the NHL, but sometimes the glamour of the pro game and the player's name provide him with sufficient credentials for a college job: former Boston Bruin Gary Doak had never attended a university when he went from the pros to head man at the University of Massachusetts in Boston.

The head coaching ranks of college baseball, soccer, tennis, and other sports are also filling with ex-pros. Steve Hamilton, a major-league pitcher for twelve years, is now baseball coach *and* athletic director at Morehead State in Kentucky. Manfred Schellscheidt, an ex-pro player and coach in his native Germany, as well as U.S. Olympic team soccer coach, now heads the nationally ranked soccer program at Seton Hall. Dick Stockton and Dennis Ralston, both successful pro tennis players, had head college coaching jobs at Trinity University and SMU, respectively.

In addition to the coaching shuttle, personnel in pro front offices and university athletic departments are beginning to move back and forth. The "People in Athletics" column has listed, among others, "L. Budd Thalman, public-relations director for the Buffalo Bills of the National Football League, to associate athletic director at Pennsylvania State University," and "Joe Dean, vice-president for promotion at the Converse Corp. . . . to athletic director at Louisiana State University." These executives do not leave their pro sports values behind when they move into college jobs—often they are hired to bring their pro savvy and selling ability to their university work. Whether this will improve athletic departments is doubtful; that it will consolidate College Sports Inc.'s control of intercollegiate athletics is inevitable.

> *"Any [college] coach who can't achieve a .500 record should be fired, especially when they're the ones who choose which teams they want to play against."*
>
> —Donna Lopiano, assistant athletic director
> at the University of Texas at Austin

Surveying the attitudes and values of pro coaches and their college colleagues, few differences stand out. The major one concerns hiring and firing. Pro coaches acknowledge that they are hired to win games and that if they don't, they will be let go. Pro coaches readily quote the line "Hired to be fired," and usually accept the latter occasion without much complaint.

College coaches, on the other hand, although they embrace most pro attitudes, moan about the pressure to win (even when self-induced) and are quick to whine if fired by their schools. Ironically, on occasion, the same coach will quietly accept being fired from a pro team but, a few years later, yell about "the unbearable pressure to win" when leaving a college job.

CHAPTER 21

The Coaches' Subculture & Old-Boy Network

"The phone rings twice before the voice answers, cold and efficient.

" 'Coach Carlen's residence,' the voice says. The caller immediately learns lesson No. 1: Football coaches, like doctors and ex-presidents, retain their titles even after they lose their jobs. Otherwise, the one-time University of South Carolina head coach would be just plain Jim."

—From an article by Richard Jablonski in the
Charleston News and Courier

ONE MAJOR RESULT of the free trade between pro and college sports has been the growth of a large coaching subculture, with its members sharing similar values and aspirations. As this group expands in size and importance, it becomes increasingly separate from other subcultures, especially the academic one. As a result, coaches in big-time sports are more loyal to their peers and profession than they are to any single employer, whether collegiate or professional. In addition, when coaches join their subculture, they see it as a lifetime commitment, and in future years, even when out of work or retired, they tend to define themselves in its terms.

Like most subculture members, coaches reinforce their beliefs and values by contrasting them with opposing groups. Program heads often regard faculty as "opponents," if not "enemies," and they claim that academics do not understand or appreciate the nature of coaches' jobs or the pressures under which they work.

Indeed, most faculty members are uninformed about coaches' duties as well as their high annual incomes—in part, because of the athletic department's "Iron Curtain" around its operations. On the other hand, coaches tend to be ignorant about the regular life of the university. Although they attended college, most were athletes and lived inside the hermetic world of the athletic department. As a result, they had minimal exposure to academic curriculum, faculty, and ordinary student life; later, as coaches, they have neither time nor inclination to explore these central parts of the university.

Like members of any subculture, coaches are more comfortable with their peers, whom they see frequently at sports events, clinics, conventions, and meetings, than with fellow employees, especially faculty, of their own schools.

Even for a subculture, however, this one is surprisingly homogeneous. Most Division I program heads are white males, in early middle to late middle age; coaches have an "old-boy network" that is truly composed of old boys. Even in the administration and coaching of women's college sports, these males predominate: a 1988 study reported that 84 percent of the directors of women's athletic programs and over half of the coaches of women's teams were men. Breaking into the coaches' subculture is difficult not only for women but also for black and minority-group men.

> *"You take all the courses and meet all the requirements and have the background, and somehow you don't get beyond first base [for a college head coaching job]."*
>
> —Prentice Gautt, a black former University of Oklahoma all-American and pro player

Coaches and athletic directors perpetuate their subculture by hiring their duplicates. In 1987, a comprehensive survey reported that of all the head coaches in football, basketball, baseball, and men's track at 278 Division I schools, only 4.2 percent were black. Of athletic directors, only two (Gene Smith at Eastern Michigan and Charles Harris at Arizona State) were not white males. In athletic department offices, 1.2 percent of the personnel was black.

The greatest surprise in this survey, however, was that the percentage of black assistant coaches—3.1 percent—was lower than the percentage of head coaches. Although highly visible as recruiters, black assistants are usually confined to that one coaching position. Moreover, recruiting is the dirtiest and most vulnerable job in college coaching.

"Once you get a label [as a recruiter]," says George Raveling, the basketball head at USC and a black, "it's hard to lose [it]."

Unfortunately, it is not simply a matter of labeling but of a more vicious racism in the coaches' subculture. Blacks work at recruiting because the majority of Division I basketball, football, and track athletes are black. Once on the athletic department's plantation, however, the black athletes are turned over to white coaches. In the SEC, in 1987, 46 percent of the over one thousand football players were black, but only eleven assistant and no head coaches were.

One of the myths of college sports is that it provides opportunities for poor blacks to make good in American society. If success is defined as brief moments of glory while carrying a football or shooting a basketball, then the myth is true for a small number of blacks. If being able to earn a lifelong living from college sports is the definition, the myth shatters.

Program heads will sometimes try to apologize for the statistics on black coaches by explaining that they, personally, want to hire more black assistants and see more black head coaches in the profession, but the booster groups won't allow it. According to this argument, boosters would not feel comfortable with black head coaches at their social functions nor would they want to channel their donations through them. If this explanation were true—and there is no hard evidence to support it—then it would be a sad and damning commentary on the nature of College Sports Inc. and, more important, the universities that house it.

The simpler explanation for this racism is that the coaches' subculture, like all homogeneous clans, particularly conservative ones, feels more comfortable photocopying itself than offering opportunities to members of outside groups.

Since the 1987 survey, organizations like the Black Coaches Association and individuals like Harry Edwards have pushed for more hirings of black head and assistant coaches in college athletics as well as in professional sports. They have made the problem more visible but they have not changed hiring practices. Even in Division I basketball (now over 290 schools, including predominantly black ones), the area with the largest number of minority-group coaches, in 1988, only *five* additional black head coaches emerged after the usual coaches' shuffle. At this rate, integration will come to college coaching some time in the twenty-fifth century.

CHAPTER 22

The Coach as Entrepreneur: Salaries, Tickets Deals, & Summer Camps

*"It might sound overly sentimental, but I like to think I'm
what America is all about."*

> —Jim Valvano, former men's basketball coach
> and athletic director at North Carolina State
> University

IF THE 1980s were the New Age of the Entrepreneur, then many college athletic coaches were at the front of the charge for the dollars. Leading the wolfpack was Jim Valvano, with an annual income of at least $750,000 (still enormous even with his recent resignation).

In the world of college coaches, Jim Valvano is less the exception than the model for his peers. Almost all NCAA Division I football and men's basketball coaches have university salaries above those of the higher-paid full professors at their schools, but, as Valvano illustrates, for these entrepreneurs their university salary line is merely the foundation upon which to build their private businesses.

Valvano's base pay from North Carolina State was $85,000. He also received over $160,000 a year and many valuable perks from Nike shoes, in part for insuring that his players wore Nikes, especially when on national TV. The N.C. State coach gives at least fifty speeches a year and is paid up to $10,000 an appearance. He also endorses various commercial products, has several TV and radio shows, runs summer basketball camps, and earns money from books and videotapes. In addition, he is half owner of an art business that sells statues of sporting figures to corporations. Valvano is a busy man, and to help him move about he has free use of a number of new cars.

Unlike many of his coaching colleagues, however, the N.C. State coach did not run his private businesses out of his university office. Valvano is incorporated as JTV Enterprises, has an off-campus suite of offices, and also employs a New York attorney, Bill Madden, to handle his financial affairs. Madden describes his client as hating to turn down any business opportunity. "And candidly, the money's good. He's just active in his community, which in his mind is America."

Into the 1990s, Valvano continues on his spectacularly entrepreneurial course. Since his university contributed only a small percentage of his annual income and served mainly as his base of operations, questions about his loyalty to his school arose. Valvano swore that he loved N.C. State—although he came close to taking the UCLA job in 1988, and interviewed for an NBA position last year—and that he would never leave. More pointed questions concern whether any university employee, like Valvano, can carry out his obligations when so much of his time and energy go into outside work.

Most schools have regulations concerning their employees' outside income and the amount of time devoted to earning it. The usual university standard is the "One-Fifth Rule": personnel, including faculty, are not supposed to spend more than one-fifth of their time (or one whole workday a week) on, or earn more than one-fifth of their annual income from, outside work. The premise for the rule is that beyond one-fifth time or income, the person no longer functions as a full-time employee of the school, fulfilling his or her duties and responsibilities.

Some entrepreneurial coaches have turned the One-Fifth Rule upside down. They earn less than 20 percent of their annual income from, and spend a minor percentage of their time on, their supposedly full-time college jobs.

> *"The University of Wyoming's new football coach will be paid more than the governor, Wyoming's congressional delegation, the university president, the chief justice of the Wyoming Supreme Court, the secretary of state, and the state attorney general."*
>
> —Item in the *Casper Star-Tribune*

Coaches' salaries are often only a small part of their annual incomes but, in actual dollars, these wages are substantial. When Dennis Erickson accepted the Wyoming job in 1985, the university paid him $80,000 a year, plus various perks. When Erickson jumped contract in

1987, the athletic director, Paul Roach, rather than go into the market for another high-salaried coach, took the job himself. (Erickson has headed football programs at four schools in the last eight years—three in the last four—and has never been fired.)

The state of Wyoming is not unusual in paying an athletic coach more than the state governor and other important public officials. Starting with the A's, in Alabama, Auburn University gives football coach Pat Dye a salary of at least $90,000 a year whereas the governor earns about $30,000 less. Arizona has a similar disparity between the salaries of the football coaches at its two largest public schools and those of its top state official. California is worse—the governor's salary is about half that of the UCLA football coach. And the list continues, with similar statistics, through the alphabet to Wyoming.

The football coach at UCLA, Terry Donahue, opposes publishing the salaries of coaches, even when, like himself, they are public employees: "[It's] an invasion of privacy. I think what a person makes is a private matter." If taxpayers' money were not being used to pay Donahue's salary, his argument would be stronger; his opinion, however, does reflect the traditional athletic department line on why financial matters, especially salaries, should be kept confidential.

Athletic directors refer to the coaches' wages as "base salary" and, for Division I-A football and big-time basketball, according to one AD, "The very low end would be $65,000 and the high end would be around $125,000." What determines the amount that an individual school pays a particular coach is less a function of supply and demand than turnover. As Colorado and Colorado State found in the 1980s, every time they replaced a coach, the base salary jumped far above the normal rate of inflation and cost of living (on which schools usually base personnel and faculty increments). When Colorado State changed basketball coaches in 1986, the base salary went from $47,200 to $60,000; at Colorado, a similar move saw the base go from $51,000 to $60,000. In addition, the new AD at Colorado State was given a base salary of $76,000 a year compared to his predecessor's $54,800.

The Athletics Arms Race also influences salary jumps. Sometimes a school within a conference will raise coaches' wages simply to keep up with the scale at their peer institutions: one or two extremely well paid or overpaid coaches can start a new upward spiral. In the early 1980s, Ohio State felt that its football and basketball head coaching salaries were lagging behind the Big Ten rates and raised them an average of 23 percent in one year. The Ohio State AD explained that he was prompted, in part, by Northwestern's having rewarded its football coach with an almost 20 percent increase for winning a total of *three* games the previous season.

Large salaries are not the exclusive preserve of football and basketball program heads at Division I schools. Coaches in nonrevenue sports now top the $60,000 mark, and in lower NCAA divisions as well as in the NAIA, some coaches approach that figure (a few years ago, Fort Hays State University in Kansas offered a $50,000 package to a basketball coach). Salary inflation has even touched rowing. The part-time coach at Temple once explained his crew's limited success with, "We're not wealthy enough to move up and go against teams with coaches who make $40,000 to $50,000 a year."

> *"If you give me fifty sideline seats, I'm not going to have to worry about driving somewhere on my vacation; I'll fly there. I won't have to worry about a hotel in Hawaii; it'll be taken care of. I won't have to worry about a whole lot of things."*
>
> —Jack Doland, former athletic director and president of McNeese State University, Lake Charles, Louisiana

Most jobs have perquisites, small extras that come with the territory. All university employees enjoy added days of Christmas, Easter, and summer vacations. Unlike other college personnel, however, many coaches' perks include the profitable sale or barter of complimentary season tickets, as well as lucrative private camps on rent-free university property. Most coaches consider their perks legitimate and ordinary, and have them written into their contracts—even when the very same perks are unavailable and forbidden to all other members of the university community.

The men's basketball coach at the University of Nevada at Las Vegas, Jerry Tarkanian, is a tenured member of his faculty with an annual base salary of at least $170,000. Among his many income supplements, which include a guarantee of 10 percent of the school's profits from NCAA men's basketball tournament appearances (the 1987 trip to New Orleans earned UNLV well over a million dollars), is the perk from his university of 234 season basketball tickets (over $40,000 face value) for the coach to dispose of as he wishes.

Tarkanian's ticket deal is only unusual in its size. Every college football and basketball coach in America receives free season tickets, although the amount varies from free seats for the coach's family at some schools to Tarkanian's horde. In recent years, college athletes have been in trouble with the NCAA for selling complimentary tickets, but the association never questions the coaches' regular sale of comps. Nor does the IRS usually inquire into the goods and services, such as free vacations, received by coaches who barter their tickets to travel agencies and other businesses.

Joe B. Hall, the former men's basketball coach at the University of Kentucky, came closest to trouble when allegations arose that he was selling many of his 322 comps at more than face value. Hall was eventually cleared of the charges but his alleged crime was scalping, not selling his free tickets.

Scalping incidents do occur, however, especially for NCAA tourney and bowl games. During the 1988 NCAA basketball championship in Kansas City, three coaches were arrested for selling their tourney comps for as much as $700 a ticket. The police later dropped the charges but, in the shadow world of illegal ticket selling, stories persist about coaches scalping their comps through third parties and other conduits.

The more serious issue with comps is what they cost the host schools. At a time of huge athletic department deficits, the "leakage" from these giveaways can be considerable. Moreover, this leakage is usually computed on the basis of the tickets' face value. Since among the coaches' freebies are some of the best locations in the house—at UNLV, Tark's comps include floor-level "Gucci seats"—the real value of the tickets, when the priority-seating price is figured in, is much higher. Coaches often realize the true value when they exchange a set of season comps for a Hawaiian vacation, but on this item the athletic department's financial statement shows only red ink.

> "You can get a thousand kids paying $200 apiece at these camps. Usually you don't have to pay, or pay much, for the facilities. . . . It can be a great deal."
>
> —Dick Vitale, former college and pro coach, presently an ESPN announcer

The summer camp perk is one of the worst abuses of the relationship between coaches and their universities, and it is also one of the least known. Not only are football and basketball camps for girls and boys very profitable, but those for soccer, gymnastics, swimming, tennis, golf, volleyball, and even wrestling can earn very good money for their coach-proprietors. Originally, the host schools owned the camps (some still do) and paid the coaches a stipend to be camp directors, but as coaches evolved into program heads and noticed the dollars generated by the camps, their entrepreneurial zeal prompted them to take over the camps and run them as private businesses. At first, coaches used locations away from their schools (some still operate this way), but later, for maximum profit, they demanded rent-free university property.

The camp perk also became part of the Athletics Arms Race. Insecure about attracting and keeping program heads, and ignoring the supply and demand of their labor market, many schools agreed to the coaches' escalating requests on this item. Some administrators even argued that the camp perk was a "free" way of increasing coaches' incomes beyond their yearly salaries; in fact, schools pay for the camp perk in lost revenue as well as in maintenance and other costs. Once the camp deal became a standard clause in a program head's contract, with the schools assuming the main business expenses of the camp operations, there was no returning to the earlier arrangements.

In its present form, the summer camp perk permits coaches to pay a nominal—or no—fee for the use of the school's grounds and facilities, i.e., the university basketball courts, football and soccer fields, swimming pools, etc., as well as the equipment therein and thereupon. In 1986, when he was football coach at the University of Arizona, Larry Smith paid his school $50 rent for the use of its football stadium, practice fields, and weight room for his private camp; he also paid the $1.88 sales tax on his $50 rental fee. This is $51.88 more than many of his fellow coaches pay their schools for similar moneymaking uses.

Schools are also generous in allowing coaches to house and feed their campers in the dorms for cost or less (for most private summer camp owners, room and board are their greatest expenses). Nevertheless, many coaches add a markup to the campers' fees for these items and make an extra profit on them. Some coaches, like Bob Knight, also do not pay the dorm bills from their camps until the last day of the fiscal year and earn significant interest on the float (as much as a year can pass between the campers' payment to the coach and the coach's to the university; $100,000 or more can sit in the coach's bank account earning interest).

Paying the camp counselors, usually a major expense for regular summer camp owners, can also cost a coach very little—thanks again to the university. The coach sets the wage scale for the counselors, sometimes paying well, often paying nothing or amazingly small salaries for ten- to twelve-hour days and six- or seven-day workweeks. Many counselors are assistant coaches, graduate student assistants, and physical education students, as well as present and former players on the coach's teams. Some coaches justify the low wages with the explanation that many of these counselors are on the current university payroll and are receiving school paychecks during the summer. In other words, these counselors are paid by the university for working at the coach's private camp!

The NCAA has tried to tighten the rules on the number of team members who can work at a coach's summer camp and the pay that they can receive because some coaches use this employment as a means of channeling extra money to athletes. In this situation, as in similar cases where recruits work for the coach, the "counselor payment" rarely comes out of the coach-entrepreneur's pocket; the money usually originates in the booster club's slush fund.

Coach-entrepreneurs also employ high school coaches as counselors. Usually these men and women want to impress and/or ingratiate themselves with the program head and are willing to work for minimum, if any, wages. Sometimes, however, the head coach will bring in a particular high school coach and pay top dollar for almost no work. Not surprisingly, this high school coach will turn out to have an outstanding prospect on his or her team. Last year, one of the NCAA's charges against the University of Kentucky basketball program was that during the school's recruiting of star guard Eric Manual it paid his high school coach almost $1,000 to give a brief talk at the Kentucky summer camp.

Coaches, however, are generous in one area: they reward their counselors with handsome warm-up suits, sneakers, and other sports gear; they also give each camper a T-shirt with the camp logo on it. But few coach-entrepreneurs pay for any of these items—they are provided free by sporting goods manufacturers as part of the coach's "shoe deal."

Unlike intercollegiate athletics, with its tremendous start-up costs and huge ongoing expenses, camps can be established and run on a small amount of capital. Because costs tend to be low—thanks to the university—summer camp profits for many coaches are outstanding, in many cases double their annual salaries.

Coaches run their camps in one-week sessions, for as many as ten weeks during a summer; campers who board pay an average of $200 to $300 a week; day campers, $150 to $250. Bill Frieder, when at Michigan, is reported to have grossed over $350,000 for his 1986 basketball summer camps. Charles "Lefty" Driesell, the former coach at Maryland, resigned from his coaching job after his star player, Len Bias, died from a cocaine-induced seizure; Driesell, however, insisted on keeping his camps at the university and, in 1986, had 875 kids pay $264 each for a $231,000 gross. Moreover, in his settlement agreement with Maryland, the school continued its $20,000 subsidy to defray Driesell's dorm and facility bill. Even when Driesell moved to James Madison University, he got to keep his Maryland camps and subsidies.

Coaches also gain a nonmonetary but valuable bonus from this sideline business. The camps both help and simplify recruiting. Many kids attend the camps for the purpose of attracting the coach's attention and eventually winning an athletic scholarship. This is especially true in nonrevenue sports like soccer where, unlike football and basketball, head coaches do not have full-time recruiting assistants scouting the country. But even in the big-time sports, a program head will often spot a youngster at his or her summer camp long before the scouts see the kid in high school games and will gain a head start in the recruiting war for that player. Steve Alford, the Indiana University all-American, first attended Bob Knight's camp as a nine-year-old.

To put the coaches' camp perk in perspective, universities do hold computer, creative writing, music, and many other kinds of summer camps with staff or faculty members as directors. In every case that this writer could find, the staff or faculty member did not operate the camp privately but acted as an employee of the university, paid on an ad hoc basis, sometimes at a prorated amount of regular salary, sometimes at a fixed amount regardless of rank or salary. Many of these university camps had very high registration fees and generated large revenues, but in each case, the university—not the person in charge—kept the profits. Moreover, these profits did not necessarily go into the budgets of the host departments. The money often moved into the school's general operating fund.

By allowing coaches to turn the sports camps into their private businesses, many schools lose out on a significant source of revenue. When coaches run the camps privately, all profits go to them but most expenses remain with the schools. The bottom line for many universities is that instead of gaining $200,000 to $300,000 from their summer sports camps for the general fund or even for the athletic department budget, they give this money to the coach-entrepreneurs. At the end of the fiscal year, do administrators, when taking money out of academic funding to cover athletic department deficits, ever remember the $200,000 to $300,000 lost to the coaches last summer?

CHAPTER 23

The Coach as Entrepreneur:
Shoe Contracts, Media Shows,
& Endorsements

"In politics in Louisiana, we'd call that [shoe contracts]
bribery. I don't know what they call it in basketball
circles. Free enterprise, I guess."

—Jack Doland, former athletic director and
president of McNeese State University

As GOOD ENTREPRENEURS, coaches try to connect their various perks
and deals. The summer camp scheme ties neatly into the shoe deal
when, as part of its shoe contract, the sporting goods manufacturer
provides the coach–camp owner with free T-shirts for every camper as
well as gear for the counselors.

The main purpose of the shoe contract, however, is to insure that
coaches outfit their teams in the company's equipment. Major sporting
goods companies regularly sign coaches to five- and six-figure annual
contracts, and although they officially call these payments "consulting
fees" (the coach is supposed to make various recommendations concerning the equipment), *the company hands out the money and the*
freebies in return for the coach's assurance that his or her players will
wear its shoes and/or uniforms for all games. When a college basketball
player, hanging in the air during a shot, is on the cover of a national
magazine—shoes and brand name clearly displayed—the manufacturer that paid the player's coach $100,000 has received more than its
money's worth.

Corporations pay in proportion to the exposure that a coach's team
has on TV and in print. Since the contracts are negotiated before the
season begins and companies cannot be certain about this year's best

teams, they hedge their bets by signing large numbers of coaches, but the program heads with the most consistently winning teams receive the best deals. Considering the dollar value of the contracts, the shoe deal creates a definite pressure to win—but coaches rarely admit that this pressure exists.

Nike, a leader in shoe deals, has contracts with over sixty college men's and women's basketball coaches, and a number of program heads in other sports. Last year's Nike contracts included $200,000 for John Thompson of Georgetown, $160,000 for Eddie Sutton, then at Kentucky, and the same amount to Jim Valvano at N.C. State, as well as $120,000 to both Jerry Tarkanian of UNLV and Jim Boeheim of Syracuse. In return for this money, these coaches fulfilled their contracts in the usual ways and also participated in a number of clinics for high school coaches sponsored by Nike (of course, the clinics help these college coaches in their ongoing recruiting). In addition, Nike rewarded these and other coaches in their stable with all-expenses-paid vacations to places like the Virgin Islands.

Other companies try to treat their coaches equally well. A few years ago, Puma signed Rollie Massimino of Villanova to a $125,000 annual contract; Converse, Adidas, and Reebok pay at least ten other men's basketball coaches $100,000 a year or more. Below the six-figure echelon, at least seventy-five NCAA Division I men's basketball coaches have contracts in the $40,000-or-higher range, and the leading women's coaches average $10,000 a year.

The sporting goods companies also make deals with every other Division I program head in basketball, as well as coaches in football and the nonrevenue sports, especially baseball, track, and soccer. The size of the deal depends on the exposure potential of the program, but even at the NAIA level, the coach receives something. Nike also has contracts with twenty-five of the most important high school basketball coaches; high school kids are part of its target market and some of these coaches will be the college program heads of tomorrow.

Shoe deals are one of the few areas where football coaches average less in payments (half or below) than their colleagues in basketball: during football games, there are fewer TV close-ups of players' shoes, and football cleats, unlike basketball sneakers, cannot be marketed as daily walking-around shoes. In addition, for football, shoe companies usually will not supply teams with free samples, whereas in basketball this is a standard, and relatively inexpensive, procedure.

Coaches in nonrevenue sports like soccer and track also do not see the six-figure contracts but often do surprisingly well, especially if they head programs that receive good exposure in the special journals, like *Soccer America,* devoted to their sports. Even in activities like swimming, equipment manufacturers like Speedo and Arena make deals with the most prominent college coaches, especially those with potential Olympic athletes in their programs.

In addition, coaches in nonrevenue sports conduct large numbers of youth clinics, often sponsored by the sporting goods companies, and flog the equipment in this way. "You can't believe all the kids out there playing soccer," Charlie Cooke, former head of promotions for Nike's soccer shoes, explained. "And companies will try anything to get coaches to push their brands of shoes."

Most coaches consider shoe contracts wonderful deals; critics have called them "influence peddling" and even "bribery." Dean Smith and Bob Knight appear to agree in part with the criticism because they turn over some of the money received from shoe companies to their universities. A few years ago, the University of Virginia tried to finesse this question when it prohibited its coaches from making private shoe deals and insisted on open bidding on all shoe and equipment contracts, with the money going to the athletic department as well as to the coaches.

Virginia's solution, however, does not attack the most serious aspect of this problem—how such deals corrupt intercollegiate athletics and the university itself.

Shoe contracts are an apt symbol for the relationship of program heads in College Sports Inc. to their athletes. Instead of exercising the coach's inherent power over the athlete for the latter's good (as when a teacher-mentor forbids a player who is failing a course from making road trips), program heads force athletes to do something—wear the shoes—solely for personal profit. Program heads do not even share these profits with the athletes who make the dollars possible—the NCAA specifically prohibits it.

When athletes complain of being "ripped off" by the college sports system, they sometimes point to coaches' shoe contracts as an example of how big money is paid to others for their hard work. The only rational response for a college athlete in this situation, other than rage, is cynicism. For many athletes, this cynicism justifies breaking NCAA rules, including accepting money from boosters. With their shoe deals, program heads, in their greed, undermine the very authority and trust necessary for success in coaching. More important, with such gross commercialization of their university positions, they emphasize the distance between College Sports Inc. and higher education.

> *"The [Virginia] Tech athletic association, which has experienced financial problems in the past two years, lost about $70,000 on the football television show [of coach Bill Dooley] despite the Hokies' Independence Bowl appearance. Dooley is being paid a $60,000 talent fee by the athletic association."*
>
> —Item in the *Roanoke Times and World-News*

TV and radio deals are another major source of income for program heads. Their usually boring, oddly scheduled (late at night or early weekend mornings), lamely produced shows sometimes earn good ratings in their local markets, but often their ratings produce the same low numbers as the religious and public service programs in similar time slots. No matter what their ratings, coaches frequently reap five- and sometimes six-figure amounts from their TV and radio contracts. As with so many aspects of coaches' income, because athletic departments or their agents intercede and supply artificial economic support, normal market forces do not prevail.

When Bill Dooley was the football coach at Virginia Tech (where his activities earned the university NCAA probation), he was paid a "talent fee" by his school's athletic program for appearing on his TV and radio shows. In other words, the success and revenue-generating power of Dooley's shows was totally separate from his pay for doing them. In fact, the shows always lost money although Dooley's "talent fee" kept increasing—in one year, from $35,000 to $60,000 for the TV show and from $15,000 to $25,000 for the radio slot. Dooley's ratings were so bad that in a year when it paid the coach an $85,000 "talent fee," the athletic program also had to lay out more than $23,000 to five TV stations to carry the coach's show.

Dooley's Virginia Tech media career gives a new definition to the term *talent* but not to *sweetheart deal*. This coach convinced his bosses that the best way to supplement his university salary was through this particular media deal, even though the cost to the athletic program was exorbitant. Such deals contain an extra bonus for the recipient—they require much less time and energy than running a summer camp and can be as lucrative.

Because the TV shows usually consist of the coach being prompted by a professional announcer to comment on a highlight film of the most recent game, and the radio programs are usually phone-ins, the coach needs almost no preparation to earn more from this deal than the annual salaries of most staff and faculty members at his university. But most coaches take their media appearances very seriously and many yearn for postcoaching careers as color commentators on local or national TV and the success of an Al McGuire or Dick Vitale.

Some program heads have shows that produce more money and cost their schools less than the Virginia Tech coach's did: when Jackie Sherrill was at Texas A. & M. he received at least $135,000 a year from the sponsors of his TV and radio shows. In Sherrill's case and in similar deals, many of the sponsors are athletic department boosters who see the payments as a way of helping their favorite athletic program. Moreover, sponsor-boosters can write off the money as a business expense (part of their companies' advertising). Athletic programs lose some large contributions this way, but at least they do not have to pay out money directly as in the "talent fee" setup.

A third kind of media deal involves those program heads who embrace the real meaning of the word *entrepreneur.* They own their shows and, like other American businessmen, make or lose money with them. Bo Schembechler was a pioneer in this area and his media earnings depended on his show's ability to sell advertising. Yet even the Michigan head was reluctant to live or die solely on his ratings: he boosted his TV revenues by selling lines on the crawl of credits at the end of his show to local businesses and individuals. He also changed the names on the crawl for different stations in different markets, thus increasing revenue by picking up boosters from locations around the state. Schembechler admitted, however, that there is a "downside" to a coach owning his show—if your team begins to lose, "your income can slip."

As in so many instances in college sports, with media deals like Schembechler's, the pressure to win does not come from the school administrators but the coach's avarice. The same pressure applies to coaches who, although they don't own their shows and work on a fixed guarantee, also get a percentage of the profits. Howard Schnellenberger, head football coach at Louisville, has just such an arrangement: his school guarantees him $90,000 a year from his TV and radio shows and, in addition, he receives one-third of the net profits above $160,000 from Louisville's football *and* basketball media shows. The school's men's basketball coach, Denny Crum, has a similar deal and it is his team that, when winning, generates the good TV ratings in the Louisville market.

Most other program heads also have lucrative media deals, financed in one of the usual ways. Bobby Bowden, football coach at Florida State, is guaranteed a minimum of $65,000 from his shows; across the state in Gainesville, the former head man at University of Florida, Galen Hall, was into six figures with his. When Mike White was football coach at Illinois (and frequently attracted the NCAA investigators' attention), he made $125,000 from his airtime. John Cooper, before he left the head football job at Arizona State, had an $80,000 media deal and reportedly has an even better one at his new school, Ohio State—a $240,000-a-year TV and radio package, which in 1988 came to $60,000 per Buckeye victory.

The TV and radio deals of men's basketball coaches, like those of their football colleagues, are also attractive, particularly in certain regions of the country. In Kentucky and Indiana, basketball program heads at the big state schools often earn six figures from their shows. In neighboring Ohio and Illinois, with fewer fanatic roundball viewers, the coaches' media deals drop to the middle five-figure range. But there are frequent exceptions to the regional rule and Bill Dooley–type arrangements occur in all states. In Georgia, only a moderate basketball area, the Bulldogs' coach, Hugh Durham, takes in at least $73,000 from his shows (the former football coach at the school, Vince Dooley, Bill's brother, earned over $100,000 from his show, but Georgia is "football country"). And in Arizona, Bill Frieder's new deal with ASU gives him $171,000 a year from his TV and radio shows.

Sometimes coaches are not satisfied with their straight media deals. When Dana Kirk headed the Memphis State basketball program, he not only earned five figures from his shows but also charged TV stations for interviews. In one instance, when his team was in the NCAA Final Four, he received $400 for a personal interview and $100 for arranging interviews with a number of his players. Kirk's scam, while unusual for a college coach, is not unknown in the world of sports. At the 1988 Olympics, many athletes and their coaches were paid—sometimes sizable amounts of money—by various news organizations, including American ones, for exclusive and not-so-exclusive interviews. In European and Latin American soccer, this practice has long occurred. Considering the hustling ability of American college coaches, in the future, Dana Kirk may be remembered as not only a convicted felon (he didn't report the income from many of his deals to the IRS) but also as a "deal innovator" in College Sports Inc.

Colleges and universities rarely object to their coaches' media deals, nor do they protest the coaches' use of athletic program property—i.e., game films—for personal profit. Many a coach assumes that he or she is the rightful owner of these films and acts in a proprietorial manner when using them on a TV show for personal profit. But these movies, usually taken by the athletic department's photographers with department equipment, featuring its stadium and team, do not legally belong to the coach. If any other individual or company, such as a TV station, tried to use the films for profit, the university's lawyers—not the coach's—would invoke the institution's copyright privileges immediately. Yet under their exemption as program heads—an exemption not granted to any other university employee—coaches are allowed to appropriate this property for their own uses and personal profit. Once again, the school bears the ultimate cost here and receives none of the revenue.

Coaches' media deals raise complex and usually ignored questions—all having to do with coaches' special and costly relationships with the university.

> "[Oklahoma football coach Barry] Switzer also makes commercials for everything from cars to air conditioners to health spas. 'He has every deal imaginable,' says another coach who knows Switzer well. 'I have never seen a guy run faster for a buck. He once bragged he made $500,000 a year.'"
>
> —Item in the *Miami Herald*

If a coach's media shows are successful, he attracts sponsors and does on-air commercials for them. In addition, the coach will often give speeches on a sponsor's behalf and serve as its representative at a variety of public occasions.

Most frequently, coaches endorse sports products but they seem willing to lend their names to almost any item or service. Penn State's

Joe Paterno, a symbol of probity in college football, has a professional agency handle his endorsements; he charges $25,000 to $100,000 for each television commercial, and $5,000 to $15,000 for a print ad. Among Paterno's nonsports clients have been Panhandle Eastern Corporation, a Texas pipeline company.

Coaches' endorsements range from national Coca-Cola ads by famous program heads to local TV spots for Mister Bee, a potato chip, endorsed by Don Nehlin, the football coach at West Virginia. However, a former Indiana University football coach, Lee Corso, set the standard for crassness when he shilled for the white minority South African government's Krugerrands during his time at I.U.

Corso's pushing the coins on his TV show points up the most troubling aspect of endorsements by coaches: in these situations, whom is the coach speaking for, himself, his school, or both? On the "Coach's Corner" shows, with the school's logo as a studio prop and its team on the screen, the coach seems very much a public spokesman for his institution. Even when endorsing a commercial product in a separate TV ad or doing a grand opening in a shopping mall, the coach is usually identified as the program head at Bigtime State U. and appears to represent the school.

Therefore, when a coach, as a university spokesman, endorses a product or service, the implication is that State U. also stands behind this commercial item. Some coaches deny that audiences make this connection, but, with the visual trappings of State U. in the ads, the tie-in between the school and the product appears very real. Sponsors certainly believe that the connection exists and are willing to pay money for their beliefs.

Jim Valvano, the leading entrepreneurial coach, has long argued that, when doing commercials, he is acting as a private individual. But in Valvano's ads, for which he earns a great deal of money, he was often identified as the head basketball coach of North Carolina State University, and he has made commercials on university property (he filmed an ad for one auto dealer in his school's basketball arena and paid a $75 rental fee for the use of the building). Nevertheless this coach disputed the connection between his university position and his endorsements, and claimed that he was not profiting from his school affiliation.

If for a TV ad a faculty member, say a professor of medicine, stood in a white coat in her department's laboratory, with her name, title, and the university's name on the bottom of the screen, and endorsed an over-the-counter cold medicine, the school would either severely reprimand her or begin proceedings for dismissal. In either case, the school would demand that the commercials stop immediately.

Coaches, however, are allowed not only to make endorsements but to earn as much money as possible from them. American colleges and universities permit no other employee or official to represent them for personal profit in this way.

CHAPTER 24

The Coach as Entrepreneur: Car Deals, Miscellaneous Freebies, & the Scheduling Scam

"Thirty-one automobiles are being donated [i.e., loaned] to the Washington State University athletic program and one of the cars is used by President Sam Smith. . . . The donation of loaned cars to athletic programs is a nationwide policy."

—Item in the *Seattle Times*

AT ONE TIME, local car dealers would sponsor the coach's media shows and include in payment the free use of a new car. But now the coach's "car deal" goes far beyond a media show tie-in, and a program head, including one in women's sports, has to be far out of the athletic department loop not to receive this job benefit. In fact, one of the generic differences between program heads and teacher-mentors is that the former have car deals and the latter try to nurse their rust-buckets through another winter.

The quantity and quality of cars that automobile dealers loan coaches, as well as the inclusion of free insurance, gas, repairs, etc., are usually directly proportional to the exposure potential of the program heads' teams. When he was Alabama football coach and AD, Ray Perkins received free use of a new Jeep Wagoneer and a Lincoln Town Car, with all the extras taken care of by the dealer. In his last year at the

University of New Mexico, Joe Lee Dunn, the football coach, drove a new Oldsmobile Cutlass free of charge and had his car replaced with a new one every two thousand miles or three months, whichever came first. A few years ago at UNLV, Jerry Tarkanian drove a new Cadillac De Ville free of charge, whereas the head women's basketball coaches (a husband-and-wife team) got to use a Volkswagen Golf. As the Washington State situation implied, almost all major coaches, as well as athletic directors and sometimes top administrators, at NCAA Division I schools have some sort of car deal with local agencies (the exceptions, like George Welsh, football coach at Virginia, often have their cars provided free of charge by their universities' foundations or booster groups). In the Big Ten last year, the athletic department at Iowa received 73 "courtesy cars," Ohio State 68, Illinois and Minnesota 43 each, etc.

Automobile dealers, however, do not donate the use of their cars simply because they are gung-ho supporters of intercollegiate athletics. Car agencies have no trouble reselling what they call "The Coach's Car," and they also receive publicity, referrals, and inquiries about the models that the coaches drive. Finally, in a neat twist, some dealers claim a tax deduction on these cars because they donated the use of them to a nonprofit educational institution!

When he was football coach at the University of Alabama, "Bear" Bryant took the car deal to a new plateau by endorsing a special fleet of 315 customized vans, with his signature on the driver's door, houndstooth upholstery (his trademark was a houndstooth hat), and a plaque with a limited-edition number on the dashboard. The vans sold for $19,000 each and the Bear got a percentage of this as well as the use of an ultra-deluxe model from the company that made the vans.

As with other coaches' hustles, everyone benefits from the car deal except the university, which loses because its representatives appear to be endorsing particular car companies and dealers. Possibly because automobile dealers have often included top administrators in their patronage, less criticism is made of the car deal than of any of the coaches' other extracurricular arrangements.

"More than $1 million could be waiting for University of Louisville basketball coach Denny Crum in nine years under a bonus plan approved by university officials this week. . . .

"But some faculty say those bonuses could hurt morale at the university. Faculty members will receive only 2% raises this year."

—Item in the *Louisville Courier-Journal*

Athletic departments and their supporters are sometimes so intimidated by and/or grateful to their coaches that, in addition to the free use of cars, they throw gifts of cash and other goodies at them. After the Nebraska Cornhuskers football team was 9–3 for the 1981 season, the school's boosters gave the coaching staff a bonus of $120,000; in the next two years, with 12–1 seasons, the bonuses grew in size. Many other coaches and coaching staffs have received similar cash thank-yous (there is no NCAA rule against this practice).

In addition to individual gifts of money, coaches often receive cash annuities. Sometimes the coach receives money when the annuity begins, and in other cases, the money kicks in at a future date. Bobby Bowden, football coach at Florida State, receives $100,000 from his annuity in 1990, and Denny Crum, the men's basketball coach at Louisville, will obtain a lump-sum $1 million in 1993 if he fulfills his long-term contract with the school. Pat Dye, at Auburn, also has an annuity that could bring him a million dollars when he is sixty-five. Howard Schnellenberger, the football coach at Louisville, collected a $500,000 annuity after the 1989 season and began work on another one.

Increasing numbers of schools are using future bonuses and annuities as an attempt to insure that a coach will not jump contract for another job. In Crum's case, the promised $1 million appears to have kept him from accepting various attractive coaching offers, including one from UCLA, his alma mater. This use of future annuities as a defensive strategy against the Coach in Motion Play also contradicts the standard coaches' complaint that schools are ready to fire them after the first losing season.

For their on-field or on-court performances, some coaches receive raises if their teams do well—Jud Heathcote at Michigan State gained a 24 percent raise in 1986 when his team made the NCAA final sixteen.

Program heads, however, also want bonus clauses in their contracts, the most common being the equivalent of one month's pay for a conference championship or a postseason bowl or tournament appearance. When John Cooper coached football at Arizona State, his bonus was one month's pay for winning the Pacific Ten title *plus* another month's salary for a bowl appearance (his team's 1986 Rose Bowl season earned him an extra $13,332). Because of his high annual salary, Denny Crum's bonus pays him over $10,000 for getting his team to the NCAA tournament. The list of these bonus-for-winning deals for coaches is long and includes those at such play-by-the-NCAA-book schools as Purdue.

The impetus for the bonus clauses comes from the coaches, not the schools. Again, the myth that the schools pressure the coaches to win is contradicted by the coaches' demand for bonus clauses in their contracts. Some coaches even tie their bonuses to home attendance. When Ron Greene was men's basketball coach at Indiana State (Larry Bird's school), he received 3 percent of all home ticket sales above $250,000; the Sycamores needed to average above 5,000 a game for Greene to see any extra money. Bill Frieder, the new men's basketball coach at Arizona State, receives $20,000 if ASU's home attendance averages 7,500 or better and $30,000 if it hits 11,000. This bonus-for-attendance practice, common in professional sports, is totally tied to winning, and only allowed for one group of university employees—coaches.

If academic staff or faculty members perform their jobs well, they receive salary raises and, very occasionally, annual bonuses. However, a bonus pegged to a quantifiable scale like a won-lost record or attendance is, by definition, impossible in university life. The academic equivalent of the coaches' bonus-for-attendance plan would be teachers receiving a percentage of the tuition revenue from their classes that attract more than the usual number of students. The educational objections to such a scheme—the bonuses would encourage huge lecture courses, taught in the most watered-down, easy-grade manner—spotlight the differences between a program head's entertainment business goals and a faculty member's teaching mission.

*"Tennessee athletic director Doug Dickey said newly hired
basketball coach Wade Houston [a black] . . . will not be
offered a membership in an all-white country club.*

*"The UT athletic department has provided the $15,000
memberships to the exclusive Cherokee Country Club to
Houston's predecessors Ray Mears and Don Devoe. Vols
football coach Johnny Majors and Dickey are members."*

—Item in an Associated Press dispatch

Coaches receive many gifts, some as large as the oil wells reportedly given to Oklahoma's Barry Switzer as well as the various stock deals that boosters have let him in on, and some as petty as the "merchant discounts" that Denny Crum has included in his contract. Some corporations appoint coaches to their boards of directors (Pat Dye of Auburn is on Colonial Bancgroup's board) and store owners often give them free and/or discounted merchandise. One midwestern basketball coach boasts that he hasn't paid for an article of clothing since junior high school or picked up the check at a restaurant since he was old enough to eat in one.

The list of gifts to coaches includes something for every taste: a $4,000 clothing allowance for Jody Conradt, women's basketball coach at the University of Texas, from Converse; the "free services . . . of an accountant and a lawyer" reported to be part of Lute Olson's contract with the University of Arizona. A free vacation is the program head's equivalent of a tie or a scarf; if the shoe company doesn't send the coach to the Bahamas, the booster club probably will. (Vince Dooley often went to Europe courtesy of the Georgia Bulldog Club.)

A more substantial gift for coaches is free or low-cost housing. Clemson provided football head Danny Ford with a beautiful home and also made payments on the $280,000 mortgage on a 137-acre farm for him. When Ford resigned after his program sparked a massive NCAA investigation, Clemson agreed to pay off the rest of the mortgage on the farm for him. Pat Dye at Auburn has a similar deal: he lives rent-free in a $500,000 house that will be his if he is still at the school next year.

Dennis Erickson, when football coach at the University of Wyoming, lived for free in a school-owned and -maintained house. He also received $5,000 a year for, to quote his contract, "decorating and aesthetic improvements purposes." Both the football and men's basketball coaches at the University of Arkansas have $10,000 housing allowances, and when Jackie Sherrill signed his Texas A. & M. pact, he was promised as much as $75,000 toward the purchase of a new home and he got to keep the house as part of his contract settlement.

As befitting their lifestyles replete with new cars and homes, most coaches like to join their local country club. But they rarely pay for expensive initiation fees, annual dues, greens fees, bar bills, and so on. The country club deal is as common as the free car arrangement—except the athletic program usually picks this one up. The majority of football and men's basketball coaches at NCAA Division I schools, as well as many program heads in nonrevenue sports, have some sort of country club deal. In 1986, the athletic department at Florida State University thought it appropriate to pay the Killearn Country Club membership, with its $3,000 initiation fee and $1,827 annual dues, for men's basketball coach Pat Kennedy. The University of Texas at Austin usually pays the country club memberships (valued in the $2,000 range) for its major coaches. Even smaller programs, like Illinois State, try to do a little something for their coaches: in 1986, the Illinois college picked up basketball coach Bob Donnewald's $320 annual YMCA membership.

However, when Wade Houston became men's basketball coach at the University of Tennessee last year, his AD was unwilling to pay the $15,000 entrance fee and $225 monthly dues to a local country club for him—not for economic reasons, but for racial ones. Eventually the university president resolved the problem by asking all athletic program personnel to resign their memberships.

Like other entertainers or business executives who are important to their enterprises, many coaches persuade their employers to carry large amounts of insurance on them. The University of Louisville pays the premium on Howard Schnellenberger's $500,000 life insurance policy as well as on his and his family's accident and medical insurance. Florida State has a $300,000 life insurance policy on men's basketball coach Pat Kennedy—$100,000 higher than Texas A. & M. took out on Jackie Sherrill. Usually the coach names the beneficiaries of these policies. In a neat extra on these insurance practices, some schools permit their coaches to draw on the cash value in and/or generated by the policies—sometimes a considerable sum of money and well hidden from inquiring reporters.

Many colleges and universities insure their faculty members, usually for the amount of their annual salaries. Some schools include the coaches in this life insurance plan; others buy special packages for athletic department personnel that include extra coverage for on-the-job injuries or fatalities, especially while traveling with a team. The University of Florida puts its coaches on a standard athletic department on-duty policy of $250,000 accidental death or dismemberment, $200,000 disability, and $25,000 medical. Florida is not alone: most NCAA Division I schools insure their athletic department personnel, particularly the program heads, for far more than they do the health and lives of their regular faculty and staff. This not only costs the universities extra money but makes a clear statement about their priorities.

Coaches, like all other businesspeople, incur expenses, and frequently their employers either reimburse them for these costs or, more generously, give them large expense accounts. According to a *USA Today* 1986 survey, Bobby Bowden, head football coach at Florida State, had a $25,000 expense account; Bowden's counterpart at Colorado, Bill Mc-Cartney, had a $10,000 expense account and the school's basketball coach received a similar amount. The University of Tennessee at Knoxville pegged its football coach's expense account at $10,000 and the men's basketball coach's at half that sum. Bill Frieder's current deal with Arizona State gives him "a discretionary expense allowance" of $25,000.

These figures are standard for many big-time Division I coaches. The trick with expense accounts is for the holder to lay off as many personal expenses as possible into them. Since coaches hardly ever pay travel costs—the car deal or an athletic department airplane or plane ticket gets them most places—or telephone bills or many other expenses, some try to spend their expense accounts on food and entertainment (although coaches can also tap into the athletic department's budget line for the latter) and on personal incidentals.

Ten thousand dollars or more a year is nice walking-around money. Nevertheless, some coaches still cheat on their expense accounts: last year, after basketball coach Gary Williams jumped from Ohio State to Maryland, his former employer suddenly discovered "$1,431 in apparent personal telephone calls [that] Williams placed to an investment broker at the university's expense." The circumstances of the Ohio State discovery—the audit coming only after this coach's Motion Play—makes one wonder what schools could turn up if they seriously investigated coaches' expense accounts.

The NCAA approves of all these gifts and expense accounts for coaches, while the association forbids them for athletes. At one time, schools could give their athletes $15 a week "laundry money," but the NCAA ended this practice in the early 1970s. In College Sports Inc., program heads are allowed and encouraged to rake in as much money as they can; the athletes who make the coaches' fame and fortune possible are ordered to stay away from the filthy lucre lest it taint their "amateur" status.

> *"That [scheduling scam] is probably as distasteful as anything in our business. If I lost a game and was benefiting from it financially, I'd find it hard to go in the locker room afterwards and face my guys."*
>
> —Andy Russo, former University of
> Washington basketball coach

In what transcends any perk or deal, some coaches, especially in Division I men's basketball, also receive money for scheduling their teams in various tournaments and games. The scheduling scam begins in one of two ways: the coach contacts or is called by a scheduling broker—a specialist in matching teams for games or tourneys; or the coach deals directly with a tournament director. After the match is made and the guarantees and other money details worked out, the broker or director gives the coach an expensive "gift" (free vacation, etc.) or pays as much as five figures for the coach to give a short speech or do a single clinic. Because of the obvious illegality of the scheduling scam as well as the IRS's interest in it, the payment to the coach is almost always in barter.

The scam usually involves preseason tourneys and games, especially when Faraway Small State visits Bigtime U. for a nice payday. At one point, the scheduling scam became so widespread that in 1987 the NCAA tried to crack down on it and prohibit coaches from receiving money in this way. In addition, the long tax evasion trial of former Memphis State coach Dana Kirk focused attention on the practice. According to many college basketball observers, the scheduling scam continues—except payoffs are less direct than before.

One of the reasons that some coaches object so strenuously to the 1990 proposal by the Presidents' Commission to cut three contests per team in basketball is that preseason games will be the first to go (schools cannot easily reduce their regular conference schedules). With fewer preseason games and tourneys, profits for program heads involved in the scheduling scam will decline. Thus, when these coaches swear that they are determined to reverse the presidents' cuts, they are acting more out of personal greed than a concern for their athletic departments' revenues.

SUMMARY: SOME MODEST PROPOSALS TO CONTROL COACHES

"Coaches—they need the same status as professors, and should be hired according to the same standards of integrity, at comparable salaries. Free them of the win-at-any-cost demands, and their priorities will straighten out quickly."

—Leonard Koppett, in the *New York Times*

MR. KOPPETT's proposal not only implies that the Type A personalities who become coaches can be transformed suddenly into calm and content "Mr. Chipses," but that the historical differences between athletic and academic departments can be bridged.

Other writers have advocated similar solutions to the Out of Control Coach problem, but all of these proposals ignore a key question about big-time college coaches: *How can program heads be given "the same status as professors" when their jobs, because of sports tradition and show business demands, are so different from faculty positions?*

In 1987, the Faculty Senate of Indiana University condemned the "teaching" methods of the school's coaches, especially Bob Knight, when it passed a resolution that said, in part, "Athletes shall not be subjected to physically or verbally abusive, intimidating, coercive, humiliating, or degrading behavior."

Many coaches, however, "teach" in precisely this way. They believe in the long-standing athletic tradition of "chewing out" players, "kicking ass," and similar techniques. If, on the other hand, a faculty member, in a classroom or any other university setting, physically or mentally abused a student, that professor would violate a number of major rules in the faculty handbook, be in very serious trouble, and, if tenured, would have provided grounds for having his or her tenure revoked. University teaching is supposed to be conducted by rational discourse, not by "kicking ass."

What is often seen as a common ground between academic teaching and college coaching—the instruction of young people—is, in fact, two very different and distinct continents. One land mass is labeled

201

"Education" and on it reside university teachers and students; the other is "Sports Entertainment," where college coaches and athletes live.

After the Indiana University Faculty Senate passed its resolution, Bill Mallory, the school's football coach, exploded, "It's totally ridiculous. I don't buy that bit about someone telling us how to run our program. We don't tell them [the faculty] how to run theirs." Mallory was correct: his world of sports entertainment is so different and separate from the faculty's educational and research missions as to have almost no areas of common interest or judgment. Mallory, however, was wrong to ignore the one connection between athletic programs and the universities that house them—the economic lifeline that keeps pumping money out of academic funding to support athletic programs.

If athletic directors and coaches would agree to run truly self-sustaining and financially independent athletic programs, employing paid athletes, not pseudostudents, few faculty members would complain about how coaches conduct their business. Moreover, coaches' incomes could fluctuate according to real market demands and not be a drain on the host schools. This solution, while logical and even viable, has never been suggested by any coach; nor, if proposed by a university, is any program head likely to accept it.

Toxic Waste

RECRUITING WARS & ATHLETIC SCHOLARSHIPS

"Be sure to say that I say that some basketball players are being paid more money to attend college than the professors who teach at the schools they attend."

—Bob Knight, men's basketball coach at Indiana University, in an interview with the *Chicago Tribune*

OVERVIEW: THE NCAA'S DEFINITION OF ATHLETIC SCHOLARSHIPS VS THE IRS'S DEFINITION OF NONCASH PAYMENTS

> *"Principle of Amateurism and Student Participation:* An amateur student-athlete is one who engages in a particular sport for the educational, physical, mental and social benefits derived therefrom and to whom participation in the sport is an avocation."
>
> —Article Three of the NCAA Constitution

ALL OF THE NCAA's rules on recruiting and athletic scholarships use the above principle as their rationale, i.e., college students play sports as an "avocation" and they are "amateurs." In the 1970s, the NCAA, in an effort to shore up its public image and to counter press charges that college athletes were "shamateurs," embraced the term "student-athlete." Currently, no college sports official or publication uses any other phrase; however, neither semantic tricks nor invocations of a long-departed amateur era (if it ever existed) can mask the professionalism of the athletes in College Sports Inc.

An NCAA "student-athlete" receives certain "benefits" in exchange for playing college sports, but athletic programs want to avoid any implication that these benefits constitute pay—this could instantly end their tax-exempt status. The *NCAA Manual* lists the permitted benefits: free tuition and fees, room and board, and course textbooks. Since at most public colleges and universities these items cost an average of $8,000 a year, and at private schools from between $15,000 to $20,000 annually, an athletic scholarship is a valuable commodity.

In addition, nice perks fatten the basic package: free tutoring, free athletic medical insurance, free rehabilitation expenses, free on-campus career counseling as well as advice from nonuniversity professionals. For a regular student, the athlete's freebies would cost thousands of dollars a year. (In 1988, the University of Iowa paid the drug rehabilitation bills for three of its basketball players: $16,522.) The free perks bring the value of the average athletic scholarship to a minimum of $10,000 and, at private schools, $20,000.

No matter what the NCAA calls these total benefits—the current preferred term is "grant-in-aid"—when the financial value and the stipulations are added up, the package looks suspiciously like a payment for services rendered: the athlete, in return for the $10,000 to $20,000 yearly package, fulfills his or her part of the deal by playing sports for the school; an athlete who refuses to play loses the "grant." Moreover, when an athlete's playing eligibility ends, the grant is usually terminated. Certainly the IRS's rules on barter and noncash payments seem to include athletic scholarships within their definition: "If you [the athlete] exchange your property and/or services [playing sports] for the property and/or services of another [an athletic program's grant and perks], you have taxable income." The IRS's rules on "educational assistance" also seem to apply: the government tells taxpayers, in this case college athletes, "You generally must include in income, as wages, any amount your employer [the athletic program] paid for educational expenses for you."

In a debate on national TV last year about whether student-athletes should be paid salaries, North Carolina State's Jim Valvano, a man who knows about making money, argued that student-athletes *"already are paid,* through scholarships worth up to $60,000 at private schools, plus [Pell] grants of up to $1,400 a year" (emphasis added).

Ironically, the NCAA itself endorses the concept of athletic scholarships and perks as noncash payments when it lists all the "extra benefits" forbidden to college athletes. The *NCAA Manual* states that "the following practices shall *constitute 'pay'* for participation in intercollegiate athletics and are expressly prohibited" (emphasis added): the first is extra "financial aid" for tuition, room and board, and books. Economists, and particularly the IRS, could argue that *any* "financial aid" in return for playing sports "constitutes pay" and that an arbitrary line—the NCAA's definition of "extra benefits" constantly changes— cannot be drawn between "pay" and "nonpay."

The *Manual* lists other forms of forbidden payments, including "complimentary admissions [to a sports event] in excess of four per student-athlete per contest." Why does the fifth "admission" become "pay," whereas the first four are proof of a student-athlete's amateur standing? When the IRS is clearer and more sensible on the question of athletic scholarships and perks as noncash payments than is the NCAA, the association is in serious trouble.

CHAPTER 25

The NCAA's Player Contracts & Its Agreements with Professional Sports

"If more people were aware that this [an athletic scholarship] is only a one-year renewal agreement based almost exclusively on athletic ability, more people would start to ask, 'How does this differ from an employer-employee relationship?'"

—Allen Sack, professor of sociology at the
University of New Haven and a former
Notre Dame football player

BURIED DEEP within the *NCAA Manual*—Section 4, Part (C), Subheading 2, Clause (F)—is a key item in the athletic scholarship agreement: "The renewal of a scholarship or grant-in-aid award shall be made on or before July 1 prior to the academic year it is to be effective. The institution promptly shall notify each student-athlete . . . whether the grant has been renewed or not renewed."

Behind this one-year-renewable rule lies an important part of the NCAA's history and its real attitude toward college athletes. Until 1973, athletic scholarships were awarded for four-year terms. Then the NCAA changed to one-year renewables because, according to its propaganda, "Some athletes . . . would compete briefly on a team, quit, and then demand that their scholarship be left intact." The NCAA never offered any statistics on this phenomenon and common sense contradicts it: from childhood, elite athletes are so programmed to play college sports and to try for subsequent pro careers that it defies credibility to suggest that a significant number were grabbing their athletic scholarships, dropping out of sports, and going full-time into academics.

207

The more probable reason behind the NCAA's change was the desire by coaches to make their practice of "running off" players simpler. With four-year athletic scholarships, coaches had to use a time-consuming and brutal system of "shit drills" to pressure unwanted players to quit school and turn in their scholarships. Darrell Royal, the famous head football coach at the University of Texas, was a master at running off: between 1961 and 1964, he awarded 207 four-year athletic scholarships yet stayed within the NCAA limit of 100 grants per team. One-year renewables accomplish the same goal without the messiness of shit drills.

The NCAA claims that the days of running off players are long over. Nevertheless, through most of the 1980s, major football programs recruited an average of 30 athletic scholarship players for their freshman class, whereas the NCAA allowed only a total of 95 football grants per school in any one year. Simple math shows the high attrition rate: over a four-year period at least 25 players, usually more, lost their grants and, in most cases, dropped out of school.

In addition, when an athlete completes four years of playing eligibility, the scholarship stops—whether the athlete is about to graduate or not (most football and men's basketball players are at least two or three semesters from their degrees). Some conferences and universities try to give nonplaying grants until the athlete graduates or leaves school, but the NCAA does not mandate this. As a result, large numbers of athletes lose their grants-in-aid as soon as their playing eligibility is over.

Thus athletes on grants are contractual employees of an athletic program. They sell their talents as sports entertainers in exchange for athletic scholarships. They cannot be compared to regular students because the latter are consumers, not sellers. Athletes are like staff members whom the university hires on the basis of their skills to do particular jobs.

Because program heads recruit and directly offer athletic scholarships to athletes, the result, as in any job recruitment, is that the hiring party—the coach—becomes the employee's—the player's—boss. Not surprisingly, many program heads feel that they can "fire" an athlete for unsatisfactory athletic performance and they do so by "yanking" his or her grant. College athletes work under a particularly unfair system because they are asked to make a four-year commitment to a program in return for one-year renewable contracts.

Since the 1973 NCAA move to one-year scholarships, many coaches in various sports have terminated grants to players or used the threat of "firing" to induce better athletic performances. Incidents occur as frequently in small as in major athletic programs. At the University of North Dakota, the men's basketball coach, after suffering his first losing season in many years, canceled the basketball scholarships of five of his players. Last year at Prairie View A. & M., a Division I-AA school, the football coach was accused of dispersing financial aid on a monthly, not yearly, basis and using it "as an incentive to boost athletic performance." In addition, some of his players said that the coach withheld their course textbooks until after the last football game and two weeks before final exams. When he gave out the books, he reportedly told the players, "All right, y'all, now you can go work on your academics."

The Prairie View A. & M. coach was exceptional in his apparent disregard of academics. More commonly, because coaches insist that their "student-athletes" focus most of their time and energies on their sports, they place their players in the school's "hideaway curriculum" and have them major in eligibility. Coaches know that an athlete taking academically serious courses could fail them, lose NCAA eligibility, and become a financial and athletic liability to a coach-employer.

Thus the leverage that one-year renewables give program heads over their players allows coaches to demand obedience not only on the field or in the gym but also in the classroom. Some program heads use this power benevolently; most employ it self-interestedly.

> *"Some of the [NCAA] members feel that if you're really going to call these people student-athletes, that the continuation of their financial-aid awards ought to be independent of their athletic performance."*
>
> —Stephen R. Morgan, NCAA director of
> legislative services at the time of the
> comment

In 1983, a number of schools tried to persuade the NCAA to reintroduce four-year athletic scholarships. Because the association is so tightly controlled by coaches and ADs, this move never made it to midfield, but the debate underlined the main issues. Those members calling for four-year scholarships invoked mainly pragmatic, not idealistic, reasons: a number of seriously injured college athletes had sued their schools for workmen's compensation and lower courts had found in favor of the athletes; legal experts advised the NCAA that four-year scholarships would not so clearly tie college athletes to athletic performance and an implied employee-employer relationship with their institutions as do one-year renewables. Four-year scholarships would also help to defuse all attempts by college athletes to form unions and to demand workers' rights (a mini movement for this had begun).

The majority of NCAA members, however, showed no inclination then or subsequently to return to four-year scholarships or, on the other hand, to abandon the "student-athlete" fiction. In a perfect illustration of Orwellian doublethink, most program heads and ADs believe in maximizing their employees' efficiency ("Sort out your best players each spring and pay them a year at a time") while simultaneously denying that their employees are really working for them ("They're students and amateurs engaged in an avocation").

> *"The court concludes that the NCAA controls over college football make [the] NCAA a classic cartel."*
>
> —United States District Judge Juan Burciaga

In its 1984 decision against the NCAA's monopoly of the televising of college football games, the Supreme Court agreed with Judge Burciaga's labeling of the association as a "cartel" and, as such, in violation of various antitrust laws.

The Supreme Court and the lower courts were mainly concerned with the NCAA's manipulation of "product"—the games—but another important characteristic of a cartel is its control of labor and wages. In the association's explicit limits on athletic scholarships and perks, the NCAA dictates the remuneration (wages) that schools can give athletes; does not allow athletes any free-market bargaining or free movement; and enforces its rules by policing its members and penalizing offenders.

These cartel rules are clearly intended to benefit the coaches and ADs who run the NCAA. Program heads invest time and money in recruiting their employees—the athletes—and, like all business people, they want to maximize their profit from their workers and benefit from all four years of player eligibility. From the day a coach signs a high school star, that athlete must work for that athletic program or face severe NCAA penalties: *if an athlete signs with one school but then chooses to go to another without the first's permission, the NCAA penalizes the athlete by barring him or her from intercollegiate sports for two years and also by canceling two years—50 percent—of his or her college playing eligibility.* Moreover, even if a coach releases an athlete from a signed letter of intent, the NCAA forces him or her to sit out a year *and also* lose one year of college playing eligibility. Thus the NCAA binds an athlete to an athletic program more closely than a professional sports contract ties a pro player to a major-league club.

Coaches feel especially protective of their star players because they spend so much money and effort to recruit them and also because their stars are their best hope of winning the college sports lottery—bowl games and NCAA tourneys. But, as in any line of work, the stars are the employees with the greatest potential mobility. To help restrict this mobility, the NCAA entered into restraint-of-labor agreements with like-minded organizations—the professional sports leagues and the United States Olympic Committee.

> *"If we have to go to court [to enforce the NFL-NCAA draft agreement], we ought to go to court and take our chances. Maybe we'll hit a judge who for once will decide to do what's right, rather than what's in the law."*
>
> —Tex Schramm, former president of the
> Dallas Cowboys and currently an
> NFL executive

The NCAA and the NFL long ago agreed that a college football player cannot enter the league until he has used up his four years of playing eligibility, or until five years have elapsed since his freshman class entered university. If a college football player wants to earn more money while still an undergraduate than his athletic department provides him, and to take the next logical step in his career—play in the NFL— officially he is not allowed to do so.

The NCAA and the NBA have a somewhat similar pact. The NCAA agreements with Major League Baseball and the National Hockey League are less restrictive, but these agreements still do not allow free labor markets or mobility for college baseball and hockey players. The NCAA has a very complicated arrangement with the United States Olympic Committee concerning Olympic sport athletes who have college eligibility remaining.

The first crack in the NCAA's agreement with pro sports came in basketball in 1971, when an underclassman, Spencer Haywood, successfully sued for admission to the NBA. Subsequently, the league permitted some undergraduates to enter by declaring them "hardship cases"—i.e., in immediate need of income. This fiction eventually wore out and, presently, any undergraduate basketball player can declare himself eligible for the NBA draft at any point in his college career.

Unfortunately for the athlete, the NCAA now waits for him at the NBA draft pass: the association says that if a college athlete declares for the NBA draft, this act immediately abolishes his "amateur" status and, if not chosen in the draft, the player cannot return to college ball. In addition, the NBA enforces its end by severely fining any team that approaches an undergraduate prior to the draft (the Portland Trail Blazers paid the league $250,000 for this offense a few years ago). This NCAA-NBA threat helps to keep undergraduates off the pro basketball labor market.

Coaches and athletic directors justify this restraint by arguing that "undergraduates are not ready physically and mentally for the pros," and that the NCAA-NBA rules are in "the players' best interests." Last year, the *Sporting News* published a study of the pro players who had left school early: the "All-Early Team" included Michael Jordan, Magic Johnson, Karl Malone, and Isiah Thomas. It was obviously in these and many other basketball players' "best interests" to pursue their profession when they felt ready.

Historically, the NCAA's collusion with the NFL has been greater than with the NBA, and the football league has long resisted allowing undergraduates on its draft lists. In the last decade, however, a number of underclassmen have challenged the restrictions that bar them from the NFL. In every recorded case, the NCAA and the NFL pretzeled their agreement to allow the athlete to leave school early. The NCAA and the NFL know that their regulation of the college sports labor market would never stand a serious court challenge, and losing such a lawsuit would eliminate the NCAA's control over *all* college athletes.

The NFL and NCAA refuse to go to court, in part, because of the case of Bob Boris—an undergraduate punter who convinced a federal court in 1984 that "the [now defunct] United States Football League's ban on hiring college underclassmen violated antitrust law." Because of the Boris case, the USFL became less hard-line than the NFL about signing undergraduates. As a result, the National Association of Collegiate Directors of Athletics threatened to deny the league the privileges received by NFL teams—total access to college coaches and players, game films and tapes, and free entrance to practice sessions and games—but the USFL went out of business before athletic programs could impose these sanctions against it. The NFL, however, has never shown much desire to change the draft rules and end its free minor-league system.

Therefore, each year the NFL and NCAA must contort themselves in new ways to allow balky undergraduates to leave college early. In 1987–88, they permitted players who signed with agents, and others who had been expelled from school for academic and disciplinary reasons, to turn pro. According to the NCAA, these players had forfeited their college eligibility and were being punished; but in fact, because these underclassmen wanted to turn pro, the NCAA and NFL rewarded them for their transgressions. *Sports Illustrated* said of this situation: "Football players deserve the same freedom as basketball players, plumbers and sportswriters to enter their profession whenever they wish. By granting that freedom only to scofflaws, the NFL is embarrassing itself."

In 1990, with more undergraduate football players wanting to turn pro—mainly because they feared a future NFL cap on bonuses and salaries for draft choices—the professional league and the NCAA further convoluted the old agreement: more undergrads can now test the pro waters than before; however, NFL commissioner Paul Tagliabue, a lawyer, promised that once the readjusted "policy is set, there is a line we will not go below"—unless an excluded collegian tries to cross the line by taking the NFL and NCAA to court, at which point the pros will lower it. (This will probably occur next year when the new NFL-sponsored international league kicks off and large numbers of American undergraduates want to play in it.)

The NCAA, however, will never agree to give athletes total freedom because of the economic consequences of such a move. When players leave college early, the money that coaches and athletic programs have invested in them stops paying dividends. Instead of your senior quarterback, a Heisman Trophy candidate, drawing huge crowds to your stadium and possibly leading the football program to the pot o' gold, when he jumps to the pros, your team is left with a shaky offense and lots of unsold tickets and canceled TV appearances (this situation occurred in 1989 at Washington State when Timm Rosenbach departed). If large numbers of college athletes played for only two or three years, this would put enormous pressure on the already fragile finances of athletic programs. Money motivates the NCAA's intransigence on the draft issue and its pressure on the NFL and NBA to maintain the current antiathlete agreements.

Baseball has a history and tradition different from those of football and men's basketball. Moreover, as a sport that loses money for most athletic departments, the financial stakes are much lower than in the revenue-producing college sports. Yet, the NCAA has tried to regulate this labor market and Major League Baseball has agreed to some of the association's demands.

Once a year, major-league teams conduct a draft of all high school seniors and college juniors; if a player does not want to sign with the team that drafted him, he can continue to play NCAA baseball on an athletic scholarship (close to 75 percent of all present major-leaguers played NCAA or other college ball). Unlike intercollegiate football and basketball players, going into the MLB draft does not cancel a college baseball player's "amateur" status. In fact, precollege as well as college baseball players can use agents, negotiate with major-league teams, turn down offers, and still play NCAA ball. The reason for this NCAA double standard is, more than likely, that the association cares less about regulating the labor of athletes in nonrevenue sports than in football and men's basketball.

The main effect of this NCAA-MLB arrangement is that it maneuvers American colleges and universities into underwriting minor-league training for the majority of professional baseball players. Chris Roberts, a second-round 1989 June draft choice, explained how the system works and why he accepted an athletic scholarship from Florida State rather than a contract with the Philadelphia Phillies: "I considered the time it would take in the minors to get to the level of, let's say, AA ball. I figure it's a choice between three years on buses, going to small towns, versus three years in college, playing almost every day," and, after that, entering the MLB draft again and being ready for AAA or major-league baseball.

Hockey, with yet another tradition and history, is least in agreement with the NCAA. Starting at the age of eighteen, a hockey player can be drafted by a National Hockey League team regardless of where that player is (Canadian junior leagues, European pro leagues, or American colleges), and once he's drafted, the NHL team retains his rights in future years. As NCAA hockey grows in number of teams, imported players from Canada, and quality of play, NHL clubs are increasingly interested in its products (20 percent of all present NHL players participated in the American college game), and every year, NHL teams draft NCAA players without regard to their college class.

This situation has long upset college hockey officials and coaches. They have lobbied for the NCAA to work out an NFL-like agreement with the NHL, but the latter group, lead by lawyer John Ziegler, has side-stepped the controversy, always arguing that the antitrust violations inherent in any NCAA-NHL labor agreement would cause problems, not solve them. NHL teams, however, taking their cue from Major League Baseball, have tended in recent years to draft undergraduates but to encourage them to obtain as much playing experience—at no cost to the NHL—with their college clubs as possible. Last year, the rights to a player still with Ferris State College in Michigan were even traded by one NHL team to another. Again, College Sports Inc., in one of its most expensive nonrevenue activities, provides a free minor league for a wealthy pro organization. And ironically, Canadian universities, because they do not offer "full ride" athletic scholarships, supply almost no players to the NHL!

As Olympic sports become increasingly professional, many NCAA athletes who compete on their nations' Olympic teams would—if NCAA rules were seriously enforced—lose their amateur status and college playing eligibility. But just as the association employs a double standard in so many other areas, it applies an extra twist to the Olympic situation.

For the fall 1988 Olympics in Seoul, the NCAA allowed "student-athletes" to drop out of school for the semester, to compete with openly professional athletes (a clear violation of NCAA rules), and to keep their NCAA eligibility for the fall and future semesters. In addition, for the Olympians, the association waived one of its basic academic rules—that college athletes take at least twelve hours of classes every semester to remain eligible. The St. Louis University faculty representative to the NCAA said that "the NCAA had long held to the belief that a college athlete must make education his top priority. The [Olympic] waiver violates everything we've been fighting for for years."

The NCAA looks ridiculous in this situation because it has long enforced its rules on amateurism in the most rigorous and picayune manner. Those schools penalized by the NCAA for giving a T-shirt to a recruit must wonder about the double standard for Olympic sport athletes.

The point of being a cartel, however, is that it allows its members to make up any rules that they like. A cartel does not guide itself by outside laws or ethics—only by self-interest. Thus, when it is in the self-interest of a majority of the coaches and ADs to declare college football or basketball players ineligible for participating on teams with paid professionals, the association will quickly enforce this rule and issue offenders the "Athlete's Death Penalty" (ending their college eligibility). However, when the NCAA's self-interest is minimal, it will not enforce the very same rule: a number of college soccer players were recently on the U.S. national team—a squad mainly composed of longtime pro players being paid for their national team stint—and the NCAA allowed the college athletes to play with the pros and also in intercollegiate games.

Being a cartel is like a child's fondest dream: make up the rules as you go along and violate them at will. The word *hypocrisy* is inadequate to describe the NCAA's rules on athletic scholarships and its enforcement of those rules.

CHAPTER 26

The NCAA's College Entrance Requirements: Trying to Put the "Student" in "Student-Athlete"

"A University of North Carolina Board of Governors committee Thursday endorsed tougher academic standards for college athletes after a study showed substantial numbers of athletes are being admitted with minimal academic skills. . . .

" 'If you could walk and chew ice, you were eligible to play basketball and football. That's where we've got to,' said committee chairman Samuel Poole."

—Item in the *Charlotte Observer*

BEFORE 1986, the only NCAA rule on an athlete's college admission and eligibility for an athletic scholarship was a C or 2.0 (out of 4.0) overall average in high school. Depending upon the player's secondary education, the C average could be meaningful or not. Since, as former major-league pitcher Jim Bouton says, "Your outstanding jock has been on scholarship since the third grade," and has received special treatment from teachers and classmates along the way, most often the athlete's C average was zero proof of his or her academic qualifications or aptitude for higher education.

In 1983, the academic counselor in charge of Iowa State's athletic department tutoring program said that 10 percent of his school's incoming football and men's basketball players were "functionally illiterate"—which he defined as reading below fourth-grade level—and that 95 percent read below tenth-grade level. Moreover, he claimed that the same situation existed in "many other major college athletic programs" and that "many universities don't test the athletes' [reading levels] because they don't want to know how illiterate some of their athletes are."

Because of the widespread "functional illiteracy" of athletes and many well-publicized cases of it, in the early 1980s the presidents of a number of major universities set out to convince the NCAA to institute tougher academic admission and grant rules for athletes. The outcome—after long debate within the association and the opposition of many coaches and ADs—was Proposal 48, passed in 1983, and first in effect in 1986. (To pass it, more presidents cast votes for their schools—or explicitly directed their ADs on how to vote—than at any previous NCAA convention.)

This new policy kept the C-or-2.0 rule but applied it to eleven "core curriculum" courses in high school, including three English and two math (previously, athletes raised their overall average by avoiding core curriculum courses and taking "blow-off" classes). In addition, Proposal 48 mandated that an athlete achieve a 700 combined score on the SAT (Scholastic Aptitude Test) verbal and math exams or a 15 on the ACT (American College Testing) exams. The SAT/ACT requirement immediately caused controversy, even though, as the president of the University of Southern California pointed out, 700 on the SAT is "an embarrassingly low score," well below the admission requirement for most college freshmen.

To put the NCAA's SAT rule in perspective, each SAT aptitude exam is scored on a 200-to-800 point range, and a student receives 200—or 400 points total on the two parts—for signing the exam sheets and answering one question. To score a combined total of 700 out of a possible 1600, a student must correctly answer 13 out of 60 math questions and 24 out of 85 verbal ones—*an average of 25 percent.* (Similar statistics apply to the ACT exam.) To receive a minimum passing grade on most exams in college courses, and on serious high school tests, a student must answer *at least 50 percent* of the questions correctly.

Throughout the early debate on the 700 SAT requirement, stories of athletes with amazingly low SAT scores surfaced. At Florida State University, two football players had earned athletic scholarships even though their SAT scores were below 450 (the median SAT scores for incoming freshmen at FSU was 1020). At Tulane University, one of the finest academic institutions in the South, John "Hot Rod" Williams (later involved in the basketball team's drugs and gambling scandal) was admitted with a 470 SAT when the median score for regular Tulane freshmen was 1121.

As newspapers throughout the country dug into this story, athletes' low SAT scores and questionable academic qualifications for college admission turned out to be less the exception than the rule. The *St. Petersburg Times* discovered that "while 96 percent of all students at the University of Florida [at Gainesville] met minimum admission standards, a significant proportion of athletes failed to meet such standards." In a ten-year period, 1976–85, more than half of the Gator football team was below the minimum standard, and that percentage was as high as 80 percent in 1985.

For many years, colleges and universities have admitted and given scholarships to academically unqualified athletes by using the rules on "special admits" (all schools accept a small percentage of applicants who do not meet the regular admission standards; often these are students, outstanding in one area like math but weak in other subjects, who have the potential to do well in university). Athletic departments long ago discovered the "special admit" loophole in the admission regulations and, increasingly, have shoved their recruits through it. At some schools, the athletic department negotiates with the admissions office over the entrance of athletes; at others, especially the big "jock factories," the athletic department decides whether to admit an athlete—based on the recruit's athletic, not academic, potential—and then has the admissions office rubber-stamp the decision. Some program heads even have "special admit" procedures for their recruits written into their contracts.

Last year, the football coach at Tennessee said that Pat Dye, the head coach at Auburn, must have a "good relationship with his registrar" because of the many Auburn recruits who had failed to make 700 on their SATs (or 15 on ACTs) but had been admitted to the school. Jim Valvano got high school basketball star Chris Washburn into North Carolina State in 1984 even though Washburn's verbal SAT was 200 and his math 270 (the median score for incoming students at this school was 1030). After Washburn dropped out of N.C. State (he was arrested for stealing various items from the dorms), the president of the university said, "We admitted Mr. Washburn because we honestly thought and believed he could do the work here." Court records revealed that Washburn had an I.Q. of 86.

Washburn was not a sole aberration in the North Carolina university system. The board of governors for the state's colleges and universities discovered that in the mid-1980s, at Washburn's school, "40% of the athletes" had SAT scores under 700, and that the same percentage prevailed at the University of North Carolina at Chapel Hill, supposedly one of the better universities in the country. At East Carolina University, 35 percent of athletic scholarship holders had scored under 600 on their SATs.

As these stories emerged, proponents of NCAA Proposal 48 argued that its tougher admission requirements would put the "student" back into the association's "student-athlete" label. Opponents attacked Prop 48's provisions, especially the 700 SAT requirement. The head of the College Board Corporation, which owns and administers the SATs, offered his perspective: "The NCAA is using the test scores in much the same way that a drunk uses a lamppost: more for support than illumination."

The most serious criticism of Proposal 48 came from black educators who argued that since many more black athletes score below 700 on the SATs than do whites, this requirement would banish great numbers of blacks from college sports. The president of Grambling State University predicted that it would lead to a kind of "apartheid," and he asked whether the NCAA was "trying to create a white organization."

Black leaders also charged that the SAT verbal exam is culturally biased against poor blacks and whites because its questions relate most directly to upper-middle-class white life. Examples of some of the exam's questions support this criticism and even the College Board Corporation criticized the NCAA for basing so much of an athlete's admission on one test.

To confuse the debate, and possibly to embarrass the presidents supporting Proposal 48, the NCAA published a study showing "that if athletes entering college in 1977 had been subjected to the [Proposal 48] requirements, a large number of those who have now graduated, particularly black students, would not have been eligible to participate in college athletics as freshmen" and possibly would not have gone to college at all. This finding did not deter the NCAA from implementing Proposal 48 but it did provide support for those educators, particularly at black schools, who argue that they can take students from deprived economic and academic backgrounds and educate them. For these opponents of Prop 48, admission requirements are less predictive of a

student's college success than is a school's commitment to undergraduate education. Temple University men's basketball coach John Chaney
says, "Don't discard a youngster because he doesn't have good grades
or test scores. Educate him."

> *"CBS's Billy Packer wonders how most college basketball
> freshmen declared ineligible under Proposal 48 become
> eligible as sophomores.*
>   *" 'I can't comprehend that marginal students all of a
> sudden become bona fide students in one year. That tells
> you that either the college boards are totally inaccurate
> barometers, or the schools have found a quick way to turn
> a marginal student into a good one, or to make a guy
> eligible is no problem.' "*
>
> —Item in *USA Today*

Like many NCAA rules, Proposal 48 initially caught defenses off
guard. Although coaches and athletic directors had three years to
prepare for it, many did not comprehend its reality until it took effect in
1986. The first results that autumn indicated that in Division I-A
football programs, 206 incoming athletes had failed to meet Proposal
48's academic standards and that 175 of them (85 percent) were black.
Similar statistics surfaced for the first group of men's basketball recruits
under Proposal 48, and lower numbers prevailed in nonrevenue sports.

Athletes in the first class of Prop 48 failures had a number of options.
If they had achieved an overall high school average of C or 2.0 but did
not maintain that average in their core curriculum and were below the
SAT/ACT requirement, they could become "partial qualifiers"—
eligible for an immediate athletic scholarship but ineligible to practice
or play their sport at their school until they passed twenty-four units
their freshman year. If they did not like Option A—it also included
losing a year of NCAA playing eligibility—they could take Option B:
pay their own way for their freshman year, make grades, then accept an
athletic scholarship and proceed with a four-year college sports career.
Obviously, many lower-income athletes could not afford Option B;
however, it presented a loophole for crooked coaches—arrange for the
recruit's parent(s) to acquire the money to pay for the athlete's first year.

If neither Option A nor B appealed or was feasible for a prospective
college athlete, he or she had a number of other options. C: Accept an

athletic scholarship from a Division II school (they kept the old 2.0 overall high school grade average requirement until 1988, when embarrassment about becoming a "dumping ground for dumb jocks" caused them to go to a modified Prop 48 rule). D: Take an athletic scholarship from an NAIA school (even embarrassment about accepting really dumb jocks has caused only minor eligibility rule changes in the NAIA). Or E: Accept a junior college athletic scholarship and later transfer, losing two years of NCAA eligibility, to a Division I school (the jucos actually lowered their admission requirements when Prop 48 began).

Many top athletes among the "partial qualifiers" (2.0 overall high school grade average) took the A train to college—accepted athletic scholarships but sat out their freshman year and lost a year of eligibility. In a 1987 survey of NCAA Division I schools, respondents reported 599 partial qualifiers on campus and 85 nonqualifiers (not even an overall C average in high school). Athletic departments were willing to accommodate partial qualifiers with NCAA-approved financial assistance; how they accommodated the reported, and the apparently larger number of unreported, nonqualifiers was not in the survey.

Jerry Tarkanian, who has always recruited what he euphemistically calls "academically high-risk athletes," enjoyed the spectacle of some famous schools "who wanted you to believe they only recruit top students, . . . they have all honor students" among their athletes, suddenly having to reveal their enrollment of academically marginal partial and nonqualifiers.

This phenomenon became known as "stockpiling": many wealthy athletic departments gave full aid to partial qualifiers and reportedly to nonqualifiers as well; the poorer programs, especially at black schools, could not begin to assume the added financial expense of having athletes on scholarship but ineligible to practice or play. Harry Edwards railed at "the ludicrous position of black schools not only being unable to recruit Blue Chip black athletes" (since desegregation, "white schools have gotten the cream of the black athletic crop"), but with Prop 48, not being able to afford some second-tier black players.

In 1988, the second year of Prop 48, the NCAA reported that the number of partial and nonqualifiers on campus had dropped to 600— but the association admitted that only two-thirds of Division I schools had answered its survey. Nevertheless the NCAA and some of its members were self-congratulatory about the positive effects of Prop 48.

One pro-NCAA newspaper article headlined, GETTING WISE: DUNCE CAPS DISAPPEARING IN YEAR 2 OF PROPOSITION 48. The football recruiting coordinator at Pitt explained, "Now that everybody realizes that Prop 48 is here to stay, people are taking the whole situation much more seriously"; coaches were only going after athletes academically prepared for college. (Apparently the men's basketball coaches at Pitt did not get the message: all five of their 1989–90 recruits failed to meet Prop 48 requirements.)

Other recruiting coordinators, however, were using different tactics to counter Prop 48. Increasingly, cheating on the SAT and ACT exams occurred. Because neither testing service has a strong security system, and the exams are often given in high school gymnasiums with high school coaches serving as monitors, cheating is not difficult. The most common ploy is to have another student take the test for the high school athlete. This switcheroo is facilitated by the fact that neither testing service insists that a student take the exam in his or her own high school. Recruiting coordinators know the best places to pull a switch—usually where an agreeable and/or paid-off high school coach is in charge—and they send recruits to the special destination. (Even though SAT and ACT procedures require that students show a photo ID card, fake IDs are easily obtainable.)

Eric Manual, former star guard at the University of Kentucky, scored no higher than the equivalent of ACT 14 on two tests he took in his hometown of Macon, Georgia. But he got a 23 on the ACT that "he" took at Lexington's Lafayette High School (in SAT terms, his scores went from 670 to 1030). Danny Woodson, University of Alabama quarterback, had an even greater jump in his ACT scores: from two consecutive 10s to a 23 (in SAT terms, from 510 to 1030). After investigating the Manual and Woodson cases, the ACT administrators invalidated the test results.

Because of embarrassments like these, cheating coaches now send surrogate test-takers to the exam on the last possible date—and then to take it only once. This avoids skyrocketing scores that attract both the testing services' and the NCAA's attention, and it also allows the surrogate to take the exam previously—in his or her own name—for practice.

When prep basketball stars Terry Mills and Rumeal Robinson became Prop 48 casualties, Mills's high school counselor and coach exclaimed, "Cheating is epidemic . . . kids have someone else take the test for them. I know that. I'd give the rest of my life's salary if some of those kids [who passed] took the test again and got the same score."

Mills and Robinson went to the University of Michigan and sat out as freshmen while they gained the necessary grades in their courses at Ann Arbor to become eligible for NCAA play as sophomores. Critics have questioned the academic seriousness of some of the courses that the Michigan athletic department, as well as many others, arrange for their athletes. The president of Lehigh University charges that "some coaches are bringing in large numbers of partial qualifiers, essentially parking them for a year in an environment in which the coaches believe they can make sure the kid is eligible." Sure enough, "The next year, he's eligible and the coach has circumvented the [academic] rules."

Partly in response to the cheating in this aspect of Proposal 48, the NCAA, at its 1989 convention, instituted Proposal 42—its latest attempt to prove the academic seriousness of intercollegiate athletics.

> *"Not only will it [Proposal 42] lead to more cheating on the SAT and ACT scores, but you'll have cheating by boosters who will pay for the [partial qualifier's] first year of school."*
>
> —Paul Evans, men's basketball coach at the University of Pittsburgh

The only difference between Prop 48 and its amended form, Prop 42, is the new stipulation that partial qualifiers can no longer receive an athletic scholarship for their freshman year, and that if they want to attend college and qualify for NCAA eligibility on campus, they have to pay their own way. NCAA officials and delegates in favor of Prop 42, like the president of the University of South Alabama, claim that it goes further than Prop 48 in upholding "standards of education." Opponents, like Georgetown's John Thompson, charge that the proposal is "racist" and further discriminates against black athletes.

An analysis of the voting pattern on Prop 42 suggests less than lofty motivations behind the "Yes" and "No" votes of many NCAA members. The majority of votes in favor of Prop 42 came from medium-size to small athletic programs that were probably less interested in academic standards than in preventing the stockpiling by the major powers that has occurred under Prop 48. Starting with Akron and proceeding alphabetically through such schools as Campbell, Canisius, Centenary,

Central Connecticut, Central Florida, and Central Michigan, the "Yes" votes accumulated. Entire conferences, such as the Missouri Valley, with schools like Bradley and Indiana State, voted in favor of the proposition because they cannot afford to have ineligible athletes on scholarship and they are tired of watching the fat cats of College Sports Inc. grow even more corpulent at their expense.

There were exceptions to this economically based voting, but even these schools usually acted out of other kinds of self-interest. Prop 42 was originally conceived by the University of Georgia during the Jan Kemp fiasco as a face-saving ploy. Georgia convinced its fellow SEC members—schools also in need of some positive publicity—to push the proposal in the NCAA. Thus, en masse, the SEC voted for the proposal (amid stories that these athletic programs were adept at hiding nonqualifiers on campus or farming them out to jucos).

Some opponents of Proposal 42 did vote against their economic self-interest: black colleges voted "No," as did Ivy League schools like Harvard and Columbia as a show of support for their black colleagues. The Big Ten, however, was typical of the self-interested opposition. Although its institutions have long bragged about their high educational standards for athletes, in reality, schools like Michigan and Illinois have been stockpiling Prop 48 partial qualifiers and want to continue the practice. Every Big Ten school except one voted "No." Northwestern University, with truly high admission requirements for athletes, a smaller athletic department budget, and a large hope that Prop 42 will bring the conference competition down to its level, voted "Yes."

Prop 42 is scheduled to go into effect in the summer of 1990; at the most recent NCAA convention, members amended it slightly to allow Prop 42 partial qualifiers "to receive normal institutional aid on a need basis." Some black coaches protested because they believe that this school aid will be in the form of loans that poor athletes will be unable to finance (as opposed to athletic scholarships that recipients do not have to pay back). However, the coach of one of the best high school basketball teams in Illinois pointed out, "Don't you think that somehow or other colleges will find a way [to totally fund these athletes], whatever they want to call it, whether it's a scholarship or [a forgiven] loan or grant, et cetera? They'll find ways to take care of kids if they want them in [their] school."

One certain effect of the 1990 amendment is that it makes it easier for universities to divert limited financial aid money to athletes and away from regular students. Even NCAA executive director Dick Schultz admits this: he told an interviewer that although he hopes schools will not engage in this diversion of financial aid, the decision is totally up to each NCAA member institution.

When Prop 42 comes on-line, athletic departments and their program heads will be ready to circumvent it. Payment schemes will be in place to enable partial qualifiers to spend their first year on campus as if they were on full athletic scholarships, and in spite of the hopes of the Northwesterns and Bradleys for greater athletic parity as a result of Prop 42, the big powers will stockpile athletes, and the lineups of the Top 20 college football and men's basketball polls in the 1990s will contain the usual suspects.

> *"The GRE General Test is a multiple-choice examination designed to measure the verbal, quantitative, and analytical skills you [college students] have developed in the course of your academic career."*
>
> —*How to Prepare for the Graduate Record Exam,* Brownstein, Weiner, Green, and Hilbert

Proponents of Proposals 48 and 42 want to insure that intercollegiate athletes are also legitimate college students. Opponents do not object to this goal, merely to the NCAA's means of achieving it—by qualifying or disqualifying an athlete on the basis of tests considered "culturally biased" *before* the athlete reaches college. Many educators, white as well as black, have long argued that they can provide a student from a "culturally deprived" background with a college education once they have that student on campus.

One simple solution to the present impasse within the NCAA on this issue would be to test athletic scholarship holders, not upon entrance to college, but after four years of university education. The logical exam for this test is the Graduate Record Examination (GRE), the Educational Testing Service's equivalent of the SAT given nationally as a way of judging applicants for graduate school admission. By all accounts, the GRE is less culturally biased than the SAT, and the exam attempts to measure the "verbal, quantitative, and analytical skills" learned in university; for example, the main preparation book for the GRE states of the math section that students "are tested not on advanced mathematical theory but on general concepts expected to be part of everyone's academic background."

Thus the GRE should satisfy both the proponents and opponents of Proposals 48 and 42: it provides a valid, nationally based test of an athlete's academic achievements, and it allows "culturally deprived" athletes four years' time to acquire the verbal and math skills to do as well on the test as other college students. (Without these skills they could not pass regular university courses—certainly not four years' worth.)

Undergraduates usually take the GRE during the fall of their fourth year in college. The exam is graded on the same scale as the SAT—200 to 800. The NCAA could require all athletic scholarship holders to take the GRE during the spring of their fourth year (the extra semester to compensate for the amount of time spent on athletics), and to achieve a minimum grade of 700. If an athlete failed to do so, rather than penalize him or her individually as Prop 48 and 42 do, the NCAA could deduct the athletic scholarship from the school's allotted total for a period of four years. If an athlete on scholarship left after his or her freshman or sophomore year, the NCAA could remove the scholarship until that athlete's playing eligibility was over, i.e., four years.

Coaches would search for the loopholes in this plan and try to squeeze athletes through them. The most obvious: have an athlete play four years and then drop out during his senior year without taking the GRE but not costing the school a scholarship. The NCAA could easily plug this hole: penalize a school for each junior and senior who does not take the GRE exam by withholding a scholarship for the amount of time that junior or senior played college sports, i.e., 3 or 4 years.

Another way to cheat would be to have someone else take the exam for an athlete. However, it would be harder to have a surrogate take the GRE than the SAT; it would be especially difficult for a regular student to pretend to be a well-known, well-publicized college football or basketball player. In addition, since GREs are administered by regular university personnel, not high school coaches, surrogate exam taking would be more difficult. The NCAA could also require that athletes take their GRE at their own university and that they show a signed driver's license as proof of identification (the NCAA has much more control over colleges than it does over high schools). Determined cheaters might slip through but not with the ease that they do on the SAT and ACT exams.

The GRE plan is so logical and so clearly answers the demands and objections of both the proponents and opponents of Props 48 and 42 that the NCAA should adopt it tomorrow. But the association won't. *For the NCAA, the plan has one major drawback—it calls the bluff of all NCAA members on the question of whether their athletes are truly receiving a college education.*

Some advocates of tying athletic scholarships to graduation rates are attempting to call the same bluff but are providing too big a loophole for athletic departments: a degree from a school's Division of Hideaway Studies is a worthless document but counts as a graduation statistic. A 700 on the GRE—like the same score on the SAT, not a major achievement—is, at least, validation by an outside testing service that the athlete acquired minimum college-level skills.

The NCAA will never accept the GRE plan or anything similar to it. It would reveal to the world that "student-athletes" have no academic clothes.

CHAPTER 27

How Athletic Departments Recruit Athletes within NCAA Rules or within the Contradictions in the Rules

"Not more than 20 percent of the football players go to college for an education. And that may be a high figure."

—Jim Walden, head football coach at Iowa State University

FOR AMERICAN high school athletes, the road to the pros and the Olympics goes through College Sports Inc. For most of these athletes, the academic quality of the school at which they enroll is far less important than the institution's athletic program, especially that program's connection to professional sports. Formal and informal studies of how athletes choose colleges suggest most prep stars want to play college sports for a coach with a winning record, on a team with a winning tradition, in the hopes of receiving the best preparation for pro or Olympic careers; and that outstanding high school athletes want to "start" as freshmen, and want to receive maximum media exposure during their college careers. They believe that if these ambitions are satisfied, they will be pro draft choices or Olympic team selections and acquire lucrative professional contracts. That very few high school athletes ever achieve their goal is irrelevant to the power of the dream and its role in their choice of a college athletic program. Basketball's Larry Brown explained how coaches use the dream: "Every kid I recruited for college felt they had an opportunity to play in the NBA and I liked them to have those expectations. So they give themselves, their trust, to you from day one, hoping to reach that goal."

All program heads, when recruiting, emphasize the number of their past players who went on to pro or Olympic careers. Their media guides and especially the special brochures sent to recruits contain photos of and sometimes testimonials from their programs' "pro connection." For many years, a standard recruiting ploy was to have a famous pro, like O. J. Simpson on behalf of USC, telephone or meet a prize recruit and describe why the sports program at the pro's old school was perfect preparation for the NFL, NBA, etc. Program heads with long winning records and with many former players now in the pros hold an attraction for recruits that younger coaches at schools with mediocre sports traditions cannot match. Thus, it is easier for successful coaches like Bob Knight and Dean Smith to run clean recruiting campaigns, whereas hungry coaches often use illegal inducements to even things up.

For all recruits who aspire to a pro career, exposure—playing time and media coverage—is an important consideration in the choice of a college sports program. Smart recruits examine the rosters and histories of programs to ascertain whether the coach is sincere in promising, "You'll start as a freshman." Recruits know that coaches who bring in high numbers of juco players send a message that these transfers will probably start before all but the most talented freshmen. Recruits in soccer, hockey, track, and swimming examine rosters for the number of foreign athletes in a program: often coaches in these sports give the prime scholarships to imports and tend to favor them over American youngsters—if only to justify the coaches' costly intercontinental recruiting trips.

Mark Tillmon, now a senior guard for Georgetown's basketball team, was leaning toward Villanova during his last year in high school. The Villanova coaches told him that he was the only guard they were recruiting but, close to the NCAA signing date, Tillmon learned that an outstanding guard from New York had announced for the Philadelphia school. Tillmon quickly lost interest in the Wildcats and signed with Georgetown—in large part because the Hoyas were graduating three guards and he thought that he would play as a freshman. As it is for most outstanding high school athletes, Tillmon's primary criterion in selecting a college was how it would further his sports, not his academic, career.

A recruit who starts for a Big East team like Georgetown takes a large step toward the NBA in part because of the TV exposure that the Big East Conference receives (in fact, the conference was created specifically for TV). A disproportionate number of players from schools like Georgetown, Villanova, Syracuse, and St. John's have won national all-American honors, thanks, in part, to this TV exposure. The TV coverage also helps Big East coaches recruit by reinforcing the apparent importance of their programs.

The role of TV coverage in recruiting, however, has an ironic side effect. Most program heads have so come to believe that TV exposure is the key to recruiting that they persuade their ADs to accept almost any terms from the networks or syndicators to get their teams on the tube. The result is often ludicrous—games beginning at odd hours, including midnight, and low payouts to schools for broadcasting rights. Thus one of the main justifications for bringing top prep athletes to a college or university—to build a profitable sports program—is negated in the very process of recruiting those athletes.

An equally strange financial debit occurs over facilities: athletic departments claim that recruits sign with schools in part because of the sports facilities at the institution. Purdue is building a $6 million indoor football practice field to help in its recruitment pitch. Other Big Ten athletic departments either already have their indoor fields or would like to construct them. The Athletics Arms Race over facilities escalates and millions are spent to impress small numbers of late adolescents. (A more cynical view is that athletic programs, like all bureaucracies, want to grow and have top-of-the-line surroundings, and that they use the recruiting excuse as a cover for their insatiable urge to expand.)

Recruits in nonrevenue sports are also said to demand state-of-the-art facilities. The men's swimming coach at Indiana University went before the school's board of trustees to argue for a new multimillion-dollar indoor pool (the school already has an Olympic-size outdoor pool). The swim coach explained: "It's very difficult for us to recruit with the [indoor] pool we have at the present time. Most of the kids are ambitious and want to swim in the Olympics. We bring kids in, they look at the facility and they aren't going to come here."

In other words, according to this coach's argument, millions of taxpayer and student dollars should be spent on a new pool to please a small number of elite athletes and to provide free training for the USOC—a wealthy organization not unlike the NFL or NBA in its use of the colleges for "minor-league" training. The I.U. swim coach got his new pool.

*"[Special summer athletic camps for high school players]
are a meat market, because the kids are on display. You
have a shopping list and you try to go in and find out
which product will meet your needs."*

—Bob Wade, former University of Maryland
men's basketball coach

Because quality recruits can turn a mediocre team into a winning one, college coaches constantly search the country for prospects. If the estimated recruiting expense per football signee is $20,000 at some schools, the above-the-table cost per signed basketball player is often over $40,000 (men's basketball teams spend about half as much on recruiting as do football programs but sign one-fifth the number of athletes). Even in the nonrevenue sports, especially with increasing intercontinental recruiting, the cost per athlete is higher than schools spend to attract the most academically talented high school graduates.

Coaches will go anywhere and do almost anything to impress an athletically gifted late adolescent. One high school all-American quarterback from El Toro, California, tells what happened when Notre Dame coach Lou Holtz came to visit. Driving the coach to his home, the high school player stopped at a gas station. "I got out and walked to the booth to pay, and when I turned around, coach Holtz, wearing a three-piece suit, was outside washing my windows! I walked over and said, 'You don't have to do that . . . ,' and he just smiled and kept washing, even my side windows." Holtz is a man who commands up to $20,000 for a public speech but he knows that his reputation and his coaching success rest on the college choices of certain seventeen-year-olds.

In their travels, coaches look not only at high school games but also at club, summer camp, and even grade school contests. During the high school season, recruiting coaches travel the scholastic circuit; during the summer, they visit athletic camps where young athletes come to "showcase" their talents. The most important camps for recruiters and prospects are not the ones run by college program heads but the all-star camps, especially Nike's ABCD and Howard Garfinkel's Five-Star Basketball Camps as well as those modeled on them.

The program heads' camps have too many "civilians"—regular kids from whom the coaches make their money—and not enough "players"; hence the level of competition for the "players" is too low. The all-star camps try to collect the best prospects in the region or the country (Nike's boast), and coaches gather to see high school hotshots compete against their peers. The camps weed out the prep athletes with inflated reputations from the kids with real talent.

Bob Wade was not the first program head to call these camps "meat markets," and most coaches go to them looking for players to fill specific team needs. In addition, coaches search for players who are not ready for college ball, and they arrange to "stash" them at prep schools or junior colleges until their college "show time" arrives.

Football summer camps are less important for recruiters than are the basketball camps because football players cannot exhibit their full talents in this situation—they are not in season shape and the camps do not duplicate football game conditions. However, the camps for soccer and other nonrevenue sports like swimming and wrestling are becoming increasingly important to recruiters, as are the women's basketball and other women's sports camps.

Some of the summer camps produce all-star teams that travel and allow the prep players to show their wares; in addition, some high school coaches organize local all-star teams for the same purpose.

Such teams can also work as a recruiting tool for big-time coaches. In Bloomington, Indiana, the company of a major Indiana University supporter generously funds an AAU high school all-star squad that features prep players whom Bob Knight is interested in or has successfully recruited. Last summer, I.U. recruits living in Columbus, Ohio, Peoria, Illinois, and Evansville, Indiana, were on the Bloomington team and at least one of them traveled back and forth to Bloomington on the sponsor's private jet. Although there are layers of buffers between the booster and the recruits, some of Knight's critics question whether the I.U. basketball program's tie-in to the AAU squad is a violation of NCAA rules. Moreover, a key management person for the all-star team is Bob Knight's adult son, Tim.

> *"Some boosters believe that stuff that is being written [in the newsletters about high school players]. Then they tell us [coaches] how screwed up we are because we didn't get this guy, that guy and the other guy."*
>
> —Willard Wells, football recruiting
> coordinator at Purdue University

In addition to the summer camps, the recruiting of high school athletes for College Sports Inc. has spawned other ancillary businesses, including national and regional newsletters devoted to the subject, and national and regional scouting bureaus set up to help schools find players and vice versa.

Some of the newsletters have thousands of subscribers and cost as much as $200 a year. Many newsletters also sell "special packages" of more detailed and/or "inside" information to schools for hundreds of dollars per package. Usually they gain their information by sending questionnaires to prospects and high school coaches, but the more enterprising newsletters also have their own scouts as well as contacts with local media. Sometimes the information is valuable to college coaches; often it is gossip about which school a particular recruit is leaning toward. The editor of one longtime newsletter admits that "we are the Rona Barretts of recruiting . . . speculation is our bread and butter." Nevertheless, every major athletic department feels that it has to subscribe to the newsletters and buy the "special packages."

More expensive are the fees paid to recruiting and scouting bureaus. These businesses operate by compiling large data bases on the current crop of high school prospects in a specific sport and selling their information to recruiting coaches, and sometimes to recruits in need of schools. The bureaus are most interested in football and men's and women's basketball, but in recent years, some have expanded into all of the nonrevenue sports. In addition, a number of bureaus are now chain operations, selling franchises to local entrepreneurs: College Prospects of America (CPOA) has affiliates in twenty-five states and makes much of its money by assembling and handling dossiers for high school players—at $389 each.

The bureaus send long questionnaires to high school athletes, coaches, and scouts and compile information about a prospect's athletic and academic abilities as well as religious, geographic, food, and other preferences. If a basketball program needs a point guard with an assist average of six per game, a three-point potential, and a liking for a warm climate, the bureau will supply a list of prep players in this category— for a hefty price. If a young hockey goalie is searching for a college team in need of help between the pipes, the bureau will provide him with a list of programs in that situation—for a fee. At one time, recruiting bureaus, operating like employment agencies, openly charged athletes who signed with schools from their lists a percentage of the value of their athletic scholarships. The NCAA now forbids this practice—it too clearly defines an athletic scholarship as pay.

*"America is the land of the free and the home of winners,
supporters [of imported athletes] say, why deny these
opportunities to foreign [college] athletes?"*

—Item in the *New York Times*

The haves of college football and basketball succeed annually by casting large recruiting nets in United States waters; the have-nots have to fish in increasingly distant regions. Gerry Faust, head football coach at Akron, signed a player from Hamilton, Ontario, Canada, and another from Devon, England, for his 1989 group. In the mid-1980s, tiny Marist College in Poughkeepsie, New York, tried to break into the basketball big time with a seven-foot-three Dutchman (Rik Smits), a seven-foot Gaudeloupean, and a six-eleven Yugoslavian. With its foreign recruitment, Marist attracted media attention and NCAA penalties (it gave the foreigners free trips and allowed them to make free long-distance calls).

For coaches to make special trips to recruit foreign athletes and to award them scholarships to an American school—not for academic or cultural reasons but solely for athletic ability—gives the lie to the NCAA's term "student-athlete." In 1988, the Seton Hall men's basketball coach signed Andrew Gaze of Melbourne, Australia. The Aussie was twenty-three, had played extensively on his national team, and during the year before coming to Seton Hall had received $25,000 from his professional team in Australia. Gaze arrived at his American college in mid-October for the start of the NCAA basketball season and returned home immediately after his team lost in the 1989 NCAA final to Michigan.

To pretend that foreign athletes like Gaze come to the United States primarily for a college education is a joke. Yet, throughout the Aussie's time in America, the Seton Hall coach and school officials vigorously denied that Gaze was a basketball-playing "hired gun" and insisted that he was a student (for his uncompleted spring semester, he was registered in courses in ethics, first-aid, youth activities, and creative movement).

To aid their entrance into American college sports, the NCAA exempts foreign athletes from the core curriculum and 2.0 GPA parts of the Proposal 48 requirements and allows them to compete if they have achieved what the association calls a "minimal academic record" in their home and regional school districts. Because recruiting coaches are well aware of this loophole in Proposal 48, they now seek increasing numbers of foreign athletes.

Some college coaches, especially in track, soccer, and hockey, have long recruited foreign athletes who come from very different sports systems and often are professionals by the time they enter an American university. In addition to their professionalism, their participation in intercollegiate athletics raises questions about the fairness of American youngsters having to compete against older foreigners, often veterans of international and Olympic contests.

The situation in soccer illustrates the problem: to play this sport seriously, most talented European, Latin American, and African youngsters join the juvenile squads of professional clubs and work up the clubs' youth team ladders, often receiving pay and/or other remunerations as they climb. By the age of nineteen or twenty, when they enroll at American colleges, foreign soccer players frequently have achieved the reserve team level, the second-to-the-top tier, and semi- to full professional status in their home countries. In addition, some have played on international youth teams. Lynn Berling-Manual, editor-in-chief of *Soccer America,* says, "It makes no sense that the NCAA has never applied its most basic definition of professionalism—having received money for playing a sport—to soccer recruits with pro backgrounds. The only reason that American coaches bring them here is to win in a hurry or to keep winning. The recruiting of foreign players has long been and continues to be a huge problem in American college soccer."

American program heads not only import athletes but sometimes take advantage of their foreignness. A coach will promise a full athletic scholarship to an import and then, when the player does not perform up to expectations, will renege, leaving the foreigner with no money thousands of miles from home. In addition, a coach will discourage an import who comes to America for a real college education from majoring in anything except NCAA eligibility.

College track has a history of problems because of foreign athletes. For much of the last two decades, the University of Texas at El Paso dominated NCAA indoor and outdoor track (UTEP won thirteen NCAA national championships) with its large contingent of African runners, and many financial and academic difficulties ensued. (A rival coach said of UTEP's and other track schools' methods, "We don't go on recruiting trips, we go on safaris.")

The situation at UTEP became a full-scale scandal in the mid-1980s when the university discovered that head track coach Larry Heidebrecht had funneled $62,150 to his star runners. Much of this money was from the "appearance fees" that track meet hosts had given him for sending his best athletes to their events. Heidebrecht eventually resigned from UTEP and left college track (only to appear at the Seoul Olympics as the personal manager of Canadian sprinter Ben Johnson).

As college recruiting becomes more intense, coaches will import increasing numbers of foreign athletes for NCAA competition, and will claim to have the foreigners' "educational interests" at heart. Critics will point to athletes like Andrew Gaze and compare them to the Hessians and other foreign mercenaries who spent time in America, collected their money, and returned home.

> *"Some of them [athletes coming from junior colleges] say they've never seen a teacher."*
>
> —Joe Graves, Utah State University academic
> counselor

Major athletic programs have long used the junior or community colleges as places to "stash" athletes who have used up their high school eligibility but are not ready for four-year colleges and universities. Usually the athletes are unprepared academically—and Prop 48 has given a new definition to "unprepared"—but also some do not measure up athletically for major college competition, and the university recruiter hopes that juco seasoning will bring them to big-time college playing level.

A number of years ago, an Oklahoma State recruiter wrote about how he visited a junior college in Kansas and talked with the football coach. The latter "had a frosh, a good-looking kid that Indiana University *had placed there,* but he [the juco coach] wouldn't give me his name because Indiana University had placed him. An agreement, even though illegal, with another university apparently supersedes alumni loyalty [the juco coach was an Oklahoma State alum]" (original emphasis).

The NCAA has rules on members stashing recruits in junior colleges; Indiana University, like most major schools, both plays within the rules (the juco officially pays the athlete's way) and continues to "place" athletes. In 1987, one of I.U.'s best football prospects, Vaughn Dunbar, an all-state high school tailback from Fort Wayne, failed to make the

Prop 48 requirements and Indiana sent him to Northeastern Oklahoma A. & M. The *Louisville Courier-Journal* headlined the story with IU FARMS DUNBAR OUT TO JUNIOR COLLEGE, and the paper also mentioned the other Hoosier players who had been on the same juco farm club and were now playing for the Big Ten team.

For many years, the NCAA allowed an athlete to spend a year at a junior college and then transfer to a four-year school, losing one year of NCAA eligibility in the process. Then, in part because of Prop 48, the association tightened the rules: athletes can only transfer after two years at and after graduating from a junior college, and they must bring transferable academic credits with them. Moreover, juco transfers now have only two years of NCAA playing eligibility.

The loophole in this requirement is that, while graduation from a juco is considered a sufficient equivalent to fulfilling Prop 48 requirements, there are junior colleges and then there are "joke colleges." Horror stories about the academic inadequacy of many junior and community colleges are common, and often these tales focus on the special courses into which athletes are funneled.

Lloyd Daniels, one of the best high school basketball players ever to come out of New York City, had a second-grade reading ability when, in 1986, the University of Nevada at Las Vegas arranged for him to enroll at Mount San Antonio Junior College in California. His juco basketball coach admitted that he put Daniels "in Reading 67. It's not even remedial reading. It's just *trying* to read." Nevertheless, Daniels made the dean's list at Mount San Antonio by taking such courses as Team Sports—Basketball and receiving academic credit for playing on the basketball team. (Daniels never made it to college ball—he kept crashing new cars loaned to him by UNLV boosters and he was arrested for buying cocaine from an undercover police agent.)

Jucos have long awarded athletic scholarships with minimal or no academic strings attached. In 1986, the National Junior College Athletic Association actually lowered the academic requirements for playing eligibility. Juco athletes could participate for one year if they were enrolled for twelve course units a semester—*enrolled,* no grade point average was necessary. To play a second year, athletes had to have a 1.75 overall average out of 4.0 in courses of their choosing (no core curriculum necessary). In addition, part-time students were allowed to play for at least one year. The jucos lowered their requirements in part as a response to the NAIA's minimal requirements and the juco coaches' protests that they were losing athletes to the competing association.

But even the brazen can be embarrassed. Many junior college presidents were upset by the negative publicity that the lowered standards generated, and, in 1988, a majority voted to tighten the rules a bit. Juco athletes now need a 1.75 to play their second semester—football players still have a first-season free ride—and they need to pass twenty-four units with a 2.0 (C) average to play a second year.

For the 1989 football season, Vaughn Dunbar, along with two of his Northeastern Oklahoma A. & M. Junior College teammates, enrolled at Indiana University. Whether any of them could score 700 on the SAT exams will never be known. However, the Indiana University athletic department vouched for their football skills and awarded them full athletic scholarships. The NCAA believes that their two years of juco education validates their academic legitimacy as university "student-athletes." Their ability to play big-time college football will be tested in various stadiums; their academic ability, depending upon the courses that their academic counselors place them in, may never be tried.

> *"That year [which a student-athlete who transfers must sit out] gives the student a chance to become part of the student body. That's necessary if the teams are to be truly representative of their student bodies, and therefore of their institutions."*
>
> —Stephen R. Morgan, NCAA director of
> legislative services at the time of the
> comment

The NCAA has never been overly clear about its rules on athletes transferring schools. The problem is the disjuncture between its ideology—athletes are students and must belong to "their student bodies"—and the reality—transfer rules are part of the NCAA's control over athletes and were written to accommodate program heads' fears about the free movement of their employees. Many coaches openly admit that if there were no transfer rules or accompanying penalties, "raiding" of other programs would go on constantly. As it is, a certain amount of low-level raiding does occur and each year a small percentage of football and basketball players, dissatisfied with one athletic program and courted by another, transfer, sit out a season, and then play for their new school.

The Southern Methodist "Death Penalty" case illustrates part of the NCAA's doublethink on the transfer issue. When, in 1986, the NCAA banned SMU from football for a year, the association also ruled that all Mustang players on scholarship could transfer to other schools without losing any eligibility and could play immediately. If "student-athletes" need a year to adjust to their new school and to become part of the "student body," then why were the football players at SMU—and athletes in other programs placed on similar NCAA probation as well as athletes at schools that discontinue teams—allowed to transfer and play immediately?

After the NCAA's ruling on SMU, hundreds of Division I football recruiters, from institutions as diverse as Texas A. & M., UCLA, and Columbia, descended upon the Dallas campus and began offering financial packages to the suddenly free SMU players. Because the NCAA had put the SMU football program temporarily out of business, the recruiters were not conducting "raids" and they proceeded with NCAA approval.

The final NCAA hypocrisy on the transfer issue is codified in the *NCAA Manual.* Buried deep in the section on "transfer provisions" is a clause stating that the rules do *not* apply to an athlete who "is a participant in a sport other than basketball, football, or men's ice hockey." In other words, all soccer players, swimmers, wrestlers, track-and-field athletes, etc., can change schools and compete the next season. The reason for this massive exception—and contradiction to the NCAA's academic justification of its transfer rule—is intra-association power politics. Most coaches in the minor sports want the same control over their athletes that the program heads in the revenue producers possess but, except for hockey coaches, they do not have enough clout within the NCAA to convince the association to extend its transfer rules to their sports.

> *"There are no reliable differences in the average number of hours per week freshman redshirts (i.e., freshmen who only practice with the varsity) spend in their sports as compared to freshman student-athletes who compete [in intercollegiate athletics]."*
>
> —*Studies of Intercollegiate Athletics,* done for the NCAA by the American Institutes for Research

One of the standard justifications for a transfer sitting out a year is that it allows him or her time to adjust to the new school. The same argument is made, with greater force, for not permitting freshmen to play inter-collegiate sports.

If a transferring "student-athlete" who has already adjusted to col-lege life at one school requires a year to feel comfortable at a new institution, freshmen, often away from home and on their own for the first time in their lives, need even more time to adjust to college, especially to difficult academic work. Yet, for almost two decades, athletic departments have chosen to ignore this transition.

For most of its history, the NCAA did not allow freshmen to play intercollegiate sports (except for brief periods during World War II and the Korean War). The reasons varied from the standard academic ones to health considerations—authorities worried that inexperienced fresh-men would get hurt playing against older athletes. Then in the 1968–72 period, counterarguments prevailed: coaches believed that freshman players could improve the quality of their varsity teams and have an immediate effect on won-lost records; athletic departments realized that they could better maximize their investment in their athletes, coaching staffs, and equipment if they eliminated costly frosh teams and put freshmen on the varsity. Freshman eligibility in all NCAA sports began in 1972. Since then, the association has never wavered from this decision, although, on occasion, some college presidents and at least one major conference have tried to begin the repeal process.

For program heads, freshman eligibility is crucial to recruiting. Coaches promise prospects that they will become "starters" as soon as they are on campus, and high school stars, seeing college mainly as a stepping-stone to the pros, require such vows. When national and local media focus on freshman "impact" players, they feed this process.

"Digger" Phelps, the men's basketball coach at Notre Dame and an opponent of freshman eligibility, says that "the reason athletes choose certain schools to attend is simple and shameful. They only want to start as a freshman and score thirty points a game. . . . They're allowing the schools to exploit them athletically, when they really should be exploit-ing the schools academically." On this issue, Phelps is an exception among his colleagues.

Freshman eligibility is not only central to recruiting but, more deeply, it is an essential part of the professionalization of college sports. In football and in soccer, a freshman can practice for an entire month and play as many as three intercollegiate games before entering his first classroom. Thus, before they become university students, these athletes have become full-time employees of College Sports Inc.

The most recent move within the NCAA to end freshman eligibility unfortunately has less to do with the education of "student-athletes" than with allowing the haves of college sports to grow even richer at the expense of the have-nots. The banning of freshmen will provide the haves with an easy way to circumvent or even abolish the academic requirements of Proposals 48 and 42: if recruits continue to score below 700 on their SATs, and if Prop 42 makes it more difficult to stockpile partial and nonqualifiers, the way out of this imbroglio is to declare all freshmen ineligible, admit them to your school regardless of their SAT scores, have them build their grade point averages in your Division of Hideaway Studies, and then suit them up for four years of intercollegiate athletics.

The new opponents of freshman eligibility reveal their true motives when they fail to embrace one of the strongest parts of Props 48 and 42: partial and nonqualifiers *cannot train or practice* with their schools' teams. Increasing numbers of NCAA coaches, including supporters of Props 48 and 42 like Bob Knight, now want to rescind this clause and allow partial and nonqualifiers to train and practice with the varsity. Bo Schembechler was also against freshman eligibility but insisted that first-year college athletes have "the opportunity to practice. . . . If they [the NCAA] don't do that, I'm not in favor of it."

If most coaches have their way, ineligible freshmen will still devote the majority of their time to their sport—often forty to fifty hours a week. As the NCAA's recent multimillion-dollar report on college athletics makes clear, "freshmen are working almost as long in their sports as other student-athletes, whether they are redshirts or players on the roster." Thus, to demand that freshmen spend forty to fifty hours a week on a demanding physical job outside of their course work is to obliterate the serious academic reasons for banning freshmen from college sports.

The athletic powers would clearly benefit from a ban on freshman eligibility because they could bear the expense of large numbers of freshman athletes on campus and at the same time have enough excellent varsity players to keep their teams at maximum strength. However, the multitude of have-not programs would face a new and major expense in maintaining nonplaying freshmen, and their varsity teams would have fewer players, less depth, and lower skill levels. These diminished have-nots would then have the impossible task of generating extra revenue to meet their increased expenses.

If the recent calls for banning freshman eligibility had come from the Missouri Valley Conference instead of the Big Ten, the sincerity and academic seriousness of the proposals would be less in question.

"Eliminate athletic scholarships; rely entirely on need-based aid with athletes treated the same as other students."

—Robert Atwell, president of the American Council on Education

Another popular proposal to solve the problems in college sports—and one that addresses some of the financial questions—is need-based grants. As college tuition costs and the expense of athletic scholarships explode, the idea of giving financial aid only to those athletes who genuinely require it appeals to some educators. Authorities such as the ACE's Robert Atwell also see this solution as a way of diminishing the commercialism of College Sports Inc.: need-based aid discontinues the awarding of grants for athletic ability and treats athletes like all other students.

Intercollegiate athletics has played with this idea before. In the early 1970s a number of college presidents proposed it and, of course, need-based-only grants have long been the rule in NCAA Division III and in the Ivy League. However, the big-time program heads and ADs have always opposed the proposal. For them, the idea triggers their worst nightmares: loss of control over athletes, and their fears of competition from other coaches. (Their opposition also illustrates that the NCAA is not seriously interested in cost cutting—need-based-only grants would instantly save athletic programs millions of dollars a year.)

Program heads worry that if their players were not on athletic scholarships, they would have much less control over them. The now-important threat of "yanking your grant" would become meaningless, and some athletes, particularly the "cannon fodder" and the "reserves," might not accept sports regimens of forty to fifty hours a week, could cause dissension on teams, and might even quit. The phenomenon of the "walk-on" could give way to that of the "walk-off."

An equal threat from the need-based plan is the coaches' fear of themselves—i.e., everyone will cheat more. They worry that if this proposal were adopted, many program heads would try to recruit ineligible athletes with illegal payments (this has occurred in Division

III and even in the Ivy League). Because coaching staffs are so adept at under-the-table payments now, extending the practice to those athletes who don't qualify for financial aid—but would not refuse it—seems inevitable to most program heads and athletic directors.

Thus College Sports Inc. refuses to accept this simple and obvious solution to many of its problems. Although university presidents and administrators are restive about the escalating expense of athletic scholarships, ADs and coaches have, in fact, introduced proposals in the NCAA for increasing the amount of "living expense" money that schools can give athletes. Need-based-only grants are such a logical idea—and so contrary to the commercialism, competitiveness, and waste of College Sports Inc.—that they will not be accepted as long as the NCAA exists in its present form.

CHAPTER 28

How Athletic Departments Recruit Athletes outside the NCAA Rules

"The worst part of recruiting is the cheating that goes on, along with having to inflate the egos of seventeen-year-old athletes."

—Bobby Bowden, football coach at Florida State University

SINCE THE NCAA began to police itself in 1952, over half of all discovered violations have concerned recruiting. Walter Byers, the association's executive director from 1952 to 1987, estimated that 30 percent of Division I schools broke recruiting rules; Bob Knight, when asked about Byers's figure, put his own estimate at 50 percent.

In 1988, *Don Heinrich's College Football,* the most authoritative annual guide, divided cheating in football recruiting into three categories and sets of percentages: (1) programs making outright illegal offers (about 15 to 20 percent of all Division I-A schools); (2) "schools that will assure a student-[athlete]'s social comfort and/or academic success if he signs" (about 65 percent); and (3) programs "that will occasionally bend a rule" (between 15 and 20 percent). According to many experts, similar statistics apply to recruiting in men's basketball as well as some nonrevenue sports. Because Don Heinrich's percentages add up to 100, the bottom line gives credence to the often-heard remark: "Everyone cheats in recruiting."

Into the mix of reasons for a recruit's choice of a school must go illegal inducements. Sometimes these are the sole reason for an athlete's signature on a letter of intent; more often, in a competition among a number of programs for a recruit, if the other elements—the coaches, media exposure, and facilities—are fairly even, the sweetness of an illegal deal will give one school the winning edge.

> *"With the million-dollar pot at the end of the rainbow, the*
> *college coach will do whatever is necessary to lure the top*
> *athlete to his school. How can we expect an athlete to*
> *have any respect for a particular coach or school, or for*
> *college athletics in general, if the bending and/or*
> *breaking of rules is condoned by those purportedly in*
> *positions of authority and leadership?"*
>
> —Dick Westervelt, sports information director
> at Stetson University, DeLand, Florida

The NCAA applies the same fictive premise—that of the "student-athlete"—to its recruiting rules as to its other regulations. When recruiting, coaches are allowed to offer a prospect only an NCAA athletic scholarship and approved perks because all other financial inducements to sign will taint an athlete's "amateurism." Most program heads, however, are realists and have no time for fiction; they endorse an NCAA rule, such as the transfer restriction on signed athletes, when it serves their self-interest, and they break the association's rules on recruiting for the same reason. At one level, their conduct is hypocritical; at another, it is a pragmatic response to a code of rules that exists partly for public relations reasons, that is illogical, and that is out of touch with the reality of College Sports Inc.

NCAA apologists also claim that recruiting regulations create a level playing field, allowing no school an illegal advantage. For program heads, however, recruiting in the 1990s is not lawn bowling but part of a vicious, high-stakes game. The goal of the game—moved toward by signing the best prospects—is to win the college sports lottery. Moreover, since program heads want to "hit the number" not only for their athletic programs but also for themselves—to greatly increase their professional standing and personal incomes—many look for "winning edges," even if illegal.

Thus the NCAA's Enforcement Division tries to regulate the high-stakes recruiting game with rules set up for an amateur era. Compounding the NCAA's problem is the fact that instead of using handcuffs, it has to wear them. As a private organization, the NCAA has no legal police powers—no authority to subpoena or arrest—and its troopers must depend on willing informants. Rumors of illegal recruiting reach high decibels but people with accurate information usually remain mute. Coaches making illegal offers will not talk and kiss away their careers; recruits who accept illegal payments are unlikely to squeal—they have no quarrel with the system and they fear retaliation from coaches if they inform. Therefore the NCAA constabulary must depend either upon athletes who attend one university but are willing to discuss their recruiting experiences with other schools, or upon former college athletes. (Last year Vincent Askew, who went to Memphis State and then the CBA, detailed the infractions committed by Kansas when that school recruited him.) But often, when these informants tell their stories, the incidents occurred years before and only the players' word serves as proof.

Whenever the NCAA Enforcement Division actually catches a program head for recruiting violations, the college sports establishment invokes the cliché "In every group there's always one bad apple." More objective observers of college sports counter with the well-worn line "It's only the tip of the iceberg." In this instance, locating the rest of the iceberg is much easier than finding the good apples.

> *"A Texas Christian [University] booster took a prospective*
> *player to a local motel, where, the [NCAA] report said,*
> *the athlete was provided with lodging, meals, and*
> *prostitutes until the signing date."*
>
> —Item in the *Chronicle of Higher Education*

The single most common recruiting violation is, to quote the NCAA, "Improper transportation or entertainment of prospective athletes or their families" during on-campus visits. This violation is primary because of the public nature of recruits' visits and the fact that many visiting athletes end up going to other schools and becoming NCAA informants. Most often, fairly small amounts of money, goods, or services are involved, and if an athletic program is apprehended, the penalty is usually light. Thus violations during recruits' visits provide the NCAA's troopers with opportunities to rack up some infraction collars and to generate publicity about how the "amateur student-athlete" code is still intact.

Violators break NCAA rules on transportation and entertainment in a number of ways: a coach provides free airline tickets for a recruit's parent(s), spouse, girl- or boyfriend, sibling(s), or other members of the athlete's entourage (the school may entertain parents and spouse once on campus but may not pay their way to campus); or a recruiting coordinator gives extra "weekend money" to a recruit and/or extra money to the hosts (the NCAA allows $20 per recruit for hosts at Division I schools and $10 at Divisions II and III).

When recent New York prep star Kenny Anderson signed with Georgia Tech, other college coaches pointed to the odd circumstances of his mother's visit to Atlanta. Georgia Tech officials said that the fiancé of Anderson's mother bought her a round-trip ticket from New York to Atlanta. Shortly before this trip, however, according to Jim Boeheim, Syracuse basketball coach, she didn't have enough money to accompany her son on his visit from New York City to Syracuse. Anderson's mother denied the Syracuse allegations; because the NCAA is a private organization and cannot subpoena the financial records of her fiancé, the association has to accept her word and drop the matter.

Once on campus, the recruit experiences forty-eight hours of high-pressure sales pitches and higher-pressure pleasures. The coaches, including the program head, try to convince the athlete that their school is the perfect choice, and the hosts, usually members of the team in the recruit's sport, make sure that the athlete's appetites, whatever they may be, are fully satisfied. A University of Texas football player recalled, "On average, I'd get probably about $300 for a weekend [of hosting] and that's conservative. . . . [The coach] would say, 'Here's enough to take [the recruit] out and show him a good time.' "

Most seventeen-year-old athletes quickly bore of business talk and try to spend as much time with their student hosts as possible. On many campuses, these also include attractive members of the opposite sex who "date" the recruit for the weekend. Often, these dates belong to a special club, organized by the athletic department, and they receive some sort of compensation for their services. The University of Florida's "Gator Getters" was one of the first of these groups but now most big-time programs have similar organizations. At the University of Texas at Austin, a Texas Angel often follows up her date with a football recruit by writing to him as often as once a day to try to convince him to sign with the Longhorns. One of the more famous incidents of a school using a female host occurred at Florida State University when a coach flew a cheerleader to Chicago to try to persuade a recruit whom she had entertained during his on-campus visit to sign. (He didn't, but Florida State incurred a minor NCAA penalty.)

Both within and outside NCAA rules, the recruiting visit is an expensive and corrupt practice. According to Wayne Duke, longtime Big Ten commissioner, it is one link in "the recruiting process, where [the athlete's] almost worshiped," and it contributes to "the compartmentalizing of [college] athletes. Viewing them as being different from the regular student body."

The recruiting visit is an athlete's first official trip to a school; most coaches and hosts, rather than present an honest picture of student life at their institution, offer a fantasy world filled with free and almost unlimited pleasures. Not surprisingly, many athletes, when they arrive on campus as freshmen, want to continue in that fantasy world and are reluctant to confront the reality of going to classes, earning grades, and observing the same rules as regular students. Of all methods devised for preparing seventeen-year-olds for life as "student-athletes," the recruiting process, and its highlight weekend visit, is probably the worst.

The NCAA bureaucracy, however, is so busy trying to enforce its rules on recruiting violations that it never takes a step back to examine the entire recruiting system. In the end, its penalties against schools for transportation and entertainment violations become the equivalent of crime statistics: quantity but not quality, infractions discovered and violators apprehended but no real movement toward ending much deeper corruption. (This phenomenon supports the argument that the NCAA's Enforcement Division is mainly a P.R. operation designed to give the public the impression that the association is trying to clean up college sports and that the NCAA is seriously interested in reform.)

> "What's the final 1985 salary structure for a high school superstar?
> " 'The figures that come to me are anywhere from $50,000 to $100,000 over a four-year period. It includes summer jobs, jobs for family members and cash payments.' "
>
> —Bob Knight, in an interview with the
> *Chicago Tribune*

The second most common type of NCAA violation is what the association describes as "improper recruiting inducements to prospective athletes, including cash payments, use of automobiles, free clothing, housing, or promises of such benefits." These violations are more serious and receive harsher NCAA penalties than those for transportation and entertainment infractions—therefore coaches work harder to hide them. Often part of the cover-up is to implicate athletes and their parents in the violations and in this way bury the NCAA's potential sources of information.

When Chris Mills, a Los Angeles prep star, went on the recruiting market in 1987, he apparently had his hand open to receive more than a basketball pass. According to his player-host for his visit to Indiana University, the L.A. high schooler said, "I have to have money. I have to have a car. I have to live in my own place." The University of Kentucky apparently satisfied Mills's demands because he signed with them and, in the spring of 1988, its athletic department started sending packages to his father in Los Angeles. One envelope accidentally opened while in the Emery depot in L.A. and $1,000 in cash fell out. Mills's father, and the Kentucky authorities, denied any wrongdoing, but the offense was so blatant that the NCAA began a major investigation of the Wildcats' basketball program. Kentucky eventually admitted its guilt.

Shawn Kemp, another Kentucky recruit in the same year as Mills, also visited Indiana, and, according to former I.U. player Rick Calloway, "He just wanted stuff. He kept saying, 'You all don't get nothing? I know you're lying'. . . . He was looking for a handout."

Even schools that promise nothing to recruits during their visits can still give very clear signals of future payoffs. Todd Mitchell, former Purdue basketball star, says that "you can just see what's going on. You see what's in the parking lot and you see where [the players] stay. Naturally, if you see six or seven guys each staying in condominiums, you're sure [that you're] not going to be staying in the back of a supermarket."

Another inducement is, according to Todd Mitchell, a summer job. The Purdue all-American knew of a player at another college who received $20,000 for a summer job "for putting in a couple of hours a week." Bob Knight once became so furious about a Chicago high school star and his mother who worked at jobs arranged by a University of Illinois booster that the I.U. coach demanded—to no avail—that the NCAA radically change its rules on recruiting.

When recruiters actually offer cash gifts, they usually do so in private, in the athlete's home, and in exchange for the player's signature on a letter of intent. David Berst, the NCAA's longtime chief cop, admitted a few years ago that "the usual [illegal] fee we find for signing a letter of intent is between $1,200 and $2,500." Berst's average applies to NCAA convictions but, in fact, his numbers seem extremely low, especially when star high school athletes are included in the statistics. John "Hot Rod" Williams said that he went to Tulane for $10,000, and the father of Clark Kellogg said that his son turned down a $100,000 four-year package deal from a rival school to sign with Ohio State.

In college sports, "signing bonuses" increased throughout the 1980s. Early in the decade, when former pro quarterback John Hadl was a recruiting coach at his alma mater, Kansas, he was accused of offering high school recruits up to $30,000 to sign with the Jayhawks. By mid-decade, SMU offered Sean Stopperich, a running back from Pennsylvania, a package worth $140,000, plus a moving allowance for his family and a job for his father in Dallas, if he would become a Mustang. At the end of the 1980s, stories of $200,000 packages circulated.

Most of the signing deals also include ownership or free use of a new automobile. David Berst of the NCAA says that the free car is often more valuable than the cash bonus ("the cars that are given to athletes can be worth from $10,000 to $15,000"). Sean Bell, who played football at Ohio State, described how the car deal usually works and why he turned one down: "It was my biggest offer, and it came from one of the alumni who owned a car dealership. He wanted something down, like five dollars, just so it would be a legal sale. I was so scared I couldn't accept it."

A generation ago in college sports, prominent boosters would promise recruits good jobs *after* their college careers were over and, at the appropriate future date, would deliver. Those promises are sometimes still made but they seem more like echoes of an innocent past than part of contemporary recruiting.

In the hard, increasingly professional world of College Sports Inc., deals are cut for the present and cash moves quickly from recruiter to athlete through sophisticated money-laundering schemes. The promise of a job four or five years down the road cannot compare to money in a parent's or family friend's safety-deposit box or in an annuity or trust fund in a parent's name. The NCAA never could police the booster's postgraduation job offer (nor was it even illegal); how can it possibly locate Cayman Island bank drops and other modern ways of transferring payoffs to recruits? The NCAA's rules and defenses are hopelessly out-of-date; the cheaters' weapons are state-of-the-art.

"As odd as it may appear, offering a job to a [high school] coach . . . in hopes of landing a player is permitted under NCAA rules. Giving the player a ride to the campus from the airport or a hamburger along the way—or paying him to play—is not."

—Bruce Lowitt and Hal Bock, Associated Press reporters

On occasion, a program head will make an illegal recruiting deal directly and entirely with an athlete; more often, a coach will bargain with a player's parent(s) or guardian(s), high school coach, or a recruiting broker. Bobby Bowden, the Florida State program head, says that a sad "occurrence in recruiting is when a family member tries to 'sell' an athlete." Often, in these situations, the family member does not want a simple sale but conducts an auction or bidding war for the child's signature.

If cash or gifts change hands, the NCAA can enter the case. Many a recruiting coach, however, has arranged for a parent to acquire, instead, a new job that can pay for a car and other goods. The NCAA has rules prohibiting such employment but unless the job offer is blatant and ridiculous—an illiterate parent suddenly lands a $75,000 position as a computer programmer with the company of a well-known booster—the association has no way of proving that the parent did not obtain his or her new job honestly.

Other family members and friends of the recruit can also benefit from such legal and frequently bestowed "gifts" as academic scholarships to the institution with which the athlete signs. The NCAA may frown upon the financial-aid package that Felonious State awards to the girlfriend of Steve Seven-Footer but the association cannot easily prove that she did not earn it. In 1989, the University of Pittsburgh, in an innovative variation on this legal gift, gave full athletic scholarships to four of the best friends and high school teammates of highly sought recruit Sean Gilbert (*USA Today*'s Prep Defensive Player of the Year). Pitt had never before awarded five football scholarships in the same year to athletes from the same high school team.

Another facilitator who can aid recruiters and benefit personally— and legally—is the player's high school coach. Usually a primary influence on a young athlete, prep coaches have become increasingly involved in the recruiting game. John Thompson of Georgetown says bluntly, "A lot of high school coaches have their hands out—a lot of them." College recruiters tell innumerable tales about high school coaches asking for everything from new sneakers to large cash payoffs in return for influencing their athletes.

But the smartest high school coaches—and the program heads who deal with them—have learned to stay within NCAA rules and focus on such payments as assistant coaching jobs in the college program in return for bringing their prep star with them. The New Jersey high school coach of Alaa Abdelnaby said that he was offered an assistant position on Lefty Driesell's staff at Maryland in return for his star's signature on a Terrapin letter of intent. The high school coach refused because "three years later, another seven-footer they're interested in comes along and I'm out of a job." (Abdelnaby went to Duke and his high school coach stayed in New Jersey.) Many prep coaches, however, have accepted such offers. Lefty Driesell defended the practice with, "I can hire anybody I want. . . . There's nothing illegal about it, absolutely nothing wrong. It's not even questionable."

Driesell is correct. The only NCAA rules that touch upon this influence peddling are the ones that prohibit program heads from offering excessive payments to high school coaches for speaking engagements or work at summer camps. The NCAA even allows Division II and III schools to employ high school and juco coaches on their coaching staffs *at the same time* as they work at their high school or junior college jobs. A number of excellent athletes have chosen to play minor college ball because their old coaches received this deal.

Even honest high school coaches are tainted by illegal and unethical recruiting practices. Because a large part of a high school coach's professional reputation and potential for advancement is based on how many of his or her athletes obtain college athletic scholarships, the majority of prep mentors tend to overlook or even condone crooked recruiting practices. One Texas high school coach explained that "it is not the [high school] coach's responsibility to act as NCAA investigator. If a player of mine shows up in a new car, I say, 'Man, what a nice car.' If the NCAA wants to look into it, they can."

Other facilitators are the "recruiting brokers." Sometimes they are professional agents who want to broaden their client base; more often, they are talent scouts who serve—usually for a hefty fee—as middlemen between the colleges and the athletes. Because the NCAA says that any high school football or basketball player who employs a professional agent automatically forfeits college playing eligibility, prep players in these sports tend to stay away from the known agents and gravitate toward the talent scouts.

Programs at schools in low-population areas often employ recruiting brokers—sometimes called "bounty hunters"—in the prime high school locations for athletes in their sports. The men's basketball program of the University of Missouri at Columbia is under NCAA investigation for using two brokers in Detroit, Michigan. Because of Mizzou's sudden influx of players from that city, the Missouri recruiting coordinator was nicknamed "Doctor Detroit."

Increasingly, when a college coach recruits a star athlete, a facilitator—parent, high school coach, or talent broker—is involved, hands out, ready to stuff the long green into pockets or bank safe-deposit boxes.

> "What I want to know is how those alumni [and boosters] know who to recruit. Isn't it strange when they're involved, that they always seem to be talking to a kid the school wants?"
>
> —Lou Holtz, head football coach at
> Notre Dame

Holtz made his astute comment in 1987. During that year, the NCAA banned all booster involvement in recruiting (some observers saw this as an attempt by coaches to deflect the blame for the increasing recruiting scandals from themselves to the boosters). The new rule limits all contact with recruits and their relatives to "institutional staff members," i.e., athletic department personnel and faculty and staff. O. J. Simpson can no longer call recruits and urge them to become Trojans; J. Deep Pockets cannot invite a prospect to his office and outline the rewards of shooting hoops for Felonious State; however, Burt Reynolds, who played football at Florida State, can promote his old school because he is an Honorary Lecturer in Drama there.

As soon as the rule was passed, sharp program heads plotted their offenses to meet this NCAA defense and to turn the reform to their advantage. Their strategy was simple: invoke the new rule to assert full control over boosters and target them onto a significant facilitator—a high school coach, a parent's closest friend, etc.—rather than onto the recruit or his parents. As Don Heinrich explains, "The go-between thus becomes the conduit for cheating." The new rule does not prohibit

J. Deep Pockets from having a cup of coffee with the best friend of the father of Steve Seven-Footer. Nor will the NCAA ever find out about the annuity in the best friend's name that J.D. opened when Steve signed with Felonious State and how the money quietly flows back to the athlete and his family.

The coaches' cheating strategies were successful and the new rule was dead meat within a year. However, the NCAA reform had the ironic side effect of raising the cost of recruiting: in addition to the necessary payoffs to recruits and their parents, now, third and sometimes fourth parties demand a facilitator's "fee."

One of two conclusions can be extracted from the failure of this NCAA rule on boosters: either the members who voted for it as a serious and enforceable reform are out of touch with the reality of College Sports Inc., or many of the coaches and athletic directors who endorsed the rule did not really intend it to work and only voted "Yes" for P.R. reasons. Either points to the same bottom line: NCAA reform of contemporary college sports, especially on issues that go against program heads' self-interest, is probably impossible.

CHAPTER 29

How Athletic Departments Pay On-Campus Athletes: Cash, Free Loans, Jobs for Jocks, Hard & Soft Tickets

"Hell, we had one player who never met his sugar daddy. . . . Every Monday, he [the player] would go to a safe-deposit box and pick up his ticket money. That's all he did. An assistant coach took care of giving the sugar daddy the tickets. He never knew who that sugar daddy was but he was generous. He was paying top dollar."

—Former NFL running back Calvin Hill, discussing the college experiences of another pro player

THE NCAA has attempted to legislate sugar daddy boosters out of the recruiting process but because their financial support is so crucial to all athletic programs, the association has no desire to bar them from College Sports Inc. When the NCAA considers rules limiting booster activity, its real agenda is not to reform intercollegiate athletics but to give coaches and ADs greater control over these supporters. Undirected boosters are loose cannons on the decks of an athletic program; carefully targeted boosters and their cash are an important asset.

When, a decade ago, the University of Houston was trying to build the best football team in the Southwest Athletic Conference, Cedric Dempsey, then athletic director at Houston, now AD at the University of Arizona and chair of the NCAA's Division I Men's Basketball Committee, reportedly told a Houston booster meeting that the University of

Texas "had a $1.5 million [slush] fund, used solely at the coaches' discretion, . . . [that Texas] A. & M. had a $2 million fund and could get more," and he implied that his department needed an equivalent fund to be competitive in the SWC.

At this same time, the athletic department at Southern Methodist University was also trying to buy the best football team in the SWC, and their boosters were amazingly generous, pouring millions into the school's athletic program, much of it for the coaches to use as they pleased. Illegal payoffs to recruits sucked up part of the money but another chunk went into regular cash payments to the football players already in school. One Dallas radio reporter estimated that "between 1980 and '86, SMU paid $1.3 million to members of the football team." Cash. At least another million or so went into perks such as new cars and free apartments.

During these years in the Southwest Conference, the University of Texas football program distributed some of the booster money through an assistant coach whom the athletes called "The Loan Professor" and "The Banker." According to former Longhorn players, not only did this coach give cash to team members, he also arranged bank loans and, when necessary, bail money.

Illegal payments, however, are hardly confined to the SWC. In the staid Big Ten, in recent years athletes at a number of schools have received large sums of money; at the University of Minnesota, football players Rickey Foggie and Valdez Baylor were given thousands of dollars by a school administrator during their Gopher careers. The practice of paying college athletes is so widespread nationally that, in 1989, when over eleven hundred current and former NFL players responded to a survey by sociologist Allen Sack, "Nearly a third [said they had] accepted illicit payments while in college" and almost half "knew athletes at their colleges who took under-the-table payments." Sack concluded that, contrary to NCAA propaganda, illegal payments are not isolated incidents but constitute a flourishing "underground economy" in college sports.

> *"A Highland Hundred [a Memphis State booster club]*
> *official used $2,100 from the [slush] fund in March 1984*
> *to pay tuition for 6-foot-9, 312-pound lineman Tim*
> *Borcky, who transferred to Memphis State from the*
> *University of Maryland [and, according to NCAA rules,*
> *had to sit out a year at his own expense].*

*". . . Borcky told NCAA investigators he paid his tuition
with $2,100 he had hidden in a shoe in his closet."*

—Item in the *Memphis Commercial Appeal*

Money is transmitted to athletes in a number of standard ways. The most old-fashioned is the "golden handshake": when a booster or coach shakes hands with a player, he slips the athlete some cash. The donor has the pleasure of pressing the flesh and receiving the recipient's "Thank you." However, the handshake is often in public and, even when private, does not conceal identities, hence the second-oldest and most frequently used method, the "golden envelope." When the player opens his locker after practice, an envelope containing cash is inside. For a number of years, a successful Big Ten football program, ignoring the obvious symbolism, used standard business pay envelopes. The advantage of the golden envelope is that identities are kept secret: if a specific booster donates the money, he cannot be traced; if the player is ever questioned about the money, he cannot finger the assistant coach who left it in his locker or put it under his dorm door. "For all that the players know or care," explains a former Big Ten assistant coach, "the Tooth Fairy brought it."

Program heads, like Mafia dons, prefer to distance themselves from the golden handshakes and envelopes, sometimes pretending—and straining observers' credulity—that they know nothing about illegal payments and that their assistant coaches and/or the boosters act independent of their knowledge. Usually only an extremely arrogant and foolish coach like Dana Kirk of Memphis State gets caught paying players directly. At Kirk's trial for tax evasion, former MSU player Keith Lee told how this coach had paid him $400 to $600 a month for four years.

Another program head convicted by the NCAA of paying his players was Bill Yeomans, longtime football head at Houston. One of his linemen, Lonell Phea, signed a sworn affidavit that Yeomans had given him at least $18,000 during his college career. Another player explained that "in Yeomans' office, he always kept an envelope in the left-side bottom drawer of his desk. It was a big envelope, and it had nothing but hundreds in it." In the 1980s, the NCAA caught Yeomans a number of times in this infraction and others, and finally the school reluctantly moved him out of coaching and into a $103,000-a-year job as head of athletic fund-raising!

Yeomans and some of his assistant coaches also moved money to their players through a newer technique: bank loans that the recipient does not have to pay back. Usually an assistant coach arranges the loan and the player signs for it, receives the cash up front or periodically, and a booster or an assistant coach makes the payments on the loan. The loan has the advantage of appearing legal (many students borrow from banks to help pay college costs) and the extra advantage to an athletic department of keeping the player financially dependent: Because the student signed the note, he is legally liable for the repayment. More than one college athlete has been forced to pay back a loan he thought was free. A former University of Texas player relates, "I went down to the bank with him [the assistant coach], met the president, filled out the papers. The president said I never had to worry about paying it back. When I left school, they called my mom and said I had a note to pay off."

Similar financial dependency can occur with annuities and other money deals agreed to at the time of signing the letter of intent. Unless the athletic program deposits the full amount in the student's account at the beginning of the player's college career, it can renege on the arrangement at any time. Many a coach has stopped the cash flow when the athlete's performance fell below expectations.

Such deals occur in all conferences and at all levels of college sports. Even hallowed Ivy League schools have ways of giving extra money to athletes. Because the Ivies award only need-based financial aid, the extent of a player's need is the loophole through which the cash can move. Bob Blackman, the last successful football coach at Dartmouth, admitted that with some of his players, he discovered "evidence of 'C.P.A.'—approved cheating on grant-in-aid applications. In one case, the [athlete's] family lived in a nicely furnished home with a two-car garage and the father ran his own business, yet the player somehow qualified for the full $4,000 grant-in-aid." (Blackman did not reveal who at his school arranged the "C.P.A.") Another Ivy League practice is the direct loan from a booster to an athlete. In the early 1980s, the Council of Ivy Group Presidents considered the case of one altruist who loaned $1,000 each to twelve athletes at Harvard, Yale, and Princeton. The presidents decided that there was nothing illegal in these loans although they asked the booster to stop such bequests.

Most illegal payments go to college football and basketball players, but some coaches in nonrevenue sports also funnel money to their athletes. An ongoing and widespread practice in college soccer is for coaches to arrange for their best players to earn a few hundred dollars a weekend by playing for ethnic league teams in such cities as Boston, New York, Chicago, and Los Angeles. Paul Kennedy, managing editor of *Soccer America,* says, "Some of the players, especially the foreigners, don't even know that taking the money breaks an NCAA rule. It's been going on so long, the players just assume that it's part of college soccer."

In other nonrevenue sports, money is moved to athletes in various ingenious ways. Arizona State was caught giving excessive financial aid to baseball players, wrestlers, and gymnasts, and also paying them for more "work-study" hours than they actually put in. However, these financial-aid tricks are becoming less popular as a way of transmitting cash to athletes: because federal money is sometimes involved and the penalties if caught far exceed NCAA wrist slaps, most athletic departments prefer cleaner exchanges, ruses such as Jobs for Jocks and the Ticket Scam.

> *"USF [University of San Francisco] basketball star*
> *Quentin Dailey said he was paid $1,000 a month for a job*
> *he didn't do. . . . It was not necessary for him to report to*
> *work. The company is owned by J. Luis Zabais, a wealthy*
> *USF alumnus."*
>
> —Item in the *San Francisco Chronicle*

High-paying, low- or no-work jobs for jocks are a college sports tradition. A few years ago, when the NCAA refused to control summer jobs for athletes, Notre Dame basketball coach Digger Phelps sarcastically commented, "Now, we can teach a kid values by having some corporate booster give him $500 an hour to arrange employee softball games." In the recent Oklahoma scandal, booster William Lambert was accused of paying a player "$6,400 for summer work that was never performed," and Lambert admitted that he "employed an estimated 100 to 150 Sooner players and assistant coaches during a period of fifteen years."

Flagrant cases such as Lambert's can cause an NCAA investigation, but ordinary and quiet overpayment for minimal work is hard to detect and harder to prove. Complicating NCAA detection is the fact that many summer jobs are in the athlete's hometown or another location away from campus. In fact, the only listing on this subject in the index of the 1988–89 *NCAA Manual* is, "Summer jobs, transportation to," and the rule warns against free transportation to the job provided by the athlete's coach or athletic program, but not illegal payments to the athlete.

Athletic departments also arrange "employment" for athletes during the school year. Cleveland State basketball star Ken "Mouse" McFadden was on his department's payroll for six months before enrolling as a student at the school. And the University of Florida football program once arranged for two of its athletes to work at booster George Steinbrenner's New York Yankees' training camp at Fort Lauderdale. Steinbrenner, never one to keep quiet about his generosity, attracted the NCAA's attention in this case and became an item in the association's indictment of Florida.

The job scam is so widespread that it even extends to the nonrevenue sports. The University of Michigan baseball program is currently being investigated by the Big Ten because of "allegations that players were paid excessively for minimal work, such as selling football [game] programs," and that they received "up to $70,000 over a period of years."

> *"Marv Goux, the [University of Southern California]*
> *assistant coach who was cited for selling the players'*
> *tickets, appeared at a football banquet after the [NCAA]*
> *penalties were announced and opened his jacket,*
> *revealing tickets pinned inside. He drew guffaws from the*
> *audience."*
>
> —Item in the *Chronicle of Higher Education*

College athletes, like their coaches, receive complimentary passes to intercollegiate sports events. Coaches sell or trade their tickets, often making a handsome profit. College players are supposed to be amateurs and the NCAA forbids them from doing what their bosses do so openly and legally. Nevertheless, for many years, college athletes have sold their free passes, often for top dollar. In addition, some coaches have arranged for players to sell their tickets to boosters at incredibly inflated prices; this funnels extra cash to the athletes and also rewards the boosters' generosity with something more tangible than a handshake.

In the mid-1980s, the NCAA calculated that "football players broke the rule [against ticket selling] 8,000 times" a season. Walter Byers, longtime head of the association, commented that the dollars earned from this commerce "have been passing me by [on the highway] in the form of TransAms and Porsches." At the University of Texas, boosters paid players as much as $600 a ticket, and one Longhorn wide receiver admitted that he made $10,000 from the sale of his free seats. Former Texas and NFL player Terry Orr explained that in college, "I lived on tickets. I really did."

The University of Texas was sufficiently embarrassed by its ticket scandal, which included NCAA penalties, that it instigated a major NCAA reform on this matter: no more "hard," or actual, tickets for athletes; instead, each player had to submit a list of four people to receive free passes, and before game time, these people had to go to a special gate, show identification, and receive their seat assignments. The Texas athletic director explained that the "pass rule . . . is a lot better than putting a hard ticket in a player's hand. Everyone you ever talked to about the issue said every kid who had an opportunity to sell tickets, sold tickets."

The NCAA instituted the "pass rule" in the mid-1980s but even the Texas AD admitted that it had "loopholes and soft spots in it." Nothing prevented a player from putting a booster's name on a pass list and receiving payment from the booster in return. The NCAA then tried to close this loophole by restricting players' lists to relatives and fellow students. Some athletic departments did not want to accept these changes and, in 1986, the association accused large numbers of athletes at various schools of violating the new pass rules. In two famous incidents that year, the NCAA penalized fifty-four football players at Tennessee and sixty at Nebraska for misusing their pass lists.

Eventually the NCAA relented and the present rule allows four free passes per player, three for relatives and/or fellow students and one for anyone whom the athlete designates. Thus the enterprising coach and player can use the open space for a sugar daddy, and also, because a relative does not necessarily have the same family name as an athlete, players can list some booster "cousins" (this latter move is illegal, but since one college football team for one game has a pass list of hundreds of names, the NCAA cannot possibly do background checks on every name on every pass list in America). At present, illegal ticket selling continues, if not at a frenetic pace, at least at a fast trot. The current Oklahoma scandal includes NCAA charges that Sooner players sold their passes for up to $600 apiece.

The pass system also has a "soft spot" available to nonjock student hustlers. At all big-time athletic schools, some young entrepreneurs earn extra money by scalping game tickets; the pass system encourages them to try to purchase places on the players' lists and sell them at scalpers' rates to other students. Because all involved are in the NCAA's approved category of "fellow students," the association cannot easily discover these transactions.

The bottom line on the players' ticket deal is similar to many other aspects of College Sports Inc.: money motivates behavior, and NCAA attempts at reform are mainly futile. Many athletes still net thousands of dollars from their free passes, and the only difference between the old "hard ticket" days and the present "soft pass" system is the more circuitous money trail and the extra "facilitators" en route.

CHAPTER 30

Athletes' Legal & Illegal Perks: Jock Dorms, Fast Cars, Free Credit Cards, & Free Phone Calls Home & to a Bail Bondsman

"Frank Layden, [former] coach of the National Basketball Association's Utah Jazz, tells a story about negotiations with one of the team's top draft choices. After agreeing to an $800,000 salary, Mr. Layden recalls, the player 'told me he wanted a gas card, a car, a job for his father, and four paid trips home.'

"How did Mr. Layden respond? 'I told him this was the NBA and we pay cash. No perks like in college.' "

—Item in the *Chronicle of Higher Education*

WHEN HE was football program head at Clemson, Danny Ford said that "one of my unhappiest moments" occurred when the school decided "to spend $2.5 million on a learning center, and [they] could have put all of that into an athletic dorm." About half of the big-time college football powers, including Clemson, have special dormitories for their players (Ford wanted a more luxurious one for his team). In men's basketball, jock dorms are less common but some major basketball schools, including Syracuse, North Carolina State, and Louisiana State, have them; other institutions, especially in the South and Southwest, house both football and basketball players in the same special facility. Many schools without jock dorms place their intercollegiate athletes in separate wings or sections of the student dormitories. In fact, only a few NCAA Division I-A institutions fully integrate the housing and dining of athletes and regular students.

Compared to the usual small rooms, spartan furnishings, and ordinary-to-awful food of the student dorms, jock housing tends toward the palatial. An individual unit for one or two athletes often consists of a nicely furnished suite—large living room, bedroom, and bathroom—with a stereo, color TV, and VCR, and the main dining room downstairs serves quality food in abundance. (The jock dorm at Alabama is nicknamed "The Bryant Hilton.") Moreover, at even those schools without jock dorms, special daily "training tables" are set up somewhere on campus for the athletes, and the free and abundant food there is far superior to what their fellow dorm residents pay to eat. At the University of Nevada at Las Vegas, the training table is often off campus—the men's basketball players can obtain a daily free meal at a number of Las Vegas casino restaurants.

Because the plushness of the jock dorm is also an important recruiting device, schools are making these facilities ever more opulent, adding such features as indoor swimming pools, state-of-the-art recreation rooms, and hotel-like maid service. The attitude of Otis Taylor, a sophomore football player at Oklahoma, is typical of many athletes: "I wouldn't want to live in any old dorm," he explained, adding that he signed with the Sooners in part because of Bud Wilkinson Hall.

The existence of jock dorms contradicts one of the most important and basic NCAA rules: *athletes are supposed to receive no more than "the same benefit [that] is generally available to the institution's [other] students"* (emphasis added). The NCAA's premise for this rule is its standard "student-athlete" line—these are amateurs, no better than their schoolmates. In 1979, it even added a specific bylaw on athletes' housing: "an institution may not provide an on-campus or off-campus housing benefit for student-athletes that is not available on the same basis to the general student body."

Yet regular college students, often paying exorbitant room-and-board bills, never live on campus in the luxury enjoyed by the athletes in the jock dorms. Moreover, even if regular students requested and could afford room and board equal to the jock dorms, their schools could not provide them with it (no college builds comparable facilities and has similar dining arrangements for "the general student body"). The blatant differences between the jock dorms and regular student accommodations contribute to the cynicism with which students often regard the athletic scholarship holders.

In the history of the NCAA, the association has penalized many institutions under its "no extra benefits" rule for giving free T-shirts and free rides to athletes, but it has rarely reprimanded a single college or university for extending much more basic and valuable room-and-board "benefits" to athletes.

For all of their superior living conditions, many athletic scholarship holders do not seem to appreciate or even like their luxurious living arrangements. Some complain, with justification, that program heads, acting like Orwell's Big Brother, use the dorms to control all aspects of the players' lives. But even in those situations where the coaches adopt a laissez-faire attitude, athletes in special facilities tend to become isolated and often destructive.

During the Len Bias scandal at the University of Maryland, the *Washington* (D.C.) *Times* investigated the living conditions at the athletes' dorm where Bias died of a cocaine-induced seizure. In an article entitled "Jock Dorm at Maryland Remembered for the Drugs," the paper described how athletic department coaches visited the dorm regularly but apparently ignored the rampant drug scene there. One former dorm resident said that the drug taking "was so common, it's hard to believe they [the coaches] didn't know." The newspaper also mentioned that "a conspicuous sideshow to the drug use in the dorm was constant vandalism" by the athletes.

The ongoing scandal at Oklahoma also involves various illegal activities, including shootings and a gang rape, in the jock dorms there. Former Sooner all-American Brian Bosworth, in his autobiography, vividly describes other violent scenes in the Oklahoma dorm and also mentions how he moved out of Bud Wilkinson Hall and into a nicely furnished $500-a-month condo thanks to a generous booster.

Leaving the dorms after freshman or sophomore year and renting an apartment is part of the rite of passage for many American college students. Athletes are no different—except often, like Bosworth, they obtain their apartments rent free or at a reduced rate. At one time, as many as thirty-three University of Texas football players lived in a local apartment complex at a 30 percent reduction in rent (the owner was a former Longhorn player). One player said that Dave McWilliams, then an assistant and now head football coach at Texas, had arranged the apartment deal for him, and that most Texas players knew about it.

Whether they live in jock dorms or in off-campus housing, college athletes receive basic "benefits" unavailable to the "general student body" of their schools. Moreover, if an athlete moves off campus, the NCAA allows an athletic department to give him or her the amount that it would have paid for the dorm bill; if the athlete has a free off-campus deal, the dorm bill money is pure profit. A regular student moving off campus pays room and board totally out of pocket.

In spite of these special deals, many program heads and ADs are now demanding new NCAA legislation to allow athletes to receive "living expense" money—direct payments of cash and/or an increase in their total financial-aid packages. Dick Schultz, the executive director of the NCAA, argues, without a hint of irony, that this additional money will enable an athlete to "live like a normal college student."

Because of this willful ignorance, the NCAA has never shown much interest in athletes' housing deals and, instead, has long targeted its "Enforcement Division" onto more obvious special "benefits" to athletes, such as free cars.

> "[Memphis State basketball coach Dana] Kirk also talked about the use of expensive cars by starting center William Bedford. Bedford has received three speeding tickets— twice driving a Lincoln and once in a Corvette—in the last six months. He also had a traffic accident in a Jaguar. All of the cars were loaned to him by boosters.
> "[Kirk said,] 'When you've got a seven-footer in your program that doesn't own a car, that's a compliment.' "
>
> —Item in the *Memphis Commercial Appeal*

The star athlete driving around campus in his new convertible is an image from college sports' basic photo album. For many years, regular students and faculty assumed, usually correctly, that athletes acquired their cars through the generosity of the athletic program and its supporters. In the old days, coaches would arrange a direct gift of or a "sweetheart deal" on a vehicle for a player with a dealer-booster (often the source of the coaches' free cars). In recent years, however, the NCAA has targeted these obvious and, according to its rules, illegal gifts. If the NCAA asks the athlete–car owner to produce the documents of purchase on the car, and the papers show that he "bought" his new TransAm from Booster Ed's Auto World for $10, the NCAA penalizes the athlete and the school. As a result, coaches have evolved the athlete's "car deal" from a simple, direct gift to a complicated and roundabout transaction.

The first opportunity for an athlete to acquire a car thanks to a college athletic program occurs with the letter of intent. In return for the athlete's signature, the parent(s) or a facilitator obtains the money to buy the car and then gives or "loans" the vehicle to the athlete. If the money in the deal is paid up front, the coach warns against paying the auto purchase price in cash and attracting the NCAA's attention; instead he advises regular payments on a car loan with money from a safety-deposit box. Coaches, however, prefer "alternative financing" for the car deal— long-term payments to the parent(s) or facilitator—because if the player fails to please athletically, the coach can "repossess" the automobile.

Once in college, an athlete without a car is unlikely to receive one for free unless he or she achieves all-American, or at least all-conference, status. More often, athletes will borrow cars from boosters or coaches. The NCAA frowns on such generosity but usually cannot discover it unless the player, like William Bedford at Memphis State, receives speeding tickets or is in a traffic accident, or unless the infraction emerges as part of a wider NCAA investigation (this happened at the University of Tennessee with a football player and a booster's Jaguar, Porsche, and Corvette).

For college athletes who want their own cars and have enough clout with their athletic departments to make their wishes come true, one method of obtaining an auto is the "booster-guaranteed" car loan. The University of Wisconsin got into trouble a few years ago when a booster agreed to underwrite $5,000 in car loans for a Badger basketball player but then let the payments fall behind. The bank became antsy, complained to the school, and the matter leaked out, implicating men's basketball coach Steve Yoder.

More common than car loans to athletes are rental car agreements. On occasion, a coach will pay for a short- or even a long-term car rental for an athlete (one of the NCAA accusations against Barry Switzer of Oklahoma). Sometimes a booster will take care of the rentals, especially if he owns the agency—the situation at the University of Cincinnati a few years ago. The rental agreement has the advantage of being less ostentatious than the free-car deal and it also allows coaches maximum control over the athletes involved. "Rent them a Hertz when they're playing well and cooperating," explains one New England assistant hockey coach. "Send them to Rent-a-Wreck on their own money when they're not."

The same short leash is used for free trips home for athletes. Because regular students pay for their own transportation home, the NCAA states that athletes must do the same. However, athletic departments so abuse this rule that it is becoming one of the NCAA's most frequently recorded violations. In the 1980s, the Arizona State track team so consistently broke this regulation and others that the athletic director had to fire the track coach and scale down the program.

> *"It's hard for me [when we play] at Las Vegas to see [UNLV players Stacey] Augmon and [David] Butler come out and get into big, fancy cars. It's hard to see them with the alligator shoes, the jewelry, the whole business, and not wonder about it."*
>
> —Kohn Smith, Utah State men's basketball coach

Kohn Smith made his remarks last year and precipitated a public shouting match with UNLV coach Jerry "Tark the Shark" Tarkanian, but the NCAA did not show much interest in his comments. A college sports observer has to assume that Smith's criticisms, as well as his call for a general "study into such matters as . . . summer employment, work compensation, the kinds of cars players are driving and the source of those cars," do not come under the heading of news nor are they apparently worthy of the NCAA's serious attention.

The fact is that college athletes, like their coach bosses, have long received presents from boosters and local merchants. In the distribution of presents, the same rule that governs all of College Sports Inc. operates—to the winners go the best freebies. A former *Louisville Courier-Journal* sports columnist explained the difference between the University of Louisville's successful men's basketball team and its mediocre football squad: "Twice in recent years I've been in the same room with all of the U. of L. basketball players and all of the football players. It's easy to pick out the basketball players because they are better dressed. I guess their parents are better off."

Only during the investigation of a major scandal, in the wake of more serious infractions, do stories of free credit cards and merchandise come tumbling out. At the University of Houston, one all-conference wide receiver testified that he was given a department store credit card and he made "numerous purchases of necklaces and diamonds and things [with it]. . . . I could never know who paid for all the stuff. I guess the football department paid for it. I know I didn't. I never even got a bill for it." Houston athletes also received free gasoline credit cards—a common part of a car deal—and were frequently given free fill-ups at a local service station.

Another perk is a free long-distance credit card or, more commonly, free use of the athletic department's WATS line. One Houston football player admitted, "I think my phone bill [on the WATS line] was about $1,400. . . . They told me to stop using it. But they never did cut it off, and I kept on using it. I didn't pay for any of it." However, the record on telephone bills was, according to the *Dallas Morning News,* set by athletes at Oral Roberts University who "charged $50,000 to university telephone credit cards."

Considering the huge long-distance bills that all athletic departments ring up, and the fact that the calls are to all parts of the country and abroad, the NCAA's ability to sift through voluminous telephone records and locate the ones made illegally by athletes is minimal. Only in cases of regular and widespread abuse does the Enforcement Division intervene and examine the bills. In the NCAA's 1980s investigation of Mississippi State University, it found long-distance violations involving athletes in such sports as women's basketball, golf, tennis, and softball. The association's only penalty in the Mississippi State case was to order its athletic department "to develop a rules-education program for its staff."

> *"For about 20 years, Richey said he allowed UT*
> *[University of Tennessee] players and their families, and*
> *UT coaches to stay free at his Gatlinburg motel and also*
> *at the Volunteer Motel, which he owned in Knoxville."*
>
> —Item in the *Knoxville Journal*

College athletes, as Princes of the Jockocracy, are frequently surrounded by fawning courtiers, a.k.a. Jock Sniffers, fans who will do almost anything to please them. For college athletes, these hangers-on are their best and most consistent source of freebies and favors.

Sam Gilbert, for fifteen years a friend of the UCLA men's basketball program, is one of the most famous supporters on record. Through the NCAA championship years, Gilbert, according to the *Los Angeles Times,* "arranged and paid for abortions for the players' friends, and helped athletes get discounts on cars, stereos, and airline tickets." Gilbert denied the abortion charges, but such ex-Bruins as Lucius

Allen, according to the *Times,* said that "when he and other players got their friends pregnant, Mr. Gilbert, if asked, would arrange and pay for an abortion."

Another generous friend of an athletic department was Trent Richey of Gatlinburg, Tennessee. In a twenty-year period up to the mid-1980s, according to the *Knoxville Journal,* he "provided $100,000 worth of free rooms to [University of Tennessee] players and their families" at his motels. The paper reported that "coaches asked him to provide the rooms free and he did so even though he suspected it violated NCAA rules."

Connected to every college sports program is its tribe of Jock Sniffers; their gifts are such an accepted part of athletes' and coaches' lives that many athletic department administrators have to remind themselves and their employees that the freebies violate NCAA rules. In this instance, ADs and administrators cannot be accused of hypocrisy: many were once college athletes and probably received similar gifts, thus they truly see nothing wrong with the practice. And to confuse the issue, the NCAA allows lots of free gifts—for example, the NCAA permits bowl game committees to give valuable presents to the players of the participating schools.

"The NCAA are their usual hypocritical selves on this one," says a Purdue University professor. "Let's see the NCAA point to one instance where ordinary students—say, all the participants in a college science fair—receive gifts like expensive watches, cameras, and engraved rings from the fair's organizing committee. However, those are the usual bowl gifts. The Rose Bowl gives each player gifts worth $750—all perfectly legal under NCAA rules."

> "Pat Horton, Lane County [Oregon] district attorney,
> suggested that some members of the university community
> 'are willing to overlook crimes being committed by a
> chosen few for what they consider to be more important
> considerations.' For the sake of a winning season [at the
> University of Oregon], he added, some would 'allow our
> football players to do basically whatever they want to do
> . . . including sodomy, attempted sodomy, and
> burglary.' "
>
> —Item in the *Chronicle of Higher Education*

The NCAA recently spent $1.75 million studying "the experiences of college or university life of student-athletes." Unfortunately—but inevitably—the survey did not inquire into the problems that college athletes have with the police and the law. One of the few studies on this subject was conducted by the *Philadelphia* (Pa.) *News* in 1986. In a survey of 350 schools for the years 1983 through 1985, it found that athletes "had been implicated in at least 61 sexual assaults [and] . . . that football and basketball players were 38% more likely to be implicated in such crimes than the average male college student."

Anecdotal evidence tends to support the *News*'s findings. However, the social and psychological reasons behind the frequent headlines of college athletes' arrests are complex. Joseph A. Pursch, a prominent M.D., suggests that because athletes receive preferential treatment from early ages, their social consciences are often underdeveloped. This doctor offers a background profile of the athlete-as-legal-offender: "At home he gets away with talking back; in school he gets good grades even when he cuts classes; and his third drunk-driving charge is covered up. Every girl in town wants to date him. And when he gets rough with a cheerleader at two o'clock in the morning, the coach smooths things out with her father."

The players on the University of Washington football team are typical of big-time college athletes. Last year, coach Don James offered an athletic scholarship to Marc Jones, a running back recently released from prison for "felony mayhem." James said that he had checked out the athlete thoroughly and "his background is probably better than most players we bring in."

When college athletes get into trouble with the police, athletic department personnel and/or boosters usually try to extricate them from it as quickly and quietly as possible. When regular students are arrested, they receive minimal or no help from university personnel and, if they are middle-class and don't have rich and powerful parents, they encounter the law as ordinary middle-class citizens. When poor black students are arrested, unless they are athletes they can expect from the police and courts what their brethren at home usually receive—trouble raising bail, representation by a public defender, and, if found guilty, a stiff sentence.

Tommy Kane, who as a junior at Syracuse in 1987 led the NCAA in touchdown receptions, grew up in one of the poorest black sections of Montreal. "A kid like Tommy Kane," says Randy Philips of the *Montreal Gazette,* "if he hadn't gotten out of Montreal would probably be in jail or have a bullet in his head right now." But because of his athletic ability, Kane made it to Syracuse University and also acquired a Cadillac. One night in April 1988, a Syracuse policewoman, while ticketing Kane's car, discovered that he had nineteen outstanding parking tickets and she ordered the car towed. The football player tried to drive away—after having closed the door on the policewoman's arm. Other police intervened and arrested Kane, charging him with "second-degree assault, a felony, and misdemeanor counts of resisting arrest and obstructing governmental administration."

If Kane had been an ordinary black student or a ghetto kid in his Cadillac (how Kane obtained the car never emerged), the court would have tried him on these charges and, if he were convicted, probably would have sent him to prison. Instead, the Syracuse district attorney offered the athlete a plea-bargain arrangement that allowed Kane "to plead guilty to disorderly conduct and harassment in exchange for 100 hours of community service, a public apology and restitution."

All students are equal in the eyes of the NCAA and the law; some students, especially "student-athletes," are more equal than others.

Local police and the courts favor athletes and help athletic departments in more ways than plea bargaining. When Chris Washburn, a basketball player at North Carolina State, was being investigated as a suspect in a dorm robbery, someone in the local police department leaked the information to the N.C. State athletic department. According to the *Raleigh News and Observer,* "The leak allowed basketball coach Jim Valvano to tell Washburn that he was a suspect before the detective in charge of the case could talk to Washburn." In some jurisdictions, Valvano's activity comes close to obstruction of justice, but the same Very Important Persons Law that extends special treatment to the player also applies to the coach, and the Raleigh police never even rapped the coach's knuckles. (Washburn pleaded guilty and received a suspended sentence.)

Athletic departments also help their athletes in legal trouble by providing free attorneys. This clearly violates the NCAA's "extra benefits" rule and, if the case is prominent enough, this freebie sometimes sparks an NCAA investigation. When Minnesota basketball player Mitch Lee was accused of rape, and the case made national headlines because of previous rape charges against other Minnesota basketball players, the coaches and boosters who helped pay Lee's legal expenses caught the NCAA's attention. The "Enforcement Division," with cooperation from university administrators, quickly uncovered the infraction, penalized the school, and gained publicity for its "vigilance."

More difficult for the NCAA to find are all the times that a coach bails out a player for a common offense, especially drunk driving, and arranges for the player's legal defense. If the coach calls a lawyer who is a booster, the expenses tend never to appear—the lawyer claims that he did it *pro bono*: "for the public good."

In 1986, the *Dallas Morning News* turned up over thirty cases of University of Texas football players receiving "free legal counsel" through the intervention of a Longhorn assistant coach. The offenses were mainly DWIs (driving while intoxicated) and traffic violations, and the lawyer claimed that he handled the cases for free. Tony Degrate, a Texas lineman and winner of the Lombardi Award, explained that one particular assistant coach was in charge of Longhorn legal difficulties: "If there was a DWI, he would go behind the scenes and set up the lawyer." Another player said, "He was the one who bailed you out of jail. I remember waiting for him in the Austin jail."

If Degrate and his teammates had been regular Texas students and had called the Office of the Students' Attorney, they would have been told, "We handle civil matters . . . no criminal matters," and they would have been advised to hire their own lawyers to get them out of jail.

Because college athletes are granted a great deal of social and legal immunity by the Very Important Persons Law, they neither behave as ordinary students are expected to behave, nor do they receive the same punishments if they misbehave. The NCAA says that athletes are entitled to only those "benefits" available to the "general student body," but the association is largely responsible for creating the huge college sports industry and the resulting climate that extends VIP treatment to athletes.

To build College Sports Inc. to its current billion-dollar state, to court the media for national attention and glorification, and then to demand that your performers, including your stars, be ordinary students and citizens is a contradiction that defies unraveling.

CHAPTER 31

Athletic Scholarships within the University Context

"By what right do you take money and give it to students whose qualifications are that they are first-rate athletes instead of students who are scholars?"

—Donald Kagan, former athletic director at Yale University

A UNIVERSITY EDUCATION, in recent times considered almost an American birthright, is becoming increasingly expensive and less feasible for many high school graduates—no matter what their academic talents and potential. Since 1980, college tuition and other costs have risen dramatically but the money available for scholarships and loans, especially from the federal government, has decreased. In 1990, the cost of a year at most state universities averages $8,000 to $10,000, and $15,000 to $20,000 at many private institutions, but family income in America averages $23,000 annually (for whites). To help meet these costs, students and their families are assuming, at a typical state school, an average indebtedness of close to $9,000 to pay for a college education. The admissions director of Indiana University says, "We have students on this campus who are looking at a $20,000 negative dowry to take into the marketplace."

Unlike athletic scholarships, student loans are neither free nor full rides but must be paid back at varying rates of interest at a future date. In addition, some student loan packages have "work-study" stipulations and the recipients must do such things as shelve books in the library to fulfill the labor requirements. Most students also work during summer vacations to earn money for their next year in college (rarely are these jobs as lucrative or as easy as those arranged for athletes). The Indiana admissions director points out that "to pay for [a state] college now by working in the summers, a student would need a job that paid the equivalent of $35,000 a year."

As a result of this oppressive financial situation, increasing numbers of qualified high school graduates are not entering higher education or are dropping out before completing their studies.

The discrepancy between college athletes and regular students (as well as would-be students) raises a troubling social question: *if universities and colleges are serious about their educational missions, why do they give enormous financial benefits to athletically talented but often academically hopeless individuals, and deny money and access to many potential teachers, doctors, lawyers, and other future leaders of American society?*

> *"The [NCAA $1.75 million] study also reported that many universities seemed more interested in and put more effort into recruiting black athletes than black students who were not athletes."*
>
> —Item in the *New York Times*

While the number of black college athletes has increased over the last fifteen years, especially at southern schools, total black enrollment in American higher education has decreased by almost 14 percent. The social implications are dire—although more blacks are graduating from high school (up 25 percent), fewer blacks, especially males, are attending college, and thus fewer black families will be able to break out of subsistence incomes or poverty.

The main reason for declining black college enrollment is financial. During a period when college costs have risen, black family income has stayed at an average of $12,000 a year. Tightening this financial vise is the decrease in federal loans to minority-group students since 1980. Moreover, those black students who could obtain loans for their college educations had assumed an average indebtedness by the late 1980s of over $10,000.

To put black college enrollment in specific terms, in 1987, in three states with very large black populations, the percentage of black students at the main campuses of the major public universities was amazingly low: at the University of Illinois, 3.8 percent; at the University of Michigan, 5.3 percent; and at Penn State, 3.7 percent.

Within this university picture of declining black enrollment and financial distress exists intercollegiate athletics. About 15 percent of black males at large state schools hold athletic scholarships but many of these men are what Professor Harry Edwards calls "black gladiators," brought to college only to play sports, not for an education. *Ironically, some schools pay for their "black gladiators" by diverting money from funds earmarked for academically motivated minority students.*

In late 1988, the NCAA reported on the University of Cincinnati's awarding of financial-aid packages to black freshmen basketball players who were Proposal 48 casualties. The men's basketball coach at Cincinnati and the university's director of financial aid had put together grants that included money from the University Honors Scholarship Fund, the State Economic Opportunity Grant, and student financial-aid discretionary funds. The NCAA noted that in this case and similar ones, "NCAA legislation actually permitted [Prop 48] partial qualifiers to receive the aid that was awarded." These athletes had failed to get over 700 on their SATs, but Cincinnati took money from its limited scholarship funds and gave it to them rather than to more academically qualified minority students. In 1990, the NCAA extended this financial aid benefit to Prop 42 partial qualifiers—thus allowing institutions to continue to divert scarce funds in this way.

Instead of trying harder to locate and educate future black teachers, doctors, et al., many schools spend large sums of money recruiting and then maintaining in college that cohort of black youth who are often the least prepared and the least interested in acquiring college educations.

> "A former MSU [Memphis State University] head
> basketball coach, Wayne Yates, said, 'I believe academic
> counselors honestly want athletes to graduate, but I've
> heard an academic counselor say he could keep a
> cockroach eligible for two years.' "
>
> —Item in the Memphis Commercial Appeal

In the last decade, newspapers have embarrassed many institutions of higher education with stories about the schools' illiterate athletes. Basketball player Kevin Ross went through four years at Creighton University only to end up in a grade school in Chicago trying to learn how to read and write. The judge who sentenced Billy Don Jackson, a former football star at UCLA, to jail for voluntary manslaughter also ordered that he learn how to read and write—skills that he never mastered before or during his years at UCLA. All-NFL player Dexter Manley admitted before a congressional hearing that he was still illiterate after four years at Oklahoma State. These horror stories and others prompted many institutions to devise plans to avoid being the school in tomorrow's headlines.

Their main initiative, throughout the 1980s, was to expand special academic advising programs for athletes. Athletic departments upgraded their longtime free tutorial services for athletes by hiring full-time academic advisors and enlarging their duties beyond tutoring. Most NCAA Division I-A schools now have an average of six full-time advisors, and some have a staffer for each sport. In addition, the full-time personnel hire large numbers of part-time assistants to do the bulk of the tutoring and "babysitting" (walking athletes to class, often taking notes for them, sometimes attending classes for them).

Penn State prides itself on its academic advising program for athletes and spends $600,000 a year on its advisors, tutors, and study hall monitors, as well as a career-development psychologist and a sports psychologist. Penn State has eight hundred intercollegiate athletes; thus it averages $750 per athlete for these NCAA-approved services. Penn State also has thirty-five thousand other students, but if they need tutoring, and the limited university services are unavailable, they have to search the bulletin boards around campus for the names of professional tutors and pay the going rate of $10 to $15 an hour. (Penn State would not reveal how much it spends on free tutoring services for regular students, but granting it a generous $1 million, this would average about $27 per student.) Moreover, as at all Division I schools, athletes can use the university-wide services but regular students are denied access to the athletic department's top-of-the-line program.

For all their recent popularity, athletic department academic advisors are not on easy street. Every day they face an insoluble problem: how to keep players eligible for intercollegiate athletics while insuring that they receive a college education. Coaches demand that players spend an enormous number of hours a week training, practicing, attending team meetings, viewing game films, traveling, and playing their sports; for most athletes, this regimen precludes spending the time and effort necessary for a decent college education. Thus, academic advisors often have to disregard the athlete's educational needs and concentrate on keeping him or her eligible, that is, within the NCAA's minimal standards of twelve credit hours per semester and a passing, usually a D, average.

If an academic advisor is high-minded and concerned about an athlete's education, the advisor soon disputes the coaches' demands on the player's time. Because ADs sympathize with their coaches, and also have the self-interest of needing winning teams, they decide most of these conflicts in favor of the coaches. Advisors who want to keep their jobs learn "to go along to get along" and to acquiesce to the coaches' commands. Bob Bradley, an academic advisor at the University of Kentucky, explained, "If a coach says of an advisor, 'I don't want him,' the advisor will be either quickly funneled out, or slowly funneled out."

An advisor's work with an athlete begins when the latter arrives on campus as a freshman; unfortunately, in many cases, this starting point is already years too late—the athlete is totally unprepared for and uninterested in college work, and is often burdened by the illusion that schoolwork is easy because compliant teachers "greased" his or her way through high school. But advisors have no real say on the college admission of athletes; their job is to make silk purses out of cauliflower ears.

The advisor's first task is to arrange the athlete's schedule of classes. Immediately a conflict between eligibility and education arises: should the athlete be allowed to take the same courses as other freshmen or be placed in the school's "hideaway curriculum" to insure eligibility? Because freshmen can play intercollegiate sports and the coaches want to suit them up, the conflict is usually resolved in favor of the "puff" courses. Even in cases where athletes request a regular course of studies, academic advisors tend to steer them toward the athletic department's approved curriculum. A freshman quarterback wants to be a premed major but ends up in phys ed courses; he complains to his advisor and is informed that premed labs are scheduled only in the afternoon, the same time that he has to be on the football practice field. A woman basketball player plans to major in prelaw but is dumped into recreation classes; when she asks why, she is told that basketball practice starts in October and she won't have time for all the work in prelaw.

Academic advisors do not inform their charges of the athletic department's unwritten policy—keep athletes away from hard majors and courses because of the possibility of failing grades and the loss of eligibility. Unlike the quarterback or woman basketball player, most freshmen athletes do not question the courses to which they are sent—usually jocks do not even fill out their own registration or class schedule forms, their advisors do. *The advising system insures that athletes will live inside the athletic department cocoon and not receive much of an education.*

Once athletes have their class schedules, the academic advisor has to make certain that they go to class and attain minimum grades. The simplest method should be to ask the athletes directly but, as one North Carolina State professor explained, "The coach asks [me], 'Is so and so in class?' and I say, 'Well, ask the student.' The coach says, 'He'll lie to us.' " Thus advisors bypass the athletes and ask the professors: since at many schools, especially the jock factories, advisors try to place athletes with faculty members who are either outright Jock Sniffers or sympathetic to athletic department needs, getting accurate information is not difficult.

If the report on the athlete is negative—he or she is not attending and/ or passing the course—often a "babysitter" is assigned to the player. At Oklahoma, when a tutor walks an athlete to a course, the expression is that the player was "eyeballed into class." If the athlete is attending but failing the course, sometimes the babysitter will stay with the athlete in class, taking notes and explaining the material to him or her. In addition, if the athlete is on a road trip with the team, sometimes the tutor will attend the class and take notes in the player's stead.

Because athletes are away from campus for as much as 25 percent to 35 percent of a semester, one of the advisor's main tasks is to arrange for them to make up missed classes. If the advising program cannot afford a legion of stenographic babysitters, the advisor tries to acquire notes from another student in the course or obtain permission to tape-record or videotape the class. But if the course has a discussion or a question-and-answer component—and most do—notes and recordings are inadequate substitutes for being present and mentally engaged in the material.

Academic advisors also try to arrange makeup exams for athletes who miss regularly scheduled ones. Again, this works against the pedagogical purpose of most courses. As Paul Lermack, a political science professor at Bradley University, explained, "An exam is partly evaluative but it's partly diagnostic as well. It lets me know how well the student is progressing." Thus when Lermack received a request that a football player be allowed to "take all four of my exams, plus the final, on the last day of the course," he refused. (Not all professors are as unobliging as Lermack: a classmate of Brian Bosworth's in a political science course at Oklahoma reported, "I don't think he went to class more than four or five times. I remember him going to the professor and managing to get a test changed because it didn't fit into his schedule. Imagine if a student tried to do that.")

With so many athletes in so many colleges and universities, inevitably some end up in courses taught by faculty who are either neutral or unsympathetic to athletic department needs. Advisors handle these professors by sending them a stream of notes or questionnaires inquiring about the athletes' progress in their courses. Professor Neil Petrie of Colorado State University believes that this system "amounts to preferential treatment" for athletes: "It requires teachers to take time from other teaching duties to fill out and return the forms for the athletes. No other students get such progress reports." If, however, a faculty member refuses to cooperate, some ADs and/or coaches send a letter—copies to the professor's department head and dean—emphasizing the athletic department's "sincere interest in the academic achievements of the school's student-athletes" and requesting the faculty member's aid in this endeavor.

There is, however, an important postscript to this athletic department "sincerity" concerning their athletes' academic progress: at most NCAA Division I institutions, once an athlete's playing eligibility is used up, the phone calls, notes, and questionnaires about academic progress abruptly stop. The athlete is usually two or more semesters away from graduation but the academic advisors no longer monitor his or her course work. An English professor at Indiana University, a school with one of the oldest and largest academic advising units for athletes, relates: "In the spring of 1989, a senior football player made his way into one of my courses, but during the semester I never received a single academic progress card for him. Finally, I phoned the athletic department and asked if there was some sort of clerical error. They said no, the player had used up his four years of eligibility and their policy in these cases was to no longer send cards. I thought, 'So much for their commitment to their athletes' education.' "

Equally questionable is the NCAA's commitment to the education of athletes with expiring eligibility. The association insists that athletic departments enroll players in the mandatory twelve units for their final semester of eligibility, but the NCAA does not require that these athletes try to pass their courses or even attend class (many do not—they play out their eligibility and drop out of school). In 1987, Brent Fullwood was Auburn's fullback in the Citrus Bowl at New Year's but had not gone to a single class since October—and in no way did this violate NCAA rules.

Auburn coach Pat Dye has never apologized for playing Fullwood and as recently as last summer he blasted his critics by replying, "Deion Sanders didn't even start to class at Florida State this past year and Tim Worley didn't darken the [classroom] door at Georgia, and he played and nobody wrote a word about it." (Georgia denied the charge about Worley; Florida State acknowledged Sanders's academic "insufficiency" and also admitted that he had played in the Sugar Bowl after flunking all of his fall semester courses.)

> *"Q. How many college football players does it take to change a light bulb?*
> *"A. Only one, but he gets three credits for it."*
>
> —Item in the *Chronicle of Higher Education*

When the Memphis State athletic scandal erupted in the mid-1980s and the fact emerged that only four basketball players, none black, had graduated from the school since 1972–73, the local head of the NAACP complained that MSU "athletes are allowed to take courses with no depth, that require no study, and lead to no degree." This is an excellent definition of the courses in most schools' "hideaway curricula" for athletes.

Almost every institution with intercollegiate teams in NCAA Divisions I and II has these special courses. Even a number of Ivy League schools have tilted a few classes toward their athletes; for many years, an easy geology course at Princeton was nicknamed "Rocks for Jocks." Depending upon the school, hideaway courses cluster in various areas, often HPER (health, physical education, and recreation), but sometimes in disciplines that at other places are perfectly respectable. At the University of Nevada at Las Vegas, two researchers found that during the early 1980s, "the departments of physical education and anthropology account[ed] for nearly half (47.7%) of the UNLV credits earned by basketball players." At institutions where anthropology is a difficult major, forensic studies or general studies will offer the courses most pleasing to jocks. Even at some academically excellent but athletically ambitious schools, athletes are steered toward certain classes—for example, at Georgia Tech, survey courses in textile and ceramic engineering. The reason for a Division of Hideaway Studies is simple: as the UNLV researchers explain, "Deprived of P.E. credits, most of the [UNLV] basketball players and some of the football players would likely be ineligible to play or to remain enrolled as students."

Traditionally, athletes have majored in physical education because it is close to their natural interests and also because athletic department personnel, including their coaches, often teach part-time in that department. If the courses are serious and well taught, the athlete receives a good education in P.E. and a legitimate college degree. Unfortunately, because often the coaches' priority is to keep the athletes eligible, P.E. courses, especially those with program heads or their assistants in charge, tend to be an area of massive academic abuse.

Spotting a hideaway curriculum course is not difficult. Usually the instructor is on the athletic department payroll as a coach or an administrator; the instructor's academic qualifications and degrees are frequently nonexistent or negligible; the instructor's teaching procedures are not standard; and the course content and exams are lighter than air. But the most convincing clue—to quote from a special faculty report at Florida State University—is "course sections . . . composed predominantly of athletes."

In the mid-1980s, hideaway curricula became more complicated for NCAA schools. In the wake of the Proposal 48 debate, the NCAA amended its "satisfactory progress" rule—twelve units and a passing average—to include the phrase "in a specific baccalaureate degree program" (until this time, many athletes were taking only miscellaneous "blow-off" courses, never declaring a major, and wandering through four years of eligibility without the hope of a degree).

Some program heads immediately located the loophole in this new version of "satisfactory progress" by gaining greater control over "a specific baccalaureate program," thus providing athletes with a major in their Division of Hideaway Studies. To secure the loophole, a number of universities moved their physical education programs from other units, such as schools of education, and gave them more autonomous status as separate divisions. In addition, to insure almost a double autonomy in case regular P.E. faculty objected to the maneuver, athletic departments began to set up such curricula as "sports management" programs within the physical education divisions. These programs, usually administered and taught by athletic department personnel, are increasingly the "specific baccalaureate degree program" of choice for athletes. Moreover, unlike almost all other academic programs in the university, sports management programs are not accredited by any outside agency and have no national validation for their degrees or checks upon their course content.

The lack of academic content of a sports management course at the University of Michigan, "PE 402—Sports Management and Marketing," a senior-level class, attracted national attention two years ago. Freelance writer Scott Shuger enrolled in the course as a regular student and then wrote about his experiences in *Sport* magazine. The class instructor listed in the catalog for "PE 402" was Don Canham, at the time Michigan's athletic director; in fact, according to Shuger, Canham's assistants and eleven guest lecturers did most of the teaching. The course had no textbook, outside readings, or regular assignments. In addition, the instructors went over the exam questions at length in class—before the tests—but still "widespread cheating" took place during tests. Most of the students were athletes, including some of the big names on Michigan's football and men's basketball teams, and "throughout the term absenteeism and lateness [were] rampant."

When Shuger published his account of "PE 402," Canham refused to read the article, but other administrators at Michigan admitted that the undercover student had scored some points. Possibly this university's problems with "sports management" began in 1984 (the year that the NCAA's amended "satisfactory progress" rule came into effect), when it removed its physical education program from the School of Education and gave it almost autonomous status as a separate division. Not surprisingly, over fifty percent of Michigan's sports management majors are on athletic scholarship.

Michigan, however, is not alone in the questionable content and grading procedures of sports management courses. At Indiana University, a student who took "P211: Introduction to Sport Management" wrote that "this course couldn't be made easier if they tried. The grading is based on 1 exam, 1 paper, and attendance. The paper is a self-analysis on what the person would like to do as a career (2 to 3 pages). The exam is multiple choice, and covers 50 vocabulary words that are passed out 2 weeks prior to the exam. Attendance accounts for 50% of the grade."

Not every NCAA Division I-A school, however, allows its athletic department to institute a hideaway curriculum for athletes. In the mid-1980s at Rice University, the athletic department and its supporters wanted to set up a half-dozen special "Business Practicum" courses for football and basketball players as a way of making the school's teams more competitive in the Southwest Conference. The head of the Rice booster club explained that the special courses "would be easier to pass than some others at Rice, and would therefore benefit athletes." Even though the school's president and the board of governors were in favor of the special courses, the faculty and some alumni and students strongly opposed the proposal. The academic purists won, the courses were never instituted, and the Owls continued to lose most of their football and basketball games. Nevertheless, throughout the 1980s, increasing numbers of the best high school students in America applied to Rice (its freshmen averaged over 1300 on their SATs), making it, by 1990, one of the most prized admissions in the country.

The incident at Rice contradicts a number of popular myths about college sports: the supposed link between the success of a school's athletic teams and the number and quality of its applicants for admission; and, as important, that big-time athletic departments will always have their way in matters of curriculum. Rice showed that the faculty, the traditional guardians of curriculum, can fight and sometimes whistle down hideaway courses.

CHAPTER 32

Tricks of Academic Aid: Within NCAA Rules, in the Spaces between the Rules, & far outside the Rules

"We're all taking kids [athletes] who don't belong in college. There's no point running a survey and saying, 'Oh boy, is Memphis State bad or is somebody else bad.' That's baloney. All of us have problems getting people through school. Everybody talks about tutoring programs and great counseling. All those kids do is major in eligibility."

—Norm Sloan, longtime Division I men's basketball coach

ALTHOUGH ATHLETES are supposed to major in a "specific baccalaureate program," at many schools, majoring in eligibility is still the preferred course of studies. To supplement hideaway curricula, academic advisors employ a large number of tricks.

The *NCAA Manual* provides them with some suggestions: "Correspondence, extension and credit-by-examination courses taken from an institution *other than the one in which a student-athlete is enrolled as a full-time student* shall not be used in determining a student's 'academic standing' or 'satisfactory progress' " (emphasis added).

Before this rule was instituted, schools would beef up their athletes' transcripts with correspondence or extension courses from compliant junior and community colleges (at times, the athletes would do zero work and receive full credit). Woody Green, a 1970s all-American football player at Arizona State, only managed during three fall semesters of Pac-10 football to pass two ASU classes, for a 0.66 average (on a 4.0 scale). Green stayed eligible by getting good grades in extension courses at Pacific College in Fresno and California Lutheran College in Thousand Oaks.

When the NCAA, as much from embarrassment as in the spirit of reform, banned such outside courses, coaches found a loophole by using these same kinds of courses at their own schools and getting the administrators who run them to "appreciate" the athletic program needs. In this scam athletes cheat by using tutor-generated and/or plagiarized work (they also use these devices in their regular university courses). With correspondence courses, since assignments are mailed in, the line between the athlete's work and the tutor's help becomes particularly blurred if ever visible.

For obvious reasons, academic advisors like correspondence courses, often justifying them as a perfect means of overcoming the problem of team travel: the athletes can work on these courses while on the road (tutors sometimes accompany the team on trips), and they are not tied to a rigorous three-times-a-week class schedule.

"You can't believe the abuses going on in our correspondence division," admits an instructor in one at a Midwest school. "Since we never see the athletes—except on TV—we have no way of knowing whether they are actually doing the work. From all that I can tell, such as the same answers from a number of athletes, or identical essays in consecutive years, as well as the high level of the completed assignments, the tutors are doing most if not all of the work for the jocks. I really resent the arrogance of the tutors—they know that even when they put down the same answer for more than one jock, we'll never turn them in because the athletic department will protect them and make maximum trouble for us."

The "moment of truth" for athletes in correspondence courses should come with their final exams—they are required to go to a "neutral" site and take a proctored exam, administered by a neutral person and sent ahead by the correspondence division. Unfortunately, the head of the athletic department's academic advising unit sometimes "convinces" the head of the school's correspondence division to allow the athletic department to be the "neutral" site and to permit the head academic advisor to be the "neutral" administrator.

Extension courses are less popular than in the old days when they could be taken at another and more compliant school's extension division, but they still have their uses for athletic departments. Instructors of extension courses are usually part-timers and their methods of teaching and the contents of their courses are not monitored by a school's regular academic departments. Thus, if an athletic department locates an "understanding" extension instructor—sometimes a person who has worked for it or is still employed as a tutor—great numbers of athletes begin appearing in that instructor's extension classes. This abuse culminates when a high grade for, say, English 100 appears on an athlete's transcript, whereas the university's English department had no control over the content and assignments in the course, and in no way certifies this grade. If the NCAA checks on the athlete's academic progress, he or she appears to have earned a B in English 100; in fact, the athlete might be semiliterate.

"Credit-by-examination" courses are somewhat more difficult for athletic departments to use. At many schools, they are only administered by regular academic departments and reserved for students who want to "test out" of a course and receive credit for it, but at some institutions, with the help of compliant administrators, athletes have "tested out" of and gained credit for courses about which they knew nothing. If an athletic department has control of a physical education department or a sports management program, it can do "credit-by-examination" in-house.

As with all scams, certain tricks of jock aid have periods of popularity and then drop out of favor. In the 1970s, extension courses were on top of the charts; in the 1980s, it was remedial classes.

Because many athletes arrive at university far behind the literacy and math levels of their classmates, athletic departments dump them into remedial programs (at many schools, some of the remedial courses are at grade school levels). For many years, according to NCAA rules, athletes could take as many remedial classes as their institution allowed and still fulfill the "satisfactory progress" requirement (some of Jan Kemp's University of Georgia athletes repeated the same remedial English class four times). Finally, in the late 1980s, the Presidents' Commission of the NCAA pushed through a change in this rule: athletes may now take only twelve hours of remedial courses, to be completed in their freshman year. The loophole in the new rule makes use of curriculum definition: if an athletic department has the necessary clout, yesterday's remedial course becomes today's regular three-unit class.

In a twist on the remedial studies ploy, last year the University of Nebraska used the school's Educational Center for Disabled Studies to shelter four of its men's basketball players (25 percent of the team). Because the players were classified as "learning disabled," rather than semiliterate, the athletic department was allowed to have instructors read exams to them and also give the players extra time to do their work, including on exams.

Often colleges and universities, sometimes very famous ones, are complicit in these academic deceptions and are as much to blame for their athletes' lack of education as are the athletic departments. Lawrence Taylor, the all-pro linebacker, tells how at the University of North Carolina at Chapel Hill, a school with an excellent academic reputation, he took "a number of courses that were ready-made for football players. You know, large lecture classes, twelve hundred people or more, with two tests, a midterm and a final, both multiple-choice. In those courses, you're gonna get what the guy sitting next to you gets. The only thing you have to do is remember not to copy the same name on your paper." The UNC athletic department steered Taylor and its other athletes to these courses but the university tolerated their existence.

Other schools allow academic departments to design majors for their undergraduate students that are not difficult until the final year. Athletes take the easy courses in these majors, fulfill all the NCAA "satisfactory progress" requirements, and then, with their eligibility used up, leave school before they have to take the hard senior courses in their major.

Another academic dodge used by regular students as well as athletes, and tolerated by many schools, is taking a course Pass/Fail. To receive the full credit units for the course, a student only needs to pass it—a D minus or better—and a "Pass" is entered on the student's transcript. Pass/Fail courses, originally popular in the 1960s as a means of allowing undergraduates to explore subjects without the grade sword hanging over them, have been abused in the 1980s by regular students and athletes who want to accumulate credit hours for minimum work. Because Pass/Fail hours count toward the twelve that an athlete needs per semester, the NCAA has no objection to this dodge, and at many schools athletes accumulate large numbers of "P" units on their records.

Athletes and regular students also fulfill their academic requirements by attending summer school, either on campus or in their hometown, and adding these hours and grades to their transcripts. Often the local school is excellent and the student's work is meaningful. In other instances, however, especially those involving athletes, the summer school credits come from a junior or community college and the scams that work with juco transfers are in play.

Some athletic departments do not even bother with juco summer schools but arrange the courses in-house or even have the juco come to them. At California State University at Chico, football players earned credit in summer P.E. courses on campus that were run by Butte Community College. According to a report in the *Chronicle of Higher Education,* "As many as 88 of the university's football players . . . did not attend [the courses]," and "some of the players, who were practicing on the campus, would have had to spend 28 hours a day in class to attend the courses they were enrolled in."

A variation on the summer school scam is the traveling course. When the men's basketball team at Ohio University went on a playing tour of Europe during the summer of 1986, the athletic department arranged for the players—as part of their tour—to take a four-credit "International Studies" course. The course was not in the school's catalog and the players earned their grades and credit hours with such tasks as keeping a diary of their travel experiences. Since they played ten games in fourteen days, their time for "International Studies" was somewhat limited.

The University of Nevada at Las Vegas offered an even more generous summer school course for its men's basketball players. During a sixteen-day, nine-game tour of the South Pacific, the athletes took a six-unit course entitled Contemporary Issues in Social Welfare, nicknamed "Palm Trees 101." Players passing this course fulfilled half of the NCAA's required twelve units to suit up for the following season.

Summer is the favorite time for athletes to become eligible for the coming year, and athletic departments offer many of their recreational and/or "puff" courses during summer school. In addition, because the coaches are often on campus for their camps, they are listed as the instructors in some of the courses. Summer school catalogs are filled with offerings such as "Jogging," "Tennis," "Karate," "Tae Kwon Do," and "Advanced Slow-Pitch Softball."

During the regular school year, athletes often receive credit for playing their sports—four units in "Intercollegiate Football" for football players, four units in "Intercollegiate Basketball" for basketball players, etc.—and they also take indoor courses like "Billiards" and

"Theory of Football." According to one report, when George Swarm, now in the NFL, played football at Miami of Ohio, he took such "courses as basketball and racquetball to try to remain eligible. When Swarm still could not meet eligibility requirements, he took a summer school course entitled 'Trees and Shrubs.' "

The bottom line on these tricks of jock aid is that most of them are perfectly legal within the NCAA's definition of academic requirements for a "student-athlete." Considering the almost unlimited possibilities within these rules, it is amazing that so many athletic departments still find it necessary to bend or break the NCAA's academic regulations to keep their athletes eligible.

> *"I knew this summer, when I came across the shortage in this young man's hours, that one way or another he would be playing football. There are certain truths in life. You don't spit into the wind, you don't tug on Superman's cape, and you don't mess around with star football players."*
>
> —Marianne Jennings, former associate dean
> of business at Arizona State University

When certain ADs and academic advisors read the NCAA's main rule on "sound academic standards," their highlighter pens mark the following: *"The phrases 'good academic standing' and 'satisfactory progress' are to be interpreted at each member institution by the academic authorities."* The NCAA justifies this rule on "states' rights" grounds— each institution is allowed to set its own academic standards (also for this reason, the NCAA does not raise the minimal grade point average required for playing eligibility). In practice, the rule deals NCAA members a wild card to win any hands involving athletes with academic problems (if a school certifies that a player with a 1.0 GPA is in "good academic standing," the NCAA accepts it).

At most big-time athletic schools, the "academic authorities" have no real power over the athletic department and its athletes. These authorities are almost always appointed by the university president and their main qualification is their willingness to do the CEO's bidding. Unless the latter is serious about, and willing to fight for, control of the athletic department, the "academic authorities" rubber-stamp the ADs list of athletes in "good academic standing." (Most university presidents, whether through lassitude, preoccupation with other tasks, or fear, prefer not to mess with their ADs.) Thus, *"interpreted at each member institution by the academic authorities"* is the athletic department's license to solve any problems caused by athletes in academic trouble.

In 1987, at Auburn, acting upon an instructor's complaint, the school's "Academic Honesty Committee," composed of four professors and three students, found starting quarterback Jeff Burger guilty of plagiarism. According to university rules, this should have resulted in Burger's academic suspension and the end of his college playing career. However, the school's vice-president for academic affairs stepped in and commuted Burger's suspension to one game. A member of the Academic Honesty Committee commented, "The athletic department is always saying that it wants athletes to be treated just like any other student. Well, we took them at their word, and for that we've been bludgeoned."

In the same year, at Arizona State University, one of the school's "academic authorities" also took her job and the NCAA mandate seriously, and as a result lost her administrative position. Marianne Jennings, an associate dean of the School of Business, ruled that a football player did not have enough credits to suit up for the fall season. The school president—a higher "academic authority"—overruled her; Jennings was then relieved of her administrative duties even though, as she pointed out, she "had received an 'excellent' job evaluation two weeks earlier."

If a college student's grades fall below his or her school's minimum average, the individual faces the prospect of flunking out. Unlike athletes, many regular students sink without a ripple and are not readmitted to the university. Athletes—at least those with playing eligibility remaining—can stay on academic probation far longer than regular students can and often, almost magically, when their sport's season starts, find themselves in "good academic standing."

A few years ago, at the beginning of the second semester at the University of Minnesota, forty football players—almost half the team—were academically ineligible to take part in spring practice. However, the "academic authority" in charge of their case admitted that although the statistic (forty players) was "technically true, in practice it will not create a problem," and that he would be surprised if most of the players "were ineligible to practice."

Basketball players at North Carolina State University have a long history of being on "academic warning" (the N.C. State term for school probation leading to suspension) and of miraculous academic recoveries. Since Jim Valvano began coaching at the school in 1980, twentynine of forty-three of his players have been on "academic warning," and in 1989 ten of twelve team members were. Some of last year's Wolfpack players had grade averages below 1.25—out of 4.0—and yet they all managed to play the entire season.

Athletes at other schools achieve even lower grade point averages but play on. Devon Mitchell, an Iowa football star in the 1980s, had a 1.0 average his sophomore year—earned with mainly Fs and one A. The A that pulled his average into the 1.0 range was in "Intercollegiate Football," i.e., for playing his sport.

If all else fails and the athlete is truly in danger of not suiting up, the athletic department can try to arrange a "retroactive" grade or some "directed studies" units. One September the assistant athletic director at the University of Florida realized that a star player had not fulfilled the NCAA's minimum eligibility requirement. To solve this dilemma, according to the *St. Petersburg Times,* the assistant AD awarded the player credit for a course that he had already taken the year before and for which he had received full credit the first time around. The course was taught by none other than the assistant athletic director.

Another standard ploy is to give the player a grade and credit for a "directed studies" course done under the supervision of a faculty member. When basketball player Russell Pierre was struggling to stay eligible at Virginia Tech, a friendly instructor (a member of the athletics board) awarded him credit hours and a C+ grade for a "directed studies" course in "House Plants"; however, because Pierre never actually completed the work, the scheme unraveled and the school was forced to declare him academically ineligible.

Often when athletic programs refuse to allow an athlete to play for academic reasons, their motivation is less a concern for educational standards than an acknowledgment of the near hopelessness of the situation—the player refuses to attend class or meet with tutors and has ignored all previous warnings. In some cases, however, academic ineligibility is used as a P.R. excuse for penalizing a player who will not obey a coach and/or is in trouble for off-the-field conduct; by invoking academic ineligibility, the athletic department appears high-minded and educationally oriented whereas the reality is more sordid.

On occasion, *players have been ineligible but have played on.* David Roberson was an all-conference end for the University of Houston and played in the Sun Bowl although he had been suspended from school. "I'll never forget," one of Roberson's teammates related, "when we went to the Sun Bowl, and one of the coaches asked Robe how many [credit] hours do you have? Robe said he didn't even have fifty-nine minutes, let alone an hour."

Because of academic failure, Roberson was later suspended from Houston for two semesters but returned to school after only one term out. He was suspended again with the transcript notation "No further enrollment should be contemplated," but the all-conference end was back in school the following season.

In 1986, the University of Houston set up a committee of administrators and faculty to investigate the academic situation of the school's athletes. The committee found that "since 1983, half of the student athletes . . . have been on academic probation, a large majority have not completed the basic English and math requirements, and 59 percent have either failed or not taken required remedial English." One of the committee members tried to put Houston's situation in perspective when he told the press that "the problems of educating student athletes are present at all major universities with football programs."

> "Norm Ellenberger is a classic example [of a coach who cheated]. The sonofagun is a great coach, a hell of a basketball coach. Why he chose to make the decisions he did, I don't know. Maybe he's lazy."
>
> —Bob Knight, commenting on his friend Norm Ellenberger

Because of the many loopholes in the NCAA Manual, the main reason that some athletic departments and coaches go beyond the rules and cheat is probably, as Bob Knight suggests, laziness. Norm Ellenberger is famous in college sports for his role in one of the worst transcript forgery cases on record. According to the NCAA, he arranged for many of the players on his University of New Mexico basketball team to receive academic credit from a number of California community colleges for extension and summer school courses that they never took and, in some cases, never even knew about. The scheme was relatively simple and involved payoffs to officials at the various colleges to approve the bogus transcripts. It continued for a number of years and the illegal credits helped keep the players eligible.

New Mexico was put on NCAA probation and Ellenberger lost his job there. He showed no remorse for his actions and continued his coaching career (he is currently an assistant at the University of Texas at El Paso and a candidate for a number of head coaching jobs). Faculty and students at New Mexico were less sanguine than the former coach about the incident. The chair of the athletic committee, a prosports faculty member, commented, "The whole episode just devastated this place. It did a great deal of damage to the integrity and the morale of this university."

In the early 1980s, academic fraud was so prevalent that half the schools in the Pac-10 were on probation for, according to conference officials, "violations of conference rules and standards in the areas of unearned credits, falsified transcripts, and the unwarranted intrusion of athletic department interests into the academic process of the respective universities." Subsequently, many big-time athletic departments became more honest and/or subtle in their strategies for keeping athletes eligible, but cheating, especially by arrogant and lazy coaches, continued.

When the University of Illinois football program needed eligibility for an outstanding quarterback named Dave Wilson, it sent the NCAA the transcript of another Dave Wilson from the player's high school. Not surprisingly, the second Dave Wilson had higher grades than the quarterback. Mainly because Dave Wilson was an outstanding player and received much media attention, the Illinois fraud was discovered.

NCAA Division I schools are not the only ones to cheat; athletic programs in other divisions bend and break the rules, too. In 1985, the Division III hockey program of the State University of New York College at Plattsburgh was penalized by the NCAA for various violations, but, according to one local reporter, the NCAA only examined the surface of this program as well as those of other small colleges. "The shame of the Plattsburgh State situation," says Sandy Caligiore, sports director of radio station WSNN in Potsdam, New York, "is that it happened in Division III, supposedly the last bastion of the amateur student-athlete."

Beyond the NCAA are the NAIA and the juco systems; academic cheating occurs in their athletic programs, too—often more openly than in the NCAA because these associations have tiny Enforcement Divisions. In 1988, the University of Wisconsin at Stevens Point had to forfeit its NAIA football title because two of its players had competed for another college the year before and had then illegally transferred to and played for the Wisconsin school. Their ineligibility was uncovered only because an NFL team drafted one of them and his previous school noticed that it was not listed on his bio sheet. Except for this accident, these NAIA athletes would have remained two more anonymous "tramp," or "gypsy," athletes, playing for various small schools for varying lengths of time—sometimes under assumed names and for a total of more than four years—and being wooed and moved about by other NAIA athletic programs.

One of the most brazen cases of academic transcript fraud occurred in 1986 at Erie Community College in Buffalo, New York. The ambitious coach of the men's basketball team admitted altering the transcripts of nine of his players so that they could win athletic scholarships to four-year colleges and make his own program appear more successful. The extent of the fraud doomed this scheme, but transcript altering—when done quietly and for one or two athletes—is much harder to detect.

The amazing aspect of these instances of outright academic fraud is that they occur at all. Some athletic directors say that "only fools cheat," and this seems true—but not for the sanctimonious reasons the ADs give. The last word on academic fraud belongs to Sandy Caligiore. When asked in an interview for this book about the extent of the corruption in the Plattsburgh State hockey program during the 1980s, he replied, "How deep do you want to go? If you want to probe two feet, you'll find stuff at two feet. If you want to go six feet, there's plenty at six feet. The NCAA couldn't get to the bottom of the corruption in Platts State if they moved their entire Enforcement Division from Kansas to upstate New York. And we're only talking about one small school in a nonrevenue sport in Division III here. If Platts State is an example of NCAA vigilance, I'd hate to think about what's going on in college sports all over this country!"

CHAPTER 33

Athletes' Graduation Rates: Phony Stats & False Solutions

"His senior season at the University of Kentucky was half over, and 6-foot-11 center Melvin Turpin was sitting in an airport terminal in Lexington when someone asked about graduation.

" 'How close are you, Melvin?'

"He paused for a moment, rubbing his chin and breaking out into a bit of a grin.

" 'How close? Oh, man, I don't know much about geography, but I'd say about here to Puerto Rico.' "

—Item in the *Louisville Courier-Journal*

IN 1985, when a Duke University official heard that the College Football Association was going to give awards to schools for graduating athletes, he exclaimed, "It's like getting a prize for breathing. You're supposed to do it. . . . What else are colleges for?" American colleges and universities are "for" many things, but during the last two decades awarding diplomas to athletes has not been one of them. From 1972–73 through 1985, Memphis State University graduated four men's basketball players (none of them black); from the early to the mid-1980s, 4 percent of the black men's basketball players at the University of Georgia graduated; and, according to a recent General Accounting Office study, "At a third of American colleges and universities with major men's basketball programs, fewer than one in five players ever graduate."

In one way, these statistics are laudable: they imply that no matter how corrupt the hideaway curricula for athletes become, many colleges and universities are unwilling to move to the next level of corruption and confer degrees upon athletes who only major in eligibility. In another, more embarrassing way, the low graduation rates contradict the NCAA's basic premise that college athletes are also students and that their primary purpose in school is to obtain an education, certified by a degree.

In the mid-1980s, in reaction to these low graduation numbers, the NCAA and allied organizations like the College Football Association tried various strategies to raise the rates. The CFA began its awards to schools with high rates and, to greater effect, both it and the NCAA began juggling their statistics: instead of basing the percentage of graduates on the total number of athletes who started in a program as freshmen, these organizations began issuing "adjusted graduation rates"—discounting from the statistical pool all athletes who transferred or dropped out of school "in good academic standing."

However, because leaving in "bad academic standing"—i.e., flunking out—usually takes a grade point average *below D,* the NCAA and CFA samples became highly skewed (those players who depart after using up four years of eligibility are often in "good academic standing"). Discounting transfers has a similar statistical effect: many transfers do not graduate from their next institution but their absence from the original pool increases the graduation rate. Finally, the NCAA and CFA gave athletes five—not the usual four—years to earn a degree and count as a successful grad stat. Not surprisingly, after this numerical sleight of hand, the NCAA and CFA graduation rates jumped significantly. (Some schools even base rates on only their senior class of athletes: such common pronouncements as, "Of our senior student-athletes, 90 percent graduated this June," can mean "We based our rates on those ten football players who made it to the senior class—out of the thirty who started in our program five years ago.")

Once the NCAA and CFA had their new stats in place, they began publicly to compare athletes' graduation rates with the percentage of regular students who obtain degrees (these average in the 90th percentile at private schools like Rice to below the 50th percentile at some state institutions). The NCAA and CFA, however, usually compared their skewed stats for athletes to the full ones that most colleges use for regular students—the percentage of *all incoming freshmen* who earn degrees after four or five years.

But beyond the statistical flaws in this comparison was a major error in logic. The NCAA and CFA ignored the fact that many regular students leave school for financial, not academic, reasons—some registrars claim that fiscal problems cause the majority of student dropouts. Athletic scholarship holders, however, never leave college because they cannot pay their tuition and other school bills. By glossing over the difference between students who drop out for financial reasons and athletes who fail academically, the NCAA and CFA invalidated their comparison of athletes' versus students' graduation rates.

On the basis of his self-proclamations, Indiana University basketball coach Bob Knight is frequently pointed to as a program head who graduates almost all of his players. Knight and the I.U. athletic department also like to contrast his apparent high rate with the much lower graduation statistic for regular Indiana students. However, if this coach's rate is calculated in the same manner as the latter group—placing in Knight's statistical pool all of the incoming freshmen and transfers to whom he has awarded athletic scholarships and giving them five years to earn their degrees at Indiana—his graduation statistic is closer to 65 than 100 percent. Similarly, when Knight's rival, Digger Phelps of Notre Dame, won his four hundredth game, Reebok Shoes placed a full-page ad in *USA Today* to congratulate him "on 400 wins and 50 victories. . . . Every one of the fifty players who *competed for four years* under Digger at Notre Dame has received a degree" (emphasis added); Reebok did not mention the number of players who dropped out of Digger's program.

Nevertheless, the percentage of Indiana and Notre Dame men's basketball players who do graduate is far above the averages at many other schools. In 1987, the *Gainesville* (Fla.) *Sun* discovered, "In the past 10 years, 673 male athletes have received scholarships to the University of Florida. Fewer than half earned degrees after five years [in school] and, in some sports, fewer than 20% graduated." This paper also noted that "in a recent five-year period, the basketball team graduated only five of 29 scholarship players—17%, just enough to fill a squad of starters."

The NCAA blames part of the low graduation rates on football and men's basketball players who sign pro contracts and drop out of school, but some studies show low rates among athletes in nonrevenue sports. The recent General Accounting Office survey reported thirty-five Division I baseball programs with graduation rates between 0 and 25 percent and another twenty-six schools below 50 percent. The same survey showed that over half the Division I men's tennis and golf programs graduated fewer than 50 percent of their athletic scholarship holders. And the graduation rates in such women's sports as basketball, track, softball, and volleyball were also below 50 percent.

The final irony on graduation rates is that as the media and the General Accounting Office demand more accurate statistics, the NCAA, ever reluctant to provide them, invokes the Buckley amendment—the law protecting the privacy of college students. The NCAA claims that releasing figures on the *total number of athletes* in a program could injure the individuals involved. The NCAA, of course, is the same organization that requires athletes to waive their rights to privacy in matters of drug testing.

> *"A wire service photograph from last month's UNLV graduation ceremonies showed [men's basketball coach] Tarkanian with five of the six seniors from this year's team, all in caps and gowns. Only two of the five players actually graduated [at the time]."*
>
> —Item in the *Los Angeles Times*

Just as colleges and universities set up hideaway curricula for athletes, some are also willing to give questionable diplomas to their players or, as in the UNLV case, "graduate" them before they actually earn their degrees. These same institutions are quick to denounce "diploma mills"—unaccredited schools that confer degrees for little or no work—and to refuse to recognize their degrees, but awarding their own baccalaureates to athletes for spending a few years in their Divisions of Hideaway Studies is acceptable to them. And as NCAA and media pressure increases on colleges to produce better graduation rates, more schools will churn out greater numbers of questionable degrees.

When the CFA announced its 1988 graduation awards, Joe Paterno, the head football coach at Penn State, warned: "I would hope that [athletes] graduated in courses that are meaningful. . . . We're getting so wrapped up in [graduation] percentages that we may be more concerned with the graduation rate than quality education." Digger Phelps has long wondered, "How many so-called student-athletes have graduated with a major that means something? That's where you're going to find the abuses being flagrant."

An athlete with a college degree does not necessarily signify an educated person, capable of earning a living in a technological society.

Not only football and basketball players with diplomas suffer from this under- or nonpreparation for the working world; many athletes in non-revenue sports, especially at Division I level, receive degrees but no education. A few years ago, the president of an Illinois graphic-arts company, and a college wrestling fan, wanted to help some recently graduated wrestlers obtain work but he "was amazed to find that the wrestlers were usually 'phys ed' majors who had no interest in anything, careerwise." The athletes also "had unrealistic expectations about jobs they might hold." The graphic-arts president related that "one guy wanted to be sales manager of my company. He had no experience or skills whatsoever. What he really wanted wasn't a job. He just wanted to be on the payroll," i.e., to stay aboard the gravy train that he and other athletes ride from an early age.

Thus graduation statistics for athletes, whether real or phony, are a sideshow to the academic problems in college sports. Low rates suggest that many athletes are not coming near a university education while playing intercollegiate sports. But high rates, because of juggled statistics and questionable degrees, offer no proof that the degree recipients gained a meaningful education.

In recent years, however, a number of national politicians have focused on low graduation rates as the central problem in college sports and have suggested some cures to those ills. The late Representative James Howard (Dem-N.J.) introduced a bill in Congress that would prohibit tax deductions for booster contributions to schools that fail to graduate 75 percent of their intercollegiate athletes. Senator Bill Bradley (Dem-N.J.) has championed legislation forcing colleges to reveal the graduation rates of their athletic scholarship holders.

These efforts are only first steps toward a solution to the academic and other frauds perpetrated by College Sports Inc. Congress might well address the question of whether *any* booster donation is a legitimate educational tax deduction, and, to be effective, Senator Bradley's legislation must prevent the NCAA and member schools from juggling and/or lying on graduation statistics.

The reality of contemporary college sports is far different from what Bill Bradley encountered during his Princeton playing days. Unless that reality is faced, no solution to the academic and other problems plaguing intercollegiate athletics will be forthcoming.

SUMMARY: TIME CONSTRAINTS, OR WHY MOST COLLEGE ATHLETES CANNOT ALSO BE STUDENTS

"When you go to college, you're not a student-athlete but an athlete-student. Your main purpose is not to be an Einstein but a ballplayer, to generate some money, put people in the stands. Eight or ten hours of your day are filled with basketball, football. The rest of your time, you've got to motivate yourself to make sure you get something back."

—Isiah Thomas, former Indiana University basketball player, presently an NBA star

ONE OF the conclusions in the NCAA's recent $1.75 million study of intercollegiate athletics was that "football and basketball players spend approximately 30 hours per week in their sports when they are in season—more time than they spend preparing for and attending class combined." The NCAA's thirty hours per week seems a low estimate. Most other studies of the time constraints on college athletes, as well as anecdotal evidence like Isiah Thomas's, point to much higher numbers.

A few years ago, the administration of Louisiana State University found that "varsity athletes spend as much as fifty hours a week in their sport." Notre Dame football coach Lou Holtz told an NCAA committee that "during the season . . . players at some schools spent as much as seven hours a day on football-related matters." Last fall, *Sports Illustrated* followed a University of Wisconsin football player through his week and noted that "football consumes 51 hours a week, classes 20 hours, studying a minimum of 25 hours. That's two full-time jobs, with plenty of overtime in both." (The player was not a pro prospect but he was in a regular course of studies.)

Professor Harry Edwards, a sociologist at the University of California, Berkeley, has done extensive research on this subject and concludes that many Division I-A football players in season spend up to "sixty hours a week" on their sport, and basketball players "fifty hours a week." Edwards succinctly explains the time dilemma of most college athletes: "Education is activist. You have to be actively involved in your

302

own education. When you're involved in sports fifty hours a week, maybe living in pain, you can't be actively involved [in your education]."

Edwards's comment also points to the unrecorded hours athletes spend: the time in recovery periods, hours passed getting over headaches and other pains acquired in scrimmages, games, etc. One former college basketball player described life under a coach who ran hard practices: "It was all you could do to drag yourself back to the dorm each day. By the time you ate and got back to your room, it was eight-thirty and all you could think about was getting your weary bones in bed and getting some sleep. Who had time to study?" This player had placed second in his high school graduating class and had wanted to be a premed major but had been channeled into phys ed. He did not graduate from college.

If the coach demands that players spend fifty or more hours a week on a sport, an athlete cannot refuse—unless he or she wants to drop the sport and lose the athletic scholarship. Football and men's basketball program heads are notorious for the time and physical demands they make on players but many of their colleagues in nonrevenue sports, sharing the program heads' win-or-die philosophy, also require constant sacrifices from their athletes. The recent NCAA survey notes that "women basketball players at major colleges spend as much time at their sport as their male counterparts."

Even in an athlete's off-season, the time required for sports does not drop significantly. Harry Edwards and most other authorities, including those who conducted the NCAA's recent study, subtract about ten hours a week from the in-season total. A former athletic director at Southern Illinois University admitted that for off-seasons, many coaches have "the mentality of 'more is better' . . . the longer the out-of-season practice period and the longer the weightlifting session, the better." In addition, new high-tech machines, rather than cut time from an athlete's training, have added to it: coaches demand longer hours on the Nautilus to increase strength and conditioning and more time spent viewing videotapes of one's own performance as well as those of opponents'.

To put the amount of time that a college athlete spends on a sport in perspective: The federal government allows a regular student receiving a work-study grant to spend *a maximum of twenty hours a week on his or her university job* (for example, shelving books in the library); the government's premise is that more than twenty hours a week would cut into the time needed for a normal course of study by a full-time student. Intercollegiate athletes, even at the NCAA's figure of thirty hours a week, are exceeding this requirement for full-time college students by 50 percent, and, at Harry Edwards's figures, by as much as 200 percent.

> *"It's like having two full-time jobs. You're on scholarship for football, so you're expected to produce in football as well as in your classes. It can make for a fifteen- or sixteen-hour day."*
>
> —Bernie Kosar, when he was quarterback at the University of Miami

Bernie Kosar is often praised as an authentic student-athlete: he entered college with excellent SAT scores and he graduated with a high GPA in finance and economics. The NCAA loves athletes like Kosar—and Bill Bradley and Byron "Whizzer" White before him—but the *Miami Herald* reporter who quoted Kosar above also pointed out that "players of Kosar's scholastic caliber are unusual. In fact, 33% of Hurricane freshmen (68 of 206) in the eight-year *Herald* study no longer were enrolled by the time they would have been seniors." (The reporter did not give the grad rates on this group but another article indicated that for the 1980–84 cohort, 24 percent graduated, with a low of 9 percent in 1982.)

Kosar articulated the main problem: student-athletes must hold "two full-time jobs," and if they are not as bright, well prepared, and determined as he was, they must neglect, if not fail, one of those jobs or both of them. Complicating their problem is the fact that for the supposed student-athlete, the two full-time jobs never end.

The NCAA allows football to begin in early August and to pause after the January bowl games, then to start again in March for thirty-six days of "spring practice," including full-contact scrimmages. Meanwhile in the off-season, football players undergo strenuous conditioning and strength programs. The college basketball season begins officially in mid-October and ends with the NCAA Final Four in early April; however, college basketball teams can take long summer tours and play in a number of preseason tournaments. None of these exhibition contests, as well as the ongoing conditioning programs and informal games, count in the NCAA official season, but they require players to take time and energy away from their studies.

In the nonrevenue sports, college baseball is played in both fall and spring, and the NCAA sanctions seventy games. College baseball teams also take two- to three-week road trips away from campus, play many exhibition games, and can compete in NCAA-approved summer leagues. Many college baseball players are in one hundred games or more a year. Other nonrevenue sports have equally long seasons: in swimming, track-and-field, golf, and tennis, athletes train all year, frequently travel to distant meets or tournaments, and miss many days of school.

The Reverend Timothy J. Healy, former president of Georgetown University, has long argued that "the length and intensity of [college sports] seasons are positively ridiculous," but he and other college presidents have made almost no progress within the NCAA to curtail the seasons (dropping three games and two weeks from the "official" basketball schedule, as the Presidents' Commission proposed in 1990, is hardly a serious reform; also this proposal does not go into effect until August 1992 and the ADs and coaches have sworn to kill it before then). Moreover, the debate has focused only on the "official" seasons and has ignored the equally serious problem of the never-ending "unofficial" season.

The NCAA sanctions both the official and unofficial seasons and yet it expects athletes to be regular students. The NCAA also permits athletes to spend time in public appearances (as long as they receive no remuneration for these) and to help promote a positive image of college sports through charity and P.R. work. A popular athlete can invest many hours in attending booster and other public functions as well as in helping coaches with clinics and other extracurricular activities.

In addition, if outstanding athletically, he or she is invited to pro and/or Olympic tryouts and training camps and, in sports like basketball, all-star games. Before the pro football draft, NFL teams hold camps around the country to test the athletes' skills and physical condition; once drafted, a player is required to attend his NFL team's spring minicamp. Meanwhile, through all of these NCAA-sanctioned distractions, athletes are expected to continue with their schoolwork.

Thus, beneath the NCAA's rhetoric about the "student-athlete," a basic and simple question exists: *How can a college athlete devote forty to sixty hours a week to a sport and also spend forty to sixty hours a week working on a meaningful college education?* Bernie Kosar, an exceptional athlete and student, tried to square this circle with fifteen- and sixteen-hour days. Kosar's very success suggests that intercollegiate athletics is a system that works for only a few. College sports, however, should function for the majority of its participants.

The NCAA, the main interest group for coaches and athletic directors, insists that it can repair this systemic failure with reforms from within the present structure of College Sports Inc. An examination of the NCAA's recent proposals for reform and, more to the point, of the NCAA as the agent of change brings into question whether the association will ever solve—or is capable of solving—the problems in college sports.

PART IV

The NCAA

THE FOX IN THE HENHOUSE

"Those are unreal people [running the NCAA] who make $80 million a year off the NCAA basketball tournament, then talk about student-athletes."

—Jackie Sherrill, former Texas A. & M.
football coach and AD

OVERVIEW: WHO IS THE NCAA?

"The NCAA is run by the athletic directors and coaches whose jobs depend on winning basketball and football games. And these people . . . also set the rules for the administration of college sports. Sound like the fox and the henhouse?"

—From a special report of the educational journal *The Kappan*

OVER EIGHT HUNDRED colleges and universities belong to the NCAA. In theory, the association represents the will of its members, keeping intercollegiate athletics in line with their educational missions. In practice, the NCAA functions mainly as a trade association for athletic directors and program heads, implementing their wishes regardless of whether these are in the best interests of the member schools.

Power in the NCAA resides in the forty-four-person Executive Council, the association's version of a board of directors. For many years, a large majority of council members have been athletic directors who serve multiyear terms and are either appointed by an athletic conference or elected at the NCAA's annual convention. The elected members, however, are preselected from a council-approved slate of delegates; Chuck Neinas, head of the College Football Association, called the Executive Council "a closed corporation. There is a nominating procedure [for it], but there are no nominations from the floor" of the convention. In the same way, few resolutions that lack the approval of the Executive Council make it to the agenda of the convention.

The council also selects a twelve-member Executive Committee to oversee the large NCAA bureaucracy and the ongoing business of the association. This committee supervises the executive director of the NCAA, who sits as an *ex officio* member on the committee and the council. The president and the various vice-presidents of the NCAA—largely figurehead positions—are almost always ex–Executive Council and/or Executive Committee members.

309

*"I was a coach for twenty-five years. I was an athletic
director for a good number of years. My background is
there; that's where I'm coming from. . . . The coaches feel
like I'm one of them; the athletic directors feel like I'm
one of them."*

—Dick Schultz, executive director of the
NCAA

The executive director is the NCAA's most visible representative, frequently speaking on behalf of the association to regional and national
media. The executive director also runs the daily business of the
NCAA, manages its over $160 million annual budget, coordinates its
many committees, and plans long-term strategy and legislation. The
NCAA executive director is very much a modern CEO and his—it has
always been a "he"—mandate is to carry out the wishes of the people
who hire him.

From 1951 to 1988, Walter Byers was executive director and helped
the association to promote its own and College Sports Inc.'s phenome-
nal growth. When Byers retired, a number of candidates from the
college sports establishment—ADs and conference commissioners—
vied to succeed him. However, a group of university presidents, unhappy with the increasing scandals in college sports, proposed one of
their own, John Ryan of Indiana University, as executive director. The
presidents believed that an educator in this important NCAA position
could help to bring intercollegiate athletics more in line with academic
goals.

But the Executive Council—which controls the selection process—
chose an athletic director from the University of Virginia for the job.
Dick Schultz's appointment was hailed by his fellow ADs as "a vote of
confidence for athletic directors" (a vote cast mainly by themselves),
and with such phrases as "he's one of us."

In his two years as executive director, Dick Schultz has proven to be
extremely hardworking, competent, publicly visible (Walter Byers was
reclusive), and mainly in sympathy with the coaches and athletic directors who put him in office. Schultz believes in reform from within the
present NCAA structure, arguing that if the association can strengthen
its various departments, it can end the financial and academic cheating
in intercollegiate athletics. He also feels that many of the difficulties in
college sports are created by the media and that better NCAA P.R. and

image making are necessary. Schultz is sincere in his beliefs but he has yet to face the basic double bind in his job: *the executive director of the NCAA is supposed to help solve the problems in college sports, but he is appointed to further the self-interests of athletic directors and program heads—the very people responsible for those systemic problems.*

CHAPTER 34

The NCAA as Empire Builder, Enforcer, and Gambler

"8 Sport [NCAA] Rule Puts Squeeze on SLU [St. Louis University]."

—Headline in the *St. Louis Globe-Democrat*

THE COLLEGE athletic establishment, like all self-interest groups, wants to grow and expand. Over the years, program heads and athletic directors have passed key NCAA legislation that ensures expansion—even though costly athletic department growth is not in the financial or academic interests of most schools.

A decade ago, the NCAA adopted a new qualifying rule for play in Division I-A football: "Members in the restructured Division I-A must now maintain an average [paid] attendance of more than 17,000 per home game over a four-year period or have a [home] stadium with at least 30,000 [permanent] seats." These economic criteria for NCAA participation force schools to spend millions of dollars to stay in the Division I-A poker game, and because winning is the best way to fill the expanded stadiums, the rule institutionalizes a win-or-die approach to college football.

When this rule came into effect in 1982, the NCAA dropped, among dozens of schools, six of the ten members of the Mid-American Conference from Division I-A football (Kent State, Bowling Green, Ohio U., Eastern Michigan, Ball State, and Northern Illinois). Subsequently, at great expense, these schools, and some others in the same situation, built back up to Division I-A status but, for most of them, football is a red-ink proposition, especially when the maintenance and debt-servicing costs on their expanded facilities are calculated.

A more pernicious and longtime NCAA regulation concerns the

312

number of intercollegiate teams a school must field to qualify for NCAA play. In 1985, the association—in spite of the rising costs in college sports—set a new minimum requirement for Division I-A participation of sixteen teams (men's and women's) in eight sports. Many schools scrambled to add teams, coaches, and athletes in various sports like track, swimming, and soccer; if an institution failed to meet the new requirement, the NCAA dropped it to "unclassified membership," barred all of its teams from NCAA play, and penalized it in various other ways.

The association's rationale for the rule is that schools should have "well-balanced athletic programs," including squads in many non-revenue-producing sports. In practice, this rule serves the college sports establishment's self-interest: ADs want their departments to be as large as possible, employing as many coaches, administrators, and athletes as possible. *The NCAA, by locking programs into a minimum number of sports and teams, deprives member institutions of a large degree of autonomy over their athletic budgets and condemns many to forever lose money on college sports.*

Since 1985, the association has fiddled with its minimum requirements: it is now thirteen teams in seven sports for Division I–A, but, according to college sports officials, the numbers will probably increase next year as the NCAA uses this rule to force smaller programs to expand their nonrevenue sports programs or quit the top division and lose the chance to participate in the men's basketball tournament.

Nonrevenue sports are aptly named, cost great sums of money, and at most schools are of no interest or benefit to 95 percent of the university community (attendance is usually low for their events and the elite athletes in these sports have exclusive use of the expensive facilities). Yet the NCAA compels members to fund nonrevenue sports and it applies the minimum-number rule to all divisions. (In recent years, the association has used the "equal opportunity for women" argument to justify this rule but considering the 1980s takeover of women's sports by NCAA male administrators and program heads, as well as the association's indifference to corecreational facilities for women, this excuse seems *ex post facto* at best.)

The NCAA's minimum-participation requirement is one of the main forces for unwarranted expansion and financial deficit in College Sports Inc. The rule forces schools who want to fund only football and basketball teams into spending millions of extra dollars on nonrevenue sports. The only university beneficiaries of this fundamental NCAA regulation reside in the athletic department.

> *"The move [of NCAA headquarters to a larger office complex] is likely to raise the eyebrows of critics who believe that the association's national office is a 'bureaucracy that's growing out of control.' "*
>
> —Item in the *Chronicle of Higher Education*

In an era when most American colleges and universities are losing increasing amounts of money on their intercollegiate sports programs, the NCAA's own revenue and spending have grown significantly. The association's main source of money is the Final Four men's basketball tournament, one of College Sports Inc.'s largest lotteries. Every year, the money in that pot o' gold increases, and every year, the NCAA bureaucracy keeps at least 50 percent of the proceeds for itself.

The NCAA spends its revenue on a variety of items. Promoting its view of college sports costs close to $5.5 million—$3.1 million for its communications department, and $2.3 million for its publishing department (according to its most recently published budget in 1988). The price for keeping its elaborate championship and committee systems going (holding championships, flying committee members to meetings, etc.) is over $18 million. To protect and police NCAA college sports, the association spends $6.14 million: $1.75 million in legal services, $1.95 million on drug testing, $1.74 million for enforcement, and $0.7 million on compliance. And there are millions for miscellaneous items like rent and insurance. When the NCAA accountants reached the bottom line for fiscal 1988, they predicted $82,011,000 in spending.

Among the most interesting items in this budget were general expenses of $2.7 million and administrative ones of $1.74 million. Probably staff salaries are covered by these expenditures but the NCAA does not disclose this; possibly the association's long-standing practice of giving interest-free loans to its employees is also part of these expenses.

In 1985, the *Washington Post* discovered that the NCAA "has provided some of its staff members with interest-free mortgage loans totaling more than $600,000 since 1978. In addition, the association has kept as much as $450,000 of its funds in accounts bearing low rates of interest at banks that provide staff members with loans at below-market rates of interest."

The main recipients of these sweetheart deals were the executive director and the controller, but other NCAA staff workers also benefited from the loan program. The Executive Committee justified the practice as an "employee fringe benefit" and explained that the loans were mainly to help staff obtain home mortgages. NCAA apologists argued that many corporations, such as computer firms in Silicon Valley, have similar programs. "The NCAA bureaucrats had trouble covering their butts on this one," commented a former faculty athletic representative. "After all, they weren't helping each other out on mortgages on the San Francisco Peninsula but in Shawnee Mission, Kansas, about as reasonable a housing market as you can find in the contiguous forty-eight."

The NCAA bureaucrats are well aware of the financial problems in college sports—the Executive Council and Committee have frequently discussed this question. In recent years, a number of university presidents have called for the association to face the financial issue, including the NCAA's own spending, directly. However, in his opening remarks to a recent NCAA convention (1989), Executive Director Dick Schultz said that "cutting sports and cutting scholarships ought to be the last step we take. . . . I think we can, back in every athletic department, review what we do, review the number of staff people we have—not just coaches, but all staff people."

Meanwhile, in Kansas, the NCAA's bureaucracy grows and grows.

> *"It punishes the innocent for the transgressions of others. It tramples due process, freely admits hearsay evidence and acts as judge, jury, and executioner. It pillories selected victims in a kangaroo court and destroys them without hard evidence. Unfettered by checks and balances, it bribes and intimidates witnesses. Relief from its vendettas is virtually impossible. . . .*
>
> *"What sounds like a description of the Gestapo or Mafia is actually a sampling of the venomous criticism that has been leveled over the years at the NCAA's enforcement division, the least understood and most maligned of the NCAA's myriad operations."*
>
> —Bill Shirley, in the *Los Angeles Times*

In the late 1960s, the NCAA's Enforcement Division had three full-time investigators. A decade later, the number had doubled and by the late 1980s more than doubled again—to fifteen full-time enforcement officers and over twenty-five part-timers, the latter mainly ex-FBI agents assigned to various parts of the country. The NCAA bureaucrats have trouble explaining this geometric progression: the propagandists, who downplay the extent of cheating in college sports and take the "only a few bad apples" line, offer no comment; the bureaucratic empire builders argue for more cops because of increasing cheating.

Many member schools are unhappy with the new horde of NCAA troopers. Donna Lopiano, assistant athletic director at the University of Texas, asked, "Why are we becoming a police state? I think it's absolutely ludicrous for a professional organization to hire ten to twenty [now twenty-five] ex-FBI agents." In addition to the expansion, controlling the new cops can be a problem. David Berst, longtime NCAA enforcement director, admitted, "It's more difficult to make sure you know what the part-timers are doing or how willing they are to do it." One agent compromised part of the SMU investigation because he illegally paid an informant.

Even the full-time investigators working out of Kansas raise troubling questions about NCAA enforcement procedures. Mike Gilleran, an ex-NCAA investigator and now the commissioner of the West Coast Athletic Conference, gave a frank explanation of how the NCAA conducts an investigation: because, as a private organization, it lacks subpoena, interrogation, and arrest powers, "ultimately everything has to be the product of a tip or a squealer." Thus investigators proceed mainly on the basis of hearsay and rumor, and the accused do not have the right to face the informants. Another favorite tactic is coercion: Gilleran admitted that if an accused school is reluctant to cooperate with an NCAA investigator, "You'll say, 'If you are prepared to spend the time and money to fight this, we are too. You won't outspend the NCAA.' "

The Associated Press, in a major study of the NCAA's Enforcement Division, noted: "It has been repeated so often, it's axiomatic, 'If the NCAA wants to look long enough and hard enough, they'll find something.' " David Berst acknowledged that "it's possible to find some type of violation anywhere, although it may be minor." The AP commented: "It is this admission that makes the question of who gets investigated particularly troublesome."

Schools in the Southwest Conference have long complained that the NCAA particularly picks on them—a number received severe penalties in recent years—and that it ignores or goes easy on athletic programs in conferences like the Big Ten with powerful allies in the NCAA hierarchy. A faculty athletic representative at a southern school claimed that there was also prejudice against some SEC members ("Look at how Florida and Kentucky always seem to get nailed") and he offered the following anecdote: "When the football program at Illinois under Mike White got totally out of hand, the school itself had to practically beg the NCAA to come in."

Association officials deny that they play favorites among conferences and schools and, in fact, most NCAA investigations seem motivated not by vendetta, but by an attempt at image repair. The NCAA attracts national media attention and applause when it descends upon high-profile athletic programs like SMU's and Kentucky's; it receives but a line of agate in the back of the sports pages when it finally raps Plattsburgh State for flagrant violations. By punishing some big-name offenders, it can keep the "few bad apples" line alive and lull the vast majority of its members—and, it hopes, the public—into believing that College Sports Inc. is basically clean.

When the NCAA begins an investigation of an athletic program, it urges the school to cooperate and it implies that cooperation will lighten the eventual penalty. The NCAA hopes that the institution, by turning on itself, will provide the hard evidence that NCAA cops are unable to obtain. The association also recommends that the school hire—sometimes for a six-figure fee—such former NCAA employees as Mike Slive and Mike Glazier, Chicago attorneys, to help prepare the case for the association's tribunal, the Committee on Infractions. Virginia Tech did this, and as a faculty member at that school observed: "It was ridiculous. You'd think a place full of Ph.D.'s could write something out for itself but apparently that's not possible when you're dealing with the NCAA. They say you have to bring in the experts—who turn out to be their old friends. So we ended up paying a small fortune to those Chicago lawyers and, as far as I can see, in the end we got the severest penalty that the NCAA could have given us."

In recent years, the careers of many NCAA "old friends" have taken off. To prevent the Enforcement Division from coming back after an investigation, a number of schools have hired away some of its personnel. Tulane, Wichita State, and Oklahoma have employed former NCAA troopers full-time to advise them on how best to avoid trouble and new penalties from the association. Other athletic programs like

Miami's have given jobs to ex-NCAA workers to interpret the association's complex and contradictory rule book and to help prevent future problems. Beyond the obvious conflicts of interest here, such employment taints the NCAA's already questionable enforcement practices.

Instead of making friends with the NCAA, some athletic programs as well as their coaches and athletes under investigation have tried to fight it in court. The NCAA Executive Council's response to this tactic was a proposal that the member institution involved in these cases pay half the NCAA's legal expenses. The Washington lawyer for the American Council on Education termed the NCAA's proposal "absolutely outrageous . . . one of those sneaky NCAA attempts to bolster its own bureaucratic mechanisms at the expense of its members . . . an attempt to undermine the independent judgment of universities and of university attorneys."

Like all large bureaucracies, the NCAA's has taken on a life of its own—often at odds with the member institutions and sometimes even in opposition to its true bosses, the athletic directors and program heads. In its 1986 article on the Enforcement Division, the Associated Press pointed out: "Universities fear that the NCAA will wield this devastating power [of severe penalties] more out of concern for its image and $57.4 million budget than for the welfare of college sports." In the years since this comment, and with the budget now over $80 million, many actions of the NCAA have confirmed these fears.

> "Big-time college sport doesn't build character, it warps it. Fixing a game is relative. [A player says] 'I got the grade changed. I don't think shaving a game by a couple of points is so bad.' "
>
> —Thomas Tutko, sports psychologist

Part of the mandate of the NCAA's Enforcement Division is to keep college sports free of gambling influences. Driven by the memory of the terrible scandals in men's basketball in the 1940s and early 1950s as well as mini scandals in the 1960s and more recently at Boston College and Tulane, the NCAA cops hope to head off all attempts at game fixing and point shaving. However, as the amount of money bet on college sports increases annually—experts currently estimate it at $2 billion—and the potential rewards to gamblers from fixed games grows, the Enforcement Division's antigambling work becomes more difficult and complex.

NCAA executive directors have always taken a hard public line against gambling. Knowing that the popularity of their sports enterprise rests on the credibility of the contests, Walter Byers and Dick Schultz have long denounced the betting on intercollegiate games. But beneath their disapproval is a dilemma for the NCAA and its member athletic programs: the fragile TV ratings for college football and men's basketball are tied to gambling. If the TV audience comes to believe that the games are fixed, they will tune out; on the other hand, millions of viewers have bet on the games and watch them mainly for that reason. If the NCAA is lax about gambling, it invites fixing and shaving; if it is too strongly antigambling and leads a national campaign against it, it could knock points off its TV ratings and watch the payouts from the networks and syndicators decrease. In this situation, as in so many others, the high ethical standards espoused by the NCAA smash into the commercial imperatives of College Sports Inc.

> *"Not realizing that the game had been canceled months earlier, Las Vegas odds-makers made Davidson's basketball team a 5¹/₂-point favorite over The Citadel on January 27. To his annoyance, Davidson's sports information director Emil Parker got a firsthand reminder the next day of the extent of gambling involvement in college sports. By Parker's count, more than 50 'fans,' frustrated by the absence of a score in their newspaper, called him [long-distance] to ask how the game came out.*
>
> *"Parker allows that he might have succumbed to the temptation to give the callers a phony score except that he was 'afraid of waking up and finding a mile-long black limo parked in my driveway.' "*
>
> —Item in *Sports Illustrated*

In the 1970s, a number of sports information directors (SIDs) began an antigambling campaign within the NCAA. Their reasons were pragmatic as well as ethical. They were tired of the constant calls from professional gamblers and ordinary bettors in search of game details, "inside information" on how teams "looked" for upcoming contests, the injury status of key players, etc. When the SIDs tried to screen their calls, the gamblers posed as newspaper reporters and other legitimate callers. Because the function of an SID is to give out information, not withhold it, they felt that the bettors were making their jobs and their lives unnecessarily difficult.

The sports information directors' professional association (CoSIDA), led by St. John's University SID Bill Esposito, came up with proposals to solve these specific problems and also to fight against the increasing amount of gambling on college sports. They suggested that the NCAA and member athletic programs not send materials to magazines that carry betting service and tip-sheet ads, and that the NCAA and its schools demand that newspapers not run betting-line/point-spread columns (e.g., "Georgetown 6 VILLANOVA"). Esposito believed that if these proposals were implemented, "the moral, law-abiding creators . . . of essential sports facts, figures and photos can starve the line sheets and betting pimps out of existence."

The coaches immediately opposed these proposals. With their obsessions about self-promotion and recruiting, program heads want maximum publicity for themselves and their teams and they were unwilling to offend any magazine or newspaper in the slightest way. Once the program heads' opposition, seconded by the ADs, was clear, most sports information directors backed down, explaining to Esposito, "Look, my coach wants the ink and I can't go against the coach."

Even the *NCAA News* admitted that Esposito's proposals failed "because coaches and administrators would not sacrifice exposure for principle." Beyond the ethical imperative, what should clearly be in the program heads' self-interest—to fight the gambling mania because of its potential for fixed games and scandals—is far less important to them than their career and program needs for maximum publicity. A number of prominent coaches like Digger Phelps and Bob Knight have taken public stands in favor of proposals similar to Esposito's but they have not made a dent in their colleagues' intransigence on this issue.

The NCAA bureaucracy also claims that it is trying to attack the gambling mania and it points to its refusal to issue tournament press credentials to writers from magazines that carry gambling ads (these reporters have to buy their own tickets and are not aided in their work by the NCAA's press officers or facilities). However, the Executive Council has never proposed legislation to make this action mandatory for member schools. Moreover, antigambling advocates charge that the NCAA will never take the next logical step and withhold tournament press credentials from reporters of newspapers that carry betting lines on college games, nor will it propose that member schools do this. In the same way, the NCAA has never seriously challenged the TV networks on their announcing of odds and point spreads for college contests (some basketball color commentators always discuss "the betting situation").

The gambling issue illustrates the basic double bind of the NCAA executive director and his bureaucrats: they claim that they are working to solve the problems in college sports and that gambling is high on their agenda, but in reality they cannot institute concrete reforms because of the self-interest of the ADs and program heads. The NCAA says that it stands for high moral behavior but, on gambling, the commercial demands of College Sports Inc.—maximum exposure for maximum dollars—overrule a strong ethical stand.

Many experts believe that because of the ever-increasing volume of betting on intercollegiate contests, a major game-fixing and/or point-shaving scandal could occur at any time. Although College Sports Inc. will be responsible and the NCAA bureaucrats will wring their hands and try to sweep up the mess, the real losers will be the colleges and universities involved, and by association, all of American higher education.

The NCAA as Predator: The Rape of the Association of Intercollegiate Athletics for Women

"I think it is interesting that an organization [the NCAA] that has been so active in fighting equal opportunity for women now wants to offer championships for them. This is not the consent of the governed.

"In certain circumstances involving men and women, lack of consent is classified as rape."

—N. Peg Burke, former president of the
AIAW, at the 1980 NCAA convention

AS WITH ALL economic cartels, the NCAA's treatment of real and potential competitors has long been predatory. In the 1940s, the National Invitational Tournament (NIT) in New York City was the premier men's basketball event and college teams could play in it as well as in the NCAA's less prestigious tourney. In 1951, the NCAA decided to eclipse the NIT: it demanded that its members enter only one of the tournaments and it began increasing the size of its field, from eight to sixteen for 1951, then to twenty-two in 1953, and eventually to the current sixty-four, leaving fewer and fewer good teams for the NIT. The result was the NIT's fall to its present state as just another exhibition basketball gathering.

The NCAA's long feud with the Amateur Athletic Union and the AAU's resulting decline was another notch on the cartel's gun. But when the association wiped out the main women's college sports group, the AIAW, it gave new meaning to the term *predatory*. The story of that takeover is crucial to an understanding of the NCAA.

*"No person in the United States shall, on the basis of sex,
be excluded from participation in, be denied the benefits of,
or be subjected to discrimination under any education
program or activity receiving Federal financial
assistance."*

—Section 901 (a) of Title IX of the Education
Amendments of 1972

The main impetus for the change in intercollegiate women's sports was Title IX, a provision in the 1972 Education Amendments that mandated equal access and opportunities for women in education. With prodding from the federal Department of Health, Education and Welfare, colleges and universities also applied the law to women's athletics and began funding them generously to move them toward parity with men's athletic programs.

In the early 1970s, the leaders of the various women's college sports programs established a national organization, the Association of Intercollegiate Athletics for Women, consciously setting up a very different kind of group from the NCAA. They wanted women's college sports to be focused on the athlete—not centered on the program head—and they emphasized that an athlete's education was more important than her athletic performance. They also preached participation, not win-or-die competition, and they saw AIAW sports as an alternative to what they called "the semiprofessional NCAA model."

They implemented their original ideas with some basic rules: no athletic scholarships; easy transfer regulations (an athlete could go to another school and play the next year); no minimum number of teams and sports required of members; and flexibility for schools to enter each of their teams at whatever level of play they chose. They also refused to set up an Enforcement Division. One official explained: "The emphasis in AIAW's system is upon cooperative self-restraint and self-policing, not upon punishment and retribution."

This utopia, where the "student-athlete" truly existed, did not last long. Pressure from some members as well as from a number of athletes forced the establishment of athletic scholarships, but compared to NCAA grants, AIAW scholarships were benign: they were for a guaranteed four years and tied to academic—not athletic—eligibility (a recipient kept her scholarship as long as she was a student in good standing and tried to participate in her sport; a coach could not revoke a grant because of inadequate athletic performance).

With athletic scholarships came increased recruiting, yet for most of its existence the AIAW held the line on this issue: schools were not allowed to pay coaches or even to give them "released time" to visit and sign recruits; in addition, members could not pay for a prospect's visit to campus. Coaches were permitted to make scouting trips but could not talk to recruits during them. In 1981, the American Council on Education noted that "women's athletics has been able to adopt a recruiting method that costs less than 5 percent of current men's expenditures in semipro institutions while retaining similar effectiveness in attracting talented athletes." The ACE saw the women's methods as the solution to many of the men's problems and warned that if the reverse occurred, "Pushing women's athletics into the same mold as men's athletics may compound the problem of the financial future of intercollegiate athletics."

As events turned out, these lines were prophetic.

> *"The AIAW's position is that its rules are set up to protect students, but college presidents and men's athletic directors don't see how an organization . . . can say that it must protect a student against her institution."*
>
> —A female observer at the 1981 NCAA convention

When the AIAW began operations, the NCAA was not particularly interested in it or in women's sports—"It's only a bunch of gals trying to be jocks" was the general attitude. But as women's sports programs grew in importance and received increasing and often separate funding from their schools, ADs began to worry about this new competitor. In 1975, the ADs prevailed upon the NCAA to try to co-opt the AIAW by proposing NCAA championships in women's events (the AIAW had its own extensive championship system).

AIAW leaders saw through this tactic, arguing that the NCAA was "really aiming at monopolizing college sports," and that under its control "women's sports would be treated like men's minor sports." They also reminded the men that AIAW programs were "a truly educational activity, instead of a semi-professional activity."

The NCAA backed away from the championships ploy; instead it went to court to try to overturn HEW's Title IX interpretation. The association claimed that HEW had exceeded its authority in applying the law to intercollegiate athletics and that this application was causing great harm to men's sports and threatening their very existence! In 1978, a federal judge dismissed the NCAA's lawsuit.

The NCAA, however, continued to fight HEW's Title IX interpretation in the courts, and it also attempted a more direct takeover of women's college sports. At its 1980 convention, instead of proposing and discussing championships for women's sports, it established a number of them by *fiat*. Christine Grant, director of women's athletics at the University of Iowa, exclaimed, "This is an outrage. To be brief, the preservation of our organization [the AIAW] is at stake," and most AIAW leaders agreed with her. Even some male NCAA delegates were appalled; one described the association's move as "an act of arrogance . . . in which six hundred men decided to be the shepherds to women's programs."

The AIAW leaders were correct about the NCAA's takeover intentions but they could not save their organization. Over the next two years, the NCAA, using its enormous economic strength, fought the AIAW for the allegiance of women's athletic programs across the country, particularly those programs at schools with men's teams affiliated to the NCAA. First, the male-dominated association, like a merchandising giant, offered discounts to institutions that enrolled their women's athletic programs with it: schools could affiliate their women's teams at no extra cost above regular NCAA dues (versus having to pay AIAW *and* NCAA dues), and they could send their teams to NCAA championships for free, the association picking up the tab (teams had to pay their own way to AIAW events). To increase the pressure on schools to choose the NCAA, the association scheduled sixteen of its women's championships on the same dates as the AIAW's. Then, to cut off a potential money source for the AIAW—the TV rights for its women's basketball championship—the NCAA tied the sale of its men's Final Four to its new women's basketball championship game, guaranteeing a major network for the event and making it more attractive to schools than the AIAW final.

In case institutions were still uncertain about switching their women's programs to the NCAA, the association also applied what Napoleon called "a whiff of grapeshot." Members began hearing rumors that uncooperative schools would soon receive visits from the NCAA cops. Christine Grant of Iowa said that "there was a widespread perception among NCAA members that they could be investigated for alleged violations of the organization's complex rules if they did not go along with the wishes of the NCAA leadership." Other AIAW leaders offered specific examples of the NCAA employing this coercive tactic.

The NCAA's assault broke the AIAW: by early 1982, over 150 members—mainly schools with men's programs in NCAA Division I— had announced that they were dropping out of the AIAW and affiliating their women's teams with the NCAA; another 91 said that they would not compete in the AIAW's championships. Because the defectors were among the wealthiest members of the AIAW, the leaders realized that the annual dues—the main source of revenue—from the remaining schools would not be sufficient to continue operations.

In June 1982, when only 95 of the 759 members said that they would send delegates to the AIAW's coming convention, the group folded. Its last president, Merrily Baker, summed up its achievement well: the AIAW treated student-athletes "as students above all else" and constructed "athletic programs and models of governance so that their [students'] time to develop as thinking and feeling human beings [was] not deformed by the demands of athletic pursuits."

Merrily Baker is now an assistant executive director of the NCAA. As she works for that still-male-dominated organization, the main bulwark of College Sports Inc., does she ever think about the AIAW alternative to commercialism and corruption in college sports? As she sees athletic programs chew up and spit out college athletes, including great numbers of women, does she remember her epitaph for the AIAW?

> *"The switch [from the AIAW] to the NCAA has put more financial pressure on institutions because women's teams must spend more money on recruiting and scholarships to remain competitive.*
>
> *"One of the things athletic directors didn't anticipate was the increase in operating budgets caused by the switch to the NCAA."*
>
> —Christine Weller, women's basketball coach
> at the University of Maryland

College Sports Inc. was not a hospitable place for women's sports. To succeed in NCAA competition, many coaches of women's teams had to become program heads and adopt the mores and expensive habits of their colleagues in men's sports. And because of the NCAA's full-scale recruiting game, the new program heads had to spend much more time and money hustling for players than under the AIAW's antirecruiting rules.

Before the switchover to the NCAA, many women's sports administrators predicted a jump in costs (at least $180,000 at the University of Texas) and most were wrong—the increase was much greater than expected. Unfortunately for women's sports, the new expenses were coupled with a shift in their sources of revenue. Under the AIAW, most school administrations as well as various levels of government had funded women's programs directly and on separate lines in the university budget. This arrangement usually did not cost athletic departments any money. However, once under the umbrella of the NCAA and merged with men's programs, the money for women's teams came out of the main athletic department budget. What had seemed attractive to ADs—to grab the women's revenue—turned into a fiscal nightmare because of the increased costs of these programs. Male athletic directors began complaining that women's sports were financially draining their departments. Considering that they had brought this situation upon themselves, their complaints rang hollow; nonetheless, their way of solving their self-inflicted problem was to cut spending on women's programs to the legal minimum.

In 1984, the Supreme Court narrowed the Title IX interpretation with its *Grove City* decision and gave ADs an excuse to cap funding on women's programs. The result was the worst possible scenario for women's intercollegiate athletics. Their programs—once student centered, sensible, prosperous, and controlled by female administrators—now became, under male ADs, stagnant. In 1987, at the main campus of the University of Arkansas, the athletic department spent one dollar in ten on women's sports, and AD Frank Broyles, very knowledgeable about college sports' financing, explained that this ratio "is similar to differences at most major colleges."

The NCAA, the catalyst of this situation, did not show much sympathy for the women's plight, and even failed them in its original area of strength—championship events. A 1987 study found that "fewer national championships—in fewer sports and in fewer divisions—are available to women [under the NCAA] than were available in 1981–82, the last year of AIAW." The NCAA's explanation was that its championship events cost a huge amount of money and that it was unable to finance them for as many women's sports in as many divisions as it wanted to. However, the NCAA's real financial problem was its obsession with deluxe travel: in 1987, for example, it held the women's ski championship in Anchorage, Alaska, although almost all of the participants were from the Lower 48.

In addition to the financial difficulties, the entry into College Sports Inc. brought increased cheating to women's sports, especially in recruiting. In 1985, the NCAA's longtime head of enforcement, David Berst, explained that "the pressure to win in Division I" was behind the multiplication of incidents and that "more coaches [of women's teams] were willing to go the extra mile for the one player that might lift them up the plateau in wins." However, Berst and his enforcement troopers were frequently frustrated by the women's unwillingness to inform on their colleagues. In a holdover from their AIAW self-policing, Berst explained, "They tend to subscribe to the thinking that they can handle the problems best by contacting each other about infractions. But they will find through experience that it won't work. The men have already found that."

By the late 1980s, with women's programs firmly bound to the NCAA and cheating incidents on the increase, many of the predictions of the AIAW leaders in the 1970s had come true: Division I women's college sports had become a minor version of men's programs, with most of the same faults and excesses. What AIAW women administrators and coaches had not anticipated was that the NCAA takeover would also end many of their jobs.

> *"In 1973, 92 percent of women's teams were coached by women. A year ago [1984], that figure had dropped to 53 percent.*
>
> *"In 1973, 95 percent of women's athletics programs were headed by women. Today 86 percent . . . are run by men."*
>
> —Patty Viverito, at the time commissioner of the
> Gateway Collegiate Athletic Conference, a
> women's sports league that no longer exists

Ms. Viverito quoted from an ongoing study done by Vivian Acosta and Linda Carpenter of Brooklyn College. The latest results (1988) do not show significant changes from the 1984–85 totals. The reason for the shift to male dominance of women's intercollegiate athletics is simple: when the NCAA put the AIAW out of business, schools placed their women's programs under the authority of their male athletic directors, thus eliminating the position of an independent women's AD. (Many institutions established a post of "Assistant Athletic Director for

Women's Sports" but, as any vice-president of any organization can attest, the assistant usually has limited power and can always be overruled by the chief.)

One slight shift from the mid-1980s figures in the Acosta/Carpenter survey has occurred in the number of female coaches of women's sports teams—it has fallen to 48.3 percent. As male coaches increasingly see positions in women's sports as excellent entries into the college coaching profession, they edge out females for these jobs. Ron Wilde became men's volleyball coach at Pepperdine University in California after starting his coaching career in charge of the women's volleyball team at Drake University in Iowa. He commented, "I knew all along the women's job was an entry-level position for a men's job," and he was pleased to move on to "one of the top programs" in the men's version of the sport.

Compounding the hiring problem for women coaches is the males' old-boy network. When Joanna Davenport headed women's athletics for the Auburn University athletic department she explained, "I've received a lot of phone calls from men who want to recommend their [male] friends for a coaching position, but I've never received a call from a female recommending another female."

Not surprisingly, male coaches also bring male sports values to their positions in women's programs. Kathryn Bunnell, a women's basketball coach and assistant athletic director at Wichita State, quit because of the shift from AIAW ideals to College Sports Inc. methods: under male program heads, "student-athletes are treated like dollar signs. That's a reality. I kept on asking, 'Why can't we treat all people equal?' I wasn't really happy fighting those kinds of battles." A more direct and dangerous abuse occurs when male coaches, acting in the Bob Knight mind-games-and-kick-ass manner, try to control their female athletes mentally and physically. A study done by a researcher at Dartmouth College found that "the incidence of abusive relationships between male coaches and female athletes could well be as staggering as that of such related phenomena as domestic violence, [and] wife abuse."

Even the NCAA's recent $1.75 million survey of athletes indicates some disturbing facts about women participants in contemporary college sports. Female basketball players spend as much time on their sport as do male players, and female athletes in other sports toil only one hour less than the basketballers. The survey also found that the percentage of female basketball players who had gone through the recruiting wars was almost the same as for the males in their sport (90 percent versus 93 percent), and that the percentage of recruited women athletes in other sports was almost as great as for the women basketball players. The researcher who did the study commented, "A lot of people think they [women college athletes] play just for fun and relaxing. I wonder if they know how competitive it is."

"Have you seen Title IX?"
"No, what's it about?"
"About equal opportunity for women athletes!"
"You mean they don't have to go to class either?"

—A winning entry in the *Chronicle of Higher Education*'s "Great Summertime Marginalia Contest"

In 1988, Congress invalidated the Supreme Court's *Grove City* decision by passing legislation that broadly interpreted Title IX, including its application to intercollegiate athletics. In the same year, Temple University, which had long fought a class-action suit against it for sex discrimination in its athletic program, settled with the female plaintiffs. Two years later, however, it is still unclear whether these cases heralded a new era in women's sports or are merely footnotes to the post-AIAW period.

The current battle in women's sports is over money: advocates clamor for equal funding with men's programs; male ADs argue that because women's teams rarely generate any ticket or TV revenue, they are not entitled to the same funding as most men's squads. Even the highest-profile women's sport, basketball, is a money loser at almost every school; in 1988, Georgetown's women's basketball team had $5,000 in revenue against $100,000 in expenses.

The NCAA's *Revenues and Expenses of Intercollegiate Athletics Programs* indicates the figures on women's sports for its most recent survey year, 1985: For schools with big-time athletic departments, the average loss on their women's teams was over $500,000. For most institutions with programs in Divisions II and III, the average losses ranged from the low thousands to close to $200,000. If athletic departments actually started to fund their women's and men's programs equally, these deficits would multiply accordingly.

The NCAA survey also shows that only in the big-time athletic departments were the women's expenses "paid [in part] by [the] men's program" and that at these schools, the average portion of total expenses paid was 42 percent. At all other institutions, the men's programs did not pick up the costs of women's sports. This contradicts one of the main myths about women's college sports—that they are bankrupting the men's programs. Although women's teams in their NCAA phase are extremely costly, their losses—mainly not paid by the men—are far less than the deficits run up by most men's squads.

If men's programs are not paying for the majority of the costs in women's college sports, who is? As usual, the main benefactor is the university, with money from the general operating fund or other sources. In addition, in a few states, legislatures have earmarked government subsidies for women's sports. Unlike during the AIAW era, however, the money from school and public sources does not go directly to the women's programs—it must pass through the athletic department books, controlled by male ADs.

Does it make sense for these university and government subsidies to continue and, if funding equal to the men's is implemented, to increase geometrically? The answer depends upon one's view of higher education, its purposes and priorities.

If women's sports programs were still student centered, as in the AIAW era, schools could justify underwriting them as a student activity. But since the NCAA takeover, an increasing number of women's programs and their expensive facilities are reserved for the exclusive use of elite athletes; therefore these programs cannot be called student activities, nor can their participants be termed regular students. Thanks to the NCAA, big-time women's programs have become another branch of College Sports Inc., as separate from their host universities and general student bodies as are the men's programs and their athletes.

Recent studies indicate that many female intercollegiate athletes are joining their male colleagues in the full-time pursuit of sports' fame and fortune. Increasing numbers of female college athletes aspire to professional careers, especially in golf, tennis, and the Olympic sports, and are willing to prepare accordingly. Many current pro women golfers and tennis players have already passed through the college ranks, and over half the women on the last U.S. Olympic team, including all of the basketball players, had held athletic scholarships. Thus, as with men's college sports, American higher education provides a minor-league system for wealthy professional organizations—the LPGA, the Women's

International Tennis Association, and the United States Olympic Committee—and receives nothing in return.

If colleges and universities were wonderfully rich institutions and could contain tuition and other student costs within reasonable limits, if they could pay graduate teaching assistants a living wage and faculty commensurate with their professional skills, then they could afford a few extra million dollars a year to subsidize nonrevenue intercollegiate athletics—male and female. Colleges and universities, however, are not wonderfully rich places and their present underwriting of women's sports has occurred during a period of serious economic difficulties in higher education. Ironically, one of the effects of their 1980s belt tightening was a cutback in funding for women's studies programs. Instead of giving millions of dollars to women's studies and benefiting large numbers of female—and male—students, they gave that money to relatively small numbers of elite women athletes and their program heads.

In the end, the same questions that should be asked about university funding of men's college sports apply to women's programs in their present and probable future state. Ever since the NCAA demolished the AIAW, the fate of women's college sports has been inextricably tied to that of College Sports Inc.

CHAPTER 36

The College Presidents Try to Reform the NCAA

"But a lot of these presidents have never had a jock on. They've never been in sports. They just get in there and come up with these foolish rules. That's scary. I worry about it."

—Bill Mallory, football program head at
Indiana University

IN 1979, as a result of a very comprehensive study, the American Council on Education called for major reforms in all phases of college sports. The ACE particularly urged presidents and ADs to bring athletic programs in line with the educational missions of their schools; athletic directors and the NCAA ignored the ACE's requests. Three years and many college sports scandals later, Derek Bok, head of Harvard University and chair of the ACE Council, appointed a committee of twenty-six presidents from schools across the country to figure out how to implement the recommendations of the ACE's study. These executives worked on their ideas for a year and then met in August 1983 to plan a definite strategy.

The outcome of their meeting was more radical than expected. One of the presidents' assistants told the *New York Times*: "They studied ways to reform the association [the NCAA] and finally threw up their hands and said, 'There isn't any way to reform it.' " Instead the ACE group proposed that a "Presidents' Board" take charge of the NCAA and that this board "have authority to veto or modify NCAA rules and to impose new rules of its own design on association members, subject to review only by a mail vote of presidents of all member institutions."

In its public statement, the ACE group explained that they were proposing this drastic move because schools had lost control of their college sports programs to athletic directors and to "the NCAA itself. . . . As a result, educational interests are often subordinated to the aims of winning games, boosting attendance, and maximizing television revenue. The consequences for academic standards and for the education of athletes are too well-known to warrant repetition."

The NCAA was outraged. Its president called the ACE proposal "undemocratic," claiming that the NCAA's structure better represented the will of its member schools than would a presidents' "banana dictatorship." Moreover, he argued, the NCAA did not need a Presidents' Board with more authority than its Executive Council because, in that group, six of the forty-six members were college presidents and nine were faculty athletic representatives. He did not mention that twenty-nine members of the Executive Council were athletic directors and that faculty representatives tend to be closer to their ADs than to their presidents.

The NCAA also counterattacked with a "Presidents' Commission" proposal of its own. It used the conclusions of a long-standing select committee to suggest a group of presidents with the power to "(1) *review* Association activities and *advise* the NCAA council, (2) *commission studies* of matters of concern, and (3) *propose* legislation" (emphasis added). Among the members of this committee were Lou Holtz, then football coach at Arkansas, Bob Devaney, AD at Nebraska, Dean Smith, basketball head at North Carolina, Roy Kramer, AD at Vanderbilt, and a number of university presidents and faculty representatives, including Charles Alan Wright, longtime chair of the NCAA's Committee on Infractions.

The ACE presidents were willing to compromise and, in late 1983, they revised their proposal to allow the actions of their Presidents' Board to be overruled by a majority vote of the NCAA convention, and to allow open nominations and voting for members of their board.

The ACE insisted, however, that its modified proposal be submitted to a vote at the January 1984 NCAA convention. That showdown with the NCAA establishment and the resulting vote turned out to be a crucial event in the history of intercollegiate athletics, the last real opportunity that American higher education had to halt the growth of College Sports Inc.

*"The failure to gain even a simple majority seemed to be a
stunning defeat for such renowned presidents as Derek C.
Bok of Harvard and the Rev. Timothy S. Healy of
Georgetown, who led the fight for the [ACE] proposal."*

—Item in the *New York Times*

Before the NCAA convention, the ACE presidents were confident of
victory, and a December poll of their constituency indicated that although the vote might be close, only 23.5 percent of the responding
presidents said that they would definitely vote "No" (another bloc was
undecided). In January, about 150 presidents attended the convention—
ADs or faculty athletic representatives served as voting delegates for
the remaining 500 schools. Nevertheless, the ACE group assumed that
the absent presidents had instructed their delegates on how to vote and
that the ACE proposal would pass.

After some rancorous debate on the proposal, the convention delegates were ready to cast their ballots. The chair requested a "voice vote"
and, hearing a louder chorus of Nays than Ayes, ruled that the proposal
was defeated. This maneuver stunned the ACE presidents and they
demanded a roll-call vote. The chair asked for a show of hands on this
ACE motion and it, too, went down. The Presidents' Board proposal
was dead.

The outraged president of California State University at Long Beach
complained to the press that "the proposal would have passed on a roll-
call vote" where delegates could not hide behind a "voice vote and an
anonymous show of hands." *New York Times* columnist George Vecsey
commented, "Now dozens of athletic directors will go back to their
schools and insist to their presidents that they followed orders and raised
their hands for Proposal 35 [the ACE Presidents' Board]."

The faculty athletic representative of a southern school, a delegate at
this NCAA convention, later recalled, "The ACE presidents and their
friends really got snookered. They assumed the good-ol'-boy AD types
play by *Roberts Rules* or something. The ACE ignored the fact that their
proposal, especially all the Presidents' Board rules, would take away
these boys' jobs, or at least end their way of doing business. The ADs
weren't about to allow that. They gave Bok and his pals a good mouthful
of red dirt to take back to their ivy halls. We've never seen them again in
the NCAA to this day."

With the defeat of the ACE's Proposal 35, the NCAA leadership

trotted out Proposal 36, the select committee's plan for a Presidents'
Commission with advisory power. The NCAA Executive Council had
endorsed this proposal, and the convention promptly approved it. The
head of North Carolina A. & T. commented that "Proposal 36 is
nothing more than a politically contrived eleventh-hour response to
35 . . . an attempt at co-optation."

By April 1984, forty-four presidents had been appointed to the commission and a chair chosen—John Ryan of Indiana University. The
commissioners promised to work to reform college sports and the
Chronicle of Higher Education reported that "freshman eligibility is
likely to be the top item on the agenda." Other important items
were "limits on seasons of play for various sports," and tightening the
rules on athletes' "satisfactory [academic] progress" toward their
degrees.

Since all these reforms conflict with the interests of most big-time
ADs and program heads, and if implemented would bring major
changes to College Sports Inc., during the next year they disappeared
from the main agenda of the Presidents' Commission. Instead the group
called for a special NCAA convention to consider new rules to punish
the cheaters—the "bad-apple" programs, coaches, and athletes—in
college sports.

In June 1985, NCAA delegates met in New Orleans for the special
convention and passed a series of rules on cheating, including the
"Death Penalty" for frequent violators (a program is discontinued for a
period of time; really it should be termed the "Penalty Box" because
schools can return from the "Death Penalty"), and the "Les Misérables" rule—if a coach cheats at one school and moves on before
NCAA penalties are imposed, the original infractions follow the coach
to his or her next school (legal experts predicted that, if enforced,
coaches would immediately challenge this rule in court). The NCAA
P.R. machine worked overtime and many newspapers wrote up the
story of the convention with such headlines as [THE] NCAA VOTE FOR
REFORM, LOUD, CLEAR.

Longtime observers of the NCAA were more skeptical and even the
association's president admitted that voting against the proposals on
cheating would be like saying no to "motherhood, apple pie and the
flag." Indiana basketball coach Bob Knight gave his pungent response:
"What do I think of the do-nothing meeting in New Orleans? Rhetoric.
That's what will come out of [these new rules]. . . . If anything good
comes out of it, I'll believe it when I see it."

> *"The measures adopted [at the special convention] will not*
> *solve the basic and systemic problems in college sports,*
> *which are [in part] its professionalization and*
> *commercialization."*
>
> —Eamon P. Kelly, president of Tulane
> University

Because of their self-proclaimed success in New Orleans, the Presidents' Commission decided to nibble away at more substantial problems in college sports—the financial deficits caused by the huge number of NCAA-approved "full ride" grants, and "student-athletes" having to participate in never-ending sports seasons. At the January 1987 NCAA convention, their proposal for cutting the number of men's basketball grants from fifteen to thirteen passed—although their plan to reduce the number of NCAA officially sanctioned baseball games from eighty to sixty failed. On the strength of what they perceived as "a wave of reform," they decided to try for cuts in football and other sports at their next special meeting, scheduled for June 1987.

The Presidents' Commission, however, underestimated the growing anger of many big-time ADs and program heads as well as their ability to organize the membership against the presidents. In a foreshadowing of future events, in January, over some procedural matters, the athletic establishment persuaded a majority of delegates to vote against the wishes of the Presidents' Commission, and they promised more opposition in June.

The pressures of attempting even minor alterations in college sports also created divisions within the forty-four-member commission. A number of presidents, influenced by their ADs and boosters, opposed any changes in the athletic scholarship system and became hostile when other members of the commission wanted to move to the next plateau and propose "need-based-only" grants and a ban on freshman participation in intercollegiate athletics. In this divided and uncertain mood, and unable to come up with any substantial proposals, the Presidents' Commission went to the special meeting in Dallas.

> *"NCAA Forum: Coaches Win Couple of Big Ones."*
>
> —Headline in the *Los Angeles Times*

No amount of NCAA P.R. could disguise the outcome of the Dallas convention. The whistle blew, the presidents received the ball and, on one of their first plays, they tried to reduce the number of grants for Division I-A football programs from ninety-five to ninety. However, the coaches' defense smashed the presidents' play and football grants stayed at ninety-five. Then their proposals for modest reductions in the number of "full rides" in nonrevenue sports—for example, in men's cross-country track from fourteen to thirteen, in women's field hockey from eleven to ten—were trounced.

When the ADs and program heads got the ball, they reversed the January reduction in men's basketball grants, going back to fifteen from thirteen. When the special meeting was over, "the clear loser," according to the Associated Press, was the Presidents' Commission. The AP reported: "There also was a sense that the NCAA's athletic directors were becoming impatient with the commission's 'ivory tower' approach to sports." Only ADs could see a cut from ninety-five to ninety football grants as an "ivory tower" move.

> *"The only area of disagreement among them [the participants at the Dallas meeting] was whether the movement for major change in college sports was dead, or just seriously wounded."*
>
> —Michael Goodwin, in the *New York Times*

In his "News Analysis" of the Dallas meeting, Goodwin pointed out that "beyond dispute . . . those who think that the world of college athletics isn't broken and doesn't need to be fixed hold a dominant hand in the NCAA." As the Presidents' Commission discovered, it is impossible to reform an organization controlled by people who believe that "everything is basically o.k." and who know that reform is against their self-interests.

After the Dallas debacle, the Presidents' Commission became semi-moribund, retreating to what it termed a "study phase" and hoping to hold "national dialogues" about the main issues in college sports. At the NCAA national conventions in 1988 and 1989, no reform proposals appeared on the agendas. In an interview last year, Peter Likens, the president of Lehigh University and a charter member of the Presidents' Commission, acknowledged his and other presidents' disillusionment with the NCAA, and the fact that "the commission has no power that's worth mentioning." (Likens was also chair of a subcommittee investigating ways to cut the enormous financial costs of college sports. At the 1989 convention, its proposals were banished to NCAA limbo.)

In the fall of 1989, prodded by increasing media attention on the corruption and contradictions in intercollegiate athletics, the Presidents' Commission roused itself and offered a number of proposals for consideration at the January 1990 NCAA national convention. Foremost was its suggestion to reduce the length of the official college football and basketball seasons: cut ten days from spring football practice, and start basketball practice as well as the playing season a month later than at present. Immediately most program heads howled in protest. Bo Schembechler, athletic director and football head at Michigan, insisted that he needed all his days of spring practice "to fill that stadium [in the fall] so that we can have 21 sports, men and women, maintain all the facilities, build them, pay the coaches." Lou Holtz, football coach at Notre Dame, also protested but commented, "I don't know if you can legislate that type of thing. There are certain people [program heads] who, no matter how much time you give them, it's not going to be enough."

The Presidents' Commission quickly backed down and, among other concessions, knocked fifteen days off its proposed month's cut in basketball. At the 1990 convention the presidents did manage to pass proposals to reduce the official NCAA basketball season by three games and two weeks and to make minor adjustments in spring football practice (the cuts do not go into effect until August 1992). The media hailed these changes as major and permanent reforms, but the reactions of most ADs and coaches indicated a different reality: members of the college sports establishment had failed to take the presidents' initiative seriously and had not prepared for the convention game; losing the vote surprised them, and afterward, they sounded their war cries.

Bob Knight questioned whether the presidents are "qualified to tell the athletic departments what the fuck to do," and he wondered why the presidents should mix in "my *business*" (his emphasis). Kentucky's Rick Pitino was even angrier and suggested "pulling out of the NCAA if the restrictions aren't rescinded. . . . I think you're going to see a lot of people [athletic programs] try to pull out of this whole thing, form their own NCAA, if it goes through. And I'd be for it."

Throughout 1990, the ADs and program heads will formulate plans to overturn the proposals and they will flood the media with their propaganda on the subject. Their counterattack will peak at the 1991 NCAA convention in Nashville; one sportswriter predicts that the scene in Tennessee "promises to be what football players like to call 'smash mouth.' " Whether the presidents' tepid cuts of 1990 will survive this convention is conjectural; whether, in future years, the Presidents' Commission can institute real reforms, such as rules to end the financial and academic fraud in College Sports Inc., is about as likely as pigs slam-dunking basketballs.

SUMMARY: THE REAL ENEMY

*"[Louisville basketball coach Denny] Crum said the new
[Presidents' Commission] measures, which go into effect
in 1992, 'won't change a thing. . . . Kids are still going
to play on their own, lift weights and condition, so they
won't have any more time to study.' "*

—Item in the *Louisville Courier-Journal*

Why has the reform-minded Presidents' Commission failed to dent the
systemic problems in College Sports Inc.? Some observers argue that
these CEOs have never understood the inner dynamics of the NCAA
and are inept at political maneuvering among its reefs and jocks. This
explanation ignores the fact that the association is tightly controlled by
the Executive Council and Committee and that a majority of the members of these bodies have long been athletic directors. No combination
of savvy moves by the presidents could ever convince these people to
renounce their self-interests.

The only way the presidents can bring about real reform is by
persuading enough of their fellow college and university heads to attend
NCAA meetings and to vote for their reforms or to send carefully
instructed delegates. (And to insist on roll-call votes—the Presidents'
Commission did succeed in making this form of balloting a more
regular NCAA procedure.)

Unfortunately, in an organization as large as the NCAA, with members holding a spectrum of opinions about college sports, convincing a
majority of presidents of the need for major and controversial changes
is not easy. In addition, many presidents of schools with Division I
programs, even if they agree on the need to control College Sports Inc.,
do not want to line up with the reformers because they fear the resulting
wrath of their ADs, coaches, athletic department boosters, and sometimes members of their boards of trustees. In the job descriptions of
university presidents, courage is rarely mentioned.

There are also many presidents who support the NCAA in its present
form, not only the CEOs of "jock factories" but also some leaders of
Division II and III institutions with athletic programs very different
from the big-time ones. These small-school presidents are often influenced by the NCAA's largesse, especially its funding of their tourna-

341

ments and championships. They know that this money would vanish if the Division I members pulled out of the association—one of the threats employed by many big-time ADs and program heads to keep the smaller schools in line on votes.

When the reasons for the weakness of the Presidents' Commission are understood, and the immutable structure of the NCAA is considered, the conclusion on NCAA reform of intercollegiate athletics becomes clear: *the association, in its present form, cannot and does not want to control the commercialism and corruption of College Sports Inc.*

At the Dallas meeting in 1987, Bo Schembechler, speaking for his fellow program heads and ADs, shouted at the reform-minded presidents, *"We are not the enemy."* Bo was wrong, but he was true to the NCAA's self-serving denials of any responsibility for the current difficulties.

PART V

Punt the Pretend

"Despite the pious halftime pronouncements we see on televised football and basketball games, in which the future of humankind is tied to the missions of universities with big-time athletic programs, these very programs contradict the fundamental aims of American higher education."

—Richard Warch, president of Lawrence
University, Appleton, Wisconsin

CHAPTER 37

Solutions to the Systemic
Problems in College Sports

"Thanking the association [NCAA], Mr. [Rowdy] Gaines
said that without an athletic scholarship at an NCAA
institution, he would have had to work his way through
college and could not have developed his swimming skills.
'I appreciate that,' he said, 'because believe me I'm
making a killing now.' Olympic fame [from the 1984
games] has made Mr. Gaines a wealthy man."

—Item in the *Chronicle of Higher Education*

TO SOLVE the systemic problems in intercollegiate athletics, American
higher education has to acknowledge and do the following:

Stop pretending that College Sports Inc. is connected to the educational
mission of American colleges and universities.

The main purpose of College Sports Inc. is commercial entertainment. At most schools with big-time programs, the athletic department
operates as an auxiliary enterprise and has almost no connection to the
academic units and functions of the school; universities should admit
that their intercollegiate athletic programs are separate commercial
businesses.

Because the elite athletes who play big-time college sports are performers, recruited and trained by the athletic department for entertainment purposes, schools should not pretend that they are regular
students.

Schools with big-time athletic programs must acknowledge that
whatever educational content once existed in intercollegiate athletics—

345

i.e., casual recreation and exercise for participating students—is no longer present in the business world of College Sports Inc.

Stop pretending that College Sports Inc. deserves its current tax-exempt status and that booster donations are for educational purposes.

Because the purpose of the campus franchises in College Sports Inc. is commercial entertainment, not education, and they operate as businesses, not educational units, the tax category of "unrelated businesses attached to tax-exempt institutions" is more appropriate for them than their current tax-free status. As "unrelated businesses," they should pay their taxes like all other "for-profit businesses."

Moreover, because the "contributions" to athletic programs are often for the purchase of such items as "priority seats" for sports events, universities should acknowledge that these "contributions" are not legitimate donations for educational purposes and do not deserve tax-exempt status.

Stop pretending that most athletic programs are financially self-supporting and that they never use public monies.

Because most athletic programs engage in creative accounting—moving as many of their expenses as possible to other parts of the university budget—they perpetuate the myth that intercollegiate athletics is self-supporting. Schools should force the franchises in College Sports Inc. to pay their legitimate expenses, such as the multimillion-dollar maintenance and debt-servicing costs on their facilities—used exclusively for their ticket sale events and by their elite athletes but usually maintained by the university and debt-serviced by student fees.

Schools should also inform federal and state governments and the taxpayers when they cover athletic department expenses with general operating funds or other money from the university-wide budget. They should admit that these financial maneuvers are their way of using tax dollars for college sports.

Stop pretending that athletic department deficits do not affect the academic programs of their host schools.

In an era when most colleges and universities operate under severe fiscal restraints, every dollar of university revenue is important.

Schools should acknowledge that when they siphon large sums of money from their budgets and other financial resources to cover athletic department deficits, they are using money that could go for academic programs, faculty, staff, and regular students.

Many athletic directors proclaim that their "tubs stand on their own bottoms" financially. The time has come to make them live up to these proclamations or scale down their operations until these claims become true. Universities must insist that covering athletic program deficits with money from academic funds is an unacceptable solution to the financial losses in College Sports Inc.

Stop pretending that program heads are college teachers and stop tolerating their conflict-of-interest entrepreneurial deals.

Big-time coaches are in the entertainment business. Few Division I program heads, especially in football and basketball, see the inside of a classroom on a regular basis; they devote their time and energies to administering their programs and promoting their careers. Their outside deals are often their major sources of income: money received for endorsing various products, for TV and radio shows, public speaking engagements, sports clinics, private summer camps, and miscellaneous hustles. Schools should treat program heads like all other university employees and demand that they either devote a major part of their time and energies to their full-time university jobs or else quit those positions.

Schools should also monitor program heads' outside income deals for conflict-of-interest violations. They should not permit coaches to receive money from sporting goods companies in return for making their athletes wear and advertise particular brands of shoes and/or equipment. They should not allow coaches, in school colors and insignias and on school property, to endorse commercial products for personal profit. They should not permit coaches the free use of university athletic facilities and dorms to run private summer camps for personal profit. They should give coaches the same privileges, and no more, that they grant to other university employees.

Stop pretending that athletes can get decent college educations.

Coaches, especially in big-time programs, frequently demand that their athletes work forty to sixty hours a week on their sports, and even in smaller programs, many coaches require athletes to spend thirty to forty hours a week in sports activity. However, full-time students, pursuing meaningful degrees, should devote at least forty to fifty hours a week to schoolwork, and students who are ill-prepared for college, including large numbers of athletes, should spend even more time on their studies.

Stop forcing "student-athletes" to try to square this time circle—to be both full-time athletes in ambitious athletic programs and full-time students in meaningful courses of study. Most talented college athletes dream of professional or Olympic careers and are willing to make great sacrifices to move toward their goals. Let them pursue their athletic dreams full-time and do not burden them with something (college studies) in which they have minimal interest and aptitude at this point in their lives.

> "We don't want people to give money to athletics at all. We've said to this community, 'If you want this [athletic] program, we're asking you to step up and take ownership of it.' We want them to buy athletics, and to give their money to academics" (original emphasis).

> —Les Wyatt, vice-chancellor of the University of Arkansas at Little Rock

If American colleges and universities actually punted the pretend, the following scenario might result:

If schools stopped pretending that College Sports Inc. is connected to their educational missions, much of the hypocrisy and corruption now associated with college sports would end. Schools could either cut loose their franchises in College Sports Inc. and have them operate as totally separate businesses employing professional athletes, or they could abolish the franchises and turn their intercollegiate athletic programs back into genuine student activities. In either situation, schools would unburden themselves of the current academic frauds perpetrated by College Sports Inc.

In the professional programs, the hired athletes would attend school only if they were qualified, if they wanted to, and for as many or as few hours as they wished. In the amateur ranks, the participants would be regular students, as responsible for their studies as every other fully enrolled student at the school. The changed situation would result in schools no longer being embarrassed by the recruiting and admission of athletes with abysmal SAT scores; no longer being hassled by NCAA concoctions like Proposal 48 or accusations that they discriminate against black athletes (as many blacks could play in College Sports Inc. as were athletically qualified); and no longer being forced to apologize for athletes who did not attend class or graduate. In addition, schools could abolish the Division of Hideaway Studies in which they now park their athletes, and they could dismantle the elaborate tutoring system that props the jocks up academically—or, better yet, continue it for regular students. If these changes occurred, there would be a great collective sigh of relief in American higher education.

If schools insisted that their athletic programs be either self-sufficient separate businesses or genuine student activities, the current financial chicanery and fraud—as well as the drain on university resources—would end. The franchises in College Sports Inc. would be separate from their schools and would have to balance their books: because athletic scholarships would no longer exist, they would save money on this expense (although they would have to pay the salaries of their players); because they would have only scouting, not recruiting, expenses, they would also cut costs on this item (although they would have to avoid bidding wars for key prospects). One solution to the latter problem—and the high cost of recruiting—was suggested by the author James Michener: hold a college draft of the best high school prospects.

Athletic programs could also try to raise revenue by demanding that the professional leagues and the USOC pay for the minor-league training of athletes. College Sports Inc. could institute a system in which a professional league and/or team pays a conference and/or college franchise a set amount for each player drafted, say, $250,000 for a first-round choice, $150,000 for a second-round choice, etc.

As separate businesses, athletic programs would have to employ coaches at real market prices—not the inflated deals now in play. They would also have to pay all of their staff and operating expenses as well as the rent, maintenance, and debt servicing on their use of university facilities—as would the coaches if they used school property for their camps and clinics. And, like every "for-profit" business in America, they would have to pay their federal, state, and local taxes.

In addition, as separate businesses, they would have to cut unprofitable parts of their operations—all those nonrevenue sports, athletes, and coaches. Unless Major League Baseball, the National Hockey League, and the USOC were willing to subsidize university teams in their sports, athletic directors would have to shrink or abolish their nonrevenue programs. At this point, the schools involved could return these sports to student activities, emphasizing participation and affordable intercollegiate play, mainly against local and regional opponents.

If American higher education actually punted the pretend, at least twenty and possibly as many as fifty franchises in College Sports Inc.— if they were managed efficiently—could survive as autonomous businesses and balance their books. To do this, ADs and program heads would have to end their longtime habits of wasteful spending; however, the knowledge that their universities would not mop up their red ink may sober them up financially. In addition, because they could concentrate their energies on football and men's basketball, they might even turn a consistent profit. (They could keep their profits, pay their athletes better, pay universities more for rent, or, if wise, bank the money against future losing seasons.)

Beyond the College Sports Inc. circle, all the other schools would have to admit that their lottery quest was over, that their chances of winning the college sports pot o' gold were as remote as when they started—in fact, further from fruition because the fat cats have grown ever more athletically powerful. When these also-ran schools scaled down their athletic programs, their ADs and coaches would have to agree to become regular university employees or move to College Sports Inc. *These colleges and universities would probably benefit the most from the transformation of intercollegiate athletics.* Because they would be the institutions that deemphasized athletics—as compared with the smaller group of schools still connected to College Sports Inc.—the general public, the various levels of government, and the private foundations would have no confusion concerning their commitment to education and would reward them accordingly.

The schools with franchises in College Sports Inc. would encounter a more problematic future. They would have to maintain the separateness of their professional athletic programs or forever risk future financial demands upon their own revenues as well as scandals involving the coaches or athletes. They could accomplish this by selling all or part of their franchises to the booster clubs and encouraging the latter to run the teams as professional sports operations (a number of schools are already well on their way to doing this). This solution would distance universities from many of the financial and ethical problems of College Sports Inc. and the boosters would be happy because they would receive what they want now—their own pro sports franchises. (Of course, whether they would be willing to support them if they lost money remains to be seen.)

The greatest problem with twenty to fifty schools having pro sports franchises in College Sports Inc. is the commercialism that will inevitably contaminate the host universities. By distancing themselves as far as possible from their franchises in College Sports Inc., these schools can try to keep the commercialism from infecting their academic missions. However, any institution with connections to College Sports Inc. forever risks poisoning its educational units with the scandals of big-time, big-money sports.

Nevertheless, punting the pretend and separating the vast majority of colleges and universities—the institutions that will go to student club sports—from the minority in College Sports Inc. will save most of American higher education from the sports commercialism that now corrupts it.

> *"If you think that I am up here because our kids graduate from school, you're foolish. I am up here because I win. I hear people say that money is bad and winning is bad. That's great. Let me win and let me have the money."*
>
> —John Thompson, men's basketball coach at
> Georgetown University and 1988 U.S.
> Olympic team coach, in an address to the
> 1988 NCAA convention

The transformation of college sports into a sane and economically viable system is not going to happen through spontaneous combustion or miraculous intervention. However, forces outside of intercollegiate athletics could intrude and hasten change—if, say, a major economic recession occurred, or if the IRS and Congress redefined the currently illogical tax rules on booster donations, or if enough university presidents banded together and imposed their educational priorities upon the NCAA. But a more likely scenario for change in college sports is reorganization from within.

In the past decade, and especially the last few years, some College Football Association members have grown increasingly greedy and unhappy with any restraints upon their activities. Possibly over an issue like the postseason football championship, or giving more money to college athletes, these schools will bolt from the NCAA and establish their own organization, enlisting some of the big-time basketball schools but excluding all small-time programs. They will set up their College Super Bowl and their own postseason basketball tournament. They will also write a new code of rules for their activities; if their past proposals within the NCAA are any indication, they will move closer to professional sports by paying athletes and having minimal academic standards for them. At this point, the Big Ten and Pacific Ten schools will have to decide whether to join the ex-CFA group or to scale down their athletic programs. Probably these conferences will reorganize, with institutions like Northwestern, Berkeley, and Stanford departing and deemphasizing intercollegiate sports, and others like Ohio State, Indiana, USC, and Arizona State going over to College Sports Inc. Similar reorganizations will occur in other conferences, except, unlike in the Big Ten and Pacific Ten, only a minority of members will be able to join the increasingly high-stakes college sports game.

At that point, the hundreds of athletic have-nots will have to decide whether to abandon their dreams of big-time sports glory or to throw more money into their attempts to compete with the elite. In the worst-case scenario, most of the also-rans will pursue the athletic chimera. In a more positive outcome, most will come to their senses and scale down their sports programs, returning them to their real students. If the latter event occurs, after the Astroturf clears, College Sports Inc. will be in its almost professional phase and its member schools will stand apart from the mainstream of the American academic community.

Whatever set of circumstances transforms intercollegiate athletics— whether punting the pretend and careful alterations or, more likely, irrational greed causing haphazard lurches—massive change will come to college sports. The present situation is too unstable and the pressures upon it too great for college sports to continue in its current form to the end of this decade.

The crucial question, however, is, how will this change affect American higher education? The hundreds of ADs and program heads with disrupted careers will not quietly pack their gym bags and leave. They will do anything to preserve their present power and wealth, even if it means harming their host institutions. If the fight becomes bloody enough, no trustee, administrator, faculty member, or student at the schools involved will remain untouched. Upon the outcome could depend the fiscal and academic integrity of many American colleges and universities.

William Atchley was president of Clemson University in the early 1980s when a college sports scandal enveloped that school. Rather than allow him to investigate fully, Clemson's board of trustees demanded his resignation, and he is now president of the University of the Pacific in Stockton, California. In an interview for this book, he summed up the tension between College Sports Inc. and American higher education: "When academics takes a backseat to athletics, you have a problem. You no longer have an institution where people with integrity want to teach, or where people with common sense and good values want to send their children to learn."

Unless American higher education solves this problem, College Sports Inc. will continue to corrupt it, and with increasing speed. The subtitle of this book is "The Athletic Department *vs* the University." If College Sports Inc. succeeds in its conquest, a future subtitle will read "The Athletic Department *is* the University."

Notes

To ascertain the accuracy of the quotes from the public record—newspapers, magazines, and journals—I have checked subsequent issues of the sources for retractions and corrections. My assumption was that persons quoted incorrectly demand and receive retractions or corrections. When I found these I dropped the quotations or used the amended form; in all other cases, I assumed that the original quotations were correct.

In quoting from the interviews done for this book, I have reproduced the speaker's words as carefully as possible, editing only for grammatical clarity. My tapes and notes of the interviews attest to the accuracy of the quotations and whether the speaker wished to be quoted for attribution or not.

The following annotations provide the sources and dates of quotes as well as additional information about various points in the text. The annotations proceed according to the order of material presented in each chapter.

Dedication, Preface, & Introduction

The *Black Beauty* quote is from the Eleanor Graham Vance adaptation, New York, 1949; it was my son's favorite book.

The Giamatti quote is from the *New York Times,* 9/13/87, and the *Louisville Courier-Journal* item about UK appeared on 12/8/85.

All of the myths and refutations about college sports reappear in the main text, and the notes for them are in the appropriate sections below.

Part I: Old Siwash in Red Ink: The Finances of College Sports

Overview

Don Tyson's remark was in the *Arkansas Gazette,* 2/18/88; the headline in the *South Bend Tribune,* 8/14/87, was a quote from the school's president; and Don Canham's comment was in the *Sporting News,* 12/5/88. The *Revenues and Expenses of Intercollegiate Athletics Programs* survey is authored by Mitchell

H. Raiborn and published by the NCAA in Mission, Kansas, 1986; the survey also contained the results of a questionnaire—the source for the item that less than 1 percent of all athletic programs defined their "fiscal objective" as earning money "to support nonathletics activities of the institution."

The Money Game: Financing Collegiate Athletics, by Robert H. Atwell, Bruce Grimes, and Donna A. Lopiano, was published by the American Council on Education, Washington, D.C., 1980. The stories about the athletic program deficits in Arkansas were in the *Arkansas Gazette,* 2/18/88 and 10/29/88; and the one about the Florida regents was in the *St. Petersburg Times,* 4/29/85. The former soccer coach made his comment during an off-the-record interview ("I'd still like to get back into college coaching," he explained, "and if I blast ADs openly, it certainly won't help the job application process"). His comment succinctly sums up an aspect of the major financial problem in college sports and is verified by other sources.

Chapter 1

Jim Valvano was quoted in the *Washington Post,* 2/21/82. The poll of sixty-five NCAA Division I presidents was done by J. Wade Gilley and Anthony A. Hickley for their *Administration of University Athletic Programs: Internal Control and Excellence,* 1985, available from the Educational Resources Information Center, Washington, D.C. The administrative relationship material is from the NCAA publication *Athletic Committees and Faculty Representatives* by Earl M. Ramer, Mission, Kansas, 1980.

Most of the facts and quotes about Don Canham were in a *Sports inc.* profile, 6/6/88. The *Ann Arbor News* material appeared 12/13/87, and the quote from the English professor was in the *New York Times,* 1/11/83. The information about Michigan being "$2.5 million in the red" in 1988–89 was made by TCU athletic director and NCAA official Frank Windegger in *Sports Illustrated,* 10/2/89.

The information on Perkins's 1986 salary and perks is from *USA Today,* 9/24/86; *Sports inc.,* 8/1/88, discussed the Alabama financial situation. The *Birmingham Post-Herald* headline appeared 6/13/88, and the article explained that part of Alabama's financial problem occurred because it is among a minority of athletic departments that pay its debt-servicing bill. The San Diego State story was in the *Chronicle of Higher Education,* 6/19/85; the Southern Illinois one was in the same journal on 5/4/88; and Canham's article was in *Sports inc.,* 8/1/88.

The information and quotes concerning the University of New Mexico's athletic department budget problems are from articles in the *Albuquerque Journal,* 8/21/85 and 9/5/85. The information on Bridgers's 1986 salary and perks is from *USA Today,* 9/24/86. The details and quotes in the Koenig story are from the *Albuquerque Journal*, 7/15/88, 7/16/88, 7/19/88, 7/20/88, 7/21/88, 7/22/88, 7/23/88, 7/24/88, 7/25/88, 7/26/88, 3/16/89, 3/17/89, and 3/23/89.

The Ray Sons column appeared in the *Chicago Sun-Times*, 7/14/88; details of Stoner's career as well as the $300,000 settlement fee were in that paper, 7/13/88, and in the *Champaign News-Gazette*, 10/23/88. Additional material as well as the quotes on Stoner's downfall were in the *Sporting News*, 6/27/88, the *Chicago Tribune*, 6/16/88, 7/12/88, 7/13/88, and the *Chicago Sun-Times*, 6/16/88. The information on Stoner's 1986 salary and perks is from *USA Today*, 9/24/86.

The *Louisville Courier-Journal* covered the $62,000 surplus story on 10/31/85 and 11/2/85, and updated it on 2/9–11/89; the Billy Reed column appeared 11/6/85. Information about the University of Louisville's Twentieth-Century Literature Conference was provided by conference officials. After the Metro Conference bonus scheme became public, one of the athletic department officials involved, Kenneth A. Lindsey, gave his $5,000 bonus to the school, and, according to the *Courier-Journal*, "Olsen never bought the car [for his wife] and the $7,500 was returned [by the Buick dealership] to the university"; however, "None of the other staff members returned their bonuses."

Chapter 2

The Beano Cook item in *USA Today* appeared 10/24/88. The statistics on college football attendance are from *Sports inc.*, 1/23/89, and the *Chronicle of Higher Education*, 2/11/87. The Arkansas coach was quoted in *Sports Illustrated*, 10/24/88; the *Lexington Herald-Leader* article was on 9/14/87; and the San Jose State information appeared in the *San Jose Mercury News*, 5/18/86 and 5/20/86.

The item about priority tickets in the *Louisville Courier-Journal* ran on 10/5/88. The San Diego State story was in the *Chronicle of Higher Education*, 9/5/84; the Boise State one in the *Idaho Statesman*, 3/2/82; the University of Missouri one in the *Jefferson City Post-Tribune*, 1/29/82; and the Louisiana State one in the *Baton Rouge Morning Advocate*, 2/23/82.

Information about University of Louisville football and basketball seating appeared in the *Louisville Courier-Journal*, 5/24/84 and 10/19/84, and the update on 1/31/89.

D. Stanley Eitzen was quoted by the *Chronicle of Higher Education*, 2/12/86; the details about the length of season and number of contests as well as the quotations used here were in that journal, 5/30/84. The Syracuse AD's comments were in *USA Today*, 1/11/90, and Denny Crum's in the *Louisville Courier-Journal* the same day.

Chapter 3

Rick Bozich's comment was in the *Louisville Courier-Journal,* 1/6/89. The *Sports Illustrated* "Special College Basketball Issue, Fall 1988" quoted the ADs' "to buy" expression. The information about current Miami guarantees and the comments from the AD were in *Sports inc.,* 1/18/88, and the *Miami Herald's* story ran on 9/17/84. The Notre Dame deficit was in the *South Bend Tribune,* 8/14/87; the Akron story and quotes were in the *Akron Beacon Journal,* 2/19/87; and the items about the Big West Conference were in *Don Heinrich's College Football,* 1989 edition.

The information and quotes about the UNLV guarantees were in the *Las Vegas Review Journal,* 1/8/83 and 1/14/84; the UNLV athletic department claims that it no longer engages in this form of creative accounting.

Chapter 4

The 1988 NCAA Final Four statistics are from the *Chronicle of Higher Education,* 4/13/88; the 44 percent distribution figure for the 1987 tournament was in that journal, 10/26/88; and Tom Hansen discussed the 1990s tournament payout in *USA Today,* 11/29/89. Information about Ole Miss's 20,000-seat guarantee was in the *Louisville Courier-Journal,* 11/16/89, and that paper quoted the Indiana AD on 11/9/88; Ole Miss's ranking when invited to the Liberty Bowl was based on the "College Football Computer Rankings" in *USA Today,* 11/21/89. The quote about the Peach Bowl sponsors was in an Indiana University News Bureau press release, 11/11/87; the *Chronicle of Higher Education* carried the story on 11/14/87, and the estimates of total bowl payouts are based on an article in that journal, 9/4/85, where "the chairman of the [then] 18 bowls groups reports that the bowls . . . altogether [in their histories] have provided more than $327 million for intercollegiate football." Using that figure as a base and adding on the subsequent annual figures in the *Chronicle of Higher Education,* the number of $400 million is reached.

Thompson's 1988 speech is in the *Proceedings of the 82nd Annual Convention of the NCAA* published by the NCAA, Mission, Kansas, 1988. The figures on the 1988 Collegiate Kickoff Classic were in *Sports inc.,* 8/22/88, and Joe Paterno's quote was in the *Chronicle of Higher Education,* 1/19/83.

The quotes and statistics about the decline in TV ratings for the major bowl games are from three issues of *Sports inc.,* 1/18/88, 6/20/88, and 7/18/88, and the TV ratings for the 1989 games were in *USA Today,* 1/13/89. That newspaper discussed the Cactus Bowl (the original name of the Copper Bowl) and Crab Bowl on 8/12/88; the Crab Bowl was postponed because of the death of a key organizer. The story about the Bluebonnet Bowl's difficulties was in *Sports inc.* on 7/25/88.

Don James made his comment about the College Super Bowl to *USA Today*, 6/2/89. The *Chronicle of Higher Education* tracked the NCAA's and CFA's arguments on 1/18/84, 7/11/84, 6/11/86, and 1/14/87. The AD of the Air Force Academy was quoted in a Scripps-Howard dispatch reprinted in the *Bloomington Herald-Times*, 6/2/89; that paper also had Wayne Duke's quote on 6/12/89.

Chapter 5

Gene Slaughter's remark was in the *Columbus Evening Dispatch*, 9/16/82. The feature in the *Chronicle of Higher Education* on the history of the televising of college football and its mid-70s situation appeared 10/20/75. The comments by educators concerning the problems of large TV revenues were in that journal, 9/2/81 and 9/8/82, and the note about the CFA helping to pay the legal fees appeared 5/2/84. The facts about the NCAA's concessions to the CFA were in the *Kansas City Star*, 6/6/82. The entire text of Judge Burciaga's decision appeared in the *Chronicle of Higher Education*, 9/22/82, and the reaction of Oklahoma's lawyer to the Burciaga decision was in the *Daily Oklahoman* on 9/16/82. The reaction of Donald Combs was in the *Chronicle of Higher Education* on 9/22/82, and Joe Paterno's comment was in the same journal on 9/29/82; the quote from Gene Slaughter was in the *Columbus Evening Dispatch*, 9/16/82.

The NCAA's argument before the Supreme Court was in the *Chronicle of Higher Education* on 3/28/84, and the texts of the Court's decisions were in that journal, 7/5/84. The *Daily Oklahoman* reaction was in that paper on 6/28/84. Keith Dunnavant's quote was in *Sports inc.*, 1/9/89, as were the statistics about Oklahoma's drop in TV revenue. The NCAA's legal costs were noted by the *Chronicle of Higher Education*, 8/8/84. Also in that journal were the Byers quote, 7/18/84; the dollar statistics on the new TV pacts and CFA distributions, 8/1/84 and 9/12/84; the facts about the 1984 Notre Dame football season, 1/9/85; the stories and quotes about Metrosports, 4/3/85, 11/12/86, and 11/19/86. The *Chicago Tribune* discussed how the syndicators hurt Northwestern on 7/22/86. The story and quotes about the Southern Conference's loss of TV money appeared in the *Charlotte Observer*, 12/2/84.

Sports inc. carried the item about the ADs' attempt to overthrow the Supreme Court decision, 12/12/88; other stories on this issue and Weistart's remarks appeared there, 6/13/88, 6/27/88, and 3/13/89. That journal also carried Dave Gavitt's comment about no revenue for basketball games, 9/18/88, and articles on college basketball ratings on 11/16/87, 2/8/88, 3/28/88, and 11/28/88. The quote from the ESPN executive was in the *Chronicle of Higher Education*, 4/4/84; the Lund quote was in that journal, 3/26/86, as were articles on declining TV ratings, 1/11/84, 4/4/84, 3/26/86, and 3/16/88.

Sports inc. carried the syndicator's remark about the conference commissioners, 3/28/88. *Indianapolis Star* sportswriter Bill Brenner wrote about the late-night tip-offs on 1/10/89, and Bob Knight's comment was in the *Bloomington Herald-Times*, 1/31/89. Neal Pilson's speech is in the *Proceedings of the 82nd Annual Convention of the NCAA*.

Chapter 6

The Fresno State–Dallas Cowboy cheerleaders incident was in the *Los Angeles Times*, 10/23/82, as was the quote from Professor Bush. The information about Bob Brodhead's background and innovations was in the *Baton Rouge Morning Advocate*, 5/22/82 and 9/30/84. The comment from the NCAA official about logos was in the *Chronicle of Higher Education*, 6/6/84; articles about Brodhead's crimes and demise at LSU were in that journal on 10/15/86 and 10/29/86, and in the *Baton Rouge Morning Advocate* on 10/30/85, 10/9/86, and 10/10/86. Brodhead went to Southeastern Louisiana to revive that school's abandoned football program; when he was unable to do so, he was let go (*Louisville Courier-Journal*, 4/26/89).

The Temple–Atlantic City story was in the *New York Daily News*, 5/19/88, and *USA Today*, 5/25/88; the latter article also ran NBC Sports' denial that it had pressured Temple to move the game.

The *Chronicle of Higher Education*, 12/3/86, had the John R. Davis comment as well as the one by the P.R. director of the Sea World Holiday Bowl. That journal also carried the San Diego State AD's "kicking and screaming" quote, 1/22/89. *Sports inc.* discussed the Rose Bowl–Burger King tie-in, 7/18/88; the San Diego State and University of Denver deals, and the Wichita State AD's comment, 8/1/88; and the Yale associate AD's criticism, 1/10/88. The Wichita State AD, Tom Shupe, admitted that he has sold space in his stadium to corporations and also that his school was the host of the recently renamed Pepsi/Missouri Valley Conference Basketball Tournament.

Bob Hammel's comment about the Old Oaken Bucket Game was in the *Bloomington Herald-Times*, 5/11/89. *USA Today* explained "Clutter" on 9/26/88; *Sports inc.* reported on SMU's problems, 7/18/88, and carried Robert E. Lehr's quote, 1/10/88.

Chapter 7

The *Chronicle of Higher Education* printed John Timothy Young's comment, 11/14/84; that journal discussed universities' tax-exempt "businesses on the side," 9/7/88, and the Michigan tax bill, 9/7/88. The *New York Times* carried J. J. Pickle's comment, 5/15/88, and *Sports inc.* the NCAA's tax bill, 3/13/89. A number of years ago, Digger Phelps began arguing that athletes should pay taxes on under-the-table payments: see the *New York Times,* 4/5/82 and 10/16/84.

Dom LaPonzima was quoted in the *Washington Post,* 9/20/82. The IRS and the priority-seating controversy was covered by the *Chronicle of Higher Education,* 9/26/84, 10/24/84, 1/16/85 (the source of the Kaplan quote), 5/7/86, and 6/26/85. *Sports inc.* followed the story on 4/11/88, 5/23/88, 7/25/88, and 10/31/88; the *New York Times* had the 80 percent compromise, 11/27/88.

Occasionally a college president raises the issue of the tax-exempt status of college sports. Chancellor Michael Heyman of the University of California, Berkeley, in an address to the June 1987 NCAA Presidents' Commission meeting, remarked, "Wouldn't it be chastening to us if the IRS decided to treat intercollegiate athletics as an unrelated business subject to tax?" When asked in an interview for this book on 6/13/88 to elaborate on his comment, Heyman replied: "It seemed to me that intercollegiate athletics are so far from any [educational] relationship to the university . . . but are similar to the NBA or the National Football League. So I would not be shocked if at least simply the logic of unrelated business was applied." Heyman was a professor of law before becoming chancellor at Berkeley; he is also the originator of the term "the Athletics Arms Race."

Chapter 8

The phrase "Unearned Revenue" for booster donations is based on the NCAA's use of this term for this kind of revenue in its *Revenues and Expenses* booklet, and is in line with the IRS's distinction between earned and passive revenue.

Atwell's comments are in the *Proceedings of the 82nd Annual Convention of the NCAA.* The NCAA statistics on booster donations are from its *Revenues and Expenses* booklet and from an article in the *Chronicle of Higher Education,* 3/3/82. The information on the Texas A. & M. Aggie Club was in the *Bryan-College Station Eagle,* 1/12/86, and the facts and quote on Sherrill's hiring are from the *Dallas Morning News,* 1/24/82. Conklin's remarks were in the *Philadelphia Inquirer,* 4/7/85.

Statistics are hard to find on the percentage of alumni (as opposed to boosters) who give to athletic programs. But taking a recent Big Ten survey, and information supplied by school alumni associations, as typical of many institutions nationally, the results show that at the University of Illinois, for example, 3,972 people gave more than one dollar a year to the athletic department's supporters' clubs and that about 50 percent of these people were alums. Thus, approximately 2,000 out of 350,000 living Illini alumni, *or half of 1 percent,* gave money in this way. Considering the nature of Big Ten schools, these percentages probably apply to most similar institutions nationally. At private schools, the percentages tend to vary according to the activity of athletic program fund-raisers and the administration's support for such activity, and the percentage probably rises to as high as 4 percent. Nevertheless, the point remains that only a very small percentage of alumni contribute to athletic programs. (The statistics on the Big Ten athletic supporters' groups come from a booklet handed out at the 1989 Big Ten Athletic Fundraisers Winter Conference, held in Columbus, Ohio, and the information on Big Ten alumni and boosters was supplied by those schools' alumni associations.)

The facts about the University of Iowa's I-Club are from the *Des Moines Register*, 12/4/83. The interview with Bruce Hinchliffe took place at Stanford on 8/14/88. The major study of the Notre Dame alumni is "Winning and Giving: Another Look," by Allen L. Sack and Charles Watkins, in *Sport and Higher Education*, Donald Chu et al., eds., Champaign, Ill., 1985. Conklin was quoted by Professor James H. Frey in "College Athletic Performance and Fund Raising: A Look at the Data," *Currents: Journal of the Advancement and Support of Education*, vol. 2, 1/85.

The article by Sigelman and Carter is "Win One for the Giver? Alumni Giving and Big-Time College Sport," *Social Science Quarterly*, vol. 60, 9/79; and Sigelman and Samuel Bookheimer did the follow-up study, "Is It Whether You Win or Lose? Monetary Contributions to Big-Time College Athletic Programs," *Social Science Quarterly*, vol. 64, 3/83. The article with the comment about UCLA fund-raising is "To the Victors Belong the Spoils? College Athletics and Alumni Giving," *Social Science Quarterly*, vol. 62, 12/81, by George Brooker and T. D. Klastorin. The *Chronicle of Higher Education*'s article about Tulane and Wichita State appeared 1/13/88. *Sports inc.* quoted the USC fund-raiser, 10/31/88.

Professor James H. Frey's comment about ADs and boosters is in his article "Boosterism, Scarce Resources, and Institutional Control: The Future of American Intercollegiate Athletics," *International Review of Sport Sociology*, vol. 17 (1982). The figures and facts about booster clubs at North Carolina schools are from articles in the *Raleigh News and Observer*, 9/13/82, 11/4/82, and 4/16/87. The information about the South Carolina booster club president was in the *Charleston News and Courier*, 3/20/88, and *The State* (Columbia), 3/20/88. Duke University has a system whereby, according to one official, the university's fund-raising office "keeps donors sorted out by their interests. . . . In the computer, an Iron Duke's name [a sports supporter] will come up as a restricted person, meaning 'he only wants to give to athletics' " (*Raleigh News and Observer*, 9/13/82).

The NCAA pamphlet is *NCAA Financial Audit Guidelines*, Mission, Kansas, 1986. Information on USC's endowed coaching and playing positions was in *Sports inc.*, 10/31/88, and on the Texas A. & M. Aggie Club, in the *Bryan-*

College Station Eagle, 1/12/86. The *Chronicle of Higher Education* story on booster money to Tarkanian appeared 3/2/83; the *Miami Herald* material, 5/29/84; and the *Des Moines Register* citation, 12/4/83. The information on the Purdue alumni was provided by that school's alumni association; because boosters make up about 50 percent of the Purdue donors to intercollegiate athletics, the percentage of Purdue alums who give to the athletic department's supporters' clubs is .0085 percent.

The Wayne Duke quote is from the *New York Times,* 3/29/81; the Don Canham one from the *Los Angeles Herald-Examiner,* 1/12/82; the SMU alumni story appeared in the *Chronicle of Higher Education,* 1/6/88; and the national statistics on contributions to higher education were in *USA Today,* 5/18/89. When asked for permission to use his name in this book, the East Coast development officer refused, explaining that one of his main duties is applying to major foundations for large amounts of grant money ("I wouldn't be doing my school or myself a favor by going public about foundation managers' prejudices"). The *Foundation News* issue was March/April 1985; *Sports Illustrated* commented on it, 6/15/87.

Chapter 9

The *Richmond Times Dispatch* item appeared 8/26/88; the information about the fees at Virginia schools and "the tea party on campus" quote are also from this source. The NCAA financial survey is *Revenues and Expenses.* The quotes from David Baker are from interviews with him 5/18/88 and 6/2/89. The NCAA pamphlet is *Athletic Committees and Faculty Representatives,* by Earl M. Ramer, Mission, Kansas, 1980.

The information about the University of Maryland is in Barbara R. Bergmann's article "Do Sports Make Money for the University?" in *Footnotes: A Publication of the American Association of University Professors,* Spring 1988. The University of Nevada at Reno incident was covered by the *Chronicle of Higher Education,* 9/7/83; that journal followed the University of Houston story on 4/9/86 and 10/22/86. The *Houston Post* discussed student reaction on 3/19/86.

Chapter 10

The item in the *Raleigh News and Observer* appeared 10/3/82; that article also discussed how academic budget lines cover coaches' salaries. The *Richmond Times Dispatch,* 8/27/84, had the statistics on Illinois and Kentucky state funding of intercollegiate athletics; the *Orange County Register* discussed state money for Cal State at Fullerton, 7/3/88; the *Anchorage Daily News* focused on the University of Alaska at Anchorage situation, 10/23/88; and for the Montana schools, see Doug Fullerton, *Revenues and Expenses of Intercollegiate Athletics: A Comparison of M[ontana] S[tate] U[niversity] and Its Peer Campuses,* April 1985, available from the Education Resources Informational Service, Washington, D.C. The court rulings on the Temple University–Title IX case were in the *Chronicle of Higher Education,* 11/24/82; that journal also discussed Washington State University's use of state funds, 7/13/81, and the Utah State situation, 9/9/87. The NCAA survey on schools using general operating funds was in the recent edition of *Revenues and Expenses.* Barbara Bergmann's quote was in her article cited above. The San Jose situation and quotes were in the *San Jose Mercury,* 5/18–20/86.

Dick Schultz's quote was in the *Richmond Times Dispatch,* 8/27/84. The Arkansas deficit was in the *Arkansas Democrat,* 6/28/88, and the *Arkansas Gazette,* 6/26/88 and 6/30/88; the *Chronicle of Higher Education* also focused on it, 7/13/88, and on the University of Wisconsin imbroglio, 3/1/89; the *Milwaukee Journal* had the results of its poll, 12/19/88.

Overview

Dick Schultz's quote was in the *Chronicle of Higher Education,* 7/1/87.

Chapter 11

Don Canham was quoted in the *Washington Times,* 2/12/87; the Michigan salary figure was in *Business Week,* 10/27/88, and the University of Georgia one in the *Atlanta Journal,* 3/8/86. The ACE comment was in *The Money Game: Financing Collegiate Athletics.*

The item about the Texas coaches and ADs was in the *Dallas Morning News,* 12/30/85. The *USA Today* study ran 9/24–25/86 and 12/9–11/86, and the list of coaches' salaries at the University of Iowa was in the *Des Moines Register,* 6/20/88. Elliott's salary is based on the *USA Today* figure of $66,000 for the previous year, 1986–87: a normal 5 percent increment moves it over $70,000. The salaries of the Iowa faculty are from *Academe: The Bulletin of the American Association of University Professors,* March/April 1988.

Professor Frey's comment was in his article "The Organization of American Amateur Sport: Efficiency to Entropy," *American Behavioral Scientist,* January/February 1978. The NCAA's statistic of 300 percent growth is in the *Revenues and Expenses* survey. The salaries of Indiana University athletic department personnel and faculty are from *IU System Salary List [1988–89],* compiled by United University Professionals–IU, Local 2254, American Federation of Teachers, and from the university's salary list deposited in the main library on the Bloomington campus. For the 1989–90 salary expenses, the I.U. athletic department would not provide dollar totals on the expenses part of its budget, but if one takes the department's "income projection" figure of $13,481,656 and assumes that, as with all athletic department budget projections, at least a balance between revenues and expenses is predicted, then the 34.57 percent ascribed to "salaries, wages, and fringe benefits" comes to $4.66 million. That the department will not release these dollar totals makes no sense; more serious and reprehensible, however, is its refusal to show the audited financial statement at the end of the fiscal year even to the Faculty Athletics Committee. But this unwarranted secrecy is not an Indiana University athletic department idiosyncrasy—this situation prevails at most NCAA schools.

Chapter 12

Don Canham's remarks are in the *Proceedings of the 82nd Annual Convention of the NCAA.* The statistic on the Michigan athletic scholarship bill was in *Business Week,* 10/27/88; the Georgia bill was in the *Atlanta Journal,* 3/8/86; and the Big Eight one in *Sports inc.,* 10/3/88. The quotes about Stanford's athletic scholarship costs are from an interview for this book with Stanford AD Andy Geiger, 6/14/88, and the statistics are from an internal Stanford administration memo dated 3/8/88 and given to the author by Mr. Geiger.

The *Chronicle of Higher Education* focused on Proposals 92 and 93 in 1/6/88, 1/20/88, and 6/15/88. William Atchley, president of the University of the Pacific and former president of Clemson University, discussed the Nebraska "county scholarship" system in an interview for this book, 6/10/88. The quote from the Nebraska assistant coach was in *Don Heinrich's College Football,* 1988 edition. The articles in the *Memphis Commercial Appeal* about Pell grants appeared 4/16/85, 8/23/85, 8/24/85, and 2/14/86. The Department of Education estimate and the quote about Alabama were in *Sports inc.,* 1/2/89.

To be fair to the student managers, most do much more complicated and time-consuming jobs than the old-time "water boys" did. Today, a student manager can spend forty to sixty hours a week on the job, mainly helping the equipment managers and the coaches, sometimes being the latters' "gofers." The job has some nice compensations—other than free tuition, room and board, etc.—such as free travel with the team, including to bowls and tournaments.

Another financial sleight-of-hand trick at public institutions is to count out-of-state athletes as in-state, lowering their tuition costs to the athletic department by thousands of dollars each. The question then becomes: who pays the difference? At some schools, the money comes out of general operating funds, at others it simply is not counted, and the taxpayers make up the difference— i.e., if it costs $8,000 to educate a single student at Northern Jock U. for a year, and the athletic scholarship bills for out-of-state athletes are lowered from $12,000 to $6,000 by counting them as in-state, then the taxpayers assume the extra $2,000.

Chapter 13

The University of Georgia athletic program travel costs were in the *Atlanta Journal,* 3/8/86. Professor James Vincent was interviewed for this book on 5/19/89.

The figures on the 1987 NCAA skiing championship were in the *NCAA Annual Reports: 1986–87,* published by the NCAA in Mission, Kansas, 1988. The dates and sites of NCAA committee meetings are listed regularly in the *NCAA News.*

Soccer teams hopscotch around the country because the NCAA chooses and seeds teams for its tournament on the basis of their total records. A team that builds a good record against national opponents will more easily gain a berth in the first rounds of the tourney, be seeded higher, and gain home field advantage over teams that remain all season within their region—thus the frantic traveling to build records. Once again, NCAA rules encourage free spending and work against cost cutting in a nonrevenue sport that loses money for almost all athletic programs. For example, the 1988 NCAA soccer champion, Indiana University, projected an income of $34,000 for 1989–90 against estimated expenses of at least $250,000.

Tom Jernstedt's comment and the Georgetown travel items were in the *Chronicle of Higher Education,* 3/21/84. The LSU–Sugar Bowl story was in the *Baton Rouge Morning Advocate,* 4/2/86; the Golden Fleece Award story in *Sports Illustrated,* 11/5/84; and the financial details of Frank Broyles's New York trip were in the *Arkansas Democrat,* 1/20/88.

Tony Barnhart discussed recruiting costs in the *Atlanta Journal,* 2/9/88, and reprinted his article in amended form in *Don Heinrich's College Football,* 1988 edition; the information and quotes here are mainly from the latter, including the quote from the football recruiting coordinator (unnamed in Barnhart's articles). Barnhart also quotes one athletic department official as saying, "Some schools don't know how much they really spend on football recruiting. Quite frankly, they don't want to know."

Pepper Rodgers's comment was in his thinly disguised *roman à clef, Fourth and Long Gone,* Atlanta, 1984. The statistic on Louisiana Tech's women's basketball team was in the *Chronicle of Higher Education,* 3/30/83, and the anecdote about the Georgia quail was in that journal, 3/26/86.

Chuck Neinas's comment was on *Fair Game,* a Public Broadcasting System program, aired 1/18/87. Details on the Chris Mills story were in *Sports inc.,* 10/10/88, and were reported in exquisite detail almost daily by the *Louisville*

Courier-Journal from May 1988 to May 1989. The life of a recruiter was outlined in a *Chicago Sun-Times* article, "Notre Dame Recruiter Rarely Takes a Break," 2/15/88. The 1981 estimate of telephone costs and recruiting personnel was in *The Money Game*. The Bill Dooley story was in *Don Heinrich's College Football*, 1988 edition; an excellent profile of this coach was in the *Roanoke Times and World-News*, 11/15/86. The story about the Cleveland State assistant coach was in the *Lake County* (Ohio) *News-Herald*, 4/12/88.

Chapter 14

The study on equipment costs was prepared in 1989 by a sports business expert at Indiana University, Bloomington. Its author kindly allowed me to quote from it but, because of the confidential nature of the study, he requested that I not use his name. I agreed to do this; however, I called equipment manufacturers to verify the prices. The prices quoted from the study are accurate as of 6/30/89.

Although the NCAA allows 95 athletic scholarship holders on Division I-A football teams, most big-time programs carry a large number of walk-ons; for example, according to the *Indiana Daily Student*, 9/26/89, the Indiana University football team had "50 walk-ons" and a "roster of nearly 145 players" in 1989. The *Louisville Courier-Journal* outlined Kentucky equipment costs, 8/28/86, and the *Atlanta Journal* had the figures on Georgia's, 3/8/86.

The *Chronicle of Higher Education* discussed Penn State's medical costs, 5/25/83, and the UNC–Chapel Hill study, 2/8/84; that journal had the Vince Dooley quote, 9/12/84; the costs of the NCAA's drug tests, 10/1/86; and the NCAA's list of banned substances, 6/27/84 (the caffeine regulation stated, "if the concentration in urine exceeds 15 micrograms per milliliter"). The *Syracuse Herald-American* also discussed the NCAA's eighty-one banned substances, 15/26/86; the *Columbus Dispatch* focused on the Ohio State drug tests, 7/31/86; the *Knoxville Journal* had the University of Tennessee costs, 9/24/86 and 7/29/87; and the *Caspar Star-Tribune* outlined the situation at the University of Wyoming, 10/18/86. The Palo Alto *Peninsula Times Tribune* discussed Simone Levant's court victory, 3/12/87; the *Raleigh News and Observer* outlined the constitutional arguments against testing, 2/21/87; and Professor Allen L. Sack eloquently opposed drug tests in his article "Random Tests Abuse [Athletes'] Dignity," *New York Times*, 5/29/88.

Chapter 15

James K. Coyne's comment was in *USA Today*, 7/28/87; the remarks of Rawlings owner Henry E. Figgie, Jr., were in the *New York Times*, 10/9/88. The statistics on helmet liability cases were in *Sports inc.*, 2/13/89; an Illinois firm, Schutt Athletic Sales Co., has stayed in the NFL game but is losing ground to Riddell, the *Chicago Tribune,* 11/16/89. The insurance costs at Oklahoma, Kansas, and Colorado were in the *Kansas City Times,* 2/3/86; Georgia's were in the *Atlanta Journal,* 3/8/86; Alabama's argument with Bobby Humphrey was in the *Louisville Courier-Journal,* 4/12/89; and the costs at Concordia College were in the *Chronicle of Higher Education,* 3/26/86. That journal covered the NCAA's catastrophic insurance plan on 4/27/83, 9/14/83, 12/14/83 (the source of the Schrader quote), 4/25/84, 1/9/85, and 7/27/88. *Sports inc.* discussed the Marc Buoniconti case, 8/1/88. Even in a relatively safe sport like soccer, according to *USA Today,* 7/28/87, "A Massachusetts college student, injured in a soccer game, sued the manufacturer of the ball for $100,000."

Chapter 16

The quotes from Herb Appenzeller were in the *Chronicle of Higher Education,* 2/20/85, and the University of Kentucky legal costs were in the *Louisville Courier-Journal,* 5/12/89 (that article placed the expenses at $356,675 through 3/31/89 and mentioned that "that figure does not include salaries of UK investigators or secretaries who have spent innumerable hours on the case"; since the legal and secretarial work continued through much of 1989, an additional $100,000 is a low estimate). The Georgia expenses were in the *Atlanta Journal,* 3/8/86. Information about Stanford's legal support of Simone Levant was provided during the interview with Stanford AD Andy Geiger, 6/14/88. The *Chronicle of Higher Education* had the NCAA's budget for 1988–89 on 10/26/88; the Dick Crum settlement, 12/9/87; and the Pepper Rodgers one, 3/30/83. That journal quoted Gordon S. White, Jr., 10/3/84, and focused on the Iowa campaign, 6/8/88. *Sports inc.* discussed the Heisman electors, 11/7/88, and *USA Today* carried the results, 12/5/88. The Georgia expenses were in the *Atlanta Journal,* 3/8/86.

Don Canham's comments about Maryland were in the *Washington Times,* 5/12/87, and *Sports inc.* discussed how athletic departments are using computers, 5/30/88. The tutor who boasted about her computer survey was well aware that she was violating the Buckley amendment and requested anonymity.

Chapter 17

Dan Blue's comment was in *Sports inc.,* 12/12/88, as was information about North Carolina State's new arena; that magazine listed the new or under-construction college sports facilities referred to in this chapter on 7/11/88 (the Cleveland State facility includes a downtown convention center), and it discussed the Tennessee fiasco, 11/16/88. The *Chronicle of Higher Education* wrote about the new arena at the University of North Carolina–Chapel Hill on 3/9/88. The plans for the new Purdue indoor football facility were in the *Purdue Alumnus,* 9/88.

John Silber was quoted by the *Chronicle of Higher Education,* 12/10/73; that journal discussed the Kent State indebtedness, 10/1/73, and the George Mason situation, 10/10/86. The Georgia debt-servicing bill was in the *Atlanta Journal,* 3/8/86, and Alabama's was in *Sports inc.,* 8/1/88; that magazine carried Bob Bockrath's comment, the information on the Boston College skyboxes, and the quote about the University of Washington's decision not to have skyboxes, 3/21/88. The *Louisville Courier-Journal* discussed the University of Kentucky skyboxes, 9/22/89.

Wayne Young's remark was in the *St. Petersburg Times,* 4/29/85. The in-house memo of the University of Cincinnati was provided by a staff member at that school, 8/18/88; it was part of the school's "Long-Range Plan for Athletics." *Sports inc.* had statistics on artificial surfaces, 7/18/88, and on Alabama's maintenance costs, 8/1/88; the *Kansas City Times* discussed the Missouri athletic program's maintenance costs, 5/5/88. The remark by C. W. "Hootie" Ingram was in the *Miami Herald,* 9/17/84. In Division III and at many smaller colleges and universities, there are multiuse gyms and fields that recreational and intercollegiate athletes share. Only for these facilities does paying some maintenance and other costs out of the main physical plant budget make sense. The *Chronicle of Higher Education* had articles on the maintenance problems of colleges and universities, 7/7/88 and 10/5/88.

Summary

Richard Lapchick's comment was in *Sports inc.,* 8/1/88; the business manager of the athletic department at the University of South Carolina was quoted by the *Charleston News and Courier,* 2/28/82. The information on and quotes about the University of North Carolina at Asheville were in the *Chronicle of Higher Education,* 9/2/87. The *Louisville Courier-Journal* carried an interesting item on 8/11/89 concerning increased enrollment and college sports: four "small state colleges that have started football this decade—Cumberland, Campbellsville, Kentucky Wesleyan, and Union—said enrollment had not increased as much as had been expected. None were making money on football."

The *Chronicle of Higher Education* had a feature article on Utica College's dropping out of Division I, 5/11/88. The *Seattle Times* covered the Seattle University story on 4/13/82; Frank DeFord included it in a *Sports Illustrated* article, 3/3/86, and Father Sullivan's comments about alumni and winning the NCAA were in that article. The *Chronicle of Higher Education* had items about the University of Baltimore situation, 11/3/82 and 4/27/83; the report on the

UB situation is "Intercollegiate Athletics and Student Activities and Recreation Programs: One College's Decision," by Dennis M. Pelletier and Katherine E. Peterson, *NASPA Journal,* Winter 1986; and the *Baltimore Sun* discussed the athletic program's demise, 4/19/83.

After completing the research for this book, I came across an interesting study on intercollegiate athletics by two political scientists, Nand Hart-Nibbrig and Clement Cottingham, entitled *The Political Economy of College Sports,* Lexington, Mass., 1985. These writers posit a very deterministic college sports universe; they call it "corporate athleticism," and describe it as hugely profitable and efficient. However, the financial losses and mismanagement of the real college sports system contradict their basic premise. If corporate America were as unsuccessful as "corporate athleticism," the Rising Sun would fly from all of our office buildings and American executives would be doing early-morning calisthenics in the courtyards.

Part II: Greed City: College Coaches' Salaries, Perks, Deals, & Scams

Overview

The Sherrill quote was in the *Bryan-College Station Eagle,* 1/12/86, and the Marcum one in *USA Today,* 9/24/86. Rick Pitino's salary at the University of Kentucky was in the *Louisville Courier-Journal* on 6/2/89; Valvano's, in *USA Today* on 4/3/89. The annual incomes of Crum, Thompson, and Tarkanian are based on the figures in *USA Today,* 12/9–11/86, and the reported increments and bonuses that these coaches have received since that year. Lute Olson's annual income and the quote from the Arizona student newspaper appeared in the *Louisville Courier-Journal,* 4/12/89. The annual incomes of Holtz, Ford, Bowden, and Erickson are based on the *USA Today* series on football coaches' incomes, 9/24–25/86, and the reported increments and bonuses that these coaches have received subsequently.

The estimates of coaches' incomes also include the value of their perks such as free houses, insurance policies, annuities, cars, etc. Because average citizens as well as university employees have to pay for these basics and amenities *out of* annual incomes, it seems fair to include these perks *as part of* the coaches' annual incomes—the IRS certainly does. The same calculation is used for the 150 basketball coaches and 100 football coaches. The statistics on them are based on the *USA Today* series on coaches' incomes in 1986 and the increments and bonuses since then. The statistics on coaches versus governors are from a chart in *USA Today,* 12/11/86, and articles in local papers such as on the Wyoming and Texas situations (see references below).

Sonny Smith's comment was reported by *USA Today,* 12/9/86. Bill Mallory's annual income is based on his annual salary of $106,570 for 1989–90;

$150,000 is a low estimate considering his TV show and ads as well as his many perks and deals. Frieder's Michigan income is based on the figures in *USA Today,* 12/9–11/86, and is also a low estimate; according to the Gannett News Service, Frieder's deal with Arizona State "could pay him as much as $700,000 a year" (quoted in the *Louisville Courier-Journal,* 9/12/89). Fisher's $370,000 package at Michigan was in *Sports Illustrated,* 4/7/89, and the article about other coaches being handed Final Four teams was by John Feinstein in the *Sporting News College Basketball 1989–90 Yearbook.*

The Ohio State basketball coach's income was in the *Washington Post,* 6/13/89; the football coach's in *Don Heinrich's College Football,* 1988 edition; and the Ohio State full professor's average in *Academe: The Bulletin of the American Association of University Professors,* March/April 1988. The average for associate professors at Ohio State was $42,000, and for assistant professors, $35,300.

The John Wooden salary information was in an article in the *New York Times,* 6/21/85; the author of that article also estimated the annual incomes of Dean Smith, Bob Knight, and Rollie Massimino as over $300,000. Considering the general inflation in coaches' incomes in the last five years, as well as the fact that Knight's 1987 team won the NCAA championship, these coaches, especially Knight, are probably now closer to $500,000 annually. Wooden generated revenue in ticket sales and TV payouts, even though alumni donations dropped during this period. The Rey Dempsey quote was in the *Los Angeles Times,* 7/13/82.

Chapter 18

The Joe Gottfried comment was in the *Dallas Morning News,* 3/22/85, and Charlie McClendon's in the *Los Angeles Times,* 7/11/82. The Jim Boeheim quote was in an article in the *Hartford Courant,* reprinted in the *Louisville Courier-Journal,* 1/9/89. The Woody Hayes Gator Bowl incident was reported in the *Chronicle of Higher Education,* 1/9/79, and articles and an obituary on Hayes in the *Cincinnati Post,* 3/12/87, discussed his personality. The book *Woody Hayes and the Hundred-Yard War* is by Jerry Brondfield, New York, 1974.

The best book on Bob Knight is John Feinstein's *A Season on the Brink,* New York, 1986; the book-length works on Knight by his best friend, Bob Hammel, and the Japanese film expert, Joan Mellen, are hagiography. Bob Knight is a particularly inappropriate role model for coaches because his success in the 1980s seems more a function of geography and demography than coaching techniques. After establishing his reputation as a winning coach in the 1970s, Knight was able to cash in on geographic and demographic good luck: to play his system and accept his mind-games-and-kick-ass method, he needs players who are middle-class and have mastered deferred gratification; in any recruiting year, there are about twenty high school seniors—white and black—in the country who have the athletic ability to play at the highest NCAA level and who are willing to endure Knight's abuse for the payoffs down the road. Fortunately for this coach, he is located in a basketball-mad region that, out of the hundreds of thousands of kids playing b-ball, will produce at least five to ten of his kind of recruits each year, and a number of these will be willing to sign with Indiana. If Knight, like most big-time college coaches, had to chase mainly black ghetto youngsters, he would be lost; when he turned down a job at New Mexico, he showed his awareness of his geographic and demographic situation. The unfortunate thing about Bob Knight as a role model is that many coaches, including those at the high school and kids' level, believe that his success is based on his method and imitate these techniques. However, because they ignore and cannot reproduce the crucial geographic and demographic component, they cannot duplicate his success and they end up mainly abusing their athletes.

The headline "Pressure to Win . . ." was in the *Dallas Morning News,* 3/22/85; the Digger Phelps comment was in the *New York Times,* 5/22/83.

The "Shug" Jordan quote was in the *Atlanta Journal,* 9/6/87. The *New York Times* had an article by Malcolm Moran about college coaches, 3/22/82, that provided useful background for the distinction between program heads and teacher-mentors (it did not use those terms).

Chapter 19

The title of the "Coach in Motion" chapter was suggested by a *Chronicle of Higher Education* article, 7/18/77, "The Old Coach-in-Motion Play." That article began, "More than 200 football and basketball coaches changed jobs during the past academic year. Some retired . . . others moved on to be head coaches at other institutions," etc. The comprehensive "People in Sports" column in the *Chronicle* every week helps chart the Coach in Motion Play, and I used it extensively for my research on the movements of big-time program heads.

The comment on Watson Brown was in the *Cincinnati Inquirer,* 11/23/83, and the information on his subsequent movements was supplied by the Vanderbilt University sports information department. The American Football Coaches Association statistics on coaches' movements were in the *Chronicle of Higher Education,* 1/13/88, and the statistic on men's basketball coaches in the *Chicago Tribune,* 12/4/88. The Penders quote was in the *Louisville Courier-Journal,* 12/25/88, and the details of Holtz's departure from Arkansas in the *Chronicle of Higher Education,* 1/4/84, in an article entitled, "Move to Minnesota Cures 'Burnout' of Former Arkansas Football Coach"—Holtz had quit Arkansas citing "burnout" but signed with Minnesota four days later. That journal, 11/26/86, is also the source of the comment "Some guys operate . . ." made by George Raveling, now men's basketball coach at USC.

The *New York Times* headline on Larry Brown was on Dave Anderson's column, 11/11/88. Anderson fumed, "But the culprit won't stand trial. Like so many other times when the police had knocked on his door, Larry Brown had skipped town."

The 1985 special convention of the NCAA passed legislation on a coach's infractions following him or her to the next job and applying to the new school as well as to the old one. This rule came into effect in 1988 and the head of the infractions committee said that the first time that the NCAA tries to apply it, "I think that the coach will have a lawyer. The school will have a lawyer. It'll be awhile before we have it all worked out" (*USA Today,* 11/16/88). Soon after, the NCAA penalized the men's basketball program at West Texas State for the sins of former coach Gary Moss, and it also levied sanctions against Moss's new school, Sam Houston State. Moss immediately went to court and the case has yet to be decided.

The *Louisville Courier-Journal* covered Joe B. Hall's resignation on 3/24/85; the article, "Personal Game Plan Dictated Hall's Timing," makes it clear that he was not fired. The details of Eddie Sutton's leaving Arkansas were in the *Arkansas Gazette,* 4/1/85; the announcements of the Richardson, Barnett, and Pollio job changes were in the *Chronicle of Higher Education* in the spring of 1985 as was the fallout from their moves in the job switching by various assistant coaches.

The next round in the Kentucky shuffle began in 1988 when Cliff Hagan, the UK AD, resigned (*Louisville Courier-Journal,* 11/16/88); that paper covered C. M. Newton's jump from Vanderbilt to the UK athletic director's job on 1/25/89, and Eddie Folger's move from Wichita State to Vandy, 3/30/89. Nolan Richardson's interest in the Ohio State job was in *USA Today,* 7/3/89. Mike Pollio quit Virginia Commonwealth in the spring of 1989 and then took the Eastern Kentucky job (*Louisville Courier-Journal,* 5/11/89); that same paper had Sonny Smith accepting the VCU job, 3/20/89, and Tommy Joe Eagles replacing him at Auburn, 4/3/89. Smith's remarks upon leaving Auburn are typical of Coaches in Motion: "I left a program that I loved. But I left because I wanted to. I felt that I could win quicker here than at Auburn" (*Chicago Tribune,* 3/21/89). Details of Lou Watson's postcoaching career at Indiana are from a faculty member in physical education at that school; Don Morton's reassignment at Wisconsin was in *USA Today,* 11/29/89, and the *Chicago Tribune,* 11/29/89; and the Don Donoher departure from Dayton was covered in the latter paper, 3/21/89. Tommy Joe Eagles's replacement at Louisiana Tech was Jerry Loyd and he came from South Plains J.C. in Texas (information courtesy of the Louisiana Tech athletic department, 9/18/89). Don Morton subsequently negotiated a $330,000 "buy-out" of his contract with Wisconsin and immediately began seeking another coaching job in College Sports Inc. (*Bloomington Herald-Times*, 12/21/89).

Chapter 20

The Gerry Faust quote was in the *Akron Beacon Journal*, 12/19/89; that paper had other stories about Faust's hiring in the same edition. Postmortems about Faust's failure at Notre Dame were in the *South Bend Tribune* on 11/29/85 and 12/19/85. Faust had a reputation at Notre Dame of going after *Parade Magazine* all-Americans, especially those with lots of glitz but not much taste for the fall mud in South Bend. Even Bo Schembechler, one of the strongest defenders of major college football, criticized Akron's hiring of Faust and its move to Division I-A; mocking the Akron president's justification, " 'We want instant respectability,' " the Michigan coach said, "I've got to laugh at that. That guy [the Akron president] shouldn't be president of a junior college" (from an AP dispatch in the *Louisville Courier-Journal*, 12/20/85).

The information about Faust's spending during his first six months at Akron was in two articles in the *Akron Beacon Journal*, 2/19/87, and the figures about the subsequent Akron athletic department budgets as well as the Broyles quote were in that paper on 6/25/87. The computer ranking for Akron's 1988 season was in *USA Today*, 12/6/88; the 1988 home attendance figures were in *Don Heinrich's College Football*, 1989 edition; and the *Sporting News 1988 College Football Yearbook* had the "worst program" comment. The Akron 1989 won-lost record and computer ranking was in *USA Today* after Akron's last game, 11/21/89. Akron is considering returning to Division I-AA, whence it came before Gerry Faust cost it millions of dollars.

The item in *USA Today* on George Perles's annuity appeared 10/20/88. Perles's jump from the Philadelphia Stars of the USFL to Michigan State was in the *Chronicle of Higher Education*, 12/15/82, and Michigan State's payment to the Philadelphia Stars of the USFL was in that journal, 3/16/83; details about Perles's 1988 offer from the Green Bay Packers were in the *Milwaukee Sentinel*, 1/28/88. The story about Warren Powers was in the *New York Times*, 1/23/78. The *Chronicle of Higher Education* discussed the clause in coaches' contracts and the NCAA rule backing it on 1/19/83.

Washington State remains an anomaly among schools on the issue of coaches jumping contracts. In 1989, it demanded that departing football coach Dennis Erickson pay the school $150,000 to settle his contract. Linda Kay and Mike Conklin of the *Chicago Tribune* explained the situation, 3/7/89: "[University of] Miami athletic director Sam Jankovich has to be kicking himself. In 1977, as athletic director at Washington State, Jankovich decreed that any coach who left the school before his contract expired had to buy himself out of the deal. That's precisely what Dennis Erickson has to do to join Jankovich in Miami. Erickson has three years left on his contract with WSU and it'll cost him $150,000 to bail out. You can bet Miami is giving Erickson a helping hand."

The Mike White information was in the *Chicago Sun-Times,* 2/1/88; in that edition, columnist Terry Boers waved goodbye to this program head with, "Don't waste a minute of your sympathy on White, whose phony charm can be rubbed off faster than the numbers on your Instant Lotto card. He's the one who made the decision to play it fast and loose with the NCAA rules." Another midwestern sports columnist wrote: "Mike White came into the Big 10 with his university waving a jaunty banner, 'The 80's belong to the Illini.' It wasn't long afterward that the first cynic said, 'They should. They're paying enough for them' " (Bob Hammel, *Bloomington* (Ind.) *Herald-Telephone,* 1/19/88; the same edition of that paper had an AP dispatch on White's contract settlement).

The Switzer settlement was in an AP dispatch in the *Louisville Courier-Journal,* 6/22/89, and the Sherrill case was in that paper, 9/10/88, and in *USA Today,* 3/6/89 and 3/28/89. Often coaches do not commit the actual violations that cause the NCAA penalty. The NCAA, for example, chastised Texas A. & M. for Sherrill's "lack of control over assistants, players, alumni and boosters." And no smoking gun was found in White's or Switzer's hand. Nevertheless, the fact remains that within the programs that these highly paid coaches headed, many NCAA violations occurred; because all of the other bucks stop at their desks, this one should too. At the very minimum, universities should fight these cases and try to invoke the penalty clauses in coaches' contracts rather than give over six-figure settlement sums. Or seven-figure ones: Clemson's "up to $1.1 million" deal with Danny Ford, including paying off the mortgage on his farm, was discussed in the *Louisville Courier-Journal,* 1/19/90.

USA Today carried Dick Vitale's comment on "high school players signing early" on 4/18/88, and his "nine out of ten" statistic on 5/19/88, as well as the quote from the NCAA Letter of Intent. As the "Toxic Waste" section on recruiting makes clear, the relationship between recruit and program head is more professional than personal; the recruit wants to play for a program head who will assure him of a future pro sports career.

The Darren Krein incident was discussed in *Sports Illustrated,* 3/27/89, and *Don Heinrich's College Football,* 1989 edition. In the end, Krein went to Miami rather than lose two years of college ball.

The Pardee item was in the *Chronicle of Higher Education,* 12/10/86; that journal tracked Larry Brown's career on 11/23/88, and explained how Dick Versace had gotten Bradley University on NCAA probation, 9/3/86. The Versace comment about Larry Brown was in *USA Today,* 6/14/88, as was information about Brown's career. Berenson's career was discussed in the

Chicago Tribune, 12/16/88; hockey expert Stan Fischler provided information on Gary Doak and also pointed out the recent migration of Craig Patrick from coach and GM of the New York Rangers to AD at the University of Denver for two years and then to the Pittsburgh Penguins as coach and GM. The "People in Athletics" items in the *Chronicle of Higher Education* appeared on 8/13/86 (Thalman) and 3/18/87 (Dean); the Donna Lopiano quote was in that journal, 5/15/85.

Chapter 21

The *Charleston News and Courier* article by Richard Jablonski appeared 2/26/82. Although there are some sociological articles on the coaches' subculture, most of the writers do not focus on program heads or the connections of college coaches with their professional colleagues. The best articles are John D. Massengale's "Coaching as an Occupational Subculture," *The Kappan,* 10/74, and George H. Sage, "An Occupational Analysis of the College Coach," in *Sport and Social Order: Contributions to the Sociology of Sport,* Ball and Loy, eds., Reading, Mass., 1975. However, college coaching has changed a great deal in the fifteen years since Massengale and Sage wrote and their conclusions are less valid each year that College Sports Inc. expands. Of greater use for this book were interviews with health, physical education, and recreation professionals; the persons interviewed spoke anecdotally and usually off the record but often had very sharp observations of the coaches' subculture.

The survey of women's athletic programs and coaches was done by Vivian Acosta and Linda Carpenter of Brooklyn College and appeared in *Sports inc.,* 5/30/88; for more details on this survey, see Chapter 35 on women's athletics.

The Prentice Gautt quote was in the *Chronicle of Higher Education,* 5/6/87; the 1987 survey on black head and assistant coaches was done by Richard E. Lapchick and Joe Panepinto and reported in the *New York Times,* 11/15/87; the George Raveling quote was in *USA Today,* 4/4/88; and the statistics on the SEC were in the *St. Louis Dispatch,* 6/29/87. An excellent article on the prejudices faced by black coaches, including from boosters, appeared in the *Charlotte Observer,* 5/31/87. The statistics on the hiring of black basketball coaches in 1988 and the black pressure groups involved were in *Sports inc.,* 7/18/88.

Chapter 22

The *Chronicle of Higher Education* had excellent articles on coaches' outside incomes and on the shoe deals in its 10/29/86 issue. Valvano's comment about his meaning to America was in the *Raleigh News and Observer,* 7/31/83; his $750,000 annual income was in *USA Today,* 4/3/89, as were his annual salary and perks, 12/9–11/86. An excellent and appropriately titled article, "Coaching for Dollars," on Valvano's outside businesses appeared in *Sports inc.*, 2/8/88. The Madden quote was in *USA Today*, 12/9/86; that newspaper covered Valvano's negotiations with UCLA, 4/1/88, and his talks with the NBA Clippers, 5/12/89.

The quote from the *Casper Star-Tribune* and the information about the football coach's salary and perks appeared on 12/15/85; AD Paul Roach's decision to hire himself as football coach was discussed in the *Chronicle of Higher Education*, 11/16/88. The statistics on the base salaries of football coaches versus governors was in *USA Today*, 12/11/86, and the Terry Donahue comment was in that newspaper, 9/25/86. The athletic director who discussed "The very low end . . ." was Doug Single, AD at SMU, in *Sports inc.*, 2/1/88. The salary jumps at the Colorado schools were in the *Denver Post*, 4/5/87; the Ohio State increases in the *Columbus Evening Dispatch*, 8/21/83; and the Fort Hayes figure in the *Arizona Daily Star*, 2/16/86. The Temple crew coach made his remark to the *Chronicle of Higher Education*, 5/28/86.

Jack Doland's comment about coaches' ticket deals was in *USA Today*, 12/10/86; Tarkanian's ticket and other deals were in the previous day's edition of that newspaper; Joe B. Hall's comps were discussed in that paper, 12/10/86, and in the *Chronicle of Higher Education*, 4/17/85. *Newsday* covered the story of the three coaches arrested for scalping, 4/3/88.

The *USA Today* quote from Dick Vitale on summer camps was in the 12/10/86 edition; the Larry Smith camp deal with Arizona was in that newspaper, 9/24/86. The Bob Knight "float" story was related by a top administrator at Indiana University, Bloomington; officials in the comptroller's office of that university would neither confirm nor deny the information, nor would they allow themselves to be quoted on the record. Probably the most amazing aspect of the Bob Knight "float" story is that he pays his camp dorm bill at all! Coaches with far less clout than Knight receive free dorm use for their campers; if Knight demanded a similar deal from Indiana University, no doubt he would receive it. As one administrator said, "If he wanted the trustees to name the damn dorm after him, they'd jump up and say, 'How big do you want the letters over the door?'"

The information about Eric Manual's high school coach receiving $500 for his speech and almost $500 in expense money was in the *Louisville Courier-Journal*, 10/19/88; the same article mentioned that recruit Shawn Kemp's high school coach also received "$500 for working one of the 1987 camp sessions." Denny Crum explained, "It's common practice by everybody who recruits kids across the country to have their coaches work in your camps. . . . There's nothing wrong with that" (*Atlanta Journal*, 5/24/85). The Bill Frieder Michigan camp deal was in *USA Today*, 12/10/86, as was some of the information on Driesell's Maryland camps. Driesell's Maryland settlement was in the *Washington Times*, 10/30/86.

Regular employees and students of a university often resent the special camp deals that coaches receive. This writer once witnessed a near riot one hundred-degree and humid Indiana summer day when, at the university's outdoor pool—for which faculty, staff, and students pay a sizable summer pass fee—a Closed sign was posted because the I.U. swimming coach was holding a swim meet for his summer camp that afternoon.

Additional information about summer camps, as well as the perspective of noncoach camp owners, was provided in an extended interview (8/8/87) with Larry McFaddin, Alf Galustian, and Mike McGlynn, owners/camp directors of Mountain View Sports Camp in Lake Placid, N.Y.

Chapter 23

The Jack Doland quote was in *Sports inc.*, 2/8/88; *Sports Illustrated* had an excellent article about the Nike shoe deals in its "Special College Basketball Issue," Fall 1988, and the information about individual coaches' agreements with Nike is mainly from that article. Coaches' deals with other companies were discussed in *USA Today*, 12/11/86; Charlie Cooke made his comment in an interview at Lake Placid, N.Y., 8/8/87. Information about Dean Smith and Bob Knight giving some of their shoe deal money to their universities was in Earl Cox's column in the *Louisville Courier-Journal*, 10/23/86. The situation at the University of Virginia was in the *New York Times*, 12/2/86.

To help coaches avoid conflict-of-interest charges, the sporting goods companies do not include formal clauses in the shoe contracts to insure the coach's "guarantee" that his or her players will wear the company's shoes. However, since the equipment managers give the players only this brand of shoes and since the coach has almost dictatorial powers over the athletes and decides whether they play or not, no college athlete is on record as having refused to wear in an intercollegiate contest the brand of shoes with which his or her coach had a contract.

The quote on Bill Dooley's TV deal was in the *Roanoke Times and World-News*, 9/28/85, as was information on Dooley's other media deals; an update on the situation was in that newspaper, 7/10/87. Additional information on Dooley was provided to me in an interview with Eric Randall, a reporter for the *Roanoke Times and World-News*, 5/18/88.

The *Miami Herald* had an excellent feature on coaches' outside deals in its 5/23/82 edition. The Sherrill, Schembechler, Cooper, and Bowden media setups were outlined there and updated in *USA Today*, 9/24/86; the *Louisville Courier-Journal* updated Schnellenberger's on 11/11/89. Cooper's new deal at Ohio State was in *Don Heinrich's College Football*, 1989 edition; the University of Georgia coaches' media deals were in the *Atlanta Journal*, 1/20/88; Bill Frieder's new ASU deal was in the *Bloomington Herald-Times*, 9/22/89; and the Dana Kirk money-for-interview story in the *Louisville Courier-Journal,* 9/4/86.

The comment about Barry Switzer's outside deals was in the *Miami Herald,* 5/23/82; the coach who made the remark was unnamed in the original story. Joe Paterno's outside deals were discussed in *USA Today,* 9/25/86, as were Don Nehlin's. The story of Lee Corso's ads for Krugerrands was related to me by Paul Strohm, editor of *Academe: The Bulletin of the American Association of University Professors.* The story about Valvano renting his university's Reynolds Coliseum for $75 was in the *Raleigh News and Observer,* 3/12/87.

Chapter 24

The item in the *Seattle Times* on the car deals appeared 10/1/86. The information on Ray Perkins's cars at Alabama and Joe Lee Dunn's at New Mexico was in *USA Today,* 9/24–25/86; the car deals of the UNLV basketball coaches were in that newspaper, 12/9/86, and Bear Bryant's vans in the *Miami Herald,* 5/23/82. The 1989 statistics on "courtesy cars" for Big Ten athletic departments was in the "Agenda Booklet" for the Big Ten Athletic Fundraisers Winter Conference in Columbus, Ohio; the most interesting number on the list was Northwestern's "0"—it is against the policy of this school to allow its coaches to accept "courtesy cars."

Denny Crum's bonus plan was in the *Louisville Courier-Journal,* 7/25/84, and the Nebraska coaches' in the *Miami Herald,* 5/23/82. Information on the annuities for Bowden, Dye, and Schnellenberger and on the bonus for Cooper were in *USA Today,* 9/24–25/86; the Heathcote raise was in that newspaper on 12/11/86, as was the Purdue bonus, and the Ron Greene attendance deal on 12/10/86. The *Indianapolis Star* had an excellent article on the decline of Greene's program, 2/8/89.

A coach's contract that illustrates the money incentives to win is Bill Frieder's current pact with Arizona State: the coach receives $20,000 if his team's season record tops .500; another $20,000 for being over .500 in the Pac-10; $3,000 if it wins one game in the Pac-10 postseason tourney or is invited to the NIT; $6,000 if it makes the NCAA tourney; $9,000 for the regional round; $12,000 for the Final Four; and $15,000 for a national championship. In addition, Frieder receives $20,000 if ASU's home attendance averages 7,500 or better, and $30,000 if it hits 11,000. When this coach implores his players to win, he has very practical reasons for his request. (The contract information was given by Frieder to a Detroit journalist and quoted in the *Bloomington Herald-Times,* 9/22/89.)

The AP item on the Tennessee country club was carried by the *Louisville Courier-Journal,* 4/10/89; Barry Switzer's oil wells were discussed in *Sports Illustrated,* 2/27/89; Pat Dye's membership on the bank board was in *USA*

Today, 9/24/86; and Jody Conradt's clothing allowance from Converse was in the 12/11/86 edition of that newspaper. The clauses in Lute Olson's contract were in the *Arizona Daily Star,* 2/18/86, and the information on Vince Dooley's European vacations in the *Miami Herald,* 5/23/82. Danny Ford's house and farm courtesy of Clemson was in *USA Today,* 9/24/86, and Pat Dye's house deal was in the *Chronicle of Higher Education,* 9/14/83. Dennis Erickson's house deal at Wyoming was in the *Casper Star-Tribune,* 12/15/85; the Arkansas housing allowances were in *USA Today,* 9/24/86 and 12/9/86; and the Texas A. & M. one in the *Bryan-College Station Eagle,* 1/12/86. The Florida State, Texas, and Illinois State country club and YMCA fees were in *USA Today,* 12/9/86, and the Tennessee one in an AP dispatch in the *Louisville Courier-Journal,* 4/11/89. That Kentucky newspaper carried Schnellenberger's insurance deal on 9/24/86; *USA Today* had Pat Kennedy's on 12/9/86; and the *Bryan-College Station Eagle* had Sherrill's on 1/12/86 as well as the explanation of how coaches draw on the cash value. The University of Florida insurance plan for coaches was in *USA Today,* 9/24/86, as were the expense accounts at Florida State, Colorado, and Tennessee. Bill Frieder's current deal with Arizona State was in the *Bloomington Herald-Times,* 9/22/89; the quote about Gary Williams's unauthorized telephone expenses was in the *Louisville Courier-Journal,* 6/24/89. Andy Russo's comment was in the "College Basketball Special Issue" of *Sports Illustrated,* Fall 1988; the NCAA's attempt to crack down on the scheduling scam was in the *Chronicle of Higher Education,* 1/21/87.

At the same 1987 meeting where the NCAA attempted to stop the scheduling scam, the association, under pressure from the Presidents' Commission, also added regulations to control coaches' outside incomes. The first rule required coaches to report such income to their presidents and athletic directors. The second prohibited them "from using the institution's name or logo in personal endorsements without prior approval." The third insisted that before they enter contracts with sporting goods manufacturers, they must obtain "prior approval." In the three years since the NCAA passed the legislation, the effect has been underwhelming. Coaches' outside incomes have increased at an even greater rate than before 1987, many have continued to use their schools' names and logos in their personal endorsements, and more coaches have earned more money with their shoe deals than ever before.

The key loophole in the legislation—wide enough for a Division III fullback to lumber through—is the "prior approval" clause. Most colleges and universities have long had similar rules on their books for all of their employees, including coaches, and have rarely enforced them for athletic department personnel. Thus, when the NCAA passed its version of these rules, it contained the old subtext: "Coach, as long as you have leverage with your school's administrators, you can do what you want." If anything, the new legislation gives coaches a wider latitude and a better excuse for their activities—"What's wrong with doing that? My university gave me 'prior approval.' "

Summary

The quote from Leonard Koppett was in the *New York Times,* 8/24/86; some of his other proposals in his "Nine Steps for College Sports" are quite sensible. The quotes from the Indiana University Faculty Senate and Bill Mallory were in the *Bloomington Herald-Telephone,* 1/25/87.

Part III: Toxic Waste: Recruiting Wars & Athletic Scholarships

Overview

The Bob Knight quote appeared in the *Chicago Tribune,* 1/13/85. The NCAA constitution is in the *1988–89 Manual of the National Collegiate Athletic Association.* A good discussion of the NCAA's use of the term "student-athlete" was in the *Washington Post,* 4/28/82. The current costs of American colleges and universities are in Chapter 31. *USA Today* reported the cost of drug treatments for the Iowa basketball players on 2/6/89; last year, the University of Tennessee paid $10,000 for drug treatments for star runner Reggie Cobb but the football player flunked a drug test in the fall (*Louisville Courier-Journal,* 10/18/89).

The quotation from the IRS rules is from the *Arthur Young Tax Guide,* 1989 edition. Valvano's comment was in *USA Today,* 12/21/88.

Chapter 25

The Allen Sack quote was in the *Chronicle of Higher Education,* 12/10/86; that journal discussed and quoted the NCAA propaganda about one-year renewables on 3/28/84. The story about Darrell Royal and the statistics on athletic scholarships at Texas were in *Meat on the Hoof,* by Gary Shaw, New York, 1972. The North Dakota incident was reported in the *Chronicle of Higher Education,* 5/18/83; the Prairie View A. & M. incident was discussed in that journal, 2/22/89, and in the *Louisville Courier-Journal,* 2/11/89 (the source of the quotes). That school announced that it was de-emphasizing football and ending athletic scholarships in 1990 "to correct an $800,000 budget deficit" (*USA Today,* 12/6/89). An example of coaches of big-time programs "firing" players occurred at Purdue last year: men's basketball coach Gene Keady got rid of three players with bad attitudes who were "not really into the game of basketball like we are. . . . [I told them] to transfer. They didn't have any choice. If I didn't want them to go, they still would be here" (*Bloomington Herald-Times*, 12/13/89).

The Stephen Morgan quote was in the *Chronicle of Higher Education*, 5/18/83, and Judge Burciaga's comment was in that journal, 9/22/82. A number of academics have written on the NCAA as a cartel, including Professors James V. Koch of Ball State University and George H. Sage of the University of Northern Colorado; their articles are listed in D. Stanley Eitzen, ed., *Sport in Contemporary Society*, 3d ed., New York, 1989. An excellent article on how the NCAA's letter-of-intent rules affected some Chicago area recruits was in the *Chicago Tribune*, 3/17/89. The Tex Schramm quote was in *USA Today*, 3/15/88; the *Sporting News* study by Mike Douchant was in the 5/29/88 issue. The Bob Boris case and the AD's reaction to it were in the *Chronicle of Higher Education*, 3/2/83, 12/14/83, and 2/8/84; the *Sports Illustrated* comment about the NFL "embarrassing itself" appeared 4/18/88. Tagliabue's quote, as well as a discussion of the NFL draft issue, was in the *New York Times*, 1/28/90.

The percentage of ex–college players in Major League Baseball remained at about 75 percent for the 1980s; Commissioner Bowie Kuhn's office did a survey in 1981 (reported in the *Chronicle of Higher Education*, 6/15/81) and that percentage has held. *USA Today*, 7/12/88, ran a comprehensive feature on this topic, and that newspaper also had Chris Roberts's quote, 7/26/89. Roberts added that he was interested in "getting an education," but considering his plan to play baseball "almost every day," and leave college after "three years," the reader is allowed a certain skepticism about his and other college ballplayers' commitment to education.

Much of the information about the NHL's relations with the NCAA was provided by Randy Philips of the *Montreal Gazette* in an interview for this book, 5/31/88. The *Chronicle of Higher Education* carried feature articles on the NCAA versus the NHL on 3/16/83 and 2/1/84. Last year, the Calgary Flames traded the rights to Tim Corkery of Ferris State to the St. Louis Blues. An interesting sidelight of the hockey situation is that Canadian universities and colleges produce almost no NHL players—there is only one presently in the league. The reason is that most Canadian schools do not give athletic scholarships and, as a result, the best young Canadian players either go into junior hockey (the professional minor league system) or into American college hockey.

The St. Louis University faculty representative, Albert E. Bender, Sr., was quoted in the *Chronicle of Higher Education*, 9/14/88. The information about the soccer players was supplied by Paul Kennedy, managing editor of *Soccer America*, in an interview for this book, 6/11/88, and an article about a college player on the current U.S. national team was in that magazine, 11/9/89.

Chapter 26

Samuel Poole's comment was in the *Charlotte Observer,* 10/11/85; Jim Bouton's was in his book *Ball Four plus Ball Five,* New York, 1981; the quote from the Iowa State academic counselor was in the *Des Moines Register,* 4/13/83. The Prop 48 debate was covered by the *Chronicle of Higher Education,* 1/22/86; the comment by the president of the University of Southern California was in the *Los Angeles Times,* 1/10/86; the statistics on the Florida State University and the University of Florida situations were in the *St. Petersburg Times,* 3/9/86; and John "Hot Rod" Williams's SAT scores were in *Sports inc.,* 11/21/88. The fact that some program heads have "special admit" clauses in their contracts was discussed by L. Jay Oliva, chancellor of New York University, in an *AGB Special Report: What Trustees Should Know about Intercollegiate Athletics,* Washington, D.C., 1989. Pat Dye's "good relationship with his registrar" was in the *Louisville Courier-Journal,* 9/23/89, and the *Raleigh News and Observer* carried stories about Chris Washburn's admission to N.C. State on 2/8/85 and 2/17/85. The statistics on admissions to other North Carolina schools were in the *Charlotte Observer,* 10/11/85. The comment by the head of the College Board Corporation was in the *Chronicle of Higher Education,* 1/22/83; and the president of Grambling's comment was in the *Los Angeles Times,* 1/14/86. Among the many articles on the cultural biases of the College Board exams, the *New York Times* had features on the subject, 1/14/83 and 6/29/88, and the *Chronicle of Higher Education,* 4/10/85; that journal also discussed the NCAA's anti–Prop 48 study on 10/17/84 and 9/12/84. John Chaney's comment was in *Sports Illustrated,* 1/23/89; that magazine also quoted another big-time coach, Jackie Sherrill at Texas A. & M., as saying, "The tests historically discriminate against those not in the mainland or streamlined," 8/24/87.

Billy Packer's comment was in *USA Today,* 8/5/88; the numbers on the first results of Prop 48 were in the *Washington Post,* 8/25/86. The NCAA survey was in the *Chronicle of Higher Education,* 5/4/88; the ACT's invalidation of Eric Manual's test was on the front page of the *Louisville Courier-Journal,* 1/26/89, but Danny Woodson's problems were in a rear page of that newspaper, 1/13/89. Harry Edwards's remarks were on *Fair Game,* a Public Broadcasting System program, aired 1/18/87; the "Getting Wise" headline was in *Newsday,* 9/30/87, and the remarks by the football recruiter at Pitt in *USA Today,* 7/22/88, as were the statistics on Pitt's 1989–90 men's basketball recruits, 8/3/89. Tarkanian's comment was in the *Chronicle of Higher Education,* 9/10/86; the quote from Terry Mills's high school counselor was in the *Ann Arbor News,* 2/27/87.

Paul Evans's comment was in *Sports Illustrated,* 2/23/89. Other coaches, even those like Bob Knight who support Prop 48, believe that Prop 42 will result in more cheating by athletic programs (AP dispatch in the *Louisville Courier-Journal*, 1/15/89). The comments of the president of Lehigh were in the *New York Times*, 1/19/89, as were those of the president of the University of South Alabama. John Thompson's protest was featured in most national media, e.g., *USA Today*, 1/16/89; that newspaper carried the votes on Prop 42, 1/17/89. Concerning Georgia's sponsorship of Prop 48 and 42, *Don Heinrich's College Football*, 1989 edition, had the following: "About the Bulldogs' use of junior colleges for signees who aren't admitted [because of Prop 48, Auburn football coach Pat] Dye said, 'They've circumvented the rule. It just doesn't make sense.' "

If schools abided by Prop 42 rules, *Sports inc.* calculated that "Division I schools could save $5 million a year . . . in scholarships now being gambled on student-athletes who may never suit up," 1/28/89.

Information and quotes about the NCAA's 1990 amendment to Prop 42 were in the *Chicago Tribune*, 1/11/90, as was the quote from Bloom high school coach Frank Nardi. Dick Schultz was interviewed by Judy Woodruff of the "MacNeil-Lehrer Newshour," 1/8/90. *How to Prepare for the Graduate Record Exam,* by Brownstein, Weiner, Green, and Hilbert, is published by Barron's; quoted material is from the 1988 edition.

The NFL does not seem to believe in NCAA graduation rates or that college athletes are receiving an education. Every year, the league gives all prospective draft choices the Wonderlic Personnel Test, an exam that tests general verbal, math, and spatial reasoning skills. The NFL examines a thousand college players who have used up their college playing eligibility and the league administers the exam. A 25 score signifies that a candidate has "management" potential—i.e., what a college graduate should possess. A 10 score is "functionally illiterate." In 1989, football players in the Big Eight averaged 19.19; in the SEC, 18.10; those at Mississippi State, 12.5; and a number of players nationally scored less than 9. The *Sporting News* had a feature article on the 1989 tests (4/17/89), and with 14 considered the level needed for a janitor's job, it related that Calvin Phillips, a wide receiver from West Virginia, scored 4 and that players from such football powerhouses as Nebraska, Florida State, Auburn, and LSU scored under 9. In examining the results for players from the Top 20 teams of the previous season, the *Sporting News* revealed that 18 percent was the average score—the equivalent of the intelligence needed for a bus driver's job—and that the pro prospects from Indiana University came out in the middle at 18.4.

Chapter 27

Jim Walden's comment was in *Sports Illustrated,* 2/27/89; an excellent listing of some of the articles on athletes' reasons for choosing schools is included in D. Stanley Eitzen, ed., *Sport in Contemporary Society,* 3d ed., New

York, 1989. Larry Brown's comment was in the *New York Times*, 5/28/89; the information on Mark Tillmon's recruiting was in the *Chronicle of Higher Education*, 4/30/86; and the *Baltimore Sun* had an excellent feature, 11/5/85, on the importance of TV in recruiting black basketball players. Even well-known program heads lust after TV: Purdue basketball coach Gene Keady justifies the Big Ten's 9:30 P.M. Monday starting times on ESPN by arguing that "to recruit players, you take any exposure you can get" (*USA Today*, 2/1/89).

The quote from the Indiana University swim coach, James "Doc" Counsilman, was in the *Bloomington Herald-Telephone*, 12/10/88. The Indiana University trustees did not give the coach a completely separate facility but placed the swim team's new pool within a proposed recreational sports facility—thus, to be funded in part by the students and in part by private donations. In theory, all I.U. students, faculty, and staff will be able to use the pool; in reality, no doubt the pool will be run as the current facility is, with I.U. public use limited to between noon and 1:00 P.M., and 9:00 to 11:00 P.M. At present, the swim team has *exclusive* use of the pool except for those three hours.

Bob Wade's comment about summer camps was in the *Chronicle of Higher Education*, 4/15/87, and the story about Lou Holtz and the California recruit was in *Don Heinrich's College Football*, 1988 edition. The life of a recruiter for a big-time school was outlined in the *Chicago Sun-Times*, 2/15/88; the *New York Times* ran an excellent feature about recruiting at the summer camps on 6/9/86. Nike makes a big P.R. point of the academic element at its camps ("ABCD" stands for "Academic Betterment and Career Development"), but as a feature article about the camp noted: "It is the ultimate sports paradox. Gathered on this bucolic Ivy League campus [Princeton], where hoops are a hobby and academics is king, are many of the big-time college basketball coaches. Their million-dollar programs . . . are riding on the decisions they make this week" (from the Scripps-Howard Service, reprinted in the *Bloomington Herald-Times*, 7/13/89). Most of the information about the Bloomington AAU team was also in that paper from April to August, 1989; other elements were supplied by Indiana University officials; the story of College Prospects of America (CPOA) was in the *Chicago Tribune*, 1/26/90.

Willard Wells was quoted in the *Los Angeles Times*, 2/11/86. The *New York Times* item about imported athletes was published 3/15/77, as was the coach's comment about "safaris." Gerry Faust's 1989 recruits were in *USA Today*, 2/9/89, and stories about the Marist College imports were in the *Chronicle of Higher Education*, 12/10/86 and 12/17/86, and also the *Poughkeepsie Journal*, 11/29/86. Andrew Gaze attracted lots of media attention after Seton Hall made the 1989 NCAA finals, but the best articles on him were by William C. Rhoden and by George Vecsey in the *New York Times*, 4/14/89 and 4/16/89. The NCAA's rules on the academic admission of foreign athletes are in the association's pamphlet *NCAA Guide to International Academic Standards for Athletic Eligibility*, Mission, Kansas, 1987, as is the quote about a "minimal academic record." Lynn Berling-Manual, editor-in-chief of *Soccer America,* made her comment in an interview for this book on 4/21/88. The *Chronicle of Higher Education* ran stories on African runners and UTEP's troubles on 4/18/84, 4/25/84, 6/6/84, 1/9/85, 4/3/85, and 7/16/86. The importing of foreign athletes has accelerated in recent years and now even obscure but expensive college sports like cross-country skiing are dominated by imports.

The comment by Joe Graves was in the *Deseret News,* 5/20/86, and the quote by the Oklahoma State recruiter was in *The Recruiting Game,* by John L. Rooney, Jr., Lincoln, Neb., 1987. The *Louisville Courier-Journal* carried the article about Vaughn Dunbar, 5/26/87; and the *Chronicle of Higher Education* tracked the juco changes in eligibility rules in its 3/26/86, 4/2/86, 5/7/86, 6/11/86, 8/13/86, and 4/6/88 issues. Part of the juco scam is that many of the basic and required courses in English and math upon which freshman athletes often flounder in four-year universities are avoided by the athlete's taking the juco version of these courses and then transferring credit in them to the four-year school. Thus equipped, many juco transfers are free to spend two years in the NCAA school's Division of Hideaway Studies.

Information about UNLV's recruiting of Lloyd Daniels appeared in the *New York Post,* 2/11/87, in the *New York Daily News,* 3/23/87, and in *Newsday,* 3/22/87 and 3/23/87. The 1989 Indiana University football recruits were in *USA Today,* 2/9/89; because Heisman Trophy candidate Anthony Thompson was at Dunbar's position, the juco transfer was redshirted in 1989. The athletic department assigned him "a personal tutor" to keep him academically eligible (*Indiana Daily Student,* 10/20/89).

Stephen R. Morgan's comment was in the *Chronicle of Higher Education,* 5/4/83; articles on the SMU transfer situation were in the *Dallas Morning News,* "Scouts Descend on SMU," 2/27/87; the *Houston Post,* 2/26/87; and *USA Today,* 6/9/87. Southern Methodist University agreed to honor the scholarships until graduation of all football players who wanted to remain at the school as regular students. Only a small minority accepted this offer of a free education. Apparently, for the vast majority of these fifty-six "student-athletes," a degree from SMU, an excellent institution, was far less important than continuing to play intercollegiate football at, as it turned out for most of them, less academically prestigious schools. Thus in an interesting test case, one group of college athletes cast a clear "vote" as to which side of the NCAA's "student-athlete" equation was meaningful to them.

Studies of Intercollegiate Athletics, done for the NCAA by the American Institutes for Research, was published in Mission, Kansas, 1989. The Digger Phelps comment on freshman eligibility was in the *Washington Post,* 9/1/84, and Bo Schembechler's in the *Bloomington Herald-Times,* 8/14/89. Robert Atwell's statement about need-based athletic scholarships was in *USA Today,* 5/19/89.

Chapter 28

The Bobby Bowden quote was in the *New York Times*, 2/14/88; the Walter Byers one in the *Washington Post*, 8/26/84; and the Bob Knight one in the *Chicago Tribune*, 1/13/85. The comment by Dick Westervelt of Stetson University was in a letter to the editor of *Sports inc.*, 11/14/88. Detailed articles on the NCAA investigation of the Kansas men's basketball program were in the *Kansas City Times*, 11/12/88, and the *Topeka Capital-Journal*, 11/11/88.

The item about Texas Christian University appeared in the *Chronicle of Higher Education*, 5/21/86; that journal had a "Summary of Most Common Rule Violations in [NCAA College] Sports" on 1/20/82, and subsequent updates have not significantly changed the statistics. The information about Kenny Anderson's recruitment by Georgia Tech was in the *New York Times*, 11/28/88, and the comment by the University of Texas football player in the *Dallas Morning News*, 3/30/86. The "Gator Getters" were discussed in the *Chronicle of Higher Education*, 9/24/73, and the "Texas Angels" in *Sports Illustrated*, 2/20/89. The story about the Florida State cheerleader was in the *Miami Herald*, 2/18/82 and 2/19/82, as well as the *Washington Post*, 4/30/82. Wayne Duke made his comments to the *Chicago Tribune*, 3/5/89; Bob Knight was quoted in that newspaper, 1/13/85. Mills's and Kemp's demands during their recruiting visits to Indiana University were reported by the *Bloomington Herald-Telephone*, 5/2/88; Kemp denied the story about him but the I.U. player who was his host said, "If that's what Shawn wants to say, fine. . . . All I did was tell them [reporters] what happened. If I had this to do all over again, I probably wouldn't have said anything. All I want to do is finish this week [at I.U.] and get out of here" (*Indiana Daily Student*, 5/3/88). The next day, the player, Rick Calloway, who was trying to leave Bob Knight's program for another school, came to see how impolitic his remarks had been, and said that "some comments were taken out of context" (*Bloomington Herald-Telephone*, 5/4/88). The references to the Emery Express package to Chris Mills's father are cited above. The Todd Mitchell quote about recruiting trips was in the *Indianapolis Star*, 5/4/88. The story about Bob Knight's anger at the University of Illinois recruiting methods was in the *Washington Post*, 11/11/84.

David Berst's comments were in the *Chicago Tribune*, 3/30/82; John "Hot Rod" Williams's remarks were in the *New York Times*, 4/6/85; and those of Clark Kellogg's father as well as Sean Bell were in the *Dayton Daily News*, 1/13/85. The John Hadl story was in the *Kansas City Star*, 7/4/82. The Dallas media were instrumental in investigating the SMU situation—dubbed "Ponygate"; a summary of Stopperich's package appeared in the magazine *Fast Lane*, 9/87. In late 1989, journalist Bruce Hunter charged that "UNLV and UCLA were offering $200,000 through anonymous representatives of their programs" to high school basketball star Chris Jackson before he signed with

LSU (reported in the *Louisville Courier-Journal*, 11/2/89); the Bruce Lowitt and Hal Bock comments were reprinted in that newspaper, 12/1/85.

Bobby Bowden's quote was in the *New York Times*, 2/14/88. The recruiting of the teammates of Sean Gilbert was in the *Louisville Courier-Journal*, 1/14/89; John Thompson's comments about some high school coaches were in the *Washington Post*, 2/7/88; the quotes by the high school coach of Alaa Abdelnaby and Lefty Driesell's reply were in the *Chicago Tribune*, 11/29/85.

The NCAA justifies the rule allowing high school and juco coaches to also work at Division II and III schools with the explanation that often these smaller programs cannot afford full-time assistant coaches and that high school and juco coaches are available part-timers willing to help out the Division II and III programs. There is some truth to this explanation—except when the high school or juco coach is hired at the same time as one of his or her star players signs with the school.

The Texas high school coach was quoted in the *Dallas Morning News*, 10/1/85; the story about Missouri basketball recruiting in Detroit was reported by *Sports Illustrated*, 2/20/89, and the *Louisville Courier-Journal*, 1/20/89. Lou Holtz's comments about boosters were in *Sports Illustrated*, 3/30/87. *Don Heinrich's College Football*, 1988 edition, had the quote about the "go-between"; and *People* magazine discussed Burt Reynolds and Florida State, 2/2/81.

Chapter 29

Calvin Hill's comment was in the *Washington Post*, 6/17/85, and Cedric Dempsey's remarks to the Houston booster club were reported in the *Houston Chronicle*, 3/15/87. Dallas radio announcer Norm Hitzges was quoted in the magazine *Fast Lane*, 9/87; the story of the Texas assistant coach was in the *Dallas Morning News*, 3/30/86. The Minnesota scandal began in the mid-1980s when Lou Holtz was the head football coach at the school; the *Chicago Tribune* covered the trial of the administrator who paid the athletes, 11/8/89, 11/10/89, and 11/15/89. Allen Sack's survey was discussed in the *New York Times*, 11/17/89.

The Tim Borcky item was in the *Memphis Commercial Appeal*, 8/4/85; the former Big Ten assistant coach is now in private business in the last college town where he coached and he insisted that his comments be off the record. The information about Keith Lee's monthly payments at Memphis State was in the *Louisville Courier-Journal*, 2/11/89; the *Houston Post* covered the University of Houston's football scandal, and among the important and quoted articles were those appearing 3/15/86, 3/22/86, 4/5/86, 3/3/87, 3/10/87, 3/15/87, 4/13/88, and 12/17/88. Yeomans eventually left the university and received a "lump-sum settlement of $217,147, plus $34,232 in retirement benefits and

$11,150 for a tax-deferred annuity" (*USA Today,* 6/2/89). The story about the University of Texas player's bank loan was in the *Dallas Morning News,* 3/30/86; Bob Blackman's quote was in *The Recruiting Game,* by John Rooney; and the story of the Ivy League altruist was in the *New York Times,* 6/25/81 and 7/30/81. Paul Kennedy, managing editor of the weekly *Soccer America,* made his comment in an interview for this book on 6/11/88; the Arizona State violations were reported in the *Chronicle of Higher Education,* 6/5/85.

The item in the *San Francisco Chronicle* about Quentin Daily appeared 6/26/82, as did an article on 8/4/82 in which Zabais "Defend[ed His] Role in the Dailey Case." Zabais "charged that the school 'threw me to the wolves' " in attempting to clear itself with the NCAA. Zabais did not dispute the facts of Dailey's no-show employment but blamed his vice-president in charge of personnel for not telling him that "Dailey wasn't working."

The Digger Phelps comment about summer jobs was in *Newsweek,* 4/22/85; the story about the generous Oklahoma booster and the summer jobs was in *Sports Illustrated,* 2/27/89, and the *Daily Oklahoman,* 1/26/89. The *Cleveland Plain Dealer* reported the "Mouse" McFadden employment at Cleveland State, 4/22/88, and the *Chronicle of Higher Education* had the Steinbrenner item, 6/5/85. The report about the University of Michigan baseball program was carried by the AP on 7/15/89 (reprinted in the *Bloomington Herald-Times*) and updated in *USA Today,* 1/24/90.

The item about Marv Goux appeared in the *Chronicle of Higher Education,* 9/29/82, and the NCAA's estimate on annual ticket selling was in that journal, 1/7/87. The *Los Angeles Times* carried an article on 5/2/82 entitled "I Was Simply Trying to Help People," in which Goux tried to explain himself. Goux mentioned that "ticket scalping activity" has "been going on [at USC] since the time of the Romans." Walter Byers's quip about the TransAms and Porsches was in the *Sacramento Bee,* 1/17/85; the information and quotes about ticket selling at the University of Texas at Austin were in the *Austin American-Statesman,* 3/23/86 and 3/30/86, and the comment by the U.T. athletic director was in that paper, 9/5/86. The ticket-selling incidents at Nebraska and Tennessee were covered by the *Omaha World Herald* on 9/4/86 and 9/7/86, as well as the *Chronicle of Higher Education,* 9/17/86.

Chapter 30

Frank Layden's quote was in the *Chronicle of Higher Education,* 9/9/87; the remark by the sophomore football player at Oklahoma was in that journal, 3/29/89; *USA Today* had statistics on schools with jock dorms, 2/15/89; and *Time* magazine mentioned the UNLV players eating at the casinos, 4/3/89. The 1979 NCAA rule on the housing of athletes was quoted in the *Louisville Courier-Journal,* 8/4/89; the article about the Maryland dorm was in the

Washington Times, 6/27/86. Brian Bosworth's autobiography is entitled *The Boz: Confessions of a Modern Anti-Hero,* New York, 1988. The nickname of the University of Oklahoma athletic teams seems apt: the "Sooners" were those people who did not abide by the government rules on land claims in the Oklahoma Territory and jumped the gun to get an advantage over their fellows. The story of the thirty-three University of Texas football players in apartments was in the *Dallas Morning News,* 3/30/86. Dick Schultz was quoted by *USA Today,* 5/12/89, and that newspaper also ran Danny Ford's comment about the jock dorms at Clemson, 1/11/90.

Dana Kirk's comment about William Bedford's cars was in the *Memphis Commercial Appeal,* 6/15/85; and the University of Tennessee situation was in the *Knoxville Journal,* 2/11/86, 5/31/86, 6/4/86, and 8/23/86. Articles on the University of Wisconsin car loan were in the *Milwaukee Journal,* 1/21/86 and 4/22/86; the NCAA penalty against Wisconsin was in the *Chronicle of Higher Education,* 7/23/86. The Barry Switzer car rental story was in the *Louisville Courier-Journal,* 12/20/88, and the University of Cincinnati one in the *Cincinnati Enquirer,* 11/4/88. Because he was committing an NCAA infraction, the New England hockey coach requested anonymity: "Since I'm the recruiting coordinator and rent lots of cars a year, my AD doesn't even know how often I loan them to players," he explained. "I rent the car, take the maximum insurance, and give the keys to a player. My only worry is that he'll get into a car wreck and the newspapers will pick it up—then the shit could hit the fan. So far that hasn't happened." The NCAA penalty against the Arizona State track program was in the *NCAA News,* 11/14/88.

Kohn Smith's remarks were quoted by the *Chicago Tribune,* 1/23/89; Earl Cox, the former *Louisville Courier-Journal* sports columnist, wrote his comment in that paper, 10/3/85. The articles on the gifts to the University of Houston football players were in the *Houston Post,* 3/15/86 and 3/20/86; the *Dallas Morning News* report on phone calls at Oral Roberts was carried by *USA Today,* 5/22/89. Oral Roberts officials denied the report but took their athletic program out of the NCAA, mainly because of the cost of big-time college sports—but they also avoided an NCAA investigation. The Mississippi State situation was in the *Chronicle of Higher Education,* 10/1/88. A year after Kohn Smith's remarks about the UNLV players, when his Utah State team came to Las Vegas for its scheduled conference visit, the UNLV players started a brawl during which Smith was punched a number of times. He commented, "Maybe it goes back to the stuff I said last year. I really meant it when I said that I was sorry. . . . I was a rookie coach and I said something stupid." Smith did not make clear whether he was "sorry" and his remarks were "stupid" because they violated the coaching fraternity's unwritten law on abstaining from whistle-blowing in public and attracting bad P.R. for college sports, or whether he was "sorry" and "stupid" because his remarks were untrue. His

1990 comments were in an AP dispatch in the *Louisville Courier-Journal*, 2/3/90.

The free motel rooms for the University of Tennessee athletes and coaches was in the *Knoxville Journal*, 2/12/86. The *Los Angeles Times* story on Sam Gilbert appeared 1/31/82; the *New York Times* had an article on it, 2/1/82. The Purdue professor who commented on the free gifts approved by the NCAA changed his mind about being quoted on the record because "I don't need any damn Black and Gold supporters calling me up at midnight and yelling at me because they saw my name and quote in your book." The professor did admit that sometimes a student at a science fair will win a prize for his or her effort but "that isn't the same as a *whole* football team getting gifts. I've never been at a science fair or any student competition where more than a few valuable prizes were given out, whereas bowl committees give gifts to over 180 players. You have to twist the 'same benefits' rule a long way to see any equivalence there."

The item in the *Chronicle of Higher Education* about football players at the University of Oregon was in the 11/3/80 issue; the *Philadelphia Daily News* study was quoted by *Sports Illustrated*, 2/27/89; the Pursch article was in the *New York Times*, 1/15/84; and Don James's remark in *Sports Illustrated*, 3/13/89. The interview with Randy Philips of the *Montreal Gazette* took place 5/31/88; and the information about Kane's arrest in Syracuse was carried by the *Montreal Gazette*, 4/14/88 and 5/25/88. The leak in the Washburn case was in the *Raleigh News and Observer*, 2/14/85; and the information in the *Dallas Morning News* about the University of Texas situation appeared 3/31/86.

Chapter 31

Donald Kagan's comment was in the *Chronicle of Higher Education*, 10/7/87. Recent articles on rising college costs were in the *New York Times*, 8/9/89, and *USA Today*, 8/10/89 (the latter article also contained a comprehensive table). Articles on students' general indebtedness as well as specific indebtedness at Indiana University were in the *Bloomington Herald-Telephone*, 5/5/89, and *[Indiana University] Campus Report*, 1/89; the quotes from the I.U. admissions director were in the *Bloomington Herald-Telephone*, 5/5/89.

The quote from the NCAA's $1.75 million study was on the front page of the *New York Times*, 4/6/89, and that newspaper had a feature article, "Ranks of Black Men Shrink at College," 2/5/89. Scripps-Howard had an excellent feature on "Black College Enrollments Keep Dropping," reprinted in the *Bloomington Herald-Telephone*, 11/4/88. Information about Big Ten enrollments was in the *Purdue University Perspective*, July/August 1987, and the *IU Newspaper*, 8/28/87. The 15 percent of black scholarship holders is a rough estimate based upon the statistics for Illinois, Michigan, and Penn State. In 1987, a total of 4,341 black undergraduates attended these schools; about 40 percent of them were males and about 300 of them held athletic scholarships. Unfortunately, the athletic departments of these schools do not furnish statistics on black athletic scholarship holders and thus 300 is an approximate figure calculated by examining the rosters of their varsity teams. Harry Edwards has long used the "gladiators" phrase; one of the first times was in *U.S. News & World Report,* 7/1/85. The NCAA report on the University of Cincinnati was reprinted in the *Cincinnati Enquirer,* 11/4/85. One Chicago black leader, Larry Hawkins, argues that schools should "give a scholarship to one non-athlete for every athlete they recruit" (*New York Times,* 6/12/86).

Wayne Yates's comment was in the *Memphis Commercial Appeal,* 6/23/85. The Kevin Ross case has attracted much media attention over the years; the latest chapter and a summary of the entire case was in the *Chicago Tribune,* 7/25/89; that newspaper carried a feature on Dexter Manley's confession of illiteracy, 9/24/89. The judge's sentence in the Billy Don Jackson case was in the *Chronicle of Higher Education,* 4/14/82; that journal profiled the Penn State advising program, 12/7/88, and carried the Bob Bradley quote, 12/4/85. The *Hartford Courant* had an informative feature on athletic department academic advisors, 2/23/86. An excellent article on how athletes get channeled into "puff" courses is Robert L. Hilliard's "It's What Happens After an Athlete Gets on Campus That Really Counts" in the *Chronicle of Higher Education,* 6/15/83; that journal also had Paul Lermack's experience with athletes, 1/11/84, and Neil Petrie's comments, 2/24/88. The North Carolina State professor was quoted in the *Raleigh News and Observer,* 2/10/85; the Oklahoma "eyeballed into class" expression was in *Sports Illustrated,* 2/27/89; and the story by Brian Bosworth's classmate in *Editor & Publisher,* 4/23/88. The professor at Indiana University who stopped receiving progress cards from the athletic department is the author of this book. The Brent Fullwood story and Pat Dye's comments were in the *Louisville Courier-Journal,* 7/1/89; that paper also carried Florida State's admission of Deion Sanders's lack of attendance in an AP dispatch, 9/30/89.

The time-honored method for academic fraud is for the athletic department, especially a coach, to pressure a faculty member to change a grade. These days, most athletic department personnel prefer more subtle and sophisticated methods but some still honor their traditions (Larry Brown so leaned on a recalcitrant history professor at Kansas that it became a *cause célèbre,* reported in the *Chronicle of Higher Education,* 2/15/84).

The light bulb joke was in that journal, 9/1/82, as was the information from the special faculty report at Florida State University, 5/9/84. The comment by the head of the Memphis NAACP was in the *Memphis Commercial Appeal,* 5/16/85, and the information about Georgia Tech in the *Atlanta Journal,*

8/8/86. The *Los Angeles Times* reported on the UNLV researchers' findings on 6/22/87; the researchers, Terry J. Knapp and Joseph F. Raney, said that "discussion with colleagues at other campuses have led [us] to believe that the problem [of special courses to keep athletes eligible] exists at almost every school that plays big-time basketball or football." One of their most important articles is "Pass One for the Gipper: Student-Athletes and University Coursework," *Arena Review*, vol. 7, 1983.

The *Chronicle of Higher Education* had a lengthy explanation of sports management programs, 11/9/88, and Michigan's response to Scott Shuger's exposé of one of its courses, 9/16/87; Shuger's article was in *Sport*, 10/87. The I.U. student who took "P211" has close ties to the athletic department and requested that his comments be off the record; this student also considered the senior-level course, "P415: Sports Promotions and Public Relations," a "puff." He wrote of the midterm and final exams, "These are a real joke. The students write them! Each one contributes 2 questions to each exam. These questions are in the form of multiple choice, true and false, and fill in the blank. Usual practice entails the students sharing their questions with each other, and therefore every student having a copy of the exams [beforehand]." The course is usually taught by the sports information director.

The *Chronicle of Higher Education* tracked the Rice University story on 11/2/83, 2/1/84, and 2/20/85. An article in *USA Today*, 11/17/87, about the "choosiest" schools in America, had the information about Rice and their freshmen's SAT scores.

An academic advisor in the athletic department of a West Coast school related the following riddle:

"How many athletic scholarship winners does it take to change a light bulb?

"None. Their tutors do it for them."

Chapter 32

Norm Sloan's comment was in the *Memphis Commercial Appeal*, 6/23/85; the information on Woody Green was in the *Arizona Republic*, 10/5/83; the Jan Kemp case attracted national media attention but the best coverage of the University of Georgia's remedial studies program was in the *Atlanta Journal*, especially on 1/15/86, 1/31/86, 2/15/86, 3/14/86, and 4/26/86. The University of Nebraska's use of the school's Educational Center for Disabled Studies for athletes was mentioned in *Time* magazine, 4/3/89, as was the story about Ohio University's basketball team's European tour. Lawrence Taylor's comment is in his book *L.T.: Living on the Edge*, New York, 1987. The situation at Chico State was in the *Chronicle of Higher Education*, 4/28/82; UNLV's "Palm Trees 101" course was in the *Las Vegas Review Journal*, 7/27/87; the summer school catalog list was in the *Chicago Tribune*, 3/10/89, as was Miami of Ohio's

"Trees and Shrubs" class, 3/7/89. The instructor in the Midwest correspondence division spoke off the record for obvious reasons.

Marianne Jennings's wonderful comment was in the *Chronicle of Higher Education*, 9/9/87, and that journal discussed her dismissal from her deanship, 10/14/87 and 12/9/87; the October article also discussed the case of Jeff Burger at Auburn, as did pieces on 9/2/87 and 11/18/87. The AP was on the Burger case early and sent out a detailed article on 8/16/87, reprinted in the *Roanoke Times and World-News*. The Minnesota eligibility problem was in the *Chronicle of Higher Education*, 2/8/84, and that journal outlined the N.C. State situation on 2/22/89; *Sports Illustrated* also covered the N.C. State academic problems, 2/27/89, as did *USA Today*, 2/10/89. The *Chicago Tribune* had Devon Mitchell's GPA at Iowa, 3/10/89; the *St. Petersburg Times* had articles on the Florida player with eligibility problems, 6/5/83, 6/9/83, 6/17/83; the Russell Pierre at Virginia Tech incident was in the *Roanoke Times and World-News*, 8/20/87.

In 1987, at the University of Oklahoma, the regular "academic authorities" gave an intercollegiate wrestler, Joe Brett Reynolds, who admitted that he had gotten another student to take an exam for him, a two-year suspension from school. However, the Board of Regents, the school's ultimate "academic authorities," reduced the suspension so that Reynolds could wrestle again for Oklahoma. The regents acted in favor of the athlete even though Oklahoma records showed that "26 of 28 students who were suspended for serious academic violations since 1981 were expelled outright" (*Chronicle of Higher Education*, 10/28/87).

David Roberson's academic ineligibility at the University of Houston was covered by the *Houston Post*, 3/16/86, 3/18/86, and 8/6/86. Bob Knight's comment about his close friend Norm Ellenberger was in *The Kappan*, 11/82; the *Chronicle of Higher Education* tracked the story, 1/7/80, 2/25/80, 6/2/80, 6/30/80, 7/20/81, and 6/9/82. Although they recorded the bogus grades, neither the University of New Mexico athletic department nor the registrar's office turned up the fraud. Only by chance, while conducting a wiretap of a suspected gambler, did the FBI hear one of Ellenberger's assistant coaches mention a forged transcript. The scam unraveled from there and not only involved UNM but also coaches and athletes at other schools, including the universities of Oregon, Oregon State, and Arizona State.

The comment about the Pac-10 in the early 1980s was in the *Chronicle of Higher Education*, 8/25/80, and that journal carried the story of Dave Wilson at Illinois on 5/11/81. The *Chicago Tribune* headlined the Wilson story on its front page, 5/3/81. The *Chronicle of Higher Education* carried articles on cheating by schools not in NCAA Division I on 10/31/84, and on Plattsburgh State, 10/16/85. The incident at the University of Wisconsin at Stevens Point was in *USA Today*, 5/10/88; the *Buffalo News* covered the Erie transcript scandal on 10/23/86, 10/24/86, and 10/25/86. The comments by Sandy Caligiore, sports director of radio station WSNN in Potsdam, New York, were in an interview for this book, 4/22/88.

Chapter 33

The Mel Turpin quote was in the *Louisville Courier-Journal*, 12/25/85, and the one by the Duke official was in the *Washington Post*, 6/16/85. The statistics on Memphis State and Georgia were in John Weistart, "College Sports Reform: Where Are the Faculty," *Academe: The Bulletin of the American Association of University Professors*, July/August 1987; this was also the source for the statistic in the Introduction that "only about 30 percent of American high school students go on to four-year colleges and universities." The summary quote about the GAO study was on the front page of the *New York Times*, 9/10/89. The information on NCAA and CFA "adjusted graduation rates" was confirmed in phone calls to the Research Department of the NCAA, and to the director of communications of the CFA, 5/30/89. The *Gainesville Sun* report was on 6/11/87. The General Accounting Office study is entitled *Student Athletes: Information on Their Academic Performance,* and was published in Washington, D.C., 5/89.

The Reebok ad for Digger Phelps was in *USA Today*, 2/6/90. The graduation statistics for Bob Knight's players were calculated by obtaining the names of all incoming freshmen and juco basketball players to whom he gave athletic scholarships since he began as coach at Indiana in 1971 and tracking them to see whether they had graduated from this school within five years. Knight's supporters will argue that many players have quit his team and left I.U. because they could not tolerate his coaching method and/or wanted to play in another college basketball system—thus their reasons for dropping out were athletic, not academic. This assertion is true but it also undercuts the line that Indiana players are serious "student-athletes." Students who are intent on obtaining a good education and a degree realize that transferring is extremely disruptive to an academic career and to be considered only as a last-resort option; if the dropouts from Knight's program were students first, why did they not continue their studies at Indiana University and work even harder on their degrees? In fact, the vast majority of Knight's players, like most participants in College Sports Inc., see themselves primarily as preprofessional athletes and place their athletic careers far above their academic ones.

The item in the *Los Angeles Times* about the UNLV "graduation" appeared 6/22/87; Joe Paterno's comment about the CFA statistics was in *USA Today*, 4/26/88; and Digger Phelps predicted abuses in graduations in *Sport* magazine, 12/82. The story about the college wrestlers was in the *Chronicle of Higher Education*, 5/21/86; that journal tracked the Howard and Bradley legislative proposals on 6/22/88, 11/2/88, and 10/25/89. The *New York Times* carried articles on Bradley's bill on 9/13/89 and 10/1/89. In addition, the author of this book had an op-ed piece in that newspaper about the Bradley bill, 9/20/89, to which the senator replied, 10/1/89.

Summary

Isiah Thomas's comment was in *Newsweek*, 1/30/89, and the quote from the NCAA report was in the "Executive Summary" of *Studies of Intercollegiate Athletics*, published by the Center for the Study of Athletics, Palo Alto, 1989. The LSU finding was in the *Baton Rouge Morning Advocate*, 7/14/86; the article about the Wisconsin football player was in *Sports Illustrated*, "Special College Football Issue," 1988, and Lou Holtz's comment was in that magazine, 11/11/85. Harry Edwards has written extensively about the time constraints on college athletes, most cogently in "The Collegiate Arms Race: Origins and Implications of the 'Rule 48' Controversy" in *The Fractured Focus*, Richard Lapchick, ed., Lexington, Mass., 1988. His comment "Education is activist . . ." was in the *Chronicle of Higher Education*, 1/26/83, as was the quote from the Southern Illinois AD, 9/3/86. The story of the player exhausted from practice was in the *Nashville Tennessean*, 6/5/85, and the quote about women basketball players was in *USA Today*, 8/9/89. Information about federally funded "work-study" grants was obtained from the bursar's office of Indiana University, Bloomington.

The *Miami Herald* article about demands on players' time as well as Bernie Kosar's comment appeared 7/1/84; the article on graduation rates was the same day. The *Chronicle of Higher Education* had features on the length of college sports seasons on 5/30/84 (the source of Father Healy's quote), 5/1/85, 2/12/86, 7/9/86, and 8/10/88.

Part IV: The NCAA: The Fox in the Henhouse

Overview

The Sherrill quote appeared in an Associated Press story in the *Louisville Courier-Journal*, 6/20/89, and the one from *The Kappan*, 5/86. To update the composition of the NCAA Executive Council: in 1988–89, the council was composed of twenty-eight athletic directors, two athletic conference commissioners, three faculty members in physical education, and five regular faculty members—all of whom had been faculty athletic representatives—six college presidents, and a lower-ranked university administrator. In addition, the Executive Committee had no presidents on it, but nine ADs, one conference commissioner, and two regular faculty members. Throughout the 1980s, the composition of these two NCAA controlling bodies was similar to the member-ships above.

The Chuck Neinas quote was in the *Los Angeles Times*, 2/21/82; the Dick Schultz quote in the *New York Times*, 1/8/89; the "vote of confidence for athletic directors" in the *Chronicle of Higher Education*, 6/17/87; and "he's one of us" in *Sports inc.* on 12/19/88.

Chapter 34

The headline in the *St. Louis Globe-Democrat* was on 4/29/82; the quote on NCAA required size of football stadiums and home attendance was in the *Chronicle of Higher Education*, 12/16/81, as was an article on the NCAA drop-ping the six Mid-America Conference schools, 2/10/82; an excellent article on the latter subject was in the *Cleveland Plain Dealer*, 2/3/82. The *Chronicle of Higher Education*, 1/30/85, explained the NCAA's sixteen-team, eight-sport rule. Since that time, the NCAA has fiddled with the rule and it is now seven sports and thirteen teams for Division I-A, and will soon increase—Tom Han-sen, commissioner of the Pacific Ten, discussed this in *USA Today*, 11/29/89.

At some schools, nonrevenue sports break through and attract good crowds and some revenue: wrestling at Iowa and some Big Eight institutions, hockey at Minnesota and some other cold weather schools, baseball in warm weather regions like Arizona, and soccer in a few places around the country. But considering the over 5,000 teams in NCAA nonrevenue sports, the exceptions tend to prove the 95 percent national rule.

The item on the NCAA's new offices was in the *Chronicle of Higher Education* on 5/25/88; the NCAA budget was in that journal, 10/26/88; the article on the NCAA's interest-free loans to employees, 11/27/85; and the Executive Committee's "blessing" of the loans, 12/18/85. *Sports Illustrated* analyzed the loan situation, 10/6/86; and the Dick Schultz quote about "cut-ting sports and cutting scholarships" was in *USA Today*, 1/9/89.

The Bill Shirley quote was in the *Los Angeles Times* on 2/23/82; an article on the growth of the NCAA's Enforcement Division appeared in *Sports Illus-trated*, 4/14/86; the *Louisville Courier-Journal* had an update on the numbers, 12/21/88; the Donna Lopiano quote was in the *Chronicle of Higher Education* on 9/11/85; Mike Gilleran's remarks were in the *Los Angeles Times*, 2/10/88; and that newspaper carried the AP feature, 12/21/86 (Berst's comments were in the story). The NCAA is open about its dependence on one school squealing on another: Stephen Morgan, a longtime enforcement official, called it a "trip mechanism" (*Chronicle of Higher Education*, 1/22/86). Discussions of some of the activities of Slive and/or Glazier appeared in the *Roanoke Times and World-News*, 8/14/87 and 6/30/87; the *Chicago Tribune*, 4/4/89; and an AP dispatch in the *Bloomington Herald-Times*, 10/20/89.

Both the faculty athletic representative at a southern school and the Virginia Tech faculty member spoke off the record—both to protect themselves and for fear of NCAA penalties against their often penalized schools. Articles about Tulane, Wichita State, and Oklahoma employing former NCAA employees appeared in *Sports Illustrated*, 2/17/84, and *USA Today*, 4/19/88 and 8/17/89. The ACE's Washington lawyer, Sheldon E. Steinbach, made his comments to the *Chronicle of Higher Education*, 1/22/86.

Dr. Thomas Tutko's remarks on gambling appeared in a *Sports Illustrated* "Special Report," 3/10/86; the figures on gambling are from that *SI* issue and a *Chronicle of Higher Education* feature, 3/2/83; the story of the Davidson SID was in *Sports Illustrated*, 2/8/82; the complaints of the SIDs appeared in the *Chronicle of Higher Education*, 4/6/83; and Esposito was quoted in an article, "Sports, Gambling and Television," by H. Roy Kaplan in Lapchick, op. cit.

Chapter 35

The N. Peg Burke quote was in the *Chronicle of Higher Education*, 1/14/80; that journal discussed the decline of the NIT, 4/3/85; the NCAA's relations with the AAU, 5/15/78 and 7/3/78; and the history of Title IX, 12/11/78 (the quote of the key provision is from that article). An update on Title IX appeared in *Sports inc.*, 10/24/88. The AIAW was formed under the auspices of the American Alliance for Health, Physical Education, and Recreation, and many of its ideas came from the view of intercollegiate athletics as recreational—not semiprofessional—activity; the quotes from the 1970s AIAW leaders were in the *Chronicle of Higher Education* on 5/12/75 and 5/22/78; and articles in that journal explaining the 1970s differences between the AIAW and the NCAA appeared 1/26/76, 5/17/76, 1/17/77, 1/23/78, and 1/22/79. The ACE quotes are in *The Money Game*; the story of the NCAA's takeover of the AIAW was in the *Chronicle of Higher Education*, 5/12/75, 1/16/78, 1/14/80 (the source of the Grant quote as well as the one from the male delegate), 1/19/81 (the quote from the female observer—unidentified in the original), 4/6/81, 1/20/82 (the source of the Merrily Baker quote), 6/2/82, 10/6/82, 10/27/82, and 11/3/82. The 1980 NCAA convention set up women's championships for the five most important women's sports in Divisions II and III; the 1981 convention extended the championships to Division I and added championships in other sports to the existing ones in Divisions II and III. The NCAA has always tried to pick up the travel tab for their championship events—except, at the time that they were putting the AIAW out of business, they were facing a budget deficit and they were considering cutting the travel subsidies to male championship events. The NAIA paralleled the NCAA in its takeover of the women's athletic programs at schools belonging to it (see the *Chronicle of Higher Education*, 3/27/78, 12/11/78, 5/12/80, 7/14/80, 10/6/82).

Christine Grant's comment about the NCAA's Enforcement Division was given under oath at the trial of the AIAW's antitrust lawsuit against the NCAA. This was the women's group's last-gasp attempt to save itself, but before the judge's final decision, it voted itself out of existence and essentially rendered the lawsuit moot. The *Chronicle of Higher Education* covered the trial, 10/27/82 and 11/3/82; the Christine Weller quote was in that journal, 2/9/83, and the estimate of increased expenses at Texas, 1/19/81. *Sports Illustrated* discussed the implications of the *Grove City* decision on 3/4/85, as did the *Chronicle of Higher Education*, 7/22/87. The Frank Broyles quote and the Arkansas situation were in the *Arkansas Democrat*, 10/7/87.

An excellent survey article, "Athletics and the University: the Post-Woman's Era," by G. Ann Uhlir, appeared in *Academe: The Bulletin of the American Association of University Professors*, July/August 1987; that article contained the facts about fewer women's championships under the NCAA than the AIAW.

Articles about the increased cheating in women's sports as well as the David Berst quotes were in the *Chronicle of Higher Education*, 5/9/84, 2/20/85, and 9/4/85. The Viverito quote was in that journal, 9/25/85, but the original text was incorrect. The writer had Ms. Viverito saying, "Today, 86 percent of all athletic departments are run by men." In fact, almost 100 percent of all athletic departments were and are run by men but, according to the survey from which Ms. Viverito was quoting, 86 percent of *women's athletic programs* were headed by males. I have dropped the incorrect parts of the quote.

The latest results of the Vivian Acosta and Linda Carpenter survey were in *Sports inc.*, 5/30/88; the Ron Wilde quote was in the *Los Angeles Times*, 7/8/87; articles on women's sports under the NCAA appeared in the *Chronicle of Higher Education*, 3/30/83 (the source of the Davenport quote), 9/25/85 (the source of the Bunnell quote), and 11/20/85 (the source of the Dartmouth study); the entry in that journal's "Great Summertime Marginalia Contest" appeared 7/21/80; and that journal also had articles on Temple's opposition to Title IX, 3/30/88, 4/13/88, 6/1/88, and 6/22/88. The figures on Georgetown's Lady Hoyas were in *Sports inc.*, 3/28/88.

Information on the NCAA's recent survey of female college athletes was in the *New York Times*, 10/9/89, as was the quote by the researcher who conducted the survey. As with all of the recent NCAA studies on the number of hours that athletes spend on sports, the totals are surprisingly low: twenty-six hours a week for women basketball players, and twenty-five for women athletes in other sports. These numbers are at odds with most other studies of this phenomenon as well as the testimony of many coaches and athletes. The NCAA survey also compared women athletes to regular women students who were heavily involved in extracurricular activities. Like the NCAA's graduation statistics that compare athletes to regular students, this comparison is basically flawed and proves much less than the NCAA intended it to. The women engaged in extracurricular activities are not on "full ride" scholarships and neither their tuition and expenses nor their activities cost the university anything (usually the activities are funded out of student activity fees). Moreover—and this is the key difference—if the grades of a woman engaged in extracurricular activity start to suffer, she can cut back on her activities and work on her courses. However, if the grades of a woman athlete decline, she *cannot decrease her sports participation hours—if she does, she will lose her athletic scholarship and have to pay her own way through school.*

Chapter 36

The Bill Mallory quote was in the *Louisville Courier-Journal,* 10/1/86; although the context was the new NCAA rules on athletes selling game tickets, his comment is apropos of the entire issue of whether university presidents should control intercollegiate athletics. As with its coverage of women's inter-collegiate athletics, the *Chronicle of Higher Education* provided the best ongoing articles on and analysis of the college presidents' attempts to reform the NCAA; that journal discussed the ACE moves on 11/9/79, 9/1/82, 9/14/83 (the quotes from the ACE presidents' report and the NCAA president's reply to it are in this issue), 9/28/83, 11/9/83 (the NCAA's counterproposal), 1/4/84 (the preconvention poll), and 1/18/84 (on the convention itself, including the quote from Edward B. Fort, the president of North Carolina A. & T.).

The other major source on the ACE presidents' attempt at NCAA reform was the *New York Times* in stories on 8/19/83, 8/22/83 (including the quote from the administrative assistant—unnamed in the original), 1/11/84 (the source of the quote on Bok and Healy), and George Vecsey's column on 1/11/84 (also the source of the Long Beach president's comment).

The faculty athletic representative of a southern school is the same gentle-man who commented on the NCAA's Enforcement Division in Chapter 35. The *Chronicle of Higher Education* covered the NCAA Presidents' Commission in items and articles on 1/20/84, and the 1985 special convention on 7/3/85 (the source of the Kelly quote); the newspaper headline, "NCAA Vote for Reform," was in the *Memphis Commercial Appeal,* 6/22/85; the NCAA president's remarks were in *Sports Illustrated,* 6/24/85; and the Bob Knight comment was in the *Chicago Tribune,* 6/25/85.

In 1985, the NCAA did not call the "Death Penalty" rule by that name. Because of subsequent use of the term in the press, especially regarding the penalties given to the SMU football program, the NCAA began to use it. (The "Les Misérables" term is an invention of this writer.) The 1985 special meeting also set up the "self-studies" that athletic programs are now supposed to do on a periodic basis. These are often cited by the NCAA, and especially its executive director Dick Schultz, as proof of the association's commitment to reform. Unfortunately, as with the NCAA's long-term *Revenues and Expenses* survey, each school is allowed to report what it wants to report, and although the NCAA provides guidelines, it has no legal power to discover the truth and thus it must accept each athletic program's "self-study." No school, for example, has yet admitted that it has a hideaway curriculum for athletes nor has the NCAA pressed any member about this massive area of abuse.

Mike Swiger, head of Synergos Management Consulting of Reston, Virginia, whose corporate clients have included Boeing and Equitable Life, has also done consulting work for athletic departments. He says of the "self-studies": "Self-assessment is one thing. But if you were doing it right, you wouldn't have any problems to begin with. And I think if there are problems, the people who are in the middle of those problems certainly aren't going to sit down and write it out and make it all public." This is especially true of unjustified, sometimes illegal, spending, and hideaway curricula. Swiger's comments were in the *Washington Times*, 2/12/87.

The *Chronicle of Higher Education* reported on the NCAA's January 1987 convention on 1/21/87, and the divisions in the Presidents' Commission on 4/8/87, 4/29/87, and 5/20/87; the *Los Angeles Times* headline appeared 7/1/87; the quotes from the AP story were in the *Bloomington Herald-Telephone*, 7/1/87; and Michael Goodwin's comments were in the *New York Times*, 7/2/87. The main *Chronicle of Higher Education* article on this special convention was published on 7/8/87; that journal covered the post-1987 convention events in articles, 1/6/88 and 1/20/88. The Likens interview was in the *New York Times*, 1/11/89, and the same newspaper carried the quotes from Bo Schembechler and Lou Holtz, 10/9/89; the Presidents' Commission proposals were discussed in *USA Today*, 10/5/89. Bob Knight's comments appeared in the *Louisville Courier-Journal*, 1/13/90, and the *Bloomington Herald-Times* on the same day. Pitino's rage was reported by the *Louisville Courier-Journal*, 1/11/90.

Summary

Denny Crum's remark was in the *Louisville Courier-Journal*, 1/11/90; Bo Schembechler's was in the *Chronicle of Higher Education*, 7/8/87.

Part V: Punt the Pretend

Chapter 37

The Warch comment was in *U.S. News & World Report*, 12/5/86; the *Chronicle of Higher Education* is the source for both the Rowdy Gaines quote, 1/23/85, and the one by Les Wyatt, vice-chancellor of the University of Arkansas, 7/13/88. James Michener worked out a draft system for high school athletes to enter college sports in *Sports in America,* New York, 1976. The Atchley interview took place at the University of the Pacific on 6/10/88.

Index